SO YOU WANNA BE A DIRECTOR?

by Ken Annakin

To Pauline and Debbie with love, and in memory of Jane.

First published in 2001 by
Tomahawk Press
PO Box 1236
Sheffield S11 7XU
England

ISBN 0-953 1926-5-2

Edited by Bruce Sachs
Designed by Steve Kirkham 01245 442215

Printed and bound in Great Britain by MPG Books Ltd., Bodmin, Cornwall

The publisher does not necessarily share the views expressed by the author.

Tomahawk Press and Ken Annakin would like to thank the following for permission to reproduce photographs:

Photos from *Third Man on the Mountain, The Sword and the Rose*, and *Swiss Family Robinson* – used by permission from Disney Enterprises, Inc.

Photos from *The Battle of the Bulge* – copyright 1965 Warner Bros. Pictures Inc. and United States Pictures Inc. All Rights Reserved.

Photos from *Monte Carlo or Bust* – Courtesy of Paramount Pictures. Copyright 2000 by Paramount Pictures. All Rights Reserved.

Photos from *Paper Tiger* – Courtesy of the Euan Lloyd Collection.

Photos from *The Longest Day* – copyright 1962 Twentieth Century Fox Film Corporation. All Rights Reserved.

Photos from *Those Magnificent Men in Their Flying Machines* – copyright 1965 Twentieth Century Fox Film Corporation. All Rights Reserved.

Photos from *Miranda, Holiday Camp, Across the Bridge, Here Come the Huggetts, The Long Duel, Hotel Sahara, The Fast Lady, Very Important Person* and *Broken Journey* – reproduced courtesy of Carlton International Media Limited.

All other photographs are from Ken Annakin's private collection.

KEN ANNAKIN

Although, to my regret, I have never worked with Ken, he was and is an essential part of the British film industry in which I grew up.

From the start I regarded him as a senior figure and, like all my contemporaries, I have always eagerly anticipated the next Annakin production. My own particular favourite amongst the long list of his achievements remains *Across the Bridge*.

As a director, Ken manages to combine many different talents. His sense of the ridiculous is in many ways unique and with the majority of his early comedies he delighted in entertaining us by illuminating various wacky forms of essentially British eccentricity. Later, of course, he gained a worldwide reputation in this particular genre with *Those Magnificent Men in Their Flying Machines*.

Comedy, though, was only one of his strengths. He was a general when he made a movie. He had to be. How else could he have planned and organised such epic films as *Battle of the Bulge* and *The Longest Day*, which he co-directed with such notable success?

Ken has always been a man of great determination, not to say ruthlessness, in his quest to attain the highest possible standard of work. He seemed tireless and, since he never spared himself, he was able to insist on an equivalent effort from those who surrounded him.

Physically, too, he is awe-inspiring, this six foot, bespectacled figure. But when I conjure him up in my mind's eye, awe is inseparable from the quirky sense of humour that plays around his lips, tinged constantly with a wonderful self-mockery.

Anyone who really wants to understand the joys and the agonies of making a movie will enjoy the vivid account Ken has set down in this captivating book.

He has been a good friend and, while we are both still on this earth, there remains, always, the enticing possibility that we might still find an opportunity to work together.

Sir Richard Attenborough

KEN ANNAKIN

According to Jean Renoir, every director makes the same film over and over again, and I'm bound to concede that he was probably right.

But how can this generalisation possibly apply to that most versatile of filmmakers, Ken Annakin, whose extraordinary range of style and subject matter has spanned the spectrum, literally from the sublime to the ridiculous — from the gravity of *The Longest Day* to the delicious nonsense of *Miranda*? Surely, this truly great master of successful, commercial cinema cannot possibly have made the kind of personal films Renoir must have been talking about?

Well, Ken's remarkable and unique achievement is that he has indeed managed, over the years, to do precisely that — his films are deeply personal, and in the most sophisticated and inventive ways, he has told and retold the same story, endlessly re-exploring a specific theme that most certainly comes out of his own formative experience.

After an 'ordinary' provincial upbringing in the dull, drab Yorkshire of the inter-war years, attending the local grammar school and then Hull University, Ken worked for three boring years as a clerk in the local tax office. Then, just like the hero of a Ken Annakin movie, he won a hundred pounds on the Derby, and escaped to a life of danger and adventure in New Zealand, Australia and, ultimately, the United States. He bummed, laboured, cycled everywhere, worked as a car salesman, compered a commercial road show, became a journalist, and even prospected for gold. Then, out of the chaos of the war, he entered the film industry.

And I can't recall a single Annakin film that doesn't explore Ken's Great Theme: Breaking Out Into The Unknown. Inevitably, the Annakin yarn is always about an individual or a group of people challenging the status quo, invariably facing hazardous consequences.

Remember his post-war holiday campers, jolly fellows and tortured souls among them, getting away from it all? Or his eccentric collection of alpine air crash victims, including a man in an iron lung who dies so that everybody else can survive, and an egocentric opera singer who destroys his voice by hollering for help across a valley? Or that beautifully understated study of a woman novelist, quietly confronting her stale marriage? Or that sexy mermaid, causing havoc all around her while savouring the delights of the big city? Or those engaging, if impossible, hoteliers, destabilising the course of World War II in the middle of the Sahara? Not to mention that merry band of outlaws!

Those were some of Ken's earlier adventurers. As his canvas grew, we shared the passionate struggles of wives and husbands in the distant colonies, first in pre-independence Malaya, then in early New Zealand; and then, when those three buffoons and their mongrel had tackled the Thames, and that awful pompous genius had popped over to Germany for a few days to escape from a P.O.W. camp, Ken gave us the most fascinating and profound of all his studies in escape.

Across The Bridge is Ken's own favourite, and its mine, too. What is fascinating about this masterpiece is that, unusually, Ken makes his central character a baddy, so that the enlightened journey into the unknown becomes a nightmare descent to hell. Fabulous stuff!

The epics continued. Two of the definitive European battles of World War II, struggles to colonial India, man and dog against the ravages of snowbound Alaska. It's tempting to recall every frame of Ken's prodigious output, but the list is far too long.

Perhaps Ken's most gloriously idiosyncratic achievement was that inspired fusing together of the zany comic strand of his work with the muscular epic. Who but Ken Annakin could have conceived — pulled off with such masterly panache — the tall story of the 1910 London to Paris Air Race, with its incredible variety of characters and stories, and all filmed for real, on land, sea and air, with hardly a trick in sight?

Ken's films are a joy and a delight, and are always a cornucopia of surprises. He is an inspiration to us all, and long may this continue.

And of course he passes the Renoir test, though you do have to look hard to spot it!!

Mike Leigh
London, August 2000

CHAPTER ONE
The Winding Road Into Film Making

Most of my movies fall into the category of commercial entertainment. I have never made art house films or movies with a message, like Oliver Stone. One or two (my favourites), like my Somerset Maugham's *Quartet* and *Trio,* and the Graham Greene short-story *Across The Bridge*, have interesting character development and something to say about life.

My other forty-nine movies were aimed mainly at making people laugh (or, at least, go out of the cinema happy); the immortalisation of World War II battles (*The Longest Day* and *Battle of the Bulge*) or pure adventure (*Swiss Family Robinson* and *Those Magnificent Men In Their Flying Machines*). Most of them showed a profit to the producing companies and for me provided mostly a Cloud Nine life with travel all over the world.

Yes, fifty-two years of film making have given me incredible experiences and angles on life, people, and places, which at this juncture, I feel might be worth sharing — even in this changed world of movie making, where stars and some directors are paid millions of dollars, and audiences flock to movies with titles like *Dumb & Dumber* and *Clueless*. And what about two young almost unknown actresses who have just been given multi-million producing contracts just because the films they were in, grossed over forty million dollars in their first three weeks of release?

It would almost seem that a well-scripted story and director who knows his stuff are no longer regarded as important in Hollywood! Yet, some people still stand in awe of 'the director' and quite often I am asked, "How did you become a director?"... in a way you feel they would really like to know.

Most young directors, I guess, making the scene today would probably answer, "Oh, I went to film school, studied old movies till they came out of my ears, then I borrowed a camera and some short ends, and at weekends shot a story me and my pals had cooked up. We flogged it around festivals. Some critic took a shine to it and a studio bought it for peanuts. They spent ten million on prints and advertising — over twenty times what we had spent — and blackmailed everyone into seeing it. The media made it a 'must', with the result every studio is after me and I'm certainly on my way to my first million!!!"

I assure you, it was never like that when we oldies were getting our first breaks, and an apt reply might be: "Good luck to you, mate. Let's see how you cope with your tenth assignment!"

As a professional, one has to be able to handle the problems of any kind of subject that comes up and attracts you. Therefore, your whole life experience and geographic background all play a vital part in your attitudes, opinions and responses. So thereby I must go ahead and write the line that always makes me cringe:

I was born and raised for the first twenty years of my life, in a small terrace house in the East Yorkshire town of Beverley. It was not the *smallest* house in an industrial neighbourhood like you still find all over Northern England, but it was bloody small, and on the wrong side of the tracks. On trips back to show my two wives and two daughters 'where it all began', I had to admit that Beverley is a very pleasant little market town, with two beautiful cathedrals and a wonderful open space called The Westwood. It has a race course (where I flew in my first plane with Sir Alan Cobham) and half-timbered Tudor houses fringed the grassland on two sides.

As I used to walk or cycle the two potholed miles to Beverley Grammar School, I used to wonder why my father would never consider moving from our 'lower' section of town, where there was a tannery that smelled pretty strong when there was an east wind, and the River Hull Drain, where they used to build trawlers occasionally. As kids we used to swim there when the water was not 'too mucky'.

So far as I could gather in my early years, my dad was very well thought of as a Government Surveyor; an opening bat in the Beverley Cricket Team, and as a competition-winning choirmaster. He had apparently built windmills at one time, but after I was born, opted for a safe nine-to-five job. Something had happened to make him lose his nerve and any thought of taking risks. I was never able to discover what it had been.

My mother, as I remember her, was beautiful, hardworking and full of fun. I recall her once telling me how she and her three sisters, when they were growing up, used to sit in the flour bins to see who could leave the daintiest bum-mark! That has always seemed to me the height of comedy. On winter evenings, I used to snuggle up to her on our sitting-room sofa and listen to visiting vocalists singing and discussing 'interpretation' of opera and oratorios with my father. My mother was raised on a farm in the Yorkshire Dales — a beautiful Land of Freedom, north of Leeds. From visits made up there in later years, I would say I got my obstinacy, straightforward 'on the nose' approach, and my love of beauty, both in women and landscape, from her.

However, I have no doubt that the seeds of wanting to create something worthwhile, organise hidden talents, and be in charge came from my unfulfilled father. During the week, he worked diligently at his routine job, but at weekends he found a rich spiritual base at the Primitive Methodist Chapel, where also on Tuesday and Friday evenings, forty or fifty Beverlonians would gather to practice choral singing under his direction. Over the years I was dragooned into singing, first with the sopranos, then the altos and finally, with the baritones. Never with the tenors! Without being conscious of it, I was absorbing my father's musical sensitivity and patient determination to create the most emotionally exciting choral effects. Whenever I hear massed choirs singing Handel's 'Messiah', I still get shivers down my spine.

My mother died suddenly under a surgeon's knife when I was thirteen, leaving me with an indescribable hole in my emotional makeup. My father did his best to interest me in accompanying his singing, and often I would accompany him as "our choir" would compete in various Northern cities. I would see how one man's creative efforts with a group of quite ordinary people, could move an audience to tumultuous applause or tears. In Leeds, Huddersfield, Manchester and Blackpool, my dad had his crowning moments and I suppose, deep in my soul, I was registering how he succeeded in his chosen art form.

At school, I was nothing special. I was good at history and English Lit because I liked the teachers. I played cricket and practiced hard to be the fastest bowler. Making the wickets fly is a great feeling — much better than anything I've ever experienced in tennis or golf. Cross-country running across the bleak open spaces of Beverley Westwood shaped me into a good long-distance runner. On two school Sports Days, I won the mile in around four minutes twenty. But the earliest moment possible — as soon as I passed the Matriculation Exams, just before my sixteenth birthday — I left school.. There was no question of going on to university — for one, we couldn't afford it and, in any case, not many Beverley Grammar School kids did — only those aspiring to be teachers. I wanted to earn money; become independent; strike out to see this exciting world that was being revealed to me in reading and on this newfangled radio set I had just built out of the shilling-a-week pocket money my father had deigned to give me.

[handwritten margin note: the world record was about 4.20 then.]

By this time, I only just tolerated my father, having discovered a number of hurtful dalliances that he had engaged in while my darling mother was alive. Obviously, I was becoming an individual with deep emotion-driven opinions — which, on looking back, I suppose, benefited me during my years as a director. But I have to admit having had my own 'affairs' —- many more than my poor old dad — I am not proud of my behaviour in my mid-and-late teens. Every year, that good well-meaning parent used to take me down for one whole week in London, where we saw every type of theatre show. What an effect that must have had on my attitude to acting, staging, drama and comedy —- and what a shit I must have been to make life hard for my dad!

On one of these trips we went for an afternoon tea at No. 11 Downing Street. Ethel, my father's sister, was married to Philip Snowden, the 'Iron Chancellor' in the first Labour Government of the UK. I remember him coming into the sitting room and tucking into a box of chocolates, saying he had just put a spoke into Churchill's wheel in a House of Commons debate.

Ethel leaned over to Dad, "You know how the press makes them out to be great enemies, but we often spend weekends together at Chequers. They have a lot of respect for each other." Snowden took another chocolate and turned to me, "And what are you going to do with your life, lad?"

I drew a deep breath. "I think I'd like to be a journalist, or something in the theatre or films."

"He's just passed his exam for the Inland Revenue," my father interjected. Snowden gave a thin-lipped smile. "You're a lucky lad. In these difficult times, security means a great deal." He must have seen my face drop, because he added, "Who knows? You could finish up as Chief Inspector! Take me, for instance. I never expected to land up here when Ethel and I were selling socialism from the street corners of Leeds!" Ethel nodded wistfully.

As we walked out into Whitehall (with the police guard saluting us), my father said, "Well, you couldn't get better advice, son. What about it?"

"I don't want to be stuck working out people's taxes all my life," I said darkly. We walked on in silence for several minutes, and then Dad said, "Well, at least, you can say you've met the highest in the land. From now on, you need never be afraid of anyone..." And that is what I never forgot from that encounter. For four long years I worked as a trainee Income Tax Inspector in the city of Hull — a boring nine-to-five job about which everyone said I should be grateful for because we were in the depths of the Great Depression.

During this period, apart from playing cricket, supporting Hull City soccer club, and chasing big-titted girls, I joined a local Concert Party, in which I used to sing baritone ballads and help out in dumb sketches. We used to tour the prisons and a local mental home. I also formed a five-piece jazz band made up of fellows from the Boy's Brigade. We practiced a lot and did a few gigs, but soon broke up because I couldn't stand the saxophonist who was a natural — a much freer performer on his instrument than me on the piano! Already I was coming to the conclusion that unless one was "the tops" it might be better to learn how to get performances out of other people, rather than sweating the impossible out of oneself.

About this time, as luck would have it, I heard of a new kind of drama course starting up at Hull University in the evenings. Assiduously, I would attend the Hull Rep every time they put on a new play, and among us regulars, the word went round that a young professor from London was setting up classes for interested local people to study plays, how they were constructed and how they reached the stage. I enrolled for ten lessons, but stayed with the course for over two years.

Professor Mayfield was a remarkable man. He loved the theatre and drama, but being a very retiring, private kind of individual, he had no desire to actually work in the theatre. He was a teacher, pure and simple, with an amazing understanding of the works of Ibsen, Chekov, Yeats and O'Neill. Mayfield would take 'The Doll's House', for example, break down the qualities of every character, and how Ibsen advanced his story and then built up his dramatic climaxes. Then we, a class of sixteen or seventeen people from every walk of life, would have to try and write similar scenes with characters based on our contemporary experiences of people and places.

Some put up a poor show with the writing, but they all loved to try and act out chosen scenes. I did quite well with the writing, but liked best to try my hand at the directing (which fortunately only one other pupil was interested in). Just imagine having live guinea pigs to work with, and no audience or money to worry about! Only our beloved professor!

I also discovered he had a yen for cycling, and being a 'bloody Southerner' had no knowledge of our wonderful Yorkshire Dales. On countless weekends, we explored the hidden corners of Wharfedale, Nidderdale, the moors around Ilkley, Keighley and Halifax (with their association with the Bronte sisters). Naturally, on these trips I was able to ask the professor every question which had cropped up in my mind — a wonderful chance for a young man living in a very arid part of the country, so far as the Arts were concerned.

In my drawer at the office, there was always a copy of a magazine called 'Picture

Show'. At any moment, I could discuss films being made in the studios both around London and Hollywood, and I knew in detail the nature of every technician's job. But how could I, stuck in Beverley and Hull, ever hope to get a chance to work in such faraway dream worlds?

When not playing theatre at the university or chatting up girls, I used to see two or three movies a week. I even tried my hand at writing film critiques and succeeded in getting one — a review of *SOS Iceberg* — published in the Hull Evening News. But my conviction that one had to be 'the best' to succeed in anything, a voice-inside definitely told me that I just didn't know enough of the outside world or have enough experience of real people, to write a play or a book or even have a chance at being a decent journalist. As for professionally directing theatre or movies, that was really "in Outer Space"!

Again, something happened to give me a break. Along with Ray, the guy at the next desk to me in the Tax Office, I bet two pounds on the Derby. Our horse won at fifty-to-one! Suddenly, I had a *hundred pounds!* For months, Ray had been nostalgically expounding the delights of New Zealand, and his regrets at ever having left it. "The most beautiful land in the world," he used to say. "A place where you can try your hand at anything, and nobody cares a damn who or what you are." Shopping around the travel agencies in my lunch hours, I found I could buy a third-class round ticket on the 'Rangitiki' to Auckland, for ninety-six pounds (and the return part would stay valid for *three years).* To hell with the safe job and security.

If I was ever to make anything of my creative urges, I had to break away. And this was going to be it, despite the long faces and dire warnings of my school friends, office colleagues, cricket buddies, my favourite girlfriend and my father. He eventually said, "Okay. So long as you keep a diary, and send me a copy as often as you can." God bless him!

There was nowhere better to study people than six weeks at sea among total strangers. I shared a cabin with Greg, a guy who was clearly 'on the run'. From the things he told me, I pieced together how he had made a killing supplying reconditioned pin-tables to clubs all over the UK, and now he wanted to put fourteen thousand miles between himself and any pursuit by creditors or from people he had perhaps 'knocked-off' machines. This was the first time I'd ever met a crook, and it was very interesting to piece together his confessions of how he had done business!

Then, there was Maggie, a fortyish, rather aristocratic divorcee, who wanted to make up for all the sex she had missed. After one fantastic evening ashore in Jamaica, at a paradise (or so it seemed to me!) called Constant Springs — dancing, Planter's punches, the lot — I was shattered when she shoved me into her cabin and stripped off all her clothes and lay down on the bunk, legs apart! Yes, legs apart!! I was absolutely shocked! So far as I could see, she had a good body, but after all she was an *old woman* compared to me! I stammered an excuse and quickly made an exit — but later I had to admit I often envied Greg who stepped into my shoes for the rest of the voyage. He used to come back to the cabin at three in the morning and regale me with detailed accounts of their carnal frolics, while I had chosen to woo a sweet Scottish lass, only a year or two older than me. Night after night in a sweaty cabin, we would kiss and grope towards a heartbreaking climax, but at the last moment, she would miraculously avoid "the blessed robin" as she called it, on the pretext that she was engaged to be married to a farmer in Christchurch! I was beginning to see how

Somerset Maugham had found his wonderful characters, and like the Master on his trips through the South Seas, I, the yet-to-be-discovered Ken Annakin, was soaking up atmosphere in Jamaica, Panama, Pango Pango, and the nightly twenty minute Technicolor sunset show over the Pacific Ocean. I was blissfully happy — probably for the first time in my life!!

The city of Auckland was a sprawl of single-story buildings spread around endless small bays, most of which were dominated by the perfectly symmetrical cone of Rangitoto, an extinct volcano. Everyone seemed even more patriotic British than the British I had left behind. The newspapers seemed full of ads for Situations Vacant. What should I go for?

On the 'Rangitiki', I had become very friendly with a couple originally from Bradford. She had been a dancer in the Folies Bergere in Paris and her husband Fred had been a drummer there. Even those romantic sounding jobs had apparently worn out their attraction and, like me, Fred and his wife were hoping to make a new start in the Land of Opportunity.

Fred had taken on a number of agencies for British products, one of which was a new type of neon sign for small shops. Meeting me in Queens Street one day, he told me he was engaging ten salesmen and that I could be one of them if I wanted. I jumped at the chance, but Fred had not counted on the reaction of his financial partner.

Vanek was a Czech immigrant who had made a fortune in manufacturing hats. The day after Fred engaged me, Vanek came into the office, took one look at me, and bawled at Fred, "Who's this long streak of nothingness?"

"He's a friend of mine from the Rangitiki," answered Fred. "He's going to be one of my sales team."

"Over my dead body," said Vanek. "I'm not having any bloody shipmates slipped into this outfit!" During this speech, he had been sizing me up. "Got any references?", he said suddenly.

Like a shot, I replied, "Of course, but unfortunately they were in the suitcase, which got lost in Customs." Then, going on the offensive, I added, "But what's all the fuss about? Either I persuade people to buy the bloody signs or I don't!"

Vanek stared at me through narrowed eyes, but Fred cut in quickly, "Ken's okay, Mister Vanek. I assure you. As a matter of fact, he was one of the star salesmen for Ewbank in England."

Vanek smiled. "Really! If you've sold vacuum cleaners for Ewbank, you'll do for me!" A pause, then "But just as a precaution, I'll get off a cable tonight to my agents in London. What territory did you work?"

I didn't like it, but now I couldn't let Fred down. "Oh, Sheffield was my HQ and the Yorkshire Dales my stamping ground," I said, without hesitation. As Vanek left, Fred and I stared at each other. "What a suspicious sod,", said Fred. "Fourteen thousand miles away and he's going to check up!"

"You shouldn't have stuck your neck out," I said. "Lying for me was stupid. After all, you're married and setting out on a new career. I'm only chasing experience."

Fred's brain was working overtime. "Maybe we could find out who his agents are and send another cable under his name saying 'Don't bother!' or..." His eyes were twinkling now. "... I could cable my pal, Jim Noakes in London and ask him to go to Ewbank Headquarters..."

I shook my head. "It's not worth it, Fred. And my bet is it's all a big bluff. It's not as though I was going to handle the firm's cash, for God's sake!"

The matter was forgotten, until three days later, Fred handed me a slip of paper with a pencilled note: "Ewbank no record of any Ken Annakin ever being employed."

"Better go and see Vanek," said Fred, looking embarrassed. With thumping heart, I crossed the road to the factory and, before the Czech had time to say anything, I blurted out, "Oh, Mister Vanek, I understand you have a cable concerning me. May I see it?"

Without any sign of the outburst I had expected, he dipped into his pocket, handed me an envelope and said, quite gently, "Yeah! Here it is, Ken."

I scanned the cable and thought quickly. I had to cover Fred.

"As a matter of fact, Mister Vanek," I said, "I lied to both you and Fred. I've never sold anything in my life. I was in the Civil Service for four years — a Tax officer. No background at all for getting a job out here. I think Fred thought "Better the Devil, you know, than some con-man he might pick up on Queen Street!"

Vanek was smiling. "This time, I believe you, Ken... and in checking on you, I was also testing Holt's integrity. Now you are both in the clear!". I grinned and asked, "So, what now?"

"See what you can do with the signs," he said, "and, if you're not good as a salesman, I'll find you some job in the factory." I thanked him and decided I had made no mistake in choosing New Zealand to try my wings.

The Lumolite signs were a flop — and I hated having to spend hours waiting for shopkeepers to deign to listen to me! But, just to prove whether it was me or the product, I tried my hand at selling several used cars, which Fred had shipped out from London. The problem here was that most of them needed maintenance (to say the least!) and we didn't have an engine-shop or crew to recondition them. After spending hours covered in grease and my fingers torn by rusty, unyielding nuts, I decided I'd better try and use my brains to make money.

I hit on an idea no one had thought of in New Zealand. It was to publish a monthly newsletter, to be posted free, to every estate agent and realtor throughout the country, informing each one of them the properties the others had for sale. All it would cost them was a fee for the ads and we would look after the rest. For two whole months Lulu (Fred's ex-dancer wife) and I drew up proposals, composed letters, collated ads, typed out foolscap pages, addressed envelopes, licked stamps, etcetera, etcetera. I have never worked such long hours even in movie making! Everyone thought 'Holtan's List' was a great original idea, but the biggest agents in Auckland and Wellington decided the 'listings' should be run by their professional association and not by three Limey interlopers!

So, having no copyright on the idea, our operation ground to a miserable halt. With the Holt's house overflowing with reams of paper, we had to accept defeat and register that however friendly the 'Pig Islanders' might be, you cannot arrive in a new country and buck the system! Now I was really out of cash and had to get a paying job, urgently! Within a week I was knocking on doors selling weekly insurance, and, believe it or not, I turned out to be quite good at this. Maybe it was because most of my prospects were women. Often I would knock on a door and a woman would appear in her dressing gown. Very often they would ask me inside and, as we drank a cup of tea, the dressing gown would invariably fall open. I swear to it. I'm not kidding, and I'm sure the same thing happened often with good-looking milkmen. The women were lonely or neglected, just eager for someone to appear and break the monotony — because remember, this was an era before housewives ever thought about going out to work.

Quickly learning to use patience, tact and charm, plus apparent expertise with figures, I was soon making good commission out of selling insurance — in fact, after three months Citizens Life and Mutual offered me a guaranteed salary and a car — up to now, I had been doing my rounds on a bicycle.

Suddenly, it was brought home to me, the reason I had come to New Zealand in the first place — to see new places and how people lived — just as Somerset Maugham, Robert Louis Stevenson and Jack London had gone on their travels. Now here was I, millions of miles away from boring old Beverley, with cash in my pockets and the summer approaching.

I bought a four shilling pair of workmen's trousers (this was before jeans came in), a woollen blanket, and a billy can, packed them into a haversack with my camera and notebook, and set off south. To all intents, I was a bum, before it became fashionable, and New Zealand was the ideal place for hitchhiking. No matter how much I might kid myself it could be a good experience to flop down for the night in some ditch or under some hedge, sure enough some good-hearted farmer would pull up beside me, ask where I was making for, and finish up taking me home.

I saw the inside of poor cow-cocky's farms and big sheep ranches. Sometimes I would try my hand at shearing woolly Merinos, and dipping them; I helped with milking, picked apples in Nelson and dug ditches — though not too much of that! In passing, I saw the geysers and hot springs of Rotorua, mingled with the Maoris (as much as they would allow me), did a stint of panning for gold in South Island, and made a kind of name as the first guy to cross the Haast Pass on a bicycle! Today a beautifully graded road sweeps through the Haast Pass, but in the Thirties, the Haast was a river that had cut an erratic course through wild granite mountains and rain forests, to finally become a raging torrent as it poured out into the Tasman Sea. I struggled up fern-fringed trails (which few New Zealanders had ever seen), cut my way through twisted lianas, struggled over rocks and several times had to cross over a tree bridge — an old kauri trunk laid over a narrow ravine.

Once my wheels got stuck in a rotted 'vein', and there was I, balancing over a four thousand foot drop, trying to free my bike. I was terrified and nearly gave up... but somehow I got the bloody bike free and pushed on. I wouldn't have missed the next two days for anything. Torrential rain poured down for forty-eight hours and I was marooned in a rough wooden hut with an old Maori forester who miraculously appeared through the surrounding tangle of tree ferns. His name was Ben Kiwaiata and over a smoky log fire and meals of dried deer meat and kumara (sweet potatoes), he gave me a cram course in the traditions and way of life of these handsome Polynesian people. According to him, they arrived in New Zealand about nine hundred years ago and lived an almost perfect communal life — although they fought battles amongst each other to keep fit and strong (he said!). They were never defeated by British troops, but were almost wiped out by measles, smallpox and influenza. In the Thirties, there were only about a hundred thousand left.

"On the surface," he said, "we are accepted as human beings, but in practice are treated as rather dumb third-class citizens." I would say that Ben's words opened up my mind to ethnic problems in general, and certainly helped me behave with more understanding when years later I had to cope with apartheid in South Africa, while shooting *Nor The Moon By Night* and *The Hellions*.

With some good hints on how to find a trail down the west side of the Pass, Ben and I said goodbye and I continued down to the Haast River. In a terrifying ten minutes, I lost my bike in the swollen waters of the Haast, but saved myself and a rucksack.

At the coast, I found one solitary farm where I was greeted like the man from Mars. I managed to hitch a lift from the weekly mail plane, but still had to trudge for two hundred miles through the lonely, but fantastically beautiful, rain forests of the West Coast. At Hokitika I settled down to write an article on my adventure — which, to my joy, was published in the Auckland Star a few weeks later. But it did seem to me that one shouldn't have to risk one's life every time one wanted to go into print, so for a while I hung out in Greymouth, where there was still talk of the Gold Rush of Ninety-eight.

A hundred years ago, masses of ships were wrecked along this coast, as 'fossikers' scrambled ashore to try and pick up the dull yellow nuggets which, for a short period, were miraculously washed up on the broad sands. I wrote about ten articles and short stories about these adventurous times, basing my writing on recorded happenings and peopling them with colourful characters out of my imagination. I sent them off home and some were published in UK magazines. The rejects, I found in one of my father's files years later.

This little stretch of authorship had been achieved without my having to risk life and limb again, but the Spirit of Adventure was rekindled when the 'Cap Pilar', a wonderful three-master schooner, dropped anchor in Wellington Harbour. Crowds flocked out to gape at the ship's romantic shape. I managed to buttonhole two young crew members and learned that they were all mostly amateurs, crazy about sailing, paying for their own keep for the privilege of 'manning the sails'. They seemed a very select closed company — a bit toffee-nosed (as we would say in Yorkshire) about their whole adventure and way of life.

Patient inquiry led me to a guy who came from Bridlington in East Yorkshire and, after some 'homesick chat', he took me to Captain McLeod. He was a genial but stern Scot who had conceived the brilliant idea of seeing the world differently and on the cheap! I told him what I was doing and that I'd like to work my passage to Australia — only one thousand miles away across the Tasman.

"I really don't need more crew," he said, "though I wouldn't mind adding two more politically minded chaps to sail with us to China."

"China?!" I asked. "Why China? And how political?" "Oh, something like the Freedom Fighters standing up to Franco in Spain," he said, obviously trying not to be too specific. I stared at him, until he blurted out, "I've always wanted to sail the China Seas, and I've a notion I might get more help from Chang Kai Chek, if I could drop him off a couple of volunteers to join his fight against the Japs and warlords." It seemed a strange proposal to me, but I told him I had nearly joined the International Brigade (which was a lie, of course), and that I had a great sympathy with the Chinese.

"Okay," he said. "You seem a bit of a freebooter like the rest of us. You can come aboard, and we'll see how you shape up in the rigging!"

Shinnying up the masts and wrapping and unfurling shrouds on madly swaying yardarms, turned out to be a tough, unrewarding job, and pretty dangerous, unless you were crazy about the sea. "Sail stations! Sail stations!" was the constant cry of Mad McLeod. "On the fore and main, set uppers and lowers!"

"Uppers and lowers, aye!" was the yelled reply of the now twenty-six crew of which I was an integral part.

The first day out, trying to hold my balance along a slack cable, looped below a yardarm swaying a hundred and twenty feet above the deck and sea, I felt a nausea such as I had never experienced. I was too terrified to vomit until back to the safety of the deck, my two new chums, Johnno and Hans, pulled me to the stern, clipped me to a railing and cried, "Now, sick your guts up, but make it to leeward, for God's sake!" After three days and a lot of weary bones, Johnno, Hans and I were relaxing in the bow.

"Don't you think it's like a giant stringed instrument?" said Johnno, pointing up. "Like fifty harps all roped together," said Hans.

"Just look at the bowsprit," said I. "One minute jutting right into the sky and the next pointing down into the depths of the deep blue swell." I had to admit there were many moments on 'The Cap Pilar' which offered the most majestically spectacular sights a man could ever experience, yet after two weeks, I felt I had absorbed enough atmosphere and beauty, to know what life must have been like in the old days, and to hell with China!

I jumped ship in Sydney, where years later I filmed *The Pirate Movie*, and had command for three whole weeks of an old two-masted schooner which I sailed and filmed all around the vast harbour! Sydney proved to be a fascinating friendly city where I might have settled down and found a job selling something or another. For a week or two, I tried getting orders for a model-photographer I was introduced to, but Bondi and other fantastic beaches with their tall, blonde, willing girls played havoc with my schedules...

Every day I became more and more intrigued by reports about a guy named Hopperman, who was trying to set a record by cycling the whole way round Australia. Now I had no ambitions to do that. But, at least, it proves you can explore Australia on a bicycle, even though it is so big — and I know all about cycling, I thought.

Australia is a very different place from the lush grasslands, forests and lakes of New Zealand. Apart from wide coastal stripes, it is a hard, hot land with snakes and iguanas, which can do you great harm. On the road to Brisbane, I once saw a woodsman with an iguana attached so strongly to his arm that he had to chop the lizard-like animal off with an axe.

"The wound will stay with me for life," he told me. "Once the bastard has bitten you, you're stuck with the wound for Eternity!" I found out also that once you become 'A Jolly Swag Man' like me, on the road, no Aussie farmer or truck driver would dream of giving you a lift, as they had insisted on doing so often in New Zealand.

"Only a stupid Pommie asshole would dream of sleeping under the open sky and get bitten by mozzies and snakes. But if that's how you want it, good luck on yer, cobber!" was the attitude of most Aussies I came across.

Great stretches of road on the New England Highway were just sun-hardened mud, and often so corrugated that I was bounced up and down on the bike like on a funfair 'cakewalk'. And when it rained, the ruts were so deep and clinging that one could barely cover a mile in an hour. On the whole, I used to average one hundred miles a day, carrying water in a billy can looped over the lamp bracket. Now, quite hardened, sunburnt and fit, I would lay over a day or two to pick tobacco, sugar and bananas. Tough work and often it meant sleeping in huts occupied by rats as well as my fellow pickers. But I made a few bob to keep me on the road and got the feel of Australia and the Aussies, better than any tourist or well-heeled sightseer.

And now, since you have been so patient, I will tell you of my first actual brush with movie making. I had pulled my bike off a dusty road near a little sawmill town of Murwillumbah.

Giant gum trees spread their barkless branches overhead and the sinuous fingers of vines wrapped themselves round my legs. I was swishing around for a place to doss, when a metallic voice yelled out: "Drop dead, cobber. You're bang in the middle of picture!"

Without a word, I dropped to my knees, almost on top of a black snake which slithered away noiselessly. I had accidentally (or perhaps as fate intended) stumbled onto the 'shoot' of one of the first Australian movies, called *Tall Timbers*. It was an adventure story set in the bush with a damsel in distress, a villain and the inevitable young hero who would have been played by 'Crocodile Dundee' Hogan today. With wide-open eyes, I watched the actors emote and the cameraman light them with tinfoil covered boards, and there was the boss man — the director himself, whom everyone obeyed and ran to carry out his every wish, the shadowy, unattainable role model of my ambitions.

I hung around and made friends with Maudie, a full-bosomed, freckled redhead, who was taking notes before and after every shot (continuity, as I now know it is called!). She told me roughly what was going on, and since I was still there when the unit wrapped, and obviously had no place to go, she took me to her bed and kept me around for three whole weeks!

During that time I helped hold on to a crocodile's tail while it snapped six inches away from the heroine's foot, and drove her in a T-model Ford in front of a forest fire. The star called in sick that day and, wonder of wonders, I doubled for him — hating the fact that I had to keep my face turned away from the camera.

Now on speaking terms with the director, Dud Duggan, I watched him line up every shot and invariably asked, "Why?" I must have been a pain in the butt to him, but he didn't want to lose the services of his Continuity Girl... while I learned what I believed was most of the whole art of movie making!

But all good things must have an end — in this case, in the shape of a lanky, weather-beaten character called Joey. Apparently, he was just back from a kangaroo hunt in the Outback, and I was about to pump him on his experiences, when Rob, the first assistant, practically ran me off the set, hissing, "Get the hell out of here, Pommy, and for God's sake lose yourself in Brisbane."

"But why?" I protested. "Duggan has said I can stick around while he puts all this stuff together."

"He may have said that yesterday," whispered Rob, almost heaving me on to my bike. "He won't want you around now, and if you care anything for Maudie, you'll scarper. That's her husband!" I vanished — having learned among many other wonderful things, the loyalty and camaraderie that springs up and holds a film unit together.

When I passed through Hollywood, a year or so later, in a homeward direction, I realised how little I had learned about real picture making. I had sailed Eastwards across the Pacific and was relaxing for a week or two in the Palisades, with a retired Yorkshire couple. Again, as fate would have it, their next door neighbour was Glenn Ford. He and his wife, Eleanor Powell, were the first real movie stars I ever met.

Over drinks in their home, I hung on to their every word and eagerly accepted an invitation to visit the MGM Studios in Culver City. For a whole day, I was given a VIP tour around a dozen indoor and exterior sets where filming was going on. My impression was of many people standing around, apparently waiting for one or another of the massive crew to come back from some mysterious errand.

I thought I could make some sense out of the setting up and rehearsing of a dance sequence directed by the fabulous Busby Berkeley. He had beautiful befeathered girls moving up and down stairways and through fountains and I found I could picture what the camera up on that crane would be registering. It must have made a deep impression on me, because in six of my first ten movies, I always managed to work in a dance sequence!

At last, I was seeing what the movie magazines like 'Picture Show' had been describing, but despite my new knowledge of people and places, I knew I was still 'on the outside' in America, with not a clue how to get inside this obviously tight magic circle of picture makers.

And I still had the wanderlust — almost like a sickness. To me, at this time, being in motion was almost the most important thing in the world, so when I found a 1930 Packard Sedan in San Pedro (in apparently good running order — for FIFTY BUCKS), I bought it and set off towards San Francisco and the northern Redwoods. For a hundred days I zigzagged my way across America, sleeping mostly in the car because cash was getting low, and I didn't really like stopping to work. The Grand Canyon, Petrified Forest, and the Painted Desert were scorched deep into my mental canvas.

I spent a week among the Indians, getting as close to them as I could, because having been brought up on Fenimore Cooper's Deerfoot stories, I felt they had had such a raw deal that even before I left Beverley, I used to include them in my prayers —- asking God to make up for the lousy deal they had obviously had. On the pretext of writing an article, I visited a trade school for young Navajos outside Albuquerque, and made friends with Skinyea, a young Indian training to be a metal worker. He took me to his mother's 'hogan' where I saw how his family lived, plucking wool from their flocks and weaving crazy zigzag designs on frameworks in the sun. I've been a sucker for Navajo rugs ever since, and one film I wrote and never succeeded to get financed, is about Cochise, the great Chief of the Apache Tribes (not Geronimo, who was a rogue). If only I could have made this movie, which I developed with more care and love than any movie I have ever been involved in, I would have felt I had done something positive for the poor Indians.

Skinyea introduced me to Pueblo Indians who have lived in the caves around Zuni for thousands of years. I tried to film some of their sacred dances, but I was spotted. We ran and tried to hide in the labyrinth of caves surrounding the place, but of course we were caught and dragged before a Council of Elders. I thought they were going to crucify Skinyea (because he should have known better). As for me, I thought I was going to be hung, drawn and quartered, but after desperate explanations (I never thought I had it in me), we were banished with only the reel of film torn from my camera. (Yes, by this time I was trying to keep some kind of documentary, 8mm record of my travels — a kind of beginning of film making, I vaguely imagined.)

One of the most scary happenings in my life occurred one night, under the stars, just outside Cameron, a lonely trading post in Arizona. Since before sunset, I had been networking with an Apache musician who had got together an orchestra.

"We had a great reception at Carnegie Hall, New York," he said. "The Yanks had never heard real traditional Indian music. Now my dream is to take the group to London. The Albert Hall. Could you get me a booking there?" So much for my boasting about Concert Party and Bands!

I grilled him about his life — especially how he had made it so far as a downtrodden Indian, and he kept telling me what his requirements would be if I could book him a tour (as if I would have been able to find the right contacts in London, at that time!).

Midnight came and, The Moment of Truth. Because I didn't want anyone hanging around my car when I slept, I had parked it about four hundred yards away in the mesquite scrub. I had not taken twenty steps toward it before I heard a rattle, then another. The whole of that quarter-mile walk was punctuated with rattles, and a terror I have never experienced before or since. I shone my torch right into the face of a coiled rattler, ready to spring. Another slithered away, rattling like a Boy's Brigade drummer. When I reached the car I hardly dare open the door in case one of the monsters slithered inside, and what if there was one inside already? It was a nightmare experience where the imagination magnified a thousand fold, a situation which was pretty dangerous anyway. But nothing is lost on a future director — on several occasions I have cast my mind back and used that memory as a measuring rod for a sequence of terror and tension I was aiming to achieve in a movie (see *The Planter's Wife*).

Another scary experience occurred along a never-ending desert road between Delta and Jericho, in Utah. I picked up a hobo. He looked quite shaggy, but I picked him up because I had sworn in New Zealand that since everyone had been so good to me on the road, that I would always stop for a hobo. (I don't do it now and haven't done so for many years!)

This guy had quick-moving eyes and smelled very high, but we talked continuously as the car bounced and kicked up the dust. He told me the technique for 'riding the rails' and the tricks of the trade for coming out with a profit after a season's harvesting. For my part, I hoped I would never again have to pick grapes, apples, bananas, lettuce or worse!

I tried to impress him with my stories of hitchhiking and cycling in New Zealand and Australia. I was boasting about the gold I'd picked up (never more than a few ounces, actually), when out of the corner of my eye, I saw him sliding a gun out from under his shirt. He was pointing it at me and laconically stroking the muzzle.

"You know," he said, "it turns out that I've had a very smooth trip with you, buddy, but this is the loneliest stretch of road I know. It was my intention to shoot you and get me a nice motey-car." As I gaped at him, he continued, "I would have shaved off all this fuzz, and buried you under all this scrub. They wouldn't have found your body for months. Lucky we're kind of birds of a feather, but if I were you, I'd be very careful about who you offer rides to in the good old USA!"

I dropped him off near the outlandish Mormon town called Jericho, and continued on my way, thinking someone up there is definitely watching over me. I guess I must be building up some kind of debt or obligation to repay. Could it perhaps mean that I am destined to turn my experiences into a novel or something creative to inspire others? My next stop was Salt Lake City.

Sailing back across the Pacific, I had developed a very cosy relationship with Mary Benning, a very pretty Mormon girl who had been doing her one year missionary service in Fiji. She must have been very short of white company, because on those hot nights on the "Mariposa" she threw herself into lovemaking with an enthusiasm I had never before experienced.

Mary invited me to stay at her parents' house in Bountiful. What a heavenly place that will be with her, I thought, but when I arrived there, only two months later, I got a very cold reception, because in two days' time Mary was going to be married! She must have been needing a man very urgently, I decided.

However, through Mary I had become very interested in Joseph Smith, the Mormon prophet, and how he founded a new religion based on finding some ancient golden plates on a hillside near Lake Erie. It seemed a very unlikely story, but according to all the records I could dig up, no one had ever proved that he didn't find the plates. Hadn't I learned on New Zealand's wild West Coast that the unbelievable is always possible (in the way those golden nuggets had been washed ashore forty years ago, so why not Joe Smith's plates of gold)? His find was a treasure indeed, for by translating the writings on the plates he had formulated a new way of living which seemed to bring joy and satisfaction to millions of people. I found Joseph Smith, Brigham Young and the whole Mormon saga fascinating, and although I was not allowed in the Temple (not having been baptised), they let me browse for several days in their unique library. There something remarkable happened.

The Mormons collect every parish register they can lay their hands on, because, if and when you become a Mormon, you have to be baptised as a proxy for all your relatives who never had the advantage of knowing Joseph Smith's heaven. I was casually thumbing through a parish register from Yorkshire when suddenly the name 'PETER ANNAKIN' jumped out at me... registered in the tiny village of Wixley, only thirty-two miles from my hometown!

This discovery gave me the start and impetus to trace this ancestor — right back to the Ukraine! He was described as a 'cordweigner' — a man who makes ropes, and apparently jumped ship off the East Coast of Yorkshire in 1745, made his way to Wixley, married and had sixteen children! Because of this clue provided me by the Mormons, I have always had a soft place in my heart for them, so when I was approached in 1987 to make a movie about Joseph Smith and his wife Emma, I jumped headlong into the fullest research, and had a ball writing the script, and was within one day of starting to shoot in Columbus, Ohio, when the promised finance vanished into thin air! I still would give anything to make this movie, which would have been my fiftieth... but I am digressing... on the question of how I ever became a director.

After more than three years on the road and high seas, I worked my passage to Liverpool, coming off the ship with exactly one shilling and sixpence (about twenty-five US cents, I would guess). My father met me at the docks, and as we drove in his little Clyno two-seater, across the Lancashire Pennines, back into my beloved Yorkshire Dales, I had the feeling that he thought it had all been a waste of time and I was a failure. However, he gave me support to try my hand at writing a book, which I laboriously typed on a dresser in the front bedroom, ten hours a day for three months. I called the book 'Breakaway Westward', and took the four hundred and twenty typed pages to London, where I literally knocked on the door of eighteen publishers. To my great joy (but secretly no surprise to me!), the House of Collins agreed to publish it, and we were about to sign a contract and start editing, when the Russo-Finnish War broke out and suddenly everything was put on hold. Great Britain was hit by its first taste of rationing — paper!! *Started in Nov 1939*

To make ends meet, I wheedled myself into a job selling flats for an estate agent just off Greys Inn Road, where I had found a boarding house for three pounds a week. It was occupied mainly by university students and young Jewish refugees from Poland and Czechoslovakia. We spent hours arguing about the writings of Marx and Engels (which I had never encountered before) and political ways to stop Hitler, Mussolini, Fascism and the war everyone said was just around the corner.

I had travelled thousands of wearisome miles to equip myself for a useful, interesting, creative career. To hell with coming events! I produced copies of articles which had been published, but neither newspaper editors nor Reuters (to whom I had a very good introduction) would give me a break, because along the way I had never learned shorthand!

I walked into the front offices of British studios like Ealing, Gainsborough and British National, but it seemed I was too old to be taken on as a clapper-boy, and although I could claim an affinity with Australian and Hollywood production, when it came down to brass tacks, I had no technical skills.

Out of desperation, I took the phone book and picked out fifty important firms with head offices in and around London. I wrote to the Managing Directors, telling them what an amazing fellow I was, with experiences that no one else could possibly have had. Surely there was a niche for me in their organisation. I received only one reply, but although I didn't realise it at the time, it was RIGHT ON THE BUTTON for the way my life was destined to go.

The Eugene Permanent Waving Company had decided to send out a travelling show to publicise their system. Some technicians had designed a very clever 'fit-up' (an expandable steel framework carrying stage curtains) which could be adapted to any theatre or town hall where they had a stage.

We were to give shows on average in three different towns per week, and my job was to get the 'fit-up' erected for the twice daily show, and by two-thirty pm, be ready and dressed in a white tuxedo, to compere the show. The show was rather unique!

The first half consisted of a demonstrated perm. I had a set speech about the history and development of adorning women's heads with curls and waves throughout the ages, and at various points in the process, I would describe exactly what was being done by Mister Elliott, our travelling hairdresser. To brighten things up, four semi-retired showgirls in our troupe would perform dances (together or solo) and our driver-cum-projectionist would show a twenty minute film. The climax of the show was my introduction of the local hairdresser's models. I would have to comment, in an amusing but informed way, on each of their creations, and finish up surrounded by a 'beauty chorus' who, under my direction, would sing OUR theme song: 'Heading Ahead for Beauty'. (Shades of my father and his primitive Methodist choir!) The job taught me to cope with every type of 'behind-the-scenes' situation, and never to fear to face, or gag, in front of an audience of anything from five hundred to three thousand!

During the interval between five and seven, we socialised with the hairdressers and their favourite models, and if I was lucky (and had the strength!), I maybe 'made out' with some pretty woman. But invariably it had to be a 'quickie' because our coach and truck usually had to leave by six am for the next town and the next twice daily show.

Over a period of nineteen months, I got to see practically every seaside town and inland city in the British Isles; worked an average of eighteen hours a day; but gained invaluable experience for a lad who was by nature a bit shy, but hoped to be in show business somehow, when the inevitable approaching war had blown over.

Eugene turned us loose just in time for me to be digging trenches in Hyde Park, when Churchill declared war over the Nazi invasion of Poland. I tried to join the RAF, but was shunted for six months into the Auxiliary Fire Service based in Soho — the centre of London's theatreland. This was another lucky break.

After three or four terrifying nights, trying to put out the fires from German bombers, things went amazingly quiet, and we became bored. Fortunately, Soho Fire turned out to have quite a smattering of professional talent: a classical composer, a guitarist, saxophonist, gag writer and pantomime queen. Between us we created 'a book' of sketches, satirical 'takeoffs' of popular stars, scenes from Movies, and Shakespeare, and much more. We had no professional producer, so I willingly stepped into the breach and rehearsed our acts. I had great satisfaction in digging out hidden talents in two of our regular firemen — and, of course, this pleased everyone. We immediately became the talk of the Fire Brigade and were commanded to give performances in Holborn, Chelsea and Hampstead.

Performing in front of fire chiefs and their wives, I learned the hard way just how far you can go with a risqué joke (risqué in those days!). The bosses had you in their power and if their womenfolk took offence, they could hand out quite a few extra duties!

My great chum was Dave Isaacs, a very lively Jew who had worked in a Leicester Square casting office. On every off-duty day, he would take me to one studio or another and we would work as extras. Imagine having a ringside seat, as famous Music Hall comics such as George Formby, Max Wall, Will Hay and the Crazy Gang worked out their shtick. One Thursday, Penn Tennyson, the director of 'Freedom Radio', came over to me and said, "You look just right for a radio announcer. Have you ever said lines?"

"Have I ever said lines?" I grinned all over my face. "I am a professional Compère!"

He gave me two pages of script and shot me in close-up. Wow! I should have been ecstatic, but I had to admit that when they called "Action!" I felt strangely inhibited — almost tongue-tied, and my heart thumped so loudly I thought sound would call "Cut!"

Suddenly, I understood the nervousness and insecurity of actors (and have never forgotten it!). As shots were being lined up, I listened to the chitchat of actors on the various sets, and decided that their way of life was full of stress, uncertainty and pitfalls. Not the ideal way to live, unless one was brilliant and had no other talents! After six months of war, the RAF decided they needed me. Following six weeks of exhausting 'square bashing', I was posted to Cosford, a big camp in the Midlands. Here as a flight mechanic I was supposed to learn how to keep Blenheim fighters in the air.

Almost immediately, I met Ron Delderfield, a budding playwright — he had had

'The Printer's Devil' performed at the Whitehall Theatre one week before the war broke out. Together, we wrote a pantomime called "Sinbad the Airman" and our CO was so amused by it that he cut my mechanics' duties to the minimum and gave me every facility to get a cast together and rehearse. Here again I found some professional talent and some very malleable amateurs.

We opened in the big canteen hall, and filled the place with so much laughter and applause that we repeated the show twenty-five times and then were sent on tour throughout Northern Command. The planes were flying without much help from me, but suddenly my flight was posted to the Middle East (so rumour had it). I spent my forty-eight hour leave with my father, who was not at all well, and seemed very embittered about everything. Again I arrived in Liverpool, but this time the Germans were giving it hell. Bombs were dropping everywhere.

I remember running across railway lines, then BLANK. Two days of my life are still missing. All anyone knows is that I was found wandering in Romford, in London's East *Essex* End, with blistered arms and torso, eyebrows singed, head with little or no hair, and a load of shrapnel up my ass.

Perhaps again the good Lord had a plan for me, because nine months later I was discharged from the hospital, and directed to Jack Beddington, Head of the Ministry of Information. Somewhere along the line it had been decided I might be more use to the war effort working in Propaganda, rather than wielding a spanner in the RAF.

"I hear you've knocked around the world quite a bit," said Jack, a rugged, no-nonsense character who had kept Shell's name to the forefront throughout the pre-war world. "What do you think you can do for us?"

I didn't really know what to say — the door seemed almost too wide open! Very hesitantly, I began... "Perhaps I could go out and write pieces showing how people all over the country are surviving in their own ways — you know, keeping their peckers up amid bombs and shortages. I've put on shows in an entertaining way to kind of illustrate themes." Then, I blurted out, "But the one thing I'd really like to do is learn every aspect of telling stories in film!"

Jack seemed to consider, a long moment. "Well, you could learn to write scripts and probably pick up film techniques at the same time."

I stared at him with open mouth. "Could I really do that, sir? If I could, I promise you, I'd work my ass off!" *(having got rid of the shrapnel)*

Jack smiled and swung in his chair. "Well, we don't actually make any of our films. The jobs are farmed out to a number of documentary companies and ex-advertising firms." He rose to his feet and looked at a board. "I could send you to Verity. They're doing some good stuff for us and are very short-handed."

I reported to Sydney Box, who became my friend, mentor, producer and guardian angel for many years. Sydney, a genial, overweight character, had not been called-up, because he had a malformed hip, but he was bright as a button, and wonderful at bringing the best out of everyone. Together with his wife Muriel (an ex-continuity girl), he had written over a thousand one-act plays that were constantly being performed in amateur theatres all over the British Empire.

"You need never starve, if you can write," said Sydney, "especially if you've given yourself a background such as yours. The question is whether your other experiences running concert parties and the like will fit you to become a director for our kind of work, so I'm going to start you at the bottom, so to speak."

I began work as a camera assistant to Reg Wyer, one of the best newsreel cameramen in the business. He taught me all the tricks of loading, focusing, and operating a Newman Sinclair, an Eymo, and eventually a studio-type Mitchell.

"If you make a boo-boo," said Reg in his high voice, "never try to hide it! They'll see it in the rushes. So, come right out with it on the spot and let's see what re-shooting has to be done."

Two weeks after starting with Reg, we were shooting an army training film called *The Sixteen Tasks of Maintaining Motorised Vehicles*. The scene needed three-camera coverage, so the director set up a brand new Arriflex (which he said he picked up from a dead German in Dunkirk).

Reg set up his Newman Sinclair (a camera driven by clockwork) and I was given an Eymo, and told to pick out the dramatic moments of a tank coming over a mined hillside. Among other things, we all had to help laying the explosives, and now at the right moment, we had to switch on 'our bombs' and photograph them.

My next lucky break was to work in a three-man team, telling the story of six British Artists and how the War had affected the content and style of their paintings. We visited the studios and homes of Henry Moore, John Piper, Henry Sutherland, John Seagrave and Matthew Smith. Henry Moore was of course becoming famous for his Underground Shelter paintings, and as the Director picked out samples to put on film, Henry turned to us and said "If you like any in that drawer, you're welcome to choose two each". That is how I started my collection with two Henry Moores for £23 each. I also loved the heavy paint-work and Rembrandt-like colouring of Matthew Smith, who at this moment seemed to be making many paintings of a long blonde-haired beauty. I acquired one of these, and showing it one afternoon to Ralph Keene, my next Director, as we were about to shoot a sequence with Land Workers. I got the most amazing reaction. He stared at the painting and said , "I *knew* the bastard was having an affair with my wife! I've got to go straight down and catch them at it!"

As he pulled on his coat he turned to me and said "You know the script and what we need, Ken. I leave you to get the shots till I'm back, hopefully tomorrow sometime!". And that is how I got my first break in Directing.

A few months later, the Ministry of Information gave me a job which couldn't have been more sexy. The powers-that-be had decided that it was much better for new mothers to breast-feed their babies, and thus save powdered milk and formula preparations which were running short. I was given twenty minutes to get this idea over persuasively, and show the mother and infant's joy in nipple sucking. I suppose today they would have given this chore to a woman director, but that species just didn't exist. However, I think my cameraman and I did a very fine job — with lots of close-ups — and the nice, full-breasted actress cast in the part seemed to enjoy herself as much as we did.

My next assignment was perhaps one of the most important changes in my career. I was chosen to work with Carol Reed on a big recruiting film for the Women's Services. It was called *We Serve.* Since Carol was one of the most respected British directors of that period, both in the theatre and movies, he was able to persuade actresses like Sybil Thorndike, Edith Evans, Margaret Rutherford, Margaret Leighton, Nora Swinburn, Joyce Redmond, and many others to work for five pounds a day, for a good patriotic cause.

One of these famous actresses, Diana Wynard, had a special interest for me, because I had seen her in *The Greeks Had A Name For It*, a show I had seen with my dad when I was fourteen. I thought she was so ethereal and enchanting that I had written her a kind of love letter — and, wonder of wonders, she had replied in her own handwriting on blue note paper!

Now, on the set of *We Serve*, I plucked up courage to tell her how I had treasured her letter. She smiled, flashed those incredible bedroomy eyes, and gave me a kiss full on the mouth. Blushing fiercely, I drifted back to the Mitchell camera I was now operating. As more and more technicians were getting called up for active service, and with only a week's instruction on this big studio camera, I was in full charge of "what went into the frame."

After a week of struggling with the wheels that you turn in opposite directions to pan and tilt a studio camera (rather like the trick of tapping your head and simultaneously rubbing your tummy), Carol slid up beside me and suddenly said, "You know, Ken, although you are putting up a good show operating, I don't think your future should be on the camera."

My face fell, but he continued, "It seems to me you have a natural aptitude for knowing where the next set-up should be." I began to feel great, beginning to ride on a cloud, as he said, "From what I've heard of your writing and directing efforts, I think you'd be better on our side of the camera!"

Nothing could have made me happier, specially since I had been completely bowled over by watching Carol's method with artistes. He never showed any irritation with their foibles and petty tantrums. Before each set-up, he would chat quietly with each actress, outlining the requirements of the scene, and listening sympathetically to their ideas. Then, he would run rehearsal, allowing them to make their own movements within the parameters he had set down for them. I learned from Carol that you can get devotion and wonderful contributions from actors when you make them feel comfortable, understood, and capable of individual interpretations of lines and actions.

Immediately, the shooting of *We Serve* was finished, a script I had been burning midnight oil to write, was accepted by the Ministry of Information. It was intended to be a mixture of reportage of war damage intermingled with the amazingly good-natured and ingenious efforts of Londoners of all ages and classes to keep up their morale. The film was timed for thirty-one minutes and this time I was a full-blown director, using whatever cameramen could be spared from other projects. In fact, I used five photographers on this movie and shot quite a few sequences myself. I was allocated an editor who had worked in studios on all types of features. Together, we assembled, edited and dubbed the film in approximately nine weeks.

I learned a tremendous amount from this experience in the cutting rooms, discovering that no matter what material you shot, it could be played about with during the editing in miraculous ways — just as Pudovkin had described in his book — "Film Techniques and Film Acting," and Eisenstein in his essays on how his Russian Revolution epic *Potemkin* had been put together.

London 1942 happened to be released throughout the cinemas in Britain, with a new RKO movie called *The Devil and Daniel Webster*. This fantastic movie, in which Walter Huston plays the Devil who buys the soul of a poor New Hampshire farmer (Gene Lockhart), and sends him a beautiful handmaiden in the form of French actress Simone Simon, became my model and inspiration to make feature movies. It was a combination of social awareness, fantasy, romance and mystery, with a unique quality which made the movie personal to everyone in the audience. The great trial scene at the end, where Daniel Webster (played by the powerful Edward Arnold) battles with the Devil for the soul of the poor farmer, in front of a jury made up on "the Quick and the Dead", is indelibly etched in my memory. Dieterle's direction has remained a yardstick for me in the judgement of movies and my personal approach... But I had to wait several more years before I could apply my new enthusiasms and ideas to a feature movie.

Perhaps it was all to the good, because for the next three years I was occupied in putting together two of the most interesting propaganda pictures that any filmmaker could ask for. The first was called *Pacific Thrust*, which I was commissioned to script and compile from material shot by war-cameramen all over the world. Its purpose was to inform British audiences what was happening in the Pacific and what the next moves of General MacArthur and Admirals Halsey and Nimitz might be at the other side of the world. I was given the run of three million feet of war material, from which I had to choose shots to create an impression of land and naval actions — in the shortest possible time — thirty minutes to be exact.

I would 'mark up' a great shot of Aussie soldiers moving under fire through the jungles of New Guinea, and maybe cut it next to a ten foot shot of Wingate's 'Chindits' picking off Jap snipers in Burma —- MacArthur wading ashore in Guam, intercut with a helicopter landing through smoke on a completely different island. So long as I could make up believable battles and naval actions which illustrated the kind of war that was being fought: 'ANYTHING WENT!' This experience proved to me that editing was something which gave one godlike power. Take a few feet shot anywhere and, as the great Eisenstein had written, so long as it was cut together with other bits of film *and meant something,* that was the game.

I spent whole nights and weekends choosing shots and cutting them together until the effect I needed was visually there. Unlike learning the magic of film making today, the war threw me into a crash course in a way nobody I know ever experienced —- because a job had to be done, and there was nobody else — no other departments to take over the work they specialised in. *I had to do it!*

In *Pacific Thrust* once the visual stories and commentary were in place there were maps to be devised with arrows that moved to show the military strategy and the next likely moves. I took my material to Jim Larkin, the only animator in Soho who had not been called up! Naturally, throughout this job I had contact with the experts in the War Office, but we had a hell of a job keeping up with the latest moves of the American forces who suddenly began to leapfrog islands at remarkable speed. Nevertheless, we delivered the film to the cinemas and, thank God, we were 'right on the button' with what was happening *that week!*

During the next two and a half years I shot fourteen documentaries and propaganda films, the most interesting being part of a series called *Know Your Enemy*. The working title of my segment was 'The Japanese Army — How it has become what it is today'. Using the same volume of war material, plus more film lying in newsreel vaults, I delved into the origins of the amazing Japanese military machine, its background in the Shinto religion, the traditions of the Samurai warriors, and pre-war atrocities in China. I was expected to rouse British audiences to anger, and show them exactly why the Japanese soldier in Burma, Okinawa, New Guinea, etc., was such a tenacious enemy, and how his training and way of thinking might lead him to behave in the future. A fascinating and somewhat awe-inspiring assignment!

On the brighter side, during the latter days of the war, I was also making documentaries to make the British public aware of the approaching problems of peace, such as the planting of new forests to replace the timber lost during the war; new ways of intense farming, if we were ever to get rid of rationing. I wrote and directed a series called *Crop Rotation* during which I made my first acquaintance with the ponderous, but wonderful, three-strip Technicolor camera. Three great British feature cameramen photographed for me — Jack Cardiff, who, like a painter, judged compositions by their colour components; Geoff Unsworth, who was an artist in judging only by the eye, the balance of daylight and artificial lights; and Cyril Knowles, who shot fast and believed only in what his light-meter told him — a great technician, also. In later years, I worked with them all on feature movies, and can only say that their approach to photography gave me the most solid basis of judging quality, and understanding exactly what I could hope to register on colour film, under all conditions.

As the Allied Forces spread like wildfire across Europe, practically anyone who could use a camera was commandeered and sent to cover the inside story of what had been Nazi Germany. I found myself riding in jeeps, through mile after mile of ruins, down the Rhine to Fribourg and the university town of Heidelberg, which I had visited as a hiker in 1933 when Nazism and Jew-baiting were just starting.

Little had I expected in those early days of hearing German students singing the Horst Wessel song, that I would see and photograph, *for a world audience,* the dreadful, mind-blowing scenes inside the concentration camp in Theresinstadt in Czechoslovakia. Amid the skeleton-like bodies, reaching out beneath eyes filled with dull desperation, I tried to use all the photographic skill and journalistic know-how that I had been lucky enough to acquire over the last four years. Because of this experience I am one of the few people who could not abide the movie *Life is Beautiful*. Comedic situations could never have happened against such a soul-destroying background, and even if they did, they should never be allowed to dull the impact of Nazi psychology. Occasionally, I see one or two of my shots in Holocaust movies, but the most lasting effect has been my intense, almost pathological hatred of anything that smells of anti-Semitism, or, for that matter, the persecution of any man, woman or child because of their creed or colour. This was a very necessary broadening of the mind for that innocent Yorkshire lad who set out to see the world on a hundred pounds and hoped vaguely to become a journalist, but finished up as a Director.

CHAPTER TWO
My Way Into
Feature Movies

Sydney Box had now moved into features while still keeping his organisation for documentary and propaganda films. His second entertainment movie was a smash hit called *The Seventh Veil* with James Mason and Ann Todd. It was a sentimental piece with a little sadism thrown in. It caught the mood of the immediate post-war period and, as a result, Sydney had been placed in charge of J. Arthur Rank's Gainsborough Studios, with a program of twenty-two movies to be made each year.

Still my great friend and advisor, he said, "We all know you're now an all-round technician, but I need to know one last thing — that you can direct professional actors as well as real people. Get hold of a subject which gives you this experience and if it is okay, I'll give you a feature!"

Another great chance. I touted around London and found the British Council urgently needed a film explaining to foreigners the working of the British legal system. In two weeks I devised three short stories which illustrated the workings of a Magistrate's Court, an Assize Court, and the famous Old Bailey where the most important murder trials took place.

The script was accepted and I was given a budget which would enable me to cast ten average-priced actors and two reasonably well known. We shot in real courts around London and Oxford and built the essential parts of the Old Bailey in the small Merton Park Studios, which Sydney's documentary company still owned. *British Criminal Justice* was shot and edited in twelve weeks, and the Council was so delighted with it that they begged me to go to South America and lecture with the film in Brazil, the Argentine and Chile.

Of course, this was to me another chance of adventure, but likely to be tricky since, despite all the string-pulling, the British Treasury would not allow any foreign travel allowance to exceed five pounds a day! But I had lived on a shoestring in my previous travels, and had devised a scheme to borrow from British Bank employees in places like Rio de Janeiro or Buenos Aires, on the promise to pay them back in pounds on their next leave in England. Thus, I was able to get a taste of Carnival in Rio, ride with the picturesque gauchos around Cordoba in the foothills of the Andes, and sneak into a strange performance of voodoo in a church outside Valpariso.

The old Spanish port was decaying and decadent, a perfect background for a shootout-pursuit kind of story which is so popular today. I drafted out a screenplay, but never used it, because on returning home, I found Sydney had other plans for me. "You passed the test handling actors, now I'm going to put you under a ten picture contract!" I gasped. "Your first movie will be *Holiday Camp*!"

Holiday camps were a phenomenon started in England just after the war by a Canadian entrepreneur called Billy Butlin. They were to provide cheap 'holidays at home' for whole families, complete with baby-sitters to relieve parents of any worries. At this time, he had built eight enormous camps, some of which accommodated as many as eight thousand people weekly throughout the summer. He kept the campers amused every hour of the day with sports instructors, comedians, clowns, top star entertainers and big bands. Everyone was taught to 'Do The Hokey-Cokey', a massive progressive dance, which used to rock the dance halls... altogether a promising background for a family-oriented movie, it seemed to me!

When Sydney took over Gainsborough Studios, most of the films they turned out had been rather like today's romance novels... very artificial, and shot almost completely in the studio. Sydney now wanted to use my documentary experience to bring realism into the treatment of the story, though he still believed that for popular cinema consumption, one had to have a good *fictional* story — in this case, six stories intertwined around the activities of a week in the 'Holiday Camp'.

To devise the script, Sydney hired Godfrey Wynn, a popular women's magazine writer, who was a great friend of the Royal Family. In order to prove he was as tough as any normal chap (he was an open homosexual), he had volunteered to join the Navy, and for two years had been on the dreaded Arctic Run, supplying arms and munitions to the Russians at Murmansk. His ship had been torpedoed twice, and he had suffered terribly from frostbite. His fingernails were completely pulped and permanently deformed. *in 1939!*

In the Butlin camp, Godfrey was a great favourite with the ladies and I grew very fond of him, until one morning he started calling me 'Darling'! I must have shown my awkwardness or displeasure, because he suddenly withdrew his arm from my shoulders. He lisped, "Oh dear, Ken, I mustn't do that, must I? Please slap my hand when I do it again ... which I guess I will!"

I grinned and we remained friends for many years. When we brought our draft screenplay back to the studio, Sydney felt it needed pepping up... so, I had my first taste of compromise and writing by committee. I remember sitting round a table with Sydney, his wife Muriel, Ted Willis (who was a left-wing playwright, later to become a Lord) and Peter Rogers (who eventually became the most successful creator of that saucy but funny British series called 'The Carry-Ons'!

At our session, everyone was asked to throw in their suggestions and add gags. Muriel's contribution, I recall, was to introduce a murderer into the camp, based on the current trial of a serial-killer called Neville Heath, whom it was alleged had lured six lonely women to their deaths. We showed the development of his sleazy relationships in the camp.

The murderer was eventually played by Dennis Price. I was also pleased with the casting of a touching comedian, Esme Cannon, with whom I had worked in Carol Reed's *We Serve*. We shot the attempted murder scene on a fake cliff in front of a painted background with strips of tinfoil strung across a painted sea, to provide the 'sea in moonlight' effect. It was all very different from my documentary experiences.

For the location shooting at Filey (which I remembered as a quiet fishing village on the East Yorkshire Coast, not more than forty miles from where I had grown up), Sydney provided me with a crew of forty expert technicians.

"Even though I have a great respect for your talents and enthusiasm, I'm not taking any risks with you, Ken," said Sydney. "I'm surrounding you with the best technicians I can find in every department."

Looking back I bless Sydney for this decision, because I was able to learn my trade and polish up my technique in the quickest and toughest possible school. If I made an error of judgement on the set, I could see (or imagine I could see!) the old hands exchanging looks and raising eyebrows.

I watched as my experienced assistants worked all day like sheepdogs among the 'Happy Campers', persuading them to give up good vacation time to be extras in the movie. Hardly anybody objected, which is the same the world over. Ordinary people love to feel they've taken part in a film. The only thing that prevents the extensive use of willing amateurs as extras has been the unions.

The shop stewards controlled the conditions of shooting throughout the British Isles at this time, and a young director had to learn very quickly how to cope with the obligatory tea breaks at ten in the morning, three-thirty in the afternoon, and having to ask their permission to work fifteen minutes extra if one was in the middle of a shot at six pm — the official end of the day!

On *Holiday Camp*, the three shop stewards even objected to the unit being housed in the holiday 'chalets' (for which the vacationers were paying good money!). They wanted to 'live-it-up' in Scarborough, a popular seaside resort some twenty miles *seven* away, complaining that the constant pep talks coming over the camp loudspeakers disturbed their concentration, and that the mass cooked food disturbed their stomachs!

They won, of course, with the result that I was told I must cut two days off my shooting schedule to pay for the extra transport and hotel accommodation for the crew. I could see life in features was going to be very different from my free and easy days in documentary, where I usually had a crew of six (at the most ten), who had always seemed as eager as I was to shoot whatever hours were needed.

"If Billy Butlin hears our lot have moved out, Gov," said my old-time location manager, "he's likely as not to withdraw all our facilities." I nodded, "I see your point, Tom, and since Billy comes around once a week to show himself off to the campers, I think you and I should make a point of showing the flag night and day!"

And so it came about that I continued to live in a chalet, overhearing all the intimate talk of families as they went to and fro. It was often very funny with a wife upbraiding her husband: "I saw the way you looked at that girl, Charlie. If I ever catch you at it with her, I'll break every bone in your bloody body!"

I registered lines like that through the thin walls of the chalets almost every night, except those when I was out dancing with one of the Red Coats (entertainment directors). She was a Welsh girl called Gwen, and because of something she told me when we were having a little 'slap and tickle' one night, months later I was able to save the finished movie from being canned!

After three weeks of shooting 'wake-up' activities, physical exercises on the beach, silly games designed solely to make holidaymakers laugh at their funny antics, beauty competitions, nightly variety shows and ballroom dancing, we returned to the studios to introduce our cast of fifteen actors into matching sets.

Our main family was called the Huggetts and was headed by Jack Warner, a popular music hall performer, and Kathleen Harrison, the very epitome of a harassed Cockney housewife. We staged a scene on the dance floor where Kathleen upbraided Jack with exactly the same words I had heard outside my chalet. In a most comic but realistic way she accused him of making eyes at Diana Dors.

At that time, Diana was a striking fifteen-year-old who had made some sort of name for herself as a Jive Queen. She had terrific joie de vivre and radiated sex, as she gyrated around. Immediately, she became the pinup girl of all the crew, especially the electricians whom I discovered all had signed postcards of her in the nude! "Why do you have to do this?" I asked her. She grinned, "Where I grew up, in Swindon, everyone was being asked to do their bit for the War Effort. I couldn't think of anything else I could do, so I had two thousand postcards printed and handed them out to GI's in the local Mecca Dance Hall. No one's ever complained, except you!"

I shook my head and put my arm around her. We worked together on and off for five or six years. I never wanted to sleep with her, but enjoyed helping her grow into a unique comedy "sexpot." She was bursting with love for everyone and every living thing. She would often come out with the dirtiest jokes, but told them with such verve and apparent innocence that no man ever felt embarrassed!

Supported by my very expert crew, the studio shooting went smoothly, apart from the Swimming Pool set, which developed a leak and soaked all our costumes stored in a room below.

We had shot the Establishing Shots for our Beauty Contest with true holidaymakers around the vast pool at Filey. Now, in a much smaller studio pool we were interweaving our actress characters. Among the group of young actresses lent to us from Rank, the most outstanding and beautiful was Hazel Court... who incidentally became a friend for life, in London, Cornwall, Italy and California. In *Holiday Camp* she played the daughter of Jack Warner and Kathleen Harrison and represented the millions of girls who had lost their men in the war, but were hanging in there. We had her winning the Beauty Contest. In real life she became a star of the Hammer Horror and Roger Corman films, an exhibition painter, sculptor, and author!

In our film, Sydney Box persuaded the beautiful, and rather unapproachable Gainsborough star, Patricia Roc, to do a one day stint as the main Beauty Judge. She responded to my direction without question... I went home feeling another milestone had been passed!

But all actors have (and should have) their own ideas about dialogue and the way a character should play. I remember going up to Sydney's office with a scene that didn't quite work. He was on the phone arguing with some union leader or other, but to my amazement managed to rewrite the dialogue of my scene perfectly before he had finished the call! He was a remarkable man of all-round talents, who had the gift of making the people he chose to work for him feel happy and fulfilled.

The grand dramatic actress Flora Robson was brought in to play some highly sentimental (almost embarrassing) scenes. She taught me how a true actress can turn on the tears at will. "Think of the saddest thing you have ever known or heard of," she said. "The tears will come without any need for camphor-sticks or other makeup tricks."

Every day I used to lunch in the special commissary provided for the contract directors of Gainsborough Studios. There were five directors who had all made names with the phoney romance-novelette-kind of pictures, which British audiences had loved during the war years: Pictures like *The Magic Box*, *Jassy*, *Madonna of the Seven Moons*, etc., with stars like Margaret Lockwood, Phyllis Calvert, Stewart Granger and James Mason. They were all a little suspicious of my documentary background and way of shooting. But Maurice Elvey, one of the Old School, turned to me one day and said, "You'll make the grade, old boy. You're obstinate, believe in yourself, and know a lot about life outside the studio. That's all you need, and I should know. I've made three fortunes as a director and lost them. The question is, do you have that same fatal flaw as me?" I frowned. "Fatal flaw? I don't understand what you mean."

Maurice gave a tight little smile as though tasting vintage wine. "I love beautiful women," he said. "Women with expensive tastes... I've had a marvellous life, old boy, living it up in the Savoy, travelling everywhere in Rolls Royces. For years, every winter I've followed the sun to the Cote d'Azur, gambled with top people in Monte Carlo... Now, I'm broke again, and because you are young and have a picture to make, I envy you like hell!"

I thought a moment. "I'm not a gambler and, at this moment can't imagine getting involved in the glamorous life you talk about — I just want to make movies about real life and real people."

Maurice shook his head. "How can you possibly hope to entertain people with unadulterated slices of real life? The kitchen sink, so to speak!". He screwed up his face.

Bernie Knowles, one of the other directors at the table, leaned forward, speaking as though to a child, "My dear fellow, it's a first principle. Audiences want escapism — beautiful women, beautiful clothes, castles in Spain, witches, crooks... that's the kind of stuff that's always filled the theatres and always will." I drew a deep breath, but before I could answer, Maurice patted me on the knee and said, "Who knows? Your friend Sydney Box seems to have different ideas. He's the new broom, and the box-office will have to prove him right, or he'll be out on his ass!"

Sydney did prove right. Audiences no longer just wanted to escape. They wanted to be told how brave they had been during the war, and what concrete rewards they could expect in the 'New World Fit For Heroes'. In three years poor old Maurice Elvey was in 'Glebelands', the charity home for broke film people, and none of the other directors at that table could get a job!

Holiday Camp turned out to be a great success, covering its cost and going into profit in less than three months after its release. But as I said earlier, it might never have been shown! Billy Butlin had been drooling at the mouth over the free publicity his camps were going to receive, but when Sydney showed him the finished film, he hit the roof. I had not been invited to the showing, but was watching from the projection booth. I signalled for the projectionist to turn down the sound...

"This bloody film will drive everyone away from my camps. How can they bring their kids and sweethearts, if they believe we let murderers stalk the camps?" he yelled. So, it was Muriel Box's bright idea of the 'Heath Murderer' that was going to sink my first effort!

"I'll fight you through every court in England, if you try to show this filthy movie!" continued Billy. I picked up the house phone and called Sydney. Cupping my hand closely around the mouthpiece, I whispered a few words to him. I saw him nod and put down the phone.

I raced downstairs to watch them come out of the elevator. It was quite a few minutes, but as the gate opened, Sydney was all smiles again. I came forward and he introduced me to Billy (who, of course, knew me quite well from the Filey shooting). "He loves the movie, don't you, Billy?" said Sydney. Billy threw me a sick smile and nodded. "It'll make a lot of money for J. Arthur Rank," he said. "I only hope it does the same for me!"

"What on earth did you tell Sydney?" said the projectionist, when I slipped upstairs to give him the customary one pound tip. I grinned, "That seven dead bodies had been fished out of the Butlin Camp pools that summer! Just think what the press would make of that story!" "But how did you know about it?" he asked. I grinned again. "Oh, through a few wasted but delightful hours with a girl called Gwen! In a rather intimate moment, she told me how she often had to go round with the night patrol collecting drunks ... and sometimes they were lying dead in the pools! She made me swear never to tell anyone, but drastic situations call for drastic action — even if it's not quite kosher."

By the time this happened, I was well into my second movie. We were having an end-of-picture party after *Holiday Camp* when Sydney, all smiles, called me across the room. He said, "I hope all this has not been too exhausting for you, old boy, because over the weekend I want you to make a trip to the French Alps." He produced a newspaper cutting, six days old, about a Dakota that had crashed on Mont Blanc. Twenty passengers had been saved by ski planes and guides, but they had had a terrifying experience.

"I've hired Bob Westerby to cook up an exciting story about a group of passengers. If you fancy making such a film, I want you to go out to Mont Blanc, find practical locations and an old Dakota which you can buy, and get it up there on a glacier or snow plateau — I leave it to your good judgement, old boy!"

Quite apart from the idea of the film, which would again be half-fiction half-documentary (ground that I still felt safest on), I loved the practical adventure side of the project. For a start, I managed to catch a mail plane to Paris. Don't forget, this was just after the war, and to catch a plane was almost impossible, unless you had a priority pass. I took the train to Lyons, and hired a car to the winter ski resort of Chamonix. There, I had the luck to walk past a photographer's shop displaying wonderful shots of glaciers and rock climbing. Inside I met George Tairraz, a simple, warm-hearted man, and perhaps the greatest French mountain photographer. As the skiing season had not started, he had time to sit down with me and talk.

In rather schoolboy French, I explained my problem and soon he was taking out photographs and telling me of his hair-raising escapes with the Maquis, the French Resistance during the war.

I shook my head. "It's no use getting me all excited about a secret ice cave, or fantastic crevasse, where it will be quite impossible to take a British unit consisting of at least twenty-eight people, who will be demanding tea and buns twice a day and a hot lunch."

Tairraz grinned, "Don't worry, I can look after that part of the operation."

The next day, he took me up the slopes of Mont Blanc via a cable railway that terminated at Les Huches, a simple Alpine-style station. About eight hundred metres away, we found a plateau where one could see nothing but icy slopes and the awe-inspiring massif of Mont Blanc. "Perfect!" I said. "And easy for a unit to work each day."

"Providing they can ski," said George with a smile. "Well, they'll just have to learn," I replied. "We can't find a site anywhere so close to acceptable living quarters... but what about the Dakota?"

"I know of quite a few that crashed near here," he said. "If we could truck one to Chamonix, maybe we could cut it into sections, winch them up the slope, and reassemble them as a set." It sounded easy, if you said it quickly!

We retraced our steps to the cable railway, and discussed our idea with the owner. "What's the maximum weight your cabin will carry?" I asked him. He threw out his hands. "Why can't you fly the plane and make a pancake landing on the plateau before the snow comes?", he asked.

"I'm pretty certain we don't have the money in the budget to buy a plane which still flies," I replied.

After taking measurements and calculating weights, we finished up with an agreement that he would be willing to transport quite large sections strapped under his "telepherique," providing we hired his cousin with a winch and Old Pierre, with his sledges! We concluded our discussions, 'knocking back' Pernods, and delicious 'saucisse montaigne' in French bread. Everything was settled, except for the little matter of finding the Dakota. Here again, luck was with me. Tairraz made some phone calls to his Maquis friends, and it was arranged I should meet a Count Guy de Saligny in Lyons. He had been a guerrilla leader and apparently knew the whereabouts of all crashed Allied planes.

The Count turned out to be a slim, athletic man — a born leader, I thought. We drove east to a military airfield at Salon in Provence, and there quite close, on a flat field which looked for all the world like one of those landscapes painted by Van Gogh, was a U.S. Army Dakota lying on its belly in good shape! The farmer would certainly like it removed from his land, and Guy clearly had influence with the local airfield authorities. A price was agreed of fifteen hundred pounds — and Guy promised that if we went ahead with the film, he would organise the cutting up and transport for a nominal fee. In fact, it was the beginning of a new career for him, because Sydney Box then decided to make a Hammond Innes story ('Snowbound') at Megeve, on a mountain range right opposite the one I had found. Guy became the French production co-ordinator for both that and *Broken Journey* — which, on returning to the studio, I discovered was to be the title of my new production!

In the remarkably short time of two weeks, Bob Westerby had knocked out a screenplay which read beautifully. He had created twelve picturesque characters: one, an opera singer worried about his throat (played by Francis Sullivan); another, a spoiled socialite (Margot Graham); and a young boxer and his manager (afraid lest his protégé's hands should get frost-bitten). They all had what seemed to be interesting gimmicks, but when I got down to filming them, I found they were cardboard characters. No matter how neatly they were dovetailed into the plot, one didn't care for them. It was a hard lesson I learned: never to trust a script which appears on the surface to be professionally written with flowery descriptions — but has no heart!

Quite unaware of this basic flaw, Bob Westerby and I sat down to accommodate the script to the actual locations I had found and photographed. We introduced the snow caves; a fantastic crevasse; a snow cliff suitable for lowering the passengers on ropes; a ski rescue plane available; sure-footed mules; and two St. Bernard dogs used for mountain rescues. The rest of the story depended on the interaction of our characters in and around the plane.

The shots inside the plane and tight exterior shots, where we could use sections of the plane as background to the actors, were scheduled to be shot in the studio. I say 'were scheduled', because I quite quickly discovered that in the feature world a director might be sent off to negotiate for a crashed Dakota, and find wonderful snow locations, but it was the production controller who eventually took hold of the script, broke it down, made a schedule, and decided, in this case, that I didn't need to take any actors at all up the slopes of Mont Blanc. Everyone was going to be so wrapped up in coats and scarves that I could use doubles for all of them on location!

I suppose he was right. Arthur Alcott was always right, from a production point of view. He was an expert, a meticulous 'breaker-downer' of the elements of a script, and how they could most economically be shot. In later years, when I had to tackle epics like *Those Magnificent Men In Their Flying Machines* and *Battle of the Bulge*, it was the way Arthur had taught me to reduce sequences to their essentials, that enabled me to plan and budget fantastic sequences economically.

Despite Sydney's determination to get *Broken Journey* made while the subject was still in the news, it wasn't until April that we got a unit up to Les Huches. The Dakota was in position, and we had local guides costumed as doubles. So we began 'sketching in' the sequences — that is playing out all the exterior scenes without getting close enough to the doubles to see their faces. During the shooting, most of the unit enjoyed themselves falling about on their skis all day, and luxuriating in the warmth and spirit of 'bonhomie' in the ski chalet at night.

It was great until bedtime, then I recall it was often quite terrifying. The wind howled and lashed the chalet walls, buffeting them like a tornado, beating down the slopes of Mont Blanc. It was easy to understand how primitive people, living under the shadow of a volcano or mountain, came to believe that there was a spirit or god living on the summit. After some nightmarish nights, when we felt we were going to be blown over the edge, I certainly felt the greatest respect for the Spirit of the Mountain. In fact, our lives became dominated by its moods!

We were sitting down to breakfast, planning our shots for the day, when Guy skied over the east ridge, waving frantically. "No Dakota!" he shouted. "Vanished into thin air!"

"Don't be ridiculous!" I replied. "It's covered with snow, or you can't have gone far enough."

"I tell you, it's gone," he said. Quickly pulling on our skis, we sped after him and, of course, he was right. There was not a sign of our precious set. Then, skiing to the south edge of the plateau, I saw it lying in pieces fifty or sixty feet below!

The rest of the day was spent winching the pieces of fuselage up the hillside and reassembling them. Everyone gave a hand except for our second camera crew, who announced it was not their kind of work and walked off.

My wife, Blanka, was so incensed that she joined the willing members of the crew, packing snow and chunks of ice under the wings with such energy, that she lost the second child we had just discovered she was carrying. I suppose I should never have let her join in the work, but there was little else for her to do on that location. She never conceived again — nor, for that matter, ever came on location — which was definitely not good for our marriage.

The plane was back in place, and staked down doubly firm and for four more days the shooting went marvellously. Suddenly, the same thing happened again — and again — and again! Four bloody times that mountain wind tore the set apart, and four times we rebuilt it with the snow beginning to melt, because it was spring.

Twenty local labourers were hired with their sleds to bring a constant supply of fresh snow from higher up the mountain. But from most angles our poor Dakota was now a droopy, sorrowful sight. We tried to explain it away by saying the real wreck must have taken a terrible punishing when it crashed, but I was disheartened and rushed through the essential longs shots, accepted the services of an ex-editor, Danny Chorlton, to finish the job, while I returned to the studio to keep contract dates with the stars.

The studio shooting had its difficulties, too. A long domed fuselage and pilot's cabin had been built in sections, so we could remove pieces when the cameraman wanted to light an artist from the most advantageous position. Nowadays we would have accepted the normal lighting through the port holes, but in those days cameramen were perfectionists, and the stars, particularly women, had been encouraged by producers to insist on the most favourable lighting for their individual features.

We finished up with our set cut into sixty-four pieces, making it as rickety and bashed about as the Dakota we had left on location. For forty-five days, we suffered in that crowded set. It was absolute hell with the twelve passengers cramped into a fuselage, no more than seven feet high and eight feet wide. You couldn't move without treading on someone or knocking a carefully set 'gobos' off a lamp.

The camera operator and I devised a metal girder on which we could mount the camera and track up end down the gangway. It was christened 'The Pencil', and enabled me to keep the camera moving for many of the shots, but one needed the patience of Job to be constantly watching the action, kneeling and balancing on that girder.

To add to our troubles, London suffered a heat wave in early June, and the studio had only the most primitive air-conditioning. Needless to say, the cast had to continue to act, wrapped up in woollen scarves and heavy coats, buttoned right up to their chins. We had a pretty makeup girl called Barbara who, in this heat, used to wear nothing but an overall. She was continually reaching over actors to mop them up, and often we would see her jump back... and perhaps affording a glimpse of goodies to brighten up our day!

One sweltering Saturday afternoon, the madly overweight Francis Sullivan (famous for his role as Mr Bumble in *David Copperfield*) had some sort of mild heart attack, and had to be carried off the set. I was left to struggle with two touchy, malicious actresses. Individually, Margot Graham and Phyllis Calvert were charming, intelligent women, but driven by the competitive star system of those days, each strove tooth and nail to come out on top and score over the other.

First, Margot would make some excuse to climb out of the set and surreptitiously pull me aside. "Darling", she would whisper, "how can I possibly play this line? She's only supposed to be a stewardess. I'm a first-class passenger accustomed to every service and comfort. The line's completely out of character". I would try to change the line to suit her. Then, a few minutes later, Phyllis would call me to her side, "Two things, darling, you've got me on my wrong side for the close-up. Ask Jack. He can never make anything of my face on this side and, darling, you can't really let Margot push that last line so hard — it makes her such a bitch."

And so it went on, wasting two hours of that Saturday afternoon, which was always a drag to work anyway. The unit was tired, and I had a secret fear that perhaps I couldn't handle the situation. Somehow, I found a way around the problem and made the two temperamental stars perform, swearing never to be caught in such a badly written scene again! When actors have true difficulties with a scene, and become argumentative and bitchy, the fault can usually be traced to an unplayable situation devised by the writer or to phoney characterisation — again, the writer! I learned a great deal about how actresses think from Phyllis Calvert, who had been a top star at Gainsborough throughout the war and continued to do solid work in various London theatres for many more years.

Margot was one hundred percent female and had learned every trick in Hollywood, when she starred as Milady deWinter in the original *The Three Musketeers* and a dozen other movies made in Hollywood. When she was feeling low, she would send one of my assistants to call me to her dressing room, and invariably I would find her sitting stark naked in front of the mirror! She would jump up, clasp me to her and unburden her woes of the moment, and when she felt a stirring down below, she would invariably break away and say, "Now, now, Kenny boy, I'm old enough to be your mum, and we don't really have the time, do we?" I would relax. The tension or anger in both of us would be over, and we would try to create something wonderful in the job we both loved best.

Given the right material, Margot was a very powerful actress. She could work herself up to tears and be very moving. I would say, "Great! Print!" And she, dabbing her eyes, would call, "No, please, darling, just another take."

"But that was perfect, Margot, darling," I would say. Beckoning me close to her side, she would whisper, "I learned from Bette Davis, in Hollywood, with any strong emotional scene, always ask for another take, because now you know how you did it, and as an actress can improve it."

It was true, and a perfect example of how most performers and creators — if they are lucky — learn from another and pass on tips to the next generation. Over the years, I have come to recognise that actors may look like normal people, but most of them are not. They are usually loveable, childlike, supersensitive, volatile, insecure Gypsies who put themselves into the director's hands rather like puppets. After all, most movies are shot completely out of continuity, and only the director knows exactly what he wants and where he is going! Recognising this, a good director should try to give these very special, insecure people, the clearly defined framework of a shot, and guide them sympathetically into the full expression of their instinctive and sensitive feeling for character. If you have cast well, both actor and director will share a 'high' — worth all the hardships, waiting and disappointments of this crazy show biz world.

I had another unpleasant lesson on *Broken Journey*. It was the first time I had to deal with stuntmen. The art director had built a set which matched part of the ice caves which Tairraz had shot on location, and Jimmy Donald, who was playing the navigator of the plane, was supposed to be leading a party down to bring help. He had to jump across a fifteen foot crevasse and Arthur Alcott had correctly decreed that I must not risk the actor, so he had brought in Jock Easton, a top stuntman to double for Jimmy Donald doing the leap.

It is normal practice that a stuntman rigs his stunt, which usually means laying down mattresses and cardboard boxes (or nowadays, an airbag) to break the fall. I knew nothing about this and when Jock casually got a prop man to lay in four mattresses, climb the rostrum and called, "Okay, let's get on with it," I got on with it... And was horrified to see him turning as he fell, and landing half on and half off the mattress.

He went as white as a sheet, and we found he'd smashed his collarbone. Jack Cox, my cameraman, muttered, "Stupid bugger. That was bound to happen one day." And I found that Jock, though one of the best, was well-known to be a hothead and very erratic. I swore from that moment to find out for myself all about rigging stunts, and to make sure I always had a level-headed expert beside me when a stunt was coming up. Here and now, I would say categorically that before anyone becomes a director, they should be made to realise that they, and they alone, are ultimately responsible for the lives of everyone on the set. If lives are not going to be lost, every director should know and be able to assess all the elements going into a stunt. Only then will he or she be able to say, at the end of their careers, "No one was ever killed on my set."

We had the usual wrap-party after *Broken Journey* and Sydney called me across and turned on his big grin. "You know, Muriel and I have taken over the studios at Islington." I nodded. He continued, "Between the two studios we've promised to turn out twenty-eight movies a year."

"Impossible," I said. "If the quality is going to be any good."

He shrugged. "Well, we can only do our best, and I'm relying on you to look after three or four." Naturally, my heart started to beat faster! What a chance! "First of all, if you're not too exhausted, I want you to take over a picture called *Miranda*. It's been shooting nearly two weeks with Danny Chorlton directing... but he's wrong casting. *Miranda* is a light, frothy comedy, but it turns out that since seeing *Citizen Kane*, Danny is obsessed with this new wide-angle/deep focus technique. The result is that when I look at rushes, I see a goldfish bowl, big and sharp in the foreground, but Griffith Jones, holding up the mermaid and showing her to his wife, Googie, are like midgets at the end of a corridor. The scenes just don't work, so I've decided to pull the plug."

I felt a prick of conscience about relieving another director of his job — I could guess how disappointed he would be. Sydney saw my disappointment.

"If you don't feel up to it, old boy, I'll find someone else!"

"When do you want me start?" I asked. "Yesterday," he said smiling angelically again.

"You can recast, change cameramen, do anything you feel necessary, but we must start up again in three days' time!"

"Give me a car and chauffeur," I said, "so I can prep the script and work out my set-ups while travelling to and from Shepperton..."

"It's a deal," beamed Sydney. "I knew I could count on my best protégé!"

Miranda was a comedy about a young London doctor vacationing in Cornwall. He finds a mermaid and brings her back to his luxury apartment, where he keeps her in the bath. The mermaid, played by the young and very sexy Glynis Johns, is a wicked little minx who causes havoc with his wife and friends. Eventually he has to agree to tip her back into the Thames. Originally, it had been a stage play, and the script was full of well-tried, funny fishy jokes. Here I had no chance to fall back on my 'documentary approach'. This was inevitably going to be a stagey-type movie, played entirely in studio sets, and a studio tank.

I'll never forget a bald-headed, old prop called Steve, whose job for one whole week was to sit up on the gantry holding a piece of piano wire, and whenever Miranda came out of the water, he had to give the wire a tug to make her tail flap! The tail was devised and manufactured by the Dunlop Rubber Company, and it fitted like a sheath over Glynis' legs. She, or a double, could swim most convincingly in it, but although Glynis was petite, she was far too heavy a load for Griffith Jones, who played the doctor. Whenever he had to lift her, he made a terrible fuss, insisting with great public show, on putting on a truss and elastic knee pads.

Although I managed to get a performance out of Griff, I have to admit that I despised him as a man. He belonged to that breed of English stage actor, which has practically passed away. He was fussy about his lines, always trying to score over the other actors. At the slightest opportunity, he upstaged his colleagues, and even when I was shooting what is called an over-shoulder shot, he would somehow manage to angle his face around so that his features were always in the picture.

One weary Saturday afternoon, shooting a scene with that most generous and superb old English actress, Margaret Rutherford, Griff sat on the edge of a desk, supposedly questioning Margaret whom he'd engaged as Miranda's nurse. He knew very well I was going to shoot a front-on close-up for his key lines, and this particular set-up was to favour Maggie. The camera operator kept asking him to keep his position in the foreground, but he continued to find reasons to play with his face turned away from her. At last, I ordered him to hold his look to Maggie, to which he replied, "It's like this, Ken, old boy, something inside me keeps saying, 'Griff, it's up to you to keep the old fizz in picture,' and that's what I intend to do!" For once I lost my cool and told him I was the director! I would look after his fizz, and he should be ashamed of himself for trying to steal the scene from an old pro like Maggie! I suppose it wasn't exactly how Carol Reed would have handled the situation, but it worked! Griff obeyed sulkily and we made the shots.

Maggie, in her own way, was a natural scene-stealer, and that is why quite often a director must break up a scene into individual close-ups or over-shoulder shots, so that they definitely favour one of the pair. That is the director's power of choice, and later he and the editor pick out the most effective sections on both actors and cut them together.

Maggie didn't have to be talking to catch your eye and make you laugh or cry, or just get a warm feeling about her! She used to do something quite unique with her mouth and lower jaw. Sometimes I would be explaining a scene to her, and would say with a smile, "At this point, you should do one of those funny things you do with your mouth." And I would try, weakly, to imitate her. With wide-open, serious eyes she would stare back at me and say, "I don't know what you mean, young man. I never do anything at all like that with my mouth." And so with Maggie, one would gently rough out the movements, rehearse the scene as little as possible, and turn on the cameras until she produced that wonderfully funny (or sad) expression that made you love her. Maggie was a completely instinctive actress — a natural who had, over the years, learned something about the mechanics of acting — the minimum necessary to play a scene on the stage with other people. But her charm or 'entertainment value' was quite individual, and not to be turned on at will. You had to set the mood of the scene, and nine-times-out-of-ten she would give you something wonderful.

There is a marvellous scene in *Miranda* where Glynis, knowing she will have to go back to the sea, presents Maggie with a handful of pearls (which one feels come straight from some fantastic ocean-bed). Maggie took the pearls, looked at them as they were the most priceless treasure and, despite her weight and age, did a spontaneous pirouette around the room, delicate as thistledown. I think we made five takes, and the last one gave me goose-pimples, so I printed it!

This was one of the great moments for which instinctively, I had known I must become a director. I had created a moment of magic. If you were to ask me now what is the greatest kick in being a director, I would probably say, "Knowing at the end of the day you have taken a bare set or piece of scenery and added something to it with actors which could never have existed without your imagination or conception or the technique to make it happen". If you're lucky enough to have many of these moments (I suppose you could call them artistic orgasms), then you feel like a true artist and completely fulfilled. You are hooked for life, and prepared to put up with all the hardships of making a movie.

By hardships, I would list first, having to get up and be ready to work by six am every morning during the shoot. If you're on location, you rush to the window and try to judge whether it's going to rain, or whether you make the fine weather call, or move into the cover set. You drive to work worrying about whether everything and everybody will be there for the day's shoot. Perhaps you may have forgotten to ask for something, such as ten monkeys, or a goldfish, a period Rolls Royce, or a bicycle rigged to run down a hill without a rider! Or even a new scene from the scriptwriter! You are worried whether things are going to work today, whether you'll be on top form with the actors and crew. If you are not, everyone knows and you can lose hours making a scene work.

If you are working in the studios, you usually labour all day in an ill-ventilated, dusty studio, or on location, stand in the snow, shiver in the rain or sweat in tropical heat. And, at the time I am talking about in England you struggled to get everything done within the framework of union rules!

During the shooting, a director's brain never stops, awake or sleeping. Our problems are no more than a businessman's worries, I guess, and you may be inclined to say, "You chose the job, mate, don't beef!" — which is true. We put up with hours of discomfort and countless worries every day, because we know the 'highs' are worth more than any money can buy!

The union 'strait-jacket' started for me in earnest on *Miranda*. I had experienced a little of studio discipline when I worked at the Shepherd's Bush Studios. I accepted now that I must shoot within certain hours, allow for fixed tea breaks, and if I wanted to go on shooting at the end of the day, I must ask the production manager to get me permission from the shop steward to perhaps work another fifteen minutes.

But at Islington I found myself and my craft in the middle of a political as well as industrial battleground. Manny Yosper, who job was to pull focus, used to sit on the camera dolly reading the communist newspaper, 'The Daily Worker' in every spare moment, and inspired by party propaganda and daily tips as to how to raise issues and upset the employer, he would find reasons to agitate among the crew! The shop steward was a pompous, power-loving sound-mixer called Mickey Hobbs, and between the two of them, they used to make my life hell. The moment the tea wagon clattered through the double doors, they would call, "Tea break," even if I was in the middle of a shot. Come one pm or six pm I might have made three of four takes of a scene, but not the one to print. An actor may have fluffed a line. The operator may not have framed the scene exactly, although that rarely occurred at Islington with my friend Dudley Lovell. However, even Dudley was dependent on the dolly pusher making the right moves. Perhaps the sound was off-mike, or perhaps I was not satisfied and believed I might get a better take, which is the director's prerogative. Unless I had asked for permission from Mickey Hobbs at the right time, as stipulated in the latest union regulation, I would not be allowed to complete a shot past one pm or six pm

After lunch this would mean starting the set-up all over again — warming up the actors, getting them in the mood, resetting lights, and reminding technicians of what they were supposed to be doing. Quite often, the shop steward's 'bloody-mindedness' would cost us at least an hour in regaining tempo, quite apart from the insult such automatic 'breaks' are to an actor who has worked himself up to a high point of creative energy. Working to petty union rules in movie-making implies that we are all machines capable of turning on emotions at the throw of a switch!

As a result of these frustrating experiences (and I was to work for two solid years at Islington), I developed a cynicism and thick skin. My temperament is such that I will always try for the best, so Mickey Hobbs and Manny Yosper made me master the art of keeping one eye on the clock while ensuring that somehow I achieved the best shots possible within the schedule, budget and enforced timetable. I learned to be a diplomat — cunning, two-faced, and tough-minded — qualities one needed to be a survivor, and occasionally the maker of a really good movie!

I can work out a shot in great detail, but the moment I start transmitting my ideas to actors and technicians, they will come up with ideas, too. They may point out that a move or a line does not work for them, or I may spot a weakness and try to shape the scene another way. All this is an essential part of movie creation, and in the best situations, the whole company becomes one team battling to get just what the director wants. I love my crews and usually they catch my spirit and will do anything for me.

Miranda cost only a hundred and seventy-five thousand pounds to make, despite the false start, and was very successful in all cinemas except America, where another film was being made called *Mr. Peabody and the Mermaid.* I remember Sydney telling me about serious threats to sue Gainsborough and discussions about the copyright of our film. But our production was firmly based on well-tried stage material, so we could not be attacked by slick American lawyers. I did make a note at the time that it would obviously be wise to check all creative ideas for an original movie script with a lawyer. Today it is even more vital if one is to survive.

Looking back, *Miranda* changed my whole approach to picture-making. It was a 'growing-up' picture, even to the extent of my behaving very cornily and falling in love with my star. Glynis was about twenty-two years old — a beautiful, stage-trained actress with a husky voice. She was full of tricks, and used to try deliberately to upset me in the belief that if we got heated and furious with each other, we would both give better performances. She needed a stimulus like some actors need a drink (or many drinks) to fortify themselves before going on. Glynis needed argument or sex, but a great deal of flirting would go on before anything happened.

She would see me looking at her on the edge of 'her mermaid pool', placing her at her most attractive angle — trying to create a legendary creature every man would like to have in *his own* bathroom — and she would give a Gianconda smile and make me feel I was the greatest. There would be long sessions in the dressing room chatting over little points: her hairdo, her dress, how to make a line funny. Yet somehow, essentially mermaidenish, and the warmer she got under the lights, the more her perfume seemed to engulf me. I began dreaming about her, seeing her face smiling up at me from the water. I arranged to share a flat in town with an actor friend, so that I could dine with Glynis and spin out the evenings discussing script, books, theatre, and our past lives.

She was married and had to go home nights, until one evening I got a call, "Please, Ken, come over now". It was around midnight. I threw on my clothes, jumped in a cab, knocked gently on her apartment door, heart thumping, and there she was in a thin negligee and a towel wrapped around her head.

"Darling", she cried, "I think I've knocked out a tooth. I won't be able to work tomorrow". My face fell. I put my hands around her face and opened her mouth and she bit me.

"Come on, you silly old fool, let's get it over and done with!" Giggling away, she ripped off the towel, and dragged me into the bedroom where the sheets were already turned back.

"I'm in charge tonight", she said, pulling off my jacket. "Drop your pants and let's see what you've got to boast about". Suddenly, I sat on the edge of the bed, looked at her laughing, mocking eyes, and in that moment, I knew it was a trap. If I played her game and made love to her, I would never be the boss again in the studio. She would wrap me around her finger, draw concessions from me, angle for extra shots that favoured her, because such was her nature — charming, crafty, selfish, one hundred percent female! We laughed the situation off. I said, "You scheming little witch! You nearly caught me... but I'm going to be one of the directors you don't have!" I gave her a kiss and a hug. "Let's be good chums, and continue our cat-and-mouse games as long as we work together".

She climbed into bed and, as I pulled the blanket over her, she threw her arms round my neck and pulled me down. "Darling", I heard her moan.

With a great effort I disentangled myself. At the door I turned. "And don't forget. Your call is six-thirty in makeup, and you'd better look better on the set than you do now, or I'll have to keep you in long shot. Kiss, kiss, Darling!"

As I let myself out her husband, Tony Forward, came out of the elevator. "So, that's why she wanted me to stay out late", he said in an emotionless sort of way.

"Don't worry, Tony, we've been having a little professional discussion about goldfish. I'm the one who got away". I gave him a wink and hurried off.

To be truthful, my heart was beating fifty to the dozen, but it turned out I needn't have lost any sleep, because the next morning Glynis, in her full war-paint, took my arm and whispered, "I should have told you, darling, Tony's gone gay! He wouldn't have cared a damn, but you must admit it would have been a giggle if he'd caught us at it!"

As a result of this intimate encounter, Glynis and I remained good friends for many years. We made seven films together, and I usually succeeded in getting the best out of her by letting her know I was fond of her and admired her skill as an actress. But I remained the boss, always conscious of her cunning and wicked sense of humour. I used to swear that she would arrive on a set in the morning, look around and think, "What can I do to upset things today?" Being aware of this, along with my assistants, I usually managed to thwart her tricks and turn her energy and perverseness into good performances on the screen.

CHAPTER THREE
Travelling... Stumbling...
Then Picking Up!

After three pictures back to back, Sydney Box allowed me to take a few weeks off. Blanka and I went to Prague, and stayed with our old friend Jiri Weiss, who had been a refugee in London and then, during the war, a respected director with the Crown Film Unit. He had been one of my inspirations and mentors when I got my first directorial break in documentaries. I remember him teaching me, step by step, how to break down an action sequence into an arrangement of smaller thumbnail sketches. By doing this, I would then know the essential visual pieces to shoot.

Jiri was also the one who made me read Stanislavsky's 'My Life In Art' and 'An Actor Prepares'. If I had stayed in the little North Country town of Beverley, where I was born, I would never have even heard of these great Russian innovators and certainly never have learned the core of my craft from them!

On a boat trip in Prague, I met a director from the Ukraine named Savchenco. He said the name Annacyn, Anyakin and Anakyn were quite common in his country! So, as we sailed down the Voltava that spring day, with the balalaikas playing and the vodka flowing, I felt a secret and special stirring of the blood from my proven Russian ancestry!

To top this fairy tale trip, I was invited to a vast open-air ballet performed by the combined Folk Dance Companies of the Red Army. Several hundred Russian young men and women danced in folk costume, one traditional number after another. I have never seen anything so vital and stimulating anywhere else in the world. It could be that I was a little over emotional, remembering that these were the heroic people who had fought Hitler to a standstill at Stalingrad, Omsk, and the banks of the Dnieper. But, whatever the reason, I jumped up and down with a vast crowd of Czechs, yelling myself hoarse in thrilled admiration.

I vowed that I would go back to England, and try to make my work as purposeful and polished as I had seen at the Russian Festival in Prague. However, on my return to London, Sydney had a script ready for me — a sequel to *Holiday Camp* called *Here Come The Huggetts*. This family became the basis for a very successful series and for the next two years I was kept with my nose to the grindstone, churning out their rather prosaic adventures in and around suburban London. I was far from thrilled with the idea, but Sydney had given me a long-term contract when he had signed me for *Holiday Camp*, and my fee was now getting into the unimaginable realms of nearly five thousand pounds a picture!

My responsibilities as a married man also began to have an influence on my actions. Blanka pointed out that neither of us had ever had a really comfortable home where we could express ourselves and put down roots. One Saturday afternoon, coming ashore from a canoe trip (yes, our pleasures were very simple in those days), she pointed to a bloody great mansion for sale at Shepperton Bend, fifteen miles outside London. I made the mistake of immediately calling up the realtor, and found that this sixteen-room 'William and Mary' house had ten acres of land, wonderful lawns, and a traditional walled kitchen garden. It could be bought for the princely sum of ten thousand pounds! At first, I threw up my hands and pooh-poohed the whole idea. "Forget it," I said to Blanka. "Where could we find ten thousand pounds?" As a camera assistant during the war I had been paid twelve pounds a week and although my rate had risen steadily, up to then we had only been able to afford a small apartment.

When I met her, Blanka had been a penniless refugee, and my good Yorkshire father had cut me out of his will for having married a "bloody foreigner." Not that he was a racist in any way... just a staunch English liberal who believed I should have found a good Yorkshire lass... certainly not someone who had studied Karl Marx! To him it was bad enough that my uncle Philip Snowden had been the 'Iron Chancellor"'in the first British Labour government.

Blanka and I now had a three-year-old daughter to support, and at most, five hundred pounds in the bank... and she wanted to buy a ten thousand pound mansion! When I pointed this out, Blanka replied with a disarming smile, "Don't give up so easily. Ask Sydney. You're his blue-eyed boy. Maybe he'll lend you the money."

Instinctively, I did not like the idea of becoming more beholden to my boss, but I suppose I was intrigued by the beautiful lawns, a mulberry tree, and ten acres of land. At some time in one's life it seems that everyone wants to own a big house and feel like country gentry! So, I approached Sydney.

"Sure, I'll lend you ten thousand, old boy, no problem. My credit is good. I'll borrow the cash from the bank against the collateral of your house, and your contract. All you need pay me is the annual interest."

I went home with my heart singing and feeling how lucky I was to have a friend like Sydney. The result was that I had to delay my dreams and ideas for 'great films', and churn out the Huggett series, because Sydney needed them. I owed him a debt and had to earn cash as quickly as possible to pay off the mortgage.

The Huggett years were not really such a bind. Jack Warner and Kathleen Harrison were a joy to work with. Jack would always come in with a new joke, and amuse us with his Maurice Chevalier imitations. Kathleen seemed to adore me and performed, marvellously and amusingly, everything I asked of her. Dinah Sheridan, Jane Hilton, Susan Shaw, Petula Clark and Diana Dors were a great team and fun to work with as well. However, the challenge was no longer there, and I was bored at home, having to work every spare moment in the garden, or decorating the sixteen rooms. As I painted ceilings and hung paper on the walls, I secretly swore that it was all Blanka's fault — even though she was helping me in these chores. So, I started a little affair with the pretty, Susan Shaw.

One Sunday evening after repairing a vast greenhouse, and trying to be fair to Blanka, I told her I was in love with Susan. To my great surprise, she laughed in my face and belittled the affair so much that I stormed out of the house for five whole days! In truth, she was right. It was only a dalliance, mainly in the studio, where I would devise complicated shots, so that I could have necking sessions with Susan in my office while the set was being lit. My high-minded approach to film making, as the be all and end all of everything, was certainly becoming wobbly at that period! I used to tell myself that I was becoming so sure of my technique that I could relax and be a more normal person.

Not that a filmmaker is ever quite normal. His values are quite different from those of other people. As you observe and create more and more characters, you mentally strip people and see how they are, both inside and out. You become analytical and critical of everyone. You have to do this, otherwise how can you hope to portray a character with any depth? That does not mean you 'don't *like* people', but as a writer or director you must find out what makes them tick. To the annoyance of your wife or friends, you may sometimes 'drift away' because you are struggling with some creative problems — trying to fathom why a character is coming out as a cardboard figure, or simply pondering the question "How can I telescope or cut those scenes to save time and catch up with the schedule?"

Sometimes a director gets lost in the thought of how to tackle the producer or the money boys about giving you the time you need to shoot those extra scenes you are convinced will make the movie, TV episode or series, a winner! Those and a hundred other thoughts are always in one's subconscious while you are 'in production'.

A director really lives a schizophrenic existence, and his wife or girlfriend often has to make excuses for his absent-mindedness, oddness, or what appears to be plain bad manners. Your friends grow to make allowances for you, and seem to put up with you because you are known to be involved in something glamourous, and there is always a chance that you will recount an amusing incident about famous people or take them vicariously to interesting places or experiences.

During the Islington/Huggett period, for most of the time, I know I felt amazingly lucky to be doing the job I adored. If Sydney had suddenly said, "We've no more money to pay you, but you can go on shooting", I'd willingly have gone on making set-ups each day — shooting, shooting, shooting just for the joy of it. But deep inside there was another side of me, feeling trapped and frustrated at not being able to move into the top class of filmmakers.

At the Denham Studios, David Lean was shooting such classic movies as *Blythe Spirit*, *Brief Encounter* and *Great Expectations*. My idol, Carol Reed was shooting *Odd Man Out* and *The Third Man* at Pinewood. At Ealing, Michael Balcon was turning out great comedies such as *The Lavender Hill Mob*, *Kind Hearts and Coronets* and *Whiskey Galore*! Without wishing to rock the boat, I appealed to Sydney and while new Huggetts were being written, he allowed me to try my hand in another studio — Elstree.

One movie was a wartime drama about a submarine and the other a thriller.

Neither had very good scripts, nor exciting casting... except for Peter Lorre! I had been thrilled to find that this famous Hollywood actor was to co-star in *Double Confession*. The trouble was that he was supposed to be the henchman of a crooked casino owner, played by the tough and very competent British actor, Billy Hartnell. Billy had given some excellent performances in the past, but the moment Peter Lorre came on the set he went on the defensive by hamming every scene most aggressively. Peter's way of countering this was to fall on his knees every so often, take my hand and cry! He would plead in apparent desperation that I should let him counter Billy, by allowing him to play his role in an offbeat, unconventional way. I admired him so much that more often than not, I let him have his way. The result was that the film was pulled completely out of joint. Lorre stole every scene and acted like the *boss* of the casino instead of the henchman! Hartnell was driven, quite justifiably, to bitter anger and even blows. I learned the hard way that a director must guard against allowing a gimmicky actor to add so much 'shtick' that he throws the balance of the whole film.

Suddenly, Sydney announced that he had acquired the rights to four of the Somerset Maugham stories, and I could have my pick. I chose 'The Colonel's Lady'"which is the story of a stuffy English country squire, who discovers that his wife has written a book of erotic poetry which is the talk of London society. Cecil Parker played the Colonel and Nora Swinburn — who remembered me from *We Serve* — played the wife whom everyone believes must have a secret lover. I can only say that Nora "made herself like putty in my hands" — it was bliss! Maugham had written a wonderful payoff line for the Colonel to say after he visits his lawyer-friend for advice:

"You want to divorce her?" queries the lawyer.

"Of course not!" bellows the Colonel. "Evie is wonderful with the servants — and keeps house impeccably." But, as he goes to the door, he turns and adds: "The one thing I'll never understand is — what on earth did the fellow ever see in her!"

Sydney felt that this was too cynical a payoff for a cinema audience, and with Maugham's permission he wrote a new scene where Nora, confronted by Cecil, says, "But the lover in my book is you — you as you were when we were courting!" They both made the scene tremendously moving, and audiences throughout Britain and the art houses in America loved it. In New York, *Quartet* ran for two whole years at the Sutton Cinema.

Maugham came down to the set a couple of times to watch the shooting. He was a shy man with a nervous stutter. He smiled broadly when I told him I had gone back to the original dialogue in the book, because his lines were more real than the lines cooked up for the screenplay by the playwright, R.C. Sheriff. "I'm not surprised," said Maugham. "In my experience, most people use simple words and often repeat themselves — like 'How nice of you to come on such a nice day.' The repetition of the word nice would worry most writers, but that is how real people speak."

In other meetings I had with Maugham, I found he was observing people all the time, and he admitted they often turned up in his short stories, just as he'd seen them. This confirmed what I had already come to believe — namely, that a sophisticated writer should be well trained: an observer of everything and everyone around him. Returning to his desk, the writer should put real people into a simple situation and allow their characters to develop and lead to an inevitably happy, sad or cynical denouement.

Sydney was rewarded for his superhuman efforts at Gainsborough by being appointed head of the larger and more modern Pinewood Studios. I followed in his trail to make two more Maugham stories in *Trio*: 'The Verger' and 'The Knowall' which gave me full scope for leading actors through the character subtleties developed by the master.

Soon after the success of *Trio*, the very active and creative producer George Brown, offered me a broad comedy with Peter Ustinov, Roland Culver, David Tomlinson, Albert Lieven, and the Hollywood musical star, Yvonne DeCarlo. The story was set during the war. Peter Ustinov owned the exotic *Hotel Sahara* somewhere in North Africa. As British, French and German troops fought their battles and exchanged territory, Peter's main object in life was to save his property and his daughter's virtue.

The script was full of good comedy situations and the cast was perfect for milking them. The only trouble I had as a director was that Peter would come on the set, go into a couple of rehearsals knowing exactly how to get the most of his part, and unless you got the shot in the can during the first or second take, he would fool around, mimicking the way other famous actors might play the scene!

Yvonne DeCarlo, on the other hand, needed at least seven full rehearsals. So, I discovered I had to take her aside and rehearse almost continuously during the time the cameraman took to light the scene. David Tomlinson (to whom I had given his first movie part in *Miranda*) had the worst habits of London theatre actors. He loved to upstage and upset other actors' performances — even to the extent of stopping in the middle of a perfect take and saying he'd seen a mouse run across the set! Roland Culver was an old stage pro who could cope with all these tricks, but Albert Lieven was a serious-minded actor trained in the Rhineheart School in Vienna, and could not understand this often stupid and sometimes vicious by-play. Yvonne DeCarlo was an excellent dancer, so I had great fun in staging her numbers with David Poltenghi, who was a choreographer with the Sadlers Wells Ballet Company.

Getting this varied troupe to give of their best became a most precarious operation. Every new set-up was a challenge, but for most of the time I revelled in it.

Hotel Sahara was a big success, especially in Germany, because it was the first time since the war that German soldiers had been portrayed as normal human beings. I was now certain that my future lay in comedies and close human dramas... with wonderful actors helping me create scintillating entertainment for world audiences.

Fate had other things in store!

CHAPTER FOUR
The First Of My
Disney Films

S itting in Pinewood's baronial style dining hall, I saw coming towards me a genial looking man with sandy hair and a droopy moustache. He reached out his hand and said, "Perce Pearce of Walt Disney Productions." He smiled like Walter Huston playing the devil in *The Devil and Daniel Webster*, and continued, "We're about to make Walt's first live-action movie in England and we'd like to talk to you about directing it."

I learned later that Perce had worked for years in the animation studios at Burbank and had been the model for Doc in *Snow White*. He was a loveable, persuasive character and had been chosen by Walt to produce *The Story of Robin Hood and His Merrie Men*. Perce sat down at my table and told me of Walt's idea for the story. He admitted it would be the fourteenth version of Robin Hood to be put on film, but the new production was to be in glorious Technicolor — a luxury in 1952; cast with top British actors, and shot mostly in Sherwood Forest and Nottingham Castle.

"It's going to be far less corny than all the previous versions and truly based on the old legends and historical records that Larry Watkins and our Research Department have been digging out for months."

He wanted to know if I could go up to Notting-ham (as he always used to pronounce it) on a scouting trip next week. My heart began beating a little faster as I saw new horizons opening for me. Wherever it was shot, this would be regarded as an American movie, and nearly every British director I knew was green with envy of American big budgets and Hollywood know-how. But something nagged my conscience. Was this the type of movie I had been setting myself up for? After all, Robin's idea of robbing the rich to give to the poor is not a bad social motivation, but the movie would be mainly action and, most likely, more Mr Disney's movie than mine. I went to consult Sydney.

His immediate response was, "Go for it, old boy. J. Arthur Rank can take a few dollars off Disney for your services, and when you're through I'll get the benefit of your greatly widened experience."

I drove through the gates of Denham Studios, gazing in awe at the four large stages, which had been built by Sir Alexander Korda, for his great series of British movies from *The Private Life of Henry VIII* (Charles Laughton) through *The Thief of Bagdad* (Conrad Veidt and Sabu), to *Things to Come* (H.G. Wells).

Two of the stages were over two hundred feet long, and I gathered from Carmen Dillon, the art director assigned to *Robin Hood*, that both stages would be completely filled. One with Robin Hood's camp in Sherwood Forest, and the other with Nottingham Castle, complete with moat.

Carmen was one of the great art directors on the European scene. Not only was she an accomplished painter, but she was able to supervise big set construction and set-dressing, down to the last nail. So much so, that sometimes when I was lining up a shot, I found her a bit of a pain in the ass because she would insist that her designs and *her* visual conception of a scene must be adhered to, whereas I regarded the sets only as a background for the actors.

The preparation for this production introduced me to a completely new way of making movies. Actually, I never met Walt until a few weeks before shooting, but I was introduced to the Disney Method, which was to sketch out practically every move in the picture before designing the set or choosing the locations.

"At Disney we have found it's much more sensible and cost-efficient to invest the time and salaries of three or four artists at a drawing board — discussing, sketching, and exploring the best ways of telling a story, rather than wasting time doing it on the set or location," said Perce Pearce. "Key technicians and all the departments are supplied with a set of sketches, and everyone knows the director's requirements."

It sounded logical, but a little like factory-line production to me. How much room was it going to leave for *my* creative input? I wondered.

When I came onto the *Robin Hood* production, practically all the camera angles and movements had been designed and storyboarded by Carmen Dillon and Guy Green, the cameraman (whom I felt privileged to work with because he had recently won an Oscar for the photographing of David Lean's *Great Expectations*). But a part of me resented being slid into a straight-jacket. What would Pudovkin, Stanislavsky, even Paul Rotha have said when presented with rules and set guidelines for their shooting? Where was all this about the director being the sole boss in charge? The King! So, on this *Robin Hood* production, quite often I had to bite my tongue or be prepared to quit.

Later, I was to discover that at least fifty percent of the reason for working this way was to enable Walt to exercise control, and supply *his* creative input from six thousand miles away. Each week during pre-production, the continuity sketches had been shipped back to Burbank and returned with Walt's suggestions and corrections. Now, these were handed to me as the Bible — even more important perhaps than the script.

On a March day in 1952, I was shooting a scene with James Hayter, testing him for the part of Friar Tuck. Jimmy had just played the title role for me in *The Verger*, and we were fooling around and going 'over the top' with the part of the jovial monk, when I turned around. There stood Walt Disney a few feet behind me. He was tall, slim, keen-eyed and wearing a tweed suit and tie — something rather unusual in the studios. As I caught sight of him, he grabbed hold of Perce Pearce and started to grill him — about his choice of director, I guessed! Perce seemed to reassure Walt and led him over to me. Walt shook hands and kind of nodded, but his eyes were over my shoulder towards Jimmy.

"You seem to have a very laid-back relationship with your actor, Annakin," he said.

"Well, we've just finished a movie together," I replied. "And we're exploring how much joviality we can get away with in this role of the hard-drinking, battling monk."

"He can be played several ways..." Walt interrupted. "I've always seen him quite clearly in *one* way. I'd like to see the stuff you've just shot."

"I'll order a special rush print from the labs, Walt," said Perce and scurried off.

Walt put his arm around my shoulder and walked me away. "I hope you're not going to be cynical about these fine old English characters. They're classics, you know, and I don't want them spoofed."

"Of course not," I replied. "Friar Tuck is very different from the realistic type of characters Jimmy has been playing, so I was trying to loosen him up and bring out his deep-voiced genial quality, which I think will be very effective in this role."

Walt was still gazing at Jimmy and nodded. "I see the character something like this..." He sat on a prop rock and began to sing the Friar's song by the river. Then he began to play a conversation with an imaginary Robin. Walt knew the lines by heart and his performance could have been put straight on film! Some of the crew gathered around and applauded him, which he acknowledged with a wave, then turned away, almost embarrassed and said, "Carry on, Annakin, I'll speak with you more when I've seen *The Verger* and the rushes of these tests."

He loved both, and a respecting and trustful relationship sprang up between us. We spent three days together on a scouting trip in Sherwood Forest and looked over a number of castles in the Midlands, most of which had had their tops blown off by Oliver Cromwell's cannons three hundred years ago. Walt was angry about this. He liked things to be tidy and just as he had imagined them in his dreams.

We talked about his Mickey Mouse days, the making of *Snow White* and his inspiration for *Fantasia* and *The Reluctant Dragon* — probably his two most avant-garde and truly creative works. I knew he was a very special man — perhaps a genius — but now I saw determination, obstinacy and a consciousness of budget, which clearly went back to his tough, early self-made beginnings. Walt wanted perfection in the realisation of his visions, but he was highly aware that if he allowed money to be wasted, there wouldn't be enough left for his boundless plans for further real-life movies, animated features, or his other dreams.

Leaving Nottingham, he said to Carmen and Perce, "I want this movie to be the truest rendering of Merrie Old England to date. But I think shooting up here on location is a sheer waste of money. Ken says he can find a forest of oaks within five miles of the studio, and your castle set, Carmen, can be much more impressive and realistic than any of these ruins we've seen. Is there such a thing as a good matte painter in England?"

I had no idea, but Carmen said, "Peter Ellenshaw is a clever young painter, and has the backing of his father-in-law, Poppa Day, who has been doing optical tricks and mattes with Korda for many years."

"Sounds good," said Walt. "We'll paint all the long shots of medieval Nottingham, the castle, Richard going to the Crusades, etc. on glass. They'll be much more fun than the real thing."

This is how my long relationship with Peter Ellenshaw began. He had been lucky in falling in love with the daughter of Poppa Day, England's most skilled and ingenious trick photographer, who had learned his trade and magic from the great French illusionist Georges Méliès. So, Poppa Day had been prepared to pass on his knowledge to Peter. He taught him how to give depth to a painting, the illusion of movement in a glass shot and how to marry special effects with painted mattes. Walt, for his part, taught Peter the use of false perspective and the importance of atmosphere in a painting. With the result that Peter became the matte genius of the world, and was eventually airlifted from London to Burbank and given a lifetime contract by Walt.

On *Robin Hood*, Peter painted twelve matte shots and I became so completely sold on this technique, that in my second film for Disney, *The Sword and the Rose*, we designed the movie to have seventy-five painted mattes. Hampton Court, Tudor mansions, Elizabethan gardens, Windsor Castle, and the exteriors from the Tower of London to Hatfield House were all painted, and no one has ever suggested that they were not real!

Walt approved Burnham Beaches as the stand-in location for Sherwood Forest, and checked all the designs of the sets and costumes with Carmen. No matter how inspired and creative you were, Walt would always have some unexpected contribution to make.

His only Achilles heel on this picture was in the casting of Joan Rice to play Maid Marion. She was an attractive brunette with a determined face and good figure, but no acting experience. She had been a waitress in a Lyons Corner House and had been discovered by a rather lecherous British producer. Walt had happened to see some of her rushes and thought she was a great little emoter. Little did he know that Marc Allegret, a French director who had little time for British actors, had regularly stuck pins into her to get any form of emotion or reactions from her! I tested six other young actresses, but Walt would not budge, mainly because he saw me as opposing him. I learned a very important lesson: if you did not want to be stuck forever with any of Walt's bright ideas or notions — 'just off the top of my head', as he would say — you should always agree with him at first and let his own good sense modify or change them later.

"The other girls may be easier to work with, Ken," he said, rubbing his moustache, "but Joan has a quality. The camera loves her. She gets my vote." Which meant she was in. Walt smiled and put his arm around my shoulder as we left the projection room. "With your documentary experience it shouldn't be beyond your skill to get a performance out of her. Treat her like a child. Spend time with her. That shouldn't be so unpleasant with those big boobs of hers." He gave me an unexpected wink. "I'll see you get extra time on the schedule."

Before I could reply, he gave a good luck wave to his first all-British crew and departed. The first day of shooting, Perce Pearce placed himself in a chair as near to the action as possible. I looked around miserably and tried to rehearse, but my temperament is such that I could not (and never have been able to) work with the feeling that someone is looking over my shoulder. The use of the camera during a shot, the order of shooting, the control of the floor, and the final look of the chosen take, have to be *my* responsibility — otherwise, they might just as well hire a robot or a traffic cop! Fortunately, Perce Pearce realised the second day that if I felt this way, he had no chance of getting a good movie. He therefore retired to his upstairs office and arranged for a series of runners to bring him progress reports every hour. Poor Perce. But, like all producers, he was able to have his say the next day when we saw the rushes — and that is how the relationship between producer and director should be.

No matter how well a movie is pre-planned or storyboarded, the director still has to give the actors freedom to add their creative touches. I was lucky to have a cast of top British actors. A good actor studies his character, works out his life story, how he thinks, how he would move and react in specific situations. Professionals like Larry Olivier, John Gielgud and, more recently, Meryl Streep and Dustin Hoffman have often delved more deeply into their character than the writer or director ever dreamed of. Consequently, when they come on to the set to rehearse, you must give them space, let them feel they have the freedom to move and create from their own instincts and background knowledge. This was never allowed for in the Disney-Carmen Dillon method, into which I had been thrown. So, I tried to rehearse in my usual way, never showing the actors the sketches, but quickly latching on to any bright ideas they might have, somehow manoeuvred them to fit as near as possible into the prearranged set-ups. Carmen would watch me like a hawk, but I couldn't criticise her, because her sets were a dream — romantic and historically accurate. She was a tremendous support in watching that costumes were correctly worn and every period prop used to advantage.

Having started my career as an assistant on the camera, I very quickly recognised the brilliance and artistry of Guy Green. Even on the larger sets, he believed in copying nature and restricting himself to one single light source. He would persuade me to shape the action so that the actors' faces were illuminated mainly by this key light, then he would add a filler here and there, but would never accept shadows falling in different directions, as happens so often when a cameraman is pushed for time or does not know how to cope.

Working with Guy, the results were usually, as we used to say, "Every frame a Rembrandt." However, his method was another kind of fence — a discipline — restricting my freedom of choice. I remember one small set — on the battlements of Nottingham Castle. Maid Marion was the only actress in the shot, and Guy worked all morning setting his single light in the ideal position.

Just before lunch (we hadn't shot a single foot of film), he walked past me and casually said, "Sorry, old boy, it doesn't work. I'll begin again after lunch."

That kind of behaviour and spendthrift attitude seems quite ridiculous today, and Guy, who became a fine director himself, would be the first to laugh about it now. But in the Forties and Fifties, it was quite common for a big set, like our Sherwood Forest, to have one or two days taken up just setting the lamps.

Film was slower, and we had to have much more light, which meant perhaps forty or fifty electricians up on the gantries, heaving heavy arcs around in great heat. In a big studio, I had to agree that this gave every good reason for the tea breaks in the morning and mid-afternoon. The electricians came off the gantries sweating like pigs and drifted back to their posts about twenty minutes later. Lamps had somehow been moved and had to be reset and with so many to play with, it's a miracle British films were ever finished.

Today, most of us rarely work in a studio. We adapt natural scenery, real city streets, real houses, prisons, night clubs, ships, etc. and pay the big money to the stars. The system works, but if one looks carefully at some of the old designed movies, they had a smoothness and satisfying visual quality often lacking today.

Robin Hood was played by Richard Todd, a popular British stage actor, who was no acrobatic movie idol like Errol Flynn or John Barrymore. He was, in fact, short like Alan Ladd, and often had to be stood on an apple box, or walk on a plank beside Maid Marion, so that one didn't notice the discrepancy in height. But Richard was a good trouper. I remember one scene where he had to swim across the castle moat under fire. I watched the prop man fasten a special cork covered backplate under Dick's shirt and, completely trustful, he jumped into the moat and started swimming. At a signal from me, an archer, supposedly the finest in Great Britain, fired an arrow. It stuck in Robin's back and he rolled over apparently mortally injured as planned, but when I cut the shot and they pulled Dick out of the water, it was found that the barb was sticking precariously right on the edge of the cork. Another quarter of an inch to the right and there would have been no more acting for Dick. This was a very serious situation for me. It was another proof that a director must never take anything on trust or hearsay. He must weigh up and judge precisely the people involved in stunts, their proposals and skills. No matter how much you want the shot, unless the risk is minimal, it is your duty to find some alternative way of achieving the action called for in the script.

The Sheriff of Nottingham was played by Peter Finch, a young actor newly arrived from Australia. He was a protégé of Laurence Olivier, but this was his first movie. In playing dialogue, Peter brought a freshness and a snide threat to the villainous character, without the histrionics of his predecessors in the role. We became great friends and over the years I was sad to see how the strain of show business made Peter hit the bottle. He drank in order to cope with theatrical challenges he had never dreamed of in the Outback, or truly prepared himself for. Movie life brought him into contact with beautiful, self-centred, ambitious leading ladies whom he invariably fell for. Apart from his last love, a Jamaican painter, I don't think he was ever as happy as his days in Denham, strutting around the stages as the Sheriff of Nottingham! We wasted one awful Saturday afternoon together. Peter came from 'Down Under', but he had lived mostly at Kings Cross, Sydney, and had never ridden a horse. In *Robin Hood* the main part of his riding was done by a double, but I couldn't avoid the moments when he had to ride into close-up, or jump onto his horse and speak lines.

In England, because we never made Westerns, the supply of trained horses and wranglers was amateurish compared to America. Peter's horse was allegedly film trained, and therefore accustomed to arc lights, wind machines, and the camera. But it was obvious the beast hated actors and directors. Every time the number board was put up in front of Peter, the horse started to perform, either moving forward or stepping back. After a number of wasted takes we decided to trick him and put the number on the end of the shot. Even then the moment Peter tried to mount from a pair of steps, the horse would sway or move off his mark. Sweating and swearing, the wrangler bent down under camera and held the horse's front hoof, while Peter tried to speak his lines convincingly. Despite this ruse, the moment Peter opened his mouth, the horse began to snort! This wasn't at all how either he or I had imagined big horse-operas! For my part, I continued to hate working with horses until 1979 when I made a true Western in Arizona. Forty riders appeared over a ridge exactly on my signal and I felt the horses could almost have said the lines!

Little John was played by James Robertson Justice — a mountain of a man who had come into films through knowing how to handle falcons. He was a natural extrovert with great energy, a loud voice and a treble ration of humour. A Scottish Highlander, he spoke eight languages, including Swahili and Arabic, which he had picked up during ten adventurous years somewhere in Africa. With careful direction he could always be relied on to "add verisimilitude" (as he used to say) to any larger-than-life character. The time came for his famous stave fight with Robin on a wooden bridge built over the studio tank. For three weeks, he and Richard Todd had rehearsed with Rupert Evans, the most expert sword master and Period 'fight-arranger' in England. After some lively exchanges of blows, James was knocked into the water as planned, and Richard jumped in after him. Without a break, they continued to parry and thrust, as choreographed, until Richard suddenly trod on a nail which penetrated his thin deerskin boot.

"Shit!" he yelled, and in trying to save himself, swiped James a mighty blow across the head.

With a cry of "Foul, not fair," James disappeared beneath the water only to reappear, angry and sputtering. "Varlet!" he cried, still in character. "Have you no respect for the pate of a Philosopher! If you've damaged the old brain box, Edinburgh University is going to lose its most distinguished Rector!" It was true James had just received a phone call in his dressing room, offering him this honour — something unheard of in the acting profession!!

After this episode, I made a number of films with James and always looked forward to lunchtime, when he would regale the whole canteen with stories: How he had dropped his rifle in front of Hitler when the Germans marched into the Rhine (he had apparently been a member of the League of Nations Police Corps in the Saar); How he had been forced to flee Arabia on a camel after penetrating a sheik's harem (he said he had been serving as the political advisor to one of the first oil sheik's). These and many other real-life experiences certainly added to 'the verisimilitude', which Jimmy was able to bring to any role!

Maid Marion was a cross I had to bear on this otherwise unique and magical experience. I tried to avoid using Marc Allegret's pin sticking techniques, but Joan Rice really was dumb and accident prone. If there was a batten lying on the floor, she'd trip over it, and the funny thing is that nobody on the crew fancied her! They would watch me going over dialogue with her word by word, or chalking numbers on the floor for her moves, and they would shake their head and sigh audibly.

One time, when she was trying to copy me slavishly (and awfully!), a North Country electrician sidled past and whispered, loud enough for her to hear, "She's nowt but a big, soft milk tart, Governor! Big tits and no drawers!" I guess he must have discovered something none of us cared to find out, but it sent her off crying again. My assistant came over and whispered, "She says if you don't like what she does she can always go back to being a waitress." But Walt wanted her, so we were chained irrevocably together until the end of the show.

Joan used to ride a bicycle to and from the local hotel and between shots would go speeding around the Denham lot. Nearly every day she fell off and came back bruised and some part of her costume hanging loose. One evening I saw her standing forlornly outside the studio door, and took pity on her. "Where's your bike?" I called.

"Smashed up, as usual," she grinned guiltily, as she climbed into my MG Midget — then the pride of my life. She lit up a cigarette. Sure enough within five minutes, I smelled burning. The wind had blown the hot ash into my rumble seat, and there was a half-inch hole smoking in the red leather. She staggered into her hotel crying again. I had to feel sorry for the poor kid!

Ten weeks into the shooting, the crew were sitting on their butts waiting for Special Effects to fix four whistling arrows on wires, so that the arrows would apparently fly through the trees and land magically beside Robin's campfire. It so happened that there had been a hold-up on the pay cheques. Young Johnny Alcott, the lowest assistant on the camera (in 1985 he won an Oscar for his brilliant photography in "*Greystoke*") began to parody a song just performed rather prissily by my old friend Tony Forward, who was playing Robin's sidekick, Scarlett:

"Off with your kirtles, and on with your rags
Robin's gone up to the office to sort out a breach,
And teach those Yankee bags,
They must pay up or get out of reach!"

The whole crew thought it hilarious and took up the chant. They were in full chorus, when who should walk in but Walt! He looked puzzled and came straight over to me. "Something wrong? Why aren't you shooting?' I explained the reason for the hold-up, and the stupid background to the singing (I couldn't tell him they were partly 'sending up' his favourite song, at the same time!). He listened carefully, and I thought, "He's not buying it", when suddenly he broke into a wide grin, and putting his hand to his mouth yelled, "Okay, fellas, I'll go rob the rich and pay the poor. But, for Pete's sake, keep this show rolling. I'd like to come back to the UK with another one next year."

We knew he was holidaying with his family somewhere in England, but no one had told us he was within a hundred miles of the studio. He looked at the rushes and had several sessions with Carmen, who was his favourite (and rightly so). Carmen went on to design both *Henry V* and *Richard III* for Sir Laurence Olivier!

I heard, through Perce, that the Master was happy, but the real reason he'd broken his itinerary was that Princess Elizabeth was going to pay a visit to Denham on the morrow. It seemed to me that every Disney executive in Europe must have got the word and turned out as his bodyguards, supporters, or just rubberneckers, while the Princess showed up on our stage accompanied only by a Lady-in-Waiting and her Equerry. Walt had shown her around the outside sets and the costume department, with Carmen explaining how they were fashioned and why. Perce sent word that we should continue shooting as normal because that is what she wanted to see. Princess Elizabeth stood quietly in a dark corner, and after about twenty minutes I saw her smile, give a friendly wave and slip out of the stage. A few moments later Walt hurried over to me. 'Excellent," he said. "She was fascinated. The only thing she wants to know is what does 'Shall I make it Chinese, Gov' mean?"

I could hardly restrain my laughter as I explained, "Well, Walt, you know the barn doors they fix on the lamps to cut off unwanted spill light? Well, they can be set with a slit either vertical or horizontal. I don't know how it is with you Americans, but our boys have heard the rumour that Chinese ladies are built differently from European women." I made a movement from side to side. "Like this — not up and down as we're all used to!" Walt gasped, "You mean to say, Ken, these fellas would use language like that in front of their future queen?"

I looked him in the eye. "Really, Walt, you can't expect British electricians to change their traditional technical terms just because of a royal visit. You did say carry on as usual!" He hurried away, shaking his head. I never knew what he told her, but he did present her with copies of *Snow White* and *Fantasia* which she told him were her favourite movies.

So far as I recall, Walt had photos taken with Robin Hood on the castle drawbridge; with the Sheriff; and the wicked Prince John in the Nottingham Square set on the lot. He posed for numerous pictures with Joan Rice on the archery field, and announced that he had clearly made the right choice with Joan as the Maid — though we all thought that she would have been better as somebody's housemaid. But most of Walt's week with us was spent at nearby Beaconsfield where he had discovered a big-scale model railway. He told me later that he had played there for hours, and that it set him thinking about building a kind of Fun Fair with a railway running around, German castles, lakes with Mississippi steamers, and pirate ships. He envisioned lots of historical characters dressed in period clothes — like those Carmen designed, plus Mickey Mouse, Donald Duck, Snow White and the Seven Dwarfs. He rubbed his moustache and said, "Maybe I'll call it Disneyland where the whole world can come and share the pleasures I have playing with all these movie toys!"

On Disney's *Robin Hood* I learned new techniques and big picture practices — one was the use of a Second Unit. Alex Bryce, an experienced action director was in charge of a unit nearly as big as mine. He took his sketches and *went* out every day to shoot scenes with galloping horses; hold-ups of the royal coach; bow and arrow fights between Robin's Merry Men and the Sheriff's hirelings. If they were working close by, I would go out at lunchtime and watch how Alex planned and broke up his fight scenes into their most effective elements.

Alex would shape-in a shot with his stunt doubles, riding into Nottingham Square, sweeping through the townsfolk and rescuing some peasant. But whenever a line of dialogue was needed, I had to match his action and set-ups with close shots of my actors. Again, my first reaction to this Hollywood practice was that it was turning an art into a factory process, but the process worked. Without that kind of division of labour, I would never have been able, in years to come, to put together big movies like *Battle of the Bulge* and *Those Magnificent Men In Their Flying Machines*.

Alex and I kept track of each other's work through our assistants, Basil Keys and Peter Bolton. Both were to play important parts on my later productions. Basil was a redheaded, quick tempered man whose father had been a famous musical star — Nelson Keys (nicknamed Bunch). Basil had inherited his sense of humour and warmth in dealing with people and had one of the quickest (but rather intolerant) brains of anyone I knew. He latched on to the main logistic problems to be faced daily and found ways to solve them without the director ever being conscious there had been any glitches.

Peter Bolton was a different type — probably the greatest assistant to ever work in British movies. He prepared meticulously for every eventuality on the floor, organised his team of assistants like a gun crew, and demanded they keep him posted about *everything* going on: the time an actor arrived; which actor needed to be coddled; which actress had the curse; who was hitting the bottle, etc. With Peter beside me, I also knew everything that was going on and could plan my shots and run the production from the floor. This had become increasingly necessary, as front office executives have changed to businessmen, ex-agents or just sharp entrepreneurs and money-launderers! It had become vital for a director, if he was to survive, to be able to take charge, run all shooting from the floor — a fact of life in the Fifties, but increasingly true now. Apart from being aware of everything, Peter Bolton could cajole and charm both cast and crew. He jollied them along in the smoothest possible ways so that I would be presented with all the elements on a platter, so to speak, all ready to cook. Just think what this means when you have to "cook up" between eight hundred to a thousand camera set-ups on a movie like *Robin Hood*, laboriously mixing ingredients together — actors, costumes, props, hairdressers, makeup, cameras, sound, lighting, and special effects. Someone had to be able to calculate when it was wise to call the tea break or lunch without the readiness of several hundred people being wasted. Peter was uncanny at this, perhaps because of his experiences on *Quo Vadis?* — a big epic he made in Rome during the Fifties with Mervyn LeRoy.

Peter had been thrown into the deep end on that production in Rome and had the task of marshalling crowds of thousands. Mervyn was a known tyrant demanding speed and perfection *plus* the impossible, all day long! At tense moments with me, Peter used to hold up his hand with one finger apparently missing. "I lost that with LeRoy," he used to say. "That time I kept him waiting five minutes for a hundred gladiators! You're getting as intolerant as he was!"

When I moved to California, I often used to see Mervyn LeRoy at the Hollywood Race Track. He looked tiny, bent, and wizened, quite incapable of bossing anyone around, but at his zenith he knew precisely what he wanted and became, if necessary, a martinet to get the shot on the screen — in the final analysis, *the only way!*

Peter Bolton taught me to be similarly tough and intolerant of amateurism. I have expected the same excellence and application from my assistants ever since. Film making is undoubtedly a profession where one learns constantly from others. Peter trained many fine British assistants, but fell by the wayside while quite young in life. He set standards for himself that were impossible to keep up year after year. His secret pride was that he would set the background, and give the action to the extras, in a way so good that no director would ever want to change it.

Like a number of conscientious first assistants, Peter burnt himself out in his search for excellence and creative service. The last I heard he was living quietly in a rose-covered cottage in Kent, mending clocks and watches. Sure, movie-making can be the most wonderful and *only* life, but to survive you have to be super tough, both mentally and physically.

When the shooting of *Robin Hood* was complete (I think the second unit shot for sixteen weeks, and I shot for twenty), the whole material was shipped to Burbank for final editing and as usual it was dubbed personally by Walt Disney with Perce Pearce, the line producer, sitting beside him, throwing in the occasional good idea.

This practice, I was assured, was not at all unusual in American production. The moguls of Hollywood — Zanuck, the Warner Brothers, Louis B. Mayer and Harry Cohn of Columbia Pictures all liked to be in at the kill and able to say if it was a good movie, "I made it." In Walt's case, since everything made in the studio emanated from him, it seemed to me he had every right to have his fun putting it all together, but it was not my idea of true picture-making or why I had chosen to be a director.

The Story of Robin Hood & His Merrie Men was chosen for a Royal Premiere in London. It was a happy, triumphant evening. My only private reservation was that despite my efforts to shake off the strait-jacket of the continuity sketches, some of the acting seemed stilted and stagey. I swore that this must never happen on my second Disney movie — which was already being mooted.

CHAPTER FIVE
Riding The Crest
of a Wave

With *The Sword and the Rose* I took part in the planning from the very first day. Larry Watkins, an ex-schoolteacher who had written the *Robin Hood* script, came over from Hollywood and did considerable research into the obscure story of Mary Tudor, the sister of Henry VIII. Walt wanted to make a movie about the colourful monarch, without repeating the stories of his eight wives — an incomparable movie which had already been made by Alex Korda, with Charles Laughton in the lead. Our movie was designed to show life and intrigues around the court, while telling a rattling good yarn. It was based on the king's determination that Mary should marry King Louis of France, rather than the English commoner she loved. Henry was to be played by James Robertson Justice, a perfect choice for *our* king, and during the picture I made sure he showed off his skill with falcons. Mary Tudor was to be played, not by Joan Rice this time, but by Glynis Johns, with whom I still had a cosy competitive relationship!

As Larry fed us the script pages from Burbank, devised and approved by Walt, I worked alongside Steven Grimes, a young British sketch artist who had been discovered by Carmen Dillon. For four months we broke down the scenes into set-ups and sketches. In this process, a director has to force his imagination to project an exact visualisation of the movie. It is a most exciting creative period, and once you have set your ideas down in pictures, you can duplicate a sheaf of copies so that every technician and every department knows exactly what you expect of them. Walt was quite right — storyboarding saves waste, and hours of explanations and, in fact, gives the director a feeling of freedom. Having contributed to the sketches he knows exactly why they were designed in a certain way, and is ready then for any actor or crew member who comes up with a new idea. He can weigh it up and measure it against his original conception, and decide whether to make any adjustments. In my experience, storyboards prevent snap decisions which sound plausible on the floor, but once committed to may lead to a dead end or even 'the road to disaster'. I have used this method of pre-production for many years — in fact, whenever the production company has been prepared to afford a process they often mistakenly regard as a luxury!

Steven expressed himself in sketches just as a writer does in words, and over the years he became a most respected art director and designer in his own right. At this period, however, he was desperately broke. Steven had a wife and two young children to support. I recall one day when he had to rush home because his wife phoned to say the bailiff's men were emptying their apartment and putting the furniture out onto the pavement! He didn't return to his drawing-board for three whole days. Like many great artists, it seemed he was condemned to live in a garret until by Herculean efforts, he raised himself from penury, and gained the heights purely by his talents. I always feel this should be a proof to sceptical parents that a son or daughter can earn a good income and a respectable position in society by following their bent as an artist.

When the script of *The Sword and the Rose* was completed, there were four important French roles to be cast. So, together with Perce Pearce, Larry Watkins and Maude Spector (the doyen of British casting directors), I flew to Paris and was established in a very luxurious suite in the fabulous George V Hotel. Through Maude's connections, we had a continual flow of actors coming to read for us, sometimes in very accented English, but every Frenchman wanted an opportunity to play in a Walt Disney movie. A young man with a long nose impressed me by his inner fire and power on the screen. His name was Gerard Oury. We cast him as the Dauphin, but as it turned out he had a dual role to play.

My nine-year-old daughter, Jane, became desperately ill during the production and was slowly wasting away in a hospital. Gerard and his wife, Danielle, became as concerned and loving as if they were part of the family. One evening, after shooting they insisted on going to Westminster Abbey, lighting candles, and arranged a special mass to be said for Jane. I swear that moment was the turning point in her life. Our desiccated child began a slow recovery, which I have always felt was a proof that there is someone up there taking notice. Down here, there is surely some overall pattern in those meetings and choices in life which often appear accidental.

In the studio, Gerard watched and asked questions about every aspect of my directing, and years later when he became a very successful comedy writer (as well as actor), he used to say, "It all began on *The Sword and the Rose.*" He learned his method from me, which means that since I was at this time very much under the influence of Walt, he learned his craft indirectly from Walt. Along a filmmaker's road to creative fulfilment, we are always scooping up ideas and skills from many different sources and people... and I see nothing wrong in that!

In Paris, on that casting trip, our Disney group had fun on a generous expense account. Between appointments, we slipped out and saw the sights, ate at Fouquets, the Tour D'Argent, and the fabulous Restaurants Claremont beside the River Seine. At night we would go down to Pigalle and see what were then considered naughty French cabarets. It was at one of these that Monique, a very charming twenty-year-old girl, came and sat on Perce's knee. I don't think anything like this had ever happened to him before, and he was so enamoured of her attentions that when we left, just before dawn, he brought her back to his suite in the George V. He established her there without apparently having any worries that we might split on him to his wife!

In the two days that followed, we saw much less of Perce, and when we left, Monique accompanied him to the airport, kissing, cuddling and promising him in the few words of English that she had learned, that she would come to London as soon as she had mastered the Linguaphone course, he had bought her. It seemed very strange behaviour for Snow White's 'Doc' and I'm sure the last thing he would have wanted in his saner moments was for Monique to have kept her promise, and shown up in London where his wife was staying!

But this closely observed 'straying' had a significant effect on my own attitudes to girlfriends. The previous summer, in Juan les Pins, while my wife had to dash off and see her father in Vienna, I had started an affair with Lucienne, who was everything an Englishman imagined a French mistress should be. She was dark, petite with clean-cut features, always chic and bright, amusing and passionately loving. Unfortunately, she was married to a rather stodgy Englishman who was well known in the city of London. Neither of us really wanted to disturb our respective households or spouses, so we had made the most discreet weekly rendezvous at friends' flats in Mayfair and Knightsbridge. Now, as a result of witnessing how Perce seemed to get away with his flirtation, I began quite openly to invite Lucienne to Pinewood Studios on the pretext of watching the shooting. Looking back, it would seem now that I wanted my crew to see what a beautiful girlfriend I had, and to show off my talent and power as a director in front of her.

I must have been quite crazy, and on looking back, quite heartless. But when you're riding as high as I was, well paid, well regarded and being given full scope for one's talents in directing big films, you feel like God! Drunk with power, you believe you can get away with murder. Fortunately, for both Perce Pearce and myself, nobody ever told Walt! He expected everyone who worked for him to be above reproach — no scandal under any circumstances. He made two visits to England during *The Sword and the Rose* production, and seemed to be very happy with what I was shooting. Walt complimented me on working closely to the sketches and said he had every confidence that I was making *his* movie — which was true.

I had learned on *Robin Hood* that if you agreed to work for Walt, you must sublimate some of your own opinions and judgements and faithfully try to interpret the Master's vision. He paid well, provided wonderful sets, actors and costumes, and clearly knew what his public wanted. Every time he came on to the set and concentrated on what I was doing, he would pick out something which might be elaborated or improved on — always something no one else had thought of. This was part of his show-biz genius.

Walt would have clearly liked to have done everything himself — written, directed, photographed, played all the parts as he had done in his early days when he created his cartoons and animated features. But he was wise enough to know that this was impractical in feature filming. In any case, neither he nor any American could have worked at this time in a British studio without big arguments with the unions — or without at least reciprocal employment for a Brit in America.

So, having checked his 'will' was 'being done' in the studio, Walt would slip off to his model trains or go off to absorb the atmosphere on Scott's famous Antarctic schooner anchored in the Thames, or to Portsmouth where Nelson's old flagship, 'Victory' was anchored. He wanted to see everything he might one day reproduce or improve on: He went to Ascot, mainly to get an impression of the top-hatted punters and bookies; Walt travelled to Edinburgh to see the castle and the Midnight Tattoo; to Inverness to see the haunts of Robby Burns; to Oban to watch the Highland games; and to Ireland to look after Leprechauns (later incorporated into *Darby O'Gill and the Little People*). Perhaps he also slipped away at this time because something was about to happen in Pinewood over which he had no control — an electrician's 'Go-Slow' strike.

The ETU Committee at the studios decided that as Disney was the most important tenant at the moment, they would cause maximum disruption by hitting *Sword and the Rose* with shock one-hour blackouts. We would be in the middle of a take when the Shop Steward would shout to his mate on the switchboard, "Pull the breakers, Dan!" Sure enough, everything would be thrown into darkness which, apart from being highly dangerous, since we were often in the middle of a sword fight or working in the tank, it was intolerable for filming.

As we came out of one of these blackouts, Perce Pearce came on to the stage and was asking me whether it might be possible to move a forthcoming sequence on to the lot, when a spanner fell from the gantry, from an electrician's pocket — accidentally, it was said! It missed Perce but struck me a glancing blow on the temple. I was knocked out for perhaps a minute, then rushed to the local hospital in Uxbridge. X-rays showed no crack in my skull and in five hours I was back on the stage directing.

Believe it or not, despite the combined efforts of Perce Pearce, Peter Bolton, and Geoff Unsworth, the cameraman, not one shot had been completed in my absence! They had tried their best, but could not agree over the interpretation of the sketches! So, for the next three weeks, despite bad headaches and nauseous feelings in my stomach, I had to carry on. To this day, massage can reveal a very tender spot at the side of my skull!

When the shooting was complete, I worked with the editor making sure everything was cut together the way I had intended, and then he departed for Burbank. There, as before, Walt decided the final cut, and supervised the music and dubbing. Again, it was at a Royal Premiere that I saw the final movie, considerably more my picture this time, but Walt had become so enamoured of Henry VIII and the almost forgotten Mary Tudor, that the story went over the heads of his usual American kiddies audience. Although beautifully mounted and historically correct, this movie was never quite as popular entertainment as Warner's *The Virgin Queen* with Bette Davis, which was released at the same time. But it has had many replays on the Disney TV Channel and video up to the present time.

Back on my Rank contract, my next two films took me to the other side of the world. First, was *The Planter's Wife*, known in America as *Outpost In Malaya*. The second was *The Seekers*, which dealt with the first pioneers in New Zealand, and was known in America as *Land of Fury*.

Earl St. John, an ex-American distributor, was now in sole charge at Pinewood and called me to say he had discovered a very topical script by a new writer called Guy Elmes. Guy had served in the Navy with Lord Mountbatten during the Burma Campaign and was fascinated with the East, especially at this time when the British were trying to stave off the attempt by Chinese infiltrators to push them out of Malaya. The plot of the script followed the efforts of a rubber planter family in their attempt to withstand the increasing threats and battles with the local Communists.

The well-know stage actor, Jack Hawkins, had been persuaded to play the lead, but since I wanted to make an internationally important film, Earl bundled me off to Hollywood to try and hook a big female star. This was most unusual for a British director and, for me, a great adventure. Due to my pre-war social acquaintance with David Niven and Eric Portman, I was able to get an introduction to Bob Coryell, head of the William Morris Talent Agency. He was a guy who had made his own way in the world, and we hit it off immediately. In the space of ten days he arranged for me to meet Norma Shearer, Loretta Young, Joan Crawford, Olivia deHavilland, and Claudette Colbert! Amazing! No agent could or would do anything like that today. We remained friends until his death in 1997.

In my bedroom in Beverley, Yorkshire, I had photos of Norma Shearer all over the walls, and now I found myself having tea with her at her Spanish-style home overlooking the blue Pacific Ocean! She was about fifty, still very beautiful, and intrigued by the idea of returning to the screen in a British movie. But she had recently married a young ski instructor and was very much in love, and, in her heart of hearts, I'm sure she was afraid of working outside a studio lot. Loretta Young and Olivia deHavilland were also charming and invited me to tea in their beautiful Beverly Hills homes. Both were involved in television and other American productions and so, politely, they passed on the project.

Under the tropical lanterns of The Luau, a popular Beverly Hills restaurant, I dined with Joan Crawford. Halfway through the evening we were holding hands and looking deep into each other's eyes. I found her still very sexy, even though she was ten years older than me. I think given a fraction more time and soft lights I could have spent a passionate night or two with her! Unfortunately, she really could not see herself playing the wife of a British rubber planter, or going on location outside America... so I didn't pursue her further.

Claudette Colbert was different. She had travelled a great deal and felt it was time to make another picture in Europe, especially with a fine actor like Jack Hawkins. She read the script, approved it, and took me to the home of George and Edie Cukor, who were the king and queen of Hollywood society at the time. Walking around their palatial home in the Palisades, I was bowled over by George's collection of Impressionist painters. The underlying purpose of the visit was for George to vet me. Apparently, I passed inspection, and after making a call to Walt, he advised Claudette to accept the role, and me as director!

Bob Coryell struck a deal acceptable to Rank, but I now had to make a stopover in New York and sell the whole project to Arthur Krim and Bob Benjamin at United Artists. The financial controller of Rank, at this time, was a tough accountant called John Davis. He had advised J. Arthur Rank not to pay American star fees without a guarantee that they would be covered by an American distribution advance.

Having got so far, I was determined to see the picture set-up and after three days of "argie-barging" Krim and Benjamin agreed to Davis' terms. I was climbing another rung to being an international director.

Returning to Pinewood, thrilled and triumphant, Earl packed me straight off to Singapore with Peter Henessey, a young cameraman I had used in my documentary days. We spent a fascinating, steamy Christmas photographing Chinese street scenes in Jahore, and Malay fishermen in the old Dutch port of Malacca.

In order to absorb atmosphere, we spent two days and nights with Angus

McKenzie, a tea-planter. We found ourselves smack in the middle of guerrilla warfare. The evenings would be spent in polite conversation, listening to his wife play the piano, knocking back scotch, and playing a few hands of bridge. Straight after breakfast, he would take us to the back door of his villa and there, laid out with their throats cut, were two Malay workers! The same thing, two days running!

"That's becoming too bloody much of a habit!" said Angus. "But we'll show those Commie buggers! This place was jungle swamp till my grandfather cleared the land and planted rubber. We've as much right to this country as any darned Chinese — or Malay, for that matter!"

Angus drove us around his enormous plantation, and on one road that looked very English, we nearly had our heads cut off! A length of piano wire had been stretched across the road — a favourite trick of the terrorists. But our host was prepared for it. His Land Rover was fitted with a strong triangular pillar — welded in front of the radiator and ready to cut through any dastardly secret weapon like piano wire!

John Dalton, the Rank Film representative for South East Asia, horrified yet fascinated us in Singapore, by recounting some of his experiences as a POW with the Japanese. He had suffered terrible beatings and privations while working on the infamous Chang-Tsu Railway — later immortalised by David Lean in his *Bridge on the River Kwai*. John arranged for us to meet more planters and to hear their experiences in combating 'the Bandits as they were called. In the screenplay of *The Planter's Wife*, I was able to incorporate many of the remarkable things these brave men and women were doing to defend themselves... while Peter shot masses of stills and filmed some valuable establishing shots, documentary fashion.

Our trip convinced us that Malaya was far too dangerous a place to bring out movie stars or a British unit, so again, on the advice of John Dalton, we made a detour home via Ceylon (now known as Sri Lanka). In the Fifties, this was one of the most beautiful tropical islands in the world. The Singhalese were a slim, graceful and most friendly, dusky people. The women were so beautiful that we quickly felt that any European women we saw looked almost gross!

We found wonderful locations to match Malaya, which John Stafford — the studio line producer — approved when he came out to join us. John was a delightful old character who was wise in film making, but believed every opportunity should be taken to enjoy oneself. He became intrigued by the talk in every British club or home about a mysterious Indian called Darna Parla, who was often seen in Colombo with different sari-clad ladies walking three paces behind him. "He's either a modern Bluebeard with a harem, or he's some kind of cult leader," was the general opinion of the white colonial population.

We discovered that Darna had recently finished building a palatial house in the mountains. He had christened it 'Shangri-La', and two of his ladies were well-known British actresses — Elizabeth Sellars and Jane Hardwicke, daughter of Sir Cedric. Through the good offices of the main cinema owner who distributed Rank Films, we managed to get an introduction to Darna and on the way to look at another location (a grove filled with hordes of monkeys). We also made a stop at 'Shangri-La'. Darla turned out to be a very handsome high-caste Indian of about forty, who received us graciously and invited us to stay overnight. During the evening we met ten of his 'handmaidens', who were mostly beautiful and clothed in rich saris. In conversation we found they were highly educated and came from rich families in Bombay, Taiwan, Hong Kong, Rhodesia and other outposts of the old British Empire. All I can say is that we found no evidence that Darna was running a harem, or even providing sexual satisfaction to any of the fourteen ladies who formed his co-operative (and whom it appeared had financed 'Shangri-La').

I think they were all women at a certain age in their lives, who had found the pressures of the world temporarily overwhelming. They wanted a period of quiet meditation... and who better to guide them than a sympathetic man who had been a journalist in London, with an encyclopaedic knowledge of literature, theatre, Eastern religions, and psychology? They were all in need of a friend, advisor, someone to lean on, who could gradually get them 'on track', in this new world where bright women were expected to become instant lawyers, politicians, financial advisors and business executives. Perhaps Darna was living off them in a way, but was certainly no Bluebeard.

Over the years I lost track of Darna Parla, but I have a strong suspicion that the violent revolution which took place in Sri Lanka, and the subsequent unrest amongst the Tamils, swept away Darna's 'Shangri-La' and broke up what was a most interesting social experience in communal living, clearly a delight to all taking part!

We came back to London, crewed up, and returned to Ceylon to shoot for eight weeks of bliss! We lived in two big colonial palaces called Mount Lavinia and the Galle Face Hotel, which though giving luxury service for their guests, still had their servants sleeping on stairways and being completely subservient to white visitors.

We used to set off at six am, when the sun rose and often had to travel two hours, passing groups of Singhalese men and women tramping to work in the fields. They would always give us a shout and a friendly wave. We would shoot till around three in the afternoon, when it always rained. Then we returned for swims in the pool or the sea.

Once again, I became involved with a most beautiful, slender Eurasian girl. Yvonne Gulampatek was married to a young Singalese businessman, but she was crazy to take part in the film. I found several spots where she could work as an extra and, after accidentally-on-purpose pressing close to each other and holding hands, we would slink away for a few romantic moments in the bush.

One evening she begged me to come to their villa, which was about two miles from the hotel. I drove out by taxi and the moment she opened the door I saw immediately what her intentions were. Her husband was out for the evening, so we clutched each other and made violent love. She taught me new forms of tender loving, which I had never experienced with any European. Suddenly, the phone rang. It was her husband and he was on his way home. Yvonne became the frightened little wife and bundled me out of the house, despite a torrential rainstorm! I staggered back along a road with no lights, suddenly fearful of snakes, monkeys, and Tamil plantation workers swinging murderous pangas on their drunken way home! My ego was shocked and soaked, and I wondered whether it had all been worthwhile, but thinking back, that evening sticks out as one of my most treasured memories!

Another unique experience was the staging of a cobra-mongoose fight. In the story, the son of the planter finds himself in the bathroom with a cobra coming down the water pipe. He is saved by his little Malay friend who runs to fetch his pet mongoose, which jumps into the fray and kills the snake, saving the boy in true Rudyard Kipling style.

We built the bottom half of the bathroom set in the zoo, and the curator provided us with a large cobra and three mongooses. The cobra was placed on the floor of the set and the first mongoose released over the set wall. It immediately took one look at the cobra preparing to strike and jumped straight over the three foot fence. The second mongoose was even more scared. The third got involved with the cobra, but latched onto the tail instead of the mouth and had to be rescued.

"I'm afraid our Singhalese mongooses are not used to fighting," said Ryland, the curator. "I'll have to get you some North-Indian variety."

We waited a week with a skeleton crew, while the mongooses were airlifted via Madras (where, we were told, they got involved with the brass section of a visiting jazz band!). However, they arrived on our set and we tried again. The first Rikki-Tikki-Tavi went over the wall, took one look at the cobra, had a little pee in the corner, and then faced the swaying reared head for what seemed like an hour, They played out a ballet of feints and sharp jabs. Then, suddenly the mongoose struck, grabbing the cobra's head in its mouth and hanging on. The cobra swung his furry assailant around and around from side to side. They writhed and collapsed in a pool of blood. I did not find this a very pleasant experience and the continuity girl refused to speak to me the rest of the day. But the script called for the scene, and on our budget there was no way one could fake that encounter.

We returned to the studios at Pinewood where Geoff Unsworth took over as director of photography, and on the stages created a wonderful black-and-white picture matching the location photography to perfection.

Claudette Colbert was a joy to work with, because she was completely professional. I felt that if by any chance I hesitated in making any set-up, she would take over most competently. The same applied with the lighting. On the first day, Claudette pointed out to Geoff exactly where her key and filler lights should be, and insisted that her face must be photographed only on the right side.

"I look like a frog when I look out right!" she used to say, so every shot had to be designed that way, which sometimes meant even modifying the set! In ordinary life, one would never have noticed a fault in her face, but from a camera viewpoint she was right.

Claudette told me she had never been called upon to do real action scenes in Hollywood, but when it came to defending the bungalow from the Chinese bandits, she quickly became adept with machine-gun and pistol. Up to this time Jack Hawkins had also only played make-believe in theatrical roles, so he willingly let Claudette guide him in gunnery. In return, Jack took her to all the best shows running in London, introducing her to Larry Olivier, John Gielgud, Edith Evans, Dame Sybil Thorndike, all with whom he had often worked. But it was to me Claudette turned to when she wanted to spend a weekend in Paris.

"I know how devotedly you drooled over those Impressionist paintings owned by George Cukor, just think what a feast we could have at L'Orangerie Galleries."

For once, I did not feel like openly hurting my wife and going off for what would inevitably turn out to be a "sexy weekend." Although my marriage had hit the rocks several times due to my determination to taste every side of life, I decided to be faithful to Blanka and therefore introduced Claudette to my very good friend Hubert Gregg (Prince John in *Robin Hood*). He was very smooth and sophisticated, and I gather they had a wonderful time together in Paris.

The Planter's Wife (titled *Outpost in Malaya* in the US) was a good action picture based on a true-life situation. Before distributing it, J. Arthur Rank made an approach to Lord Templer, who was Commander-in-Chief of the British Forces in Malaysia. He looked at the movie and said, "Annakin's done a great job in catching the situation as it was, but I have to say if the buggers had only fought half as hard as he shows them, I wouldn't have had to spend seven stinking years in the jungle!"

The Seekers (known in America as *Land of Fury*) was not my greatest triumph as a filmmaker, but an enjoyable experience in living — something I was beginning to recognise as just as important as the actual movie process. George Brown, who had produced *Hotel Sahara*, had been pressing me for some time to join him in another film, but one way or another I did not go for any of the scripts he was offering me. However, he had got hold of a young cockney comedian called Tommy Steele, and had produced (without me directing!) a very successful comedy called *Tommy the Toreador*. So when George came to me with a pioneering story called *The Seekers*, I listened to him... especially since it was set in New Zealand, my old stomping ground. It was based on a novel which was historically true, but the script which playwright Bill Fairchild was writing seemed to me to be full of clichés and boring characters. However, I felt I could put these things right on the location shoot. Suddenly, to my horror, George and John Hargreaves, the studio accountant, went off on a spotting trip to New Zealand without me, and came back with figures proving that we could make the whole picture cheaper at Pinewood. I was furious, but already committed by contract.

Morris Carter, a fine art director who had also been taken on the scouting trip, made fabulous paintings to show what he could build in the studio, and knowing the success we had had with studio sets on *Robin Hood* and *Sword and the Rose*, I tried hard to cooperate with him and make things work.

Jack Hawkins and Glynis Johns were cast as the young pioneers. Glynis was fine with me, but Jack, much as I liked him, seemed too old and well fed. Noel Purcell, an amusing Irishman, and Ken Williams (who later had great success in the *Carry On* series) were interesting supporting characters. George also imported eight genuine Maoris from New Zealand, plus an opera singer named Mara TeWiata, to play the Polynesian Chief. I planned my set-ups with the usual care and tried to make the actors feel comfortable, but the geysers, hot springs and signal fires did not seem very convincing in the studio!

One of the most interesting sequences to shoot was a night battle on the Pinewood lot. The trouble was that it was October and a thick mist came up every night at eleven, making it bitterly cold. I had to drive two hundred stuntmen, wearing nothing but jockstraps, into naked action until six in the morning, when dawn light made shooting impossible. Throughout the night I plied them with rum and offered every inducement I could think of, if they would only carry on and look like fierce Maori warriors! Unfortunately, when the material was all edited, you could not tell who were the good Maoris and who the enemy! Even though it would not have been historically correct, I should have devised some distinctive clothing or markings... another lesson learned the hard way!

Suddenly, George Brown revealed a very devious plan. In his own mind, he had apparently known very well that we could not finish the picture without going to New Zealand, so he now threw himself at the mercy of the unions and begged them to let him send out a skeleton crew of only sixteen people and no sound recordists (although everyone must have known there was dialogue still to be shot).

To my astonishment, George managed to persuade the Studio Works Committee (with bribes of free holidays in Spain!) to allow this to happen. So, we set off on a seventy-two hour flight with Jack Hawkins, Noel Purcell and, oh yes, Laya Raki... I had forgotten her! The script called for a beautiful Maori princess, so we tested all the beautiful young Asians we could find in London, including Tsi Chin, a lovely Indonesian model who figured in all the glossy magazines at that period... but she proved to be no actress.

Suddenly, George said he had found just the right girl... a German-Javanese cabaret performer with a nice smile, good legs, and so far as I could judge, attractive breasts. But although her agent in Munich assured us that she had starred in several German movies, it turned out that she had never played a scene face to face with another actor. She could speak lines, but whenever Jack Hawkins had to kiss her, she broke out into embarrassed laughter! The whole unit found her a bit of a joke, but on location, in a little one-horse town called Whakatane, she seemed very desirable company. Several guys were deceived by what they took to be Laya's 'come-on' look, and were surprised to be haughtily rebuffed, until they decided she was saving herself for the producer ... which is often too true with actresses. However, in this case this might not have been so, because poor George was struggling day and night to keep this picture turning!

One hot afternoon we were shooting on the picturesque Lake Rotoiti, and Laya, as an uninhibited Maori maiden, had to run across the rocks and swim underwater, apparently naked. I can recall the frustrating hold-ups while waiting for the wardrobe mistress to fix feathers (at Laya's insistence) on her nipples! Suddenly, the cameraman announced that the light was too yellow to shoot, and as though released from a trap, Laya set off swimming for an island in the middle of the lake. I think she wanted to show us that at least she was a champion swimmer! Immediately, Peter Henessey, Dave Harcourt, the camera operator and I leapt in after her, and eventually caught up with her. She seemed to want to play, so we surrounded her and threatened to pull off her feathers. Suddenly, a spluttering 'porpoise' appeared amid us — George Brown, coming to the defence of his princess! He blustered, and tried to force us to go back and shoot something, but the light had definitely gone, and perhaps we could still have fun with Laya!!

The unique semitropical locations of North Island were beautiful and fun to work in. But here there was something I had never experienced — deep rumblings in the crew against the producer. The unit was seething because George had cut the crew to the absolute minimum. For me, this was an important lesson. George was behaving like a general who had got himself into an almost impossible corner, and now had to use fair means or foul to win the battle – or, in this case finish the picture!

However, British unionism caught up with us and punished us in a way I'd never experienced, then or since. We had come to this great showplace of Rotorua to shoot the big geyser, which only blows off once a day — regularly as clockwork at eleven am. Here we were, having travelled halfway round the world with camera all set up and Noel Purcell and Jack Hawkins costumed and ready to play a scene backgrounded by the geyser. Then, Nobby Clark, the shop steward, refused to allow us to shoot! Why? Because George was late with providing the morning tea-wagon! A tremendous argument ensued, and the geyser blew. Because of his ridiculously tight schedule, there was nothing more for George to do but to move us on to the next location, where we staged a fantastic sequence with four traditional war canoes filled with Maoris in grotesque war paint. The same evening we 'immortalised' Jack watching beautiful Maori women swaying rhythmically and swinging their pois (coloured straw balls) in front of their whares (decorated houses). Quite a day!

As part of a race where Jack Hawkins is challenged to prove his superiority over a young Maori champion, they had to swim down a raging torrent. The Maori tries to cheat by shortcutting Jack by diving over a large waterfall. I had managed to persuade a Maori Olympic athlete to dive over the two hundred foot high Huka Falls, while Jack's British double negotiated the river rapids. It was shaping up as a sensational sequence, but when it came to fake Jack's close-ups in a safe shallow stream, which we disturbed by high pressure water from the nozzles of fire pumps, Jack unfortunately trod on a sharp stone. He howled like a wolf and said we should have had the riverbed swept (as they would have done on a London stage, I presumed he meant!)

The twelve day shoot (including travel!) was over but George now decided that in order to get the missing geyser shot and a number of other documentary shots depicting the creation of New Zealand, Peter Hennessy, Steve Clayton, the camera assistant, and I should stay on. What a break! Flying in a crop-dusting plane to the northernmost point of North Island, we filmed Maoris building a small settlement around what was alleged to be the oldest tree in the world — a twelve hundred year old kauri. On the East Coast we filmed millions of cormorants nesting on rocks so slippery with guano, that we slid sixty feet down the cliff holding on to the camera tripod! It was a miracle no bones were broken!

At the little port of Wairoa, we hired a small trawler and sneaked out to the forbidden White Island — the volcanic centre of the whole of New Zealand. It was a ghoulish dangerous place consisting of nothing but a crust of sulphur laced with foul-smelling vent holes. We were told that twenty-six people had lost their lives there until visits were banned. However, our skipper knew the secret paths. We followed in his footsteps (literally!) across this eerie smoking island, until we reached a small cone.

"The heart of the volcano," said our guide. Fixing up our tripod on the rim, we looked down into a swirling fiery mass only twenty feet below. Steve Clayton, like a gunner doing his normal routine, stepped around the crater rim to check the focus on the lens, lost his balance, and almost dragged the tripod and the three of us to a horrible death! We rolled over on the hot crust, receiving only small burns, which only ceased to irritate after we dashed back to the ship and jumped into the crystal clear sea.

Flying back from New Zealand, I made a stopover in Hawaii, visiting the famous Waikiki Beach, watching hula-dancing and generally enjoying Hawaiian food and hospitality, but the thing that impressed me most and amazed me, were the number of Japanese on the island and the number of people who clearly had mixed blood. White American guys were going around with Japanese girls, Polynesians were becoming light-skinned with straight noses, and slit eyes were cropping up in the most unlikely faces! Hawaii was clearly a big ethnic melting pot where, from what I could discover, a new hybrid breed of people were getting on with their lives without any more than normal problems. It was an eye-opener for me — the shape of the world to come. If so, it presented me with a big career problem!!

Before leaving for New Zealand I had persuaded Earl St. John to option a best-selling book for me called 'The Hidden Flower' by Pearl S. Buck. It was a charming love story based on a young Englishman meeting a girl in Tokyo before the war. She was gentle, submissive, but intelligent and wonderful in bed. The Englishman seemed to feel about her exactly as I had felt about the beautiful Yvonne in Ceylon... and he was fascinated with the Japanese way of living. The couple went through ethnic and cultural difficulties with her family, but love and perseverance were winning through, until he brought her back to his hometown, in the stuffy cathedral city of Salisbury, England. His staid family and friends made no concessions to the girl's different way of thinking and traditional background. The young man was blackballed in British clubs, and eventually their relationship was made so unbearable that the girl fled back to Japan, where I planned to give the movie a modern Romeo and Juliet ending.

Now, on returning to Pinewood, I told Earl that much as I appreciated his faith in me — he was offering me the long-coveted chance to both direct and produce! I really felt that 'The Hidden Flower' was old hat, an issue which for half the world was passé — solved — dead!

"Certainly in Hawaii," I told him. "And most probably throughout California where Asians and people of European stock are flooding together to seek the sun, no one is going to care about race or colour!" Looking back, I realise how wrong I was, because mixed marriages still pose a problem to most parents. But I think I had reached a point in my upward climb, when I had to falter... or make some career mistake!

I cast my mind back. After leaving Beverley Grammar School at sixteen, and being forced by my father to train as an Income Tax Inspector (!!!), my great role model in life had been a cheery, vital, rugger-playing Yorkshireman named Bramley. He was an Oxford graduate with a fine analytical brain, but had somehow landed himself into a safe Civil Service job in Hull. He said he was content so long as he could relieve the boring routine of examining tax returns by long vacations abroad, doing unusual things like climbing the Matterhorn, dog-sledding in the Arctic, or diving for treasure off Old Troy... pitting himself against experiences he would never normally have. With wide eyes and much envy, I used to listen to his tales in the local pub.

"Life is a series of forked roads," Bram used to say. "One goes the safe way, you know, the other goes into the unknown. It may be dangerous, but we only have one life and it should be lived to the full. Take my advice, when faced with two roads, always take the more dangerous one!"

From the time I first broke the shackles and sailed off to New Zealand and Australia, I had always taken this maxim to heart. Whenever I came to a decision, I would consciously say, "What would Bram do?" and usually my choice had led to adventure, fun and personal development. My only serious aberration was my rejection of 'The Hidden Flower', and the new fields the project opened out to me. Suddenly, I was playing for safety, and imagining dangers that didn't exist. I flunked out, and threw out of joint the run of good luck I'd been blessed with for the last ten years.

CHAPTER SIX
Marking Time...
Big Success... then ????

I had just passed on 'The Hidden Flower', when I heard Walt Disney was ready to start another live-action movie in Britain — *Rob Roy* based on Sir Walter Scott's classic novel. He claimed to have found wonderful locations during a summer trip to Scotland and now approached the Rank Organisation to lend me out again. Back in the saddle again, I thought, but John Davis, who had now been promoted to Head of the whole Rank Organisation, killed the offer without even consulting me. "We've let you out too often to make money for the Americans," he said. "You still have two pictures to make for us under your original Sydney Box contract."

"But you have nothing important for me," I said. "And Walt will bring the film into Pinewood, and you'll make money..."

"No use arguing," said John. "And I'll sue you if you think of breaking your contract."

Earl St. John, still nominally Head of Production, was bitterly disappointed for me, and quickly brought me together with Paul Soskin, who was preparing an exciting adventure movie called *Elephant Bill*. It was set in Burma, and told the story of a remarkable elephant called 'Bandoola'. During the war, Bandoola had been instrumental in the rescue of some twenty thousand women and children from the advancing Japanese Army.

The book had been written by an old Burma hand, Colonel Williams, and told a fascinating story from the time when Bandoola was a baby; how he was trained to work in the great teak forests; and how his Oozie (trainer/keeper) discovered his intelligence was much greater than the other elephants. He taught him to use his amazing ballet-like sensitive footwork to negotiate the most precarious mountain trails. The climax of the story was the use of this skill and devotion in leading sixty other pack elephants and five hundred refugees over an impregnable mountain range into India.

CHAPTER SIX *Marking Time... Big Success... then ????*

The script was fascinating... Earl sent me off on a scouting trip to Burma and Sri Lanka. I found great elephants... but the unions back home demanded a minimum crew of 45, which was ridiculous because the elephants would never have performed with a chattering crew around them! After many arguments, John Davis said "No way!"

I felt that my luck had run out. I was not allowed to work for any other company but Rank, so I joined up with three friends to take over the concession at a seaside spa, consisting of a repertory theatre, a concert party show, and a pier-restaurant, at Ventnor in the Isle of Wight.

I helped run the theatre and put on the concert party show, which was fun. With the comedy routines set for the season, the professionals we engaged took over, and my trips to the island became mere excuses to indulge in one-night stands!

I did not like what I was becoming... Blanka still clearly loved me and would do anything for me. My daughter Jane was growing up adorable and looking to me for guidance which I could not give. Why? Because I clearly didn't have the answers, even for myself.

Blanka was two years older than me — a graduate of universities in both Vienna and Prague. She had an excellent brain, and was highly erudite in matters psychological, political, and socialist. When we had first come together she had expanded my horizons, and our sex relationship had always been good. However, she was a worrier — a pessimist with a nagging social conscience, whereas I was by nature an optimist — happiest in the fantasy world of scriptwriting, and getting my biggest kicks out of audience applause — either for laughs, tears or shared adventures.

A strong sense of self-preservation told me that if I wished to continue movie making and be successful, I must not be coerced into tackling the psychological and social message subjects Blanka wanted to steer me into. I had to stick to the people and things I really understood and had gut feelings about.

Suddenly, Sydney Box came up with a suggestion that looked as if it might break my deadlock with Rank and Pinewood. Though no longer an active producer, he was managing the affairs of his family, which now included Peter Rogers — who had married Betty Box — my producer at Islington. Peter had been around even in the days we were shooting *The Huggetts*, but at that time we had regarded him as just Betty's consort, run-around driver, and occasional gag man. We had always known he had a funny outlook on life and an amusing turn of phrase, but now, under Sydney's guidance, he had written a crazy comedy set in an 'Arabian Nights' kind of country. Most of the action took place around a sheik's desert palace. "I'm sure the two of you together can make a glamourous, risqué, escapist comedy-adventure," said Sydney with his usual encouraging smile.

Having polished the script and added as many gags as we could, Peter and I began auditions to find twelve beautiful girls for the sheik's harem. In a Pinewood oak-panelled office, we sat for a week behind a large desk and viewed the girls as they paraded past us. We would ask the attractive ones to sit down and tell us about their acting or modelling careers, which, of course, were usually very slight. Then, usually one of us would say: "I wonder if we could see a little more of you? If you've brought a bikini, would you please slip into the anteroom and change?"

Most of them *had* brought bikinis and would come out and give us a very pleasant parade. One very beautiful girl called Shirley was not content with this, however. To our amazement, we saw her reaching behind the bra, slipping it off, coming straight towards us. She said, "Now, which of you two really make the decisions?" She gave us a saucy smile. "Or is it both? I don't really care, because I'm determined to get this part."

By this time, she had come around the desk, reached for my hand and put it under her very lovely right breast.

"Not bad, eh?" she said, looking down enchantingly. Then, she went around to Peter and repeated the ploy with, "I need this job more than all the others you've seen, I guess," she murmured.

Peter gulped. "Uh, well, yes." And he couldn't resist one of his funny lines, "But, darling, I really don't go for tits, I'm a bottom man myself."

With that, she stood in front of us with her legs astride, and put her thumbs on the side of the bikini. "That's okay with me, darling." Peter jumped up, ran to her, turned her around and sent her off in the direction of the anteroom. As soon as she closed the door he said, "I don't know about you, Ken, but I'm fucking that one."

"Okay with me," I said. "Good luck and I'll see you after lunch." Although I had enjoyed the incident tremendously, I could not bring myself to take advantage of a girl who was really at our mercy.

As though to punish the Rank Organisation and to get even with them for not having given me a big movie such as *The Million Dollar Bank Note*, which Ronnie Neame was making, or *The Purple Plain* which Bob Parrish, an ex-Hollywood director, had been given with a fantastically large budget for that time, I demanded the right to build the most fanciful Arabian palace, with gilded arches and white fluted columns, such as the Pinewood construction shop had never been asked for!

We failed to persuade either of the big Rank stars — Dirk Bogarde or Kenny More — to play the lead, and finished up with Donald Sinden, who had a good sense of comedy and timing, but it put us in the Second Division, so to speak! I made a discovery of an Australian actor called Bill Kerr, who was working at that time as straight man to the brilliant English comic, Tony Hancock. But my best coup was to insist on some kind of international name, and Earl St. John helped me in hooking Akim Tamiroff, a Hollywood Russian who had been nominated for an Oscar in *For Whom The Bell Tolls*. He created a marvellously funny sheik and was supported brilliantly by Dora Bryan, who has been making the British laugh for over twenty years.

Martin Miller, a screwball Czech refugee, and Ferdy Mayne, who had played an Arab for me in *Hotel Sahara*, provided the broadest comedy around a secret weapon which the sheik was developing in his desert stronghold — this was thirty years before Saddam Hussein, and we thought it all a big joke — how times change!!

The desert set caused us tremendous photographic problems because it was so bare — not even a palm tree in sight! I had given my old friend and mentor from documentary days, Reg Wyer, his first chance to shoot a movie on the new Eastman Color film, and he made the mistake of trying to be too co-operative and economical by accepting the overhead rig for the lamps that had been used for *Purple Plain*. We died when we saw our rushes with great arc-circles all over the backing!

Reg tried to remedy this by piling in more lamps to even out the light, but the temperature on the studio floor rose higher than in a real desert, and we nearly blew up the whole studio! It taught me a lesson never to allow a designer to land me with a large studio backing without foreground pieces to break it up.

The movie was glamourous and eventually went out under the title *You Know*

What Sailors Are. It cost around a quarter of a million dollars (in 1954) and did good average business in the UK, and is still getting laughs in various parts of the world. A few months ago, I was lecturing at Ohio University and a student stood up and said, "Please tell us about the making of *You Know What Sailors Are*".

I said, "How, in heaven's name, could you know anything about that turkey?"

He said, "Oh, I have a 16 mm copy and have run it at least twenty times. My friends and I have had some of our biggest laughs watching it."

Nice to hear but for me *You Know What Sailors Are* stands out as the movie on which I discovered that farce is not my strongest talent! I know how to build scenes to release the 'big laugh', but I prefer to rely on sly humour, and on comedy arising from the observation of the funny things people do in real life.

About this time, Bert Batt and other assistants began calling me 'The Smiling Tiger', which was okay... but could it mean that in striving to be a perfectionist I was becoming intolerant? My greatest strength (and joy) had always been the ways in which I could get the best out of both crews and cast and keep them happy. If they were beginning to be wary of me...? I was becoming a very mixed-up chappie. Suddenly, fate, or more simply Sydney Box (again!), came up with "a break" which pulled me right out of the 'Slough of Despond' and the worry that I was not using my talents to the full. Sydney had acquired a Graham Greene short story called 'Across The Bridge' and had adapted it with the idea of starring Charles Laughton ... but the material was too thin, sad, and uncompromising. No studio apparently wanted it. But John Stafford turned up again, and told Sydney of his great personal friendship with Graham Greene — which I learned later was based on their shared experiences in Roman brothels!

John suggested that Graham might be prepared to let Guy Elmes write a new first half to the story, and possibly we could hook a younger star in the shape of Rod Steiger — a vital young actor, who had just made a hit in *On The Waterfront*.

Sydney agreed to sell the script to John, and our old friend Earl St. John put up the money for the rewrite. Guy concocted a wonderful first half to the story, telling how Carl Shaffner, a big financier came to be on the run to Mexico. He then became involved with the Mexican police chief and acquired the dog which became his only friend and conscience... as in Graham's story.

I remember Guy and I arguing for hours with John over the first draft script, because he was dead against our attempts to add colour and a little sex to the adventures in Mexico. He insisted that in the second half we keep within the framework of monk-like austerity, as established in Greene's original story. It could be that John was afraid of facing Graham and wanted to stay in his good books at all costs, or he genuinely felt we were trying to vulgarise a classic and unique character study. Certainly, I had never seen John come on so strongly!

In shooting the movie, I followed the story line as laid down by John, and I will never know whether we might have had more commercial success with Guy's more sexy version, but one thing is sure, I could never complain at the tremendous and permanent acclaim the movie won throughout the world.

Rank finally agreed to finance the film and pay Rod Steiger's fee, but no one seemed to have realised the picture could not be shot in England! The new story started in New York, travelled by train south to the Mexican border, and required an old frontier bridge crossing the Rio Grande, and a small Mexican village at the other side. Earl St. John looked at me and said, "Is your bag packed? You'd better go off and see what these very non-British locations ought to look like!"

Flying to New York, I made contact with a small documentary company who could shoot establishing shots as the train leaves Grand Central Station and travels across the country. We'd never have got union permission in either country to pick up those shots economically! Then I 'rode the rails' down to San Antonio — which was exactly what Carl Shaffner was to do. In this Spanish-style city I was lucky enough to find Paco, a very bright and knowledgeable driver, who took me all along the border, zigzagging in and out of Mexico between Laredo and El Paso. I sketched and photographed bridges, bars, motels, trains, police stations, cars and costumes. In all, I brought back over six hundred stills which became 'the Bible' for the look of the picture. From Paco, I learned all about local customs, and politics. I recall very clearly him saying they had a Senator in Texas who could solve all America's problems if they would only put him in the White House. His name was Lyndon Johnson!

Back in Pinewood, John Stafford persuaded Earl that Spain would be the most suitable and economical place to reproduce the location photos I had brought back. John had worked with a very practical Spanish art director named Julio Molina, and I happened to have kept in contact with an ex-Technicolor camera-assistant and still photographer, Johnny Cabrera, who was now in Spain making a profession of finding locations for the big Bronston epics like *El Cid* and *The Fall of the Roman Empire*.

So, we immediately phoned our two friends and within twenty-four hours I was off again — on a scouting trip that was to introduce me to wonderful places like Cadiz, the Rhonda Valley, Seville, Granada, and Cordoba — with its multi-arched mosque *Ronda* built by the Arabs a thousand years ago. Finally, we found the village of Lora del Rio, which had a metal girder bridge almost exactly like the one I had seen near Laredo.

In ten days of much travelling and discussion, we had come to an area where I could stage all the exteriors in the movie (with a few adjustments) and I had cemented friendships with Julio, Johnny and Julio Mercado (our driver) which lasted through three more of the movies I made in Spain. This led me into another romantic liaison! As we visited these various towns, after a late Spanish meal, my three friends would invariably take me to see flamenco dancing. It was in Seville that I met Marucha, a dark Spanish beauty of around twenty, who spoke not one word of English, but who laughed and joked and danced with me in a way that made me feel completely at one with the world — and very sexually aroused! She refused to come back to my hotel, but promised to spend a lot of time with me when the unit came out on location.

Over the phone, I reported progress to John Stafford, and he agreed that Julio should start building sets immediately because there was only four weeks before Rod Steiger would be 'on the clock'. On my return to London, Rod turned up and proved to be quite a difficult customer. He had never been to London before and immediately set up house with a weird hippie he had picked up in Schwab's coffee house on Sunset Boulevard!

For two whole weeks Rod argued with me about the inner meaning and psychological motivations of Carl Shaffner. Thank God I had been introduced by Blanka to the basic theories of Freud and Jung or I would have been completely lost! Rod had studied at the Actors Studio in New York, and had become completely hooked on 'The Method'. Since it had stood him in such good stead in *On The Waterfront*, he was certain he was right about almost everything. Gradually, as I was able to tune in to his wavelength, I became convinced that he was going to give a great performance — even if just to show he could out Brando Brando! Rod never looked at the script again, merely asked me which scene it was we were about to shoot — then threw himself into it!

Sometimes he would lose the sense of time completely, and just emote. I would let him strut and shout, stumble and sob, always checking in my mind what character I could cut away to when editing — usually the dog! This was the only way to get the best out of the remarkable Rod Steiger. It was no good restricting him with stopwatches or petty directing instructions. I particularly recall one scene in the village square where he is completely down and out and the kids are baiting him. Rod howled like a dog and such tears of chagrin came to his eyes, that I have never been to a projection of the movie where the audience did not have their handkerchiefs out!

Shooting *Across The Bridge* was the happiest time I had ever experienced. The village of Lora del Rio took us into its bosom — it was ours to shoot, adapt, and do whatever we wanted. I felt a new exhilaration, setting out each day like a painter — knowing the shape of what I was going to shoot, but not the details. Like Rod, I was free to create, completely attuned to every nuance of the story and characters. I have never been more relaxed, nor have I ever had less sleep!

My crew were all old friends, Reg Wyer, Dudley Lovell (my favourite operator), Yvonne Axworthy, one of the best continuity girls in the world, Johnny Cabrera on second camera, Pepe Lopez, a very bright English-speaking Spanish boy who became one of the top first assistants for Dino DeLaurentiis; Nick Anson, and Harry Edgar, both prop men who knew exactly what I wanted and when I wanted it.

In the evenings we used to travel to and fro to Seville, which was about an hour's journey. I would dance the night away with Marucha, while the other guys drank, picked up girls, or watched flamenco dancers. I remember Nick got so involved with some dancers, that he wandered off with them and, according *to his* version, was kept prisoner for one whole delightful night. He staggered back to the bridge of Lora Del Rio somewhere around noon the next day. Since we were all old buddies, and his work had been so well 'covered' by other members of the crew, I had never really missed him.

Rod was devoted to realism. I remember one scene where he escaped from the police into the river, and then had to crawl in the mud (which we felt was visually symbolic of how low this big city businessman had sunk). Rod made such a meal of crawling, that Dudley, the camera operator, got temporary sunstroke and I had to take over the operating. Back to where I started in film making!

The second star of the picture was really a mongrel Spaniel dog called Dolores. We had discovered her in London's Battersea Dog's Home, and she had been lovingly trained by a Cockney barrow-boy. We had no difficulty in taking Dolores to Spain, but we had a hell of a time getting her back into England for the shooting at Pinewood. The authorities thought they were giving us a great concession in allowing the dog to be quarantined on the studio lot, but neither Dolores nor her keeper enjoyed the six months she had to stay there! One of Dolores' greatest moments in the movie is when she spots a scorpion climbing up the sleeping Rod's leg. We had a genuine Mexican scorpion borrowed from the zoo —- a dangerous-looking black monster whom Rod hated and feared so much that we had to make a false leg for it to crawl up. Dolores' touching expressions and whimpers of warning were obtained mainly by dangling food in front of her, but when the shots were edited you fully believed she loved Rod and had saved his life.

Rod practiced his 'Method' technique even more assiduously in the studio shooting, and I remember one day when he had to sweat with fear on the train. He insisted on running four times round the stage before jumping into the carriage seat and yelling, "Shoot!" A highly respected British actor, Bernard Lee (who later made a name for himself playing 'M' in the Bond movies) watched Rod with great scepticism. "These bloody Yanks," he moaned. "The poor buggers don't get enough opportunities to play in legitimate theatres, so have to fall back on stupid mechanical gimmicks!" So much for Method Acting — some actors need it, others who are instinctive performers devise their own inner motivations..

Rod was a generous and inspiring co-actor towards the Canadian, Bill Nagy, who had to play some of the most dramatic scenes on the train, and in the motel with this restless unconventional star. The situation in the story was that Rod, fleeing London after a tip-off that Scotland Yard was investigating his double bookkeeping, decides to travel the least conspicuous way (by train) to Mexico, where he has stashed away a few millions. The news of his fraudulent dealings breaks while he is on the train south, and in a panic Rod decides to change identities with a fellow traveller not unlike him. He gets the man (Bill Nagy) drunk, then throws him out of the carriage window, only to find soon afterwards that the Nagy character is much hotter than he is, having killed a South American president! So, Rod has to go back and search for the body. He finds Nagy holed up in a motel and badly injured, but quite cold-bloodedly he forces the helpless man to give him back his original passport. I provided the framework for the development of tension between these two characters, but it was Rod who gave the acting tips to Nagy so they would dovetail into his style. In later years I understand he worked the same kind of 'double-act' with Sidney Poitier when they played together *In The Heat of the Night*.

Throughout the years, I have watched and admired Rod's performances and recognised quite a few of the mannerisms that have become his 'stock-in-trade' gestures. His approach to a character is always full of deep psychological research. I always feel that in learning my trade I was fortunate and privileged to experience Rod's 'method' when I did.

Across the Bridge opened in London to great critical acclaim, gaining the most wonderful notices I have ever had. One critic called the picture "the Saviour of Pinewood Studios". John Davis acclaimed me as Rank's greatest director! For six months afterwards I had to attend all his studio lunches when he was trying to impress investors, or the politicians whom he was courting in the hopes of getting a knighthood!

In the US the film had a limited release, mainly because the tiny Rank Sales Organisation could not compete with the majors for theatre space... on top of which, I was told Rod Steiger made a complete fool of himself in a TV interview with Johnny Carson. There was a side to Rod that scorned publicity and hated the Establishment. Claire Bloom, whom he later married, used to say he loved to pretend that he was just a wino and a bum, which of course ties up with the choice of buddy he brought with him to London during the shooting! However, in this TV interview, Rod pulled faces, pretended to be a mental case and said that he had such terrible experiences in Europe, that he'd had to go for hourly sessions with his analyst!

This cannot have helped the film, but on the plus side, I have to say whenever I worked with stars like Hank Fonda, Yul Brynner, John Wayne, Edward G. Robinson or Vittorio de Sica, they would say, "You directed *Across The Bridge*, eh? What a movie!". Even now, it remains my favourite Annakin movie.

My next encounter with Graham Greene was when John Stafford came to me and said the great novelist had said we could turn his latest book 'Loser Takes All' into a movie. I jumped at this opportunity to make a satirical comedy, and to work with Graham, who had scripted movies like *The Fallen Angel* and, *The Third Man*.

In 'Loser Takes All' Graham had based his main character on Sir Alexander Korda, he told me, having observed him closely over the years of working for him. In the story, the Korda-like character calls his favourite accountant, Bertrand to his penthouse office in Mayfair. In appreciation of his finding a loophole to cheat the shareholders, Korda rewards the accountant by suggesting he switches his approaching wedding and honeymoon to Monte Carlo — all expenses paid. When Bertrand breaks the news to his fiancee, she is not impressed. All her friends are in London and she has always dreamed of a normal English marriage in a local church. However, the Korda character continues to expand his offer with promises of trips on his yacht, etc... and we find the two lovers established in the best suite of the palatial Hotel de Paris, with a balcony looking down on the famous casino. The Korda character never turns up to give the bride away, as he had also promised. There is no yacht in the harbour, and after two days, their credit runs out at the hotel.

So, our accountant hero, being a mathematician, decides to try his luck in the casino, where, as fate would have it, he meets the devil in the form of an old gambler, who gives him a system to beat the roulette tables. Our hero makes millions in a few nights, but his bride never sees him! He becomes so obsessed with winning that she turns for comfort and love to a penniless student. The moment Bertrand realises he has lost her, the Korda character appears in the casino bar. At first, he does not recognise the successful gambler Bertrand has become, but when he does, he leads him back to his yacht and takes the greatest trouble in instructing him how to win back his bride. The ploy succeeds, but Bertrand has to become a poor man again... It was really a modern parable about greed, with Graham turning accepted human values topsy-turvy.

Graham wanted Trevor Howard to play the accountant, and Orson Welles to play Korda. One night he took me along to the Globe Theatre where Orson was playing in his experimental production of 'Moby Dick', without any stage props. It was a fantastic theatrical concept, and Orson was, as usual, magnificent... We went round backstage after the show, where Orson, all sweaty and excited, listened as Graham told him how he was caricaturing Korda. Orson threw his head back in great guffaws and accepted the part on the spot. Of course, Trevor, who had established a name for himself in *Brief Encounter* and Graham's *Third Man*, accepted, as well.

Unfortunately, the new head of British Lion, Sir Arthur Jarratt, was a very square fellow who didn't believe the subject was commercial, but wanted desperately to take a swipe at Korda, under whom he felt he had suffered in the way of broken promises, much the same as Bertrand in our story! He refused point-blank to provide the finance with Trevor in the cast, saying he was box-office poison. According to him, Orson Welles was a crazy man, whom no normal cinema-goer wanted to see! "How about David Niven for Bertrand?" I suggested. "Washed up," said Jarratt, in the sweeping way of a distributor. This was in the mid-Fifties, and David went on to make winners like *Separate Tables, The Guns of Navarone, Pink Panther*, and **my** *Paper Tiger* ... among twenty other mostly good movies.

The only name Jarratt would consider was Rossanno Brazzi, the Italian who had just made a hit in David Lean's *Summertime,* opposite Katharine Hepburn. Brazzi was handsome and sexy, but completely wrong for the character. A flamboyant know-all, a 'coxcomb' as Shakespeare would have called him. Brazzi was the complete opposite of the ordinary 'little man' Bertrand was supposed to be... but Graham and John Stafford were persuaded that there was no deal without Brazzi. They caved in. In addition, we all had set our hopes on Audrey Hepburn, but for economic reasons we had to settle for my old chum, Glynis Johns, who was going through a bad period and beginning to show her age. The only member of the cast who excited me now was Alec Guinness, who was being tempted to play the Korda role.

Graham persuaded John Stafford that it was vital for me to see Monte Carlo and the casino table habitues, *through his eyes*. So, we were immediately booked into the Hotel de Paris for the writing and polishing of the script. It was a fantastic experience. The hotel was even more grand than the George V, where I had stayed in Paris while casting *Sword and the Rose*. Our suite overlooked the casino where many of our movie scenes were to take place. We would have an early breakfast on the terrace, and discuss the next section of the book to be adapted. Graham would write till around twelve-thirty midday, while I wandered round Monte Carlo, soaking up atmosphere and looking for possible locations.

Graham would not show me the morning's work until revised, but was happy to discuss it while strolling into the casino to watch the types gambling in what the locals call 'The Kitchen' — the first public room after you pass through the gilded portals. Back on the terrace for a leisurely lunch, I would pump Graham about his writing techniques. He said the backgrounds to his stories were never created out of his imagination, but were always places where he had travelled or had experienced 'lowlife' — even the opium dens of China. "How do you create your characters?" I asked.

"Never like your friend Willie Maugham, who's notorious for meeting people and putting them directly into a story. That's not creative writing," said Graham. "I love watching people for their appearance, dress, mannerisms, opinions, but my fiction characters are made up of composites from many sources. Even aspects of *you* may pop up in some future novel of mine!"

He liked to work from eight to twelve, but was always prepared to break earlier if he had written his eight hundred words — his daily quota, whether he was working on a story, novel, script or newspaper article. I have to admit, I was not always comfortable in Graham's presence. You could never make a loose statement or observation without his picking it up and putting you through the hoop if your thought was lazy, untidy or ill-informed. In many ways, Graham was like a university don, and since my education was acquired in grammar school, and in what I always used to call 'my World University', there were times when I could not compete in dialectical dissertations with Graham. Nevertheless, I worked at it and usually scrambled through!

On our second night in the casino, whom should we run into but Sir Alexander Korda, propping up the bar! I was a little embarrassed because of Graham's portrayal of him, but Korda shook me by the hand and said he admired several of my films, and kidded Graham about his caricature. "I hear you are trying to get my dear friend Alec Guinness to play me," he said. "I'm very flattered as I'm sure he will create some amusing mannerisms and exaggerate my idiosyncrasies — probably even more than you!" He put his hand to his crown of grey hair. "Of course, you may have to put him in a wig or postpone production a few years", he laughed.

Two days later, we heard from Alec's agent that he was passing on Graham's script and going to play in *The Swan* which Korda was producing! This nearly sunk our project, but a couple of weeks later, we offered the part to Robert Morley, who jumped at the chance to play such a legendary figure.

Wearing my writer's cap, I will always be grateful to have had the chance to see how Graham worked, and to hear his observations as we explored the hills around Tourette and Vence. We drank Pernod in bars, where the tarts hung out, in the old part of Nice (Graham loved doing that!) and explored his beloved brothels. We had drinks, too, with Onassis in his large Monte Carlo apartment, The next morning, Graham arranged for us to meet Onassis on his 'Christiana', his massive yacht which was berthed in the Port of Monaco. I had never seen anything like the Communications Room, where he showed us, with obvious pride, how he kept in touch with his fleet of oil tankers, no matter where in the world they were at sea. After this visit Graham smiled and said, "I wanted you to meet, so that when you have to portray a phenomenally rich character — a really big operator — you have a model."

Another day we had tea in the fairy-tale palace of the Grimaldi family, who have presided over Monaco for two hundred years. The handsome Prince Rainier showed us his collection of vintage cars. I'm sure if we'd been able to spare the time, he would have driven us round every hairpin bend above the principality in each of the cars!

Here again, I saw through Graham's eyes (and our discussion afterwards) how and what a true writer should observe and store in his memory for future use. Until this time I had been lucky to mix with people from all walks of life — but not the rich and famous. Now, I was starting to fill that gap!!

After eight weeks of preparation in London, I returned to the Cote D'Azur with a mixed French and British crew. We took over the exclusive Monaco Sporting Club for a couple of days shooting, with our two stars performing against luxurious Mediterranean backgrounds. But even Perinal could not make Glynis look beautiful or young enough. Out of desperation, Brazzi decided that the only way to bring back her spirit and looks, was sex. He broached the situation with me, and when he stated quite flatly that the only way to make Glynis beautiful for the picture was to "sacrifice himself", I knew what he meant, and nodded.

Glynis fell for his Italian smooch, and in three or four days began to look young and beautiful. It was only in London, at the end of the picture, when she discovered that she could have been pregnant with Brazzi's child, that she cursed herself as the biggest fool alive — especially when Brazzi made excuses and disclaimed all responsibility! "To think that I should fall for that Via Veneto crap!" she said to me. "When you, of all people, know I've been twisting guys round my finger for years!"

But for all of us there had been many sunny romantic days, as our two lovers rode up and down those olive tree lined Riviera lanes or played boules with the locals in the old square at Tourette. I fell in love with the whole South of France way of life, and did not rest until a few years later, when I was able to acquire a magnificent home overlooking the blue Mediterranean.

On *Loser Takes All*, for the first time ever, I had a heavy-handed editor who seemed to be trying to prove the editor makes the movie! Finally, he made such a mess of putting together a comedy sequence with mirrors, that I fired him and brought in a girl who had only assisted on a previous picture, but whom I knew I could trust. That again is a lesson every director should learn. Choose your editor most carefully, because although *you* know your material will cut together perfectly, there may be executives and lawyers who sneak into rough-cut showings in the early stages and your credibility as a director can be completely undermined by an overly ambitious editor. Then you may find yourself fighting an uphill battle, with most likely a very poor release for your movie and possibly no future offers!

Loser Takes All was a so-so success, with mixed notices. Despite the wrong casting, the seeds of failure lay in the novel with its 'topsy-turvy' moral standpoints. It turned out that although the book was brilliant and funny, cinema audiences had no sympathy for a girl who felt deserted by her husband during the few days he was amassing millions. The Glynis Johns character walked away from Bertrand because she felt he was no longer the nice simple guy she had fallen in love with. However, we all know that in real life, many women remain in unbearable relationships, especially if the man has loads of money.

CHAPTER SEVEN
More Adventures... And Promise of a New Start

Despite *Loser Takes All*, Sir Alexander Korda did not hold it against me that I had 'roasted' him on the screen. In fact, he appeared to take it as a great joke. "I could have told you when we met in Monte Carlo," he said. "If you were seeking a big commercial success, it would never come with a Graham Greene satire. He's almost a genius, but sometimes too clever-clever for the average cinema audience."

I had now worked out the long-term contract with which Sydney Box had originally tied me to Rank, so I decided that I would like a change and work for Korda, because despite financial troubles, he seemed to be involved in much more classy and exciting movies.

Sydney, as my agent, arranged a meeting for me at Korda's Piccadilly Headquarters. He received me in a high, beautifully panelled room, and within ten minutes made me feel that I was the one director he had been waiting for! If Sydney had the power of making crews work happily together, Alex had the Hungarian schmaltz, erudition, imagination and gift of gab to bewitch bankers and insurance companies like the Prudential, to invest millions of pounds to build studios and back his epic movies.

"What kind of subject would you like to make, dear boy?" said Alex, warming his hands at the cheerful log fire.

"Well, I'm pretty good with comedy," I said, "but I think I'd like to make a Rudyard Kipling adventure like 'Kim' or 'Jungle Book' or a classic fantasy love story like 'Hassan' by James Elroy Flecker."

"All too expensive these days, dear boy," said Korda. "Over the years, I've watched your work, and know you have a fine realistic sense of film making. Did you ever see my pre-war documentary *Conquest of the Air?*"

"Of course," I replied. "And I saw your *Things to Come*."

"You keep swinging back to fiction," smiled Alex. "I would like you to tell the very real story of the first flight over the Atlantic."

"You mean the almost successful crossing by Alcock and Brown?" I asked. Alex nodded. "A little known but fine British achievement!"

"Sure, sure," I replied. "And I've always been interested in small aeroplanes, ever since I was scared out of my wits in an Immerman roll, with a Hollywood dancer!" Alex was intrigued as I told him of my thrilling flights with Loretta Finlay in pre-war California, and how I could think of nothing more wonderful than staging all the hazards which Alcock and Brown overcame in their flight from Newfoundland to Ireland.

"Snow weighing down the wings, frozen controls; the scene where Alcock has to walk out on the wing and is nearly blown away by the gale; Brown being forced down in fog to within ten feet of the waves and making a brilliant manoeuvre which saves them! This is all wonderful stuff for a movie!" said Alex, his eyes gleaming.

I was under his spell, and a deal was struck. Ian Dalrymple, an old documentary writer, was to collaborate with me on the screenplay, and young Lord Brabourne, the son-in-law of Lord Mountbatten would produce.

During pre-production, I made my first contact with Alex's brother, Vincent, who was not the dreamer or financial wizard that Alex was, but a practical designer architect and construction genius. I was to meet him some years later on *The Longest Day*, but here at Shepperton, he threw himself into designing and making working models and mock-ups of the plane which would be the heart of our movie. Chris Challis was hired to work out all the trick flying shots, and Kenneth More and Denholm Elliott were cast as Alcock and Brown — perfect casting. Five months preparation went ahead at Shepperton, and I was even supervising the dressing of the first set, when the blow fell!

Korda had been forced into bankruptcy, and the receiver refused to allow us to continue the production, even though over a hundred thousand pounds had been spent. My fascination with old aeroplanes had become almost an obsession, but I was not able to do anything about that until some ten years later when I created an opportunity to make *Those Magnificent Men In Their Flying Machines*.

Alex was completely shattered by his financial crash and could not understand why the City had chosen this moment to close him down, when he had four reasonably priced winners in preparation. Lord Brabourne and Ian Dalrymple tried to salvage something with the receiver. Apparently, he agreed for our unit to stay together and make a low-budget comedy called *Raising A Riot* — all set around an old windmill.

Ken More agreed to switch his contract to this movie and I was asked to take over the direction. The idea of 'going back' to a small family comedy did not thrill me, and when I discovered a young woman called Wendy Toye had actually been preparing this project for months. I turned the offer down flat.

It seemed to me highly immoral that because I had a valid contract I should push out someone who had been hoping to make her debut as a director. As it turned out, she did not establish herself as a feature director, though the movie was quite amusing because of Ken More's antics with a group of kids.

When the phone didn't ring again for months, I began to feel I should not have been so squeamish. Obviously as Bram would have said, I'd taken 'a wrong road again', when suddenly I received a call from John Davis to meet him at Pinewood.

Although he had been furious that I should even consider deserting the Rank stables for Sir Alexander Korda, he still felt that I had done such a great job on *Across The Bridge*, that he now offered me a two-picture contract, with freedom to choose the first subject, so long as John Stafford was the producer.

I jumped at the offer, because John was a good friend, sympathetic, knowledgeable, and normally quite easy to manipulate — something which a creative director prays for in a producer!

For our first film, we chose a novel which Rank had just acquired called "The Singer, Not The Song", a drama set in Mexico between two priests. Guy Elmes and I adapted the story and produced a script designed to star Brando and Peter Finch.

Peter, who was now a top international star, jumped at the part. But getting a script to Brando turned out to be almost impossible. I flew to New York to track him down, but this time I found no friendly, helpful agent like Bob Coryell, but a hard-faced, stonewaller named Freddie Fields, who at that time was running CMA, the top agency in America.

I tried the back door approach, using my friendship with Rod Steiger to contact Brando direct, but he was sailing around the South Seas looking for his island retreat, and so was unreachable. "To hell with the Americans," said John Davis. "I'm going British with Dirk Bogarde who's under contract anyway!"

I was heartbroken because although Dirk was a fine actor, the story was based on a gargantuan struggle between a heavyweight Catholic Archbishop in Mexico City and a young enlightened country priest. I had learned a hard lesson about wrong casting (with Brazzi!) and I refused flatly to go along with Dirk as the intolerant Archbishop. Ever the diplomat, John Stafford came up with a solution to the impasse. "Let's make the second picture first," he said. "Then maybe J.D. will simmer down and we can inveigle Brando into playing the Archbishop!"

"What is the second picture?" I asked him, puzzled. "'Nor The Moon By Night'" — I've just been reading the novel and I think you'll love it." He hid behind a cloud of cigar smoke. I looked at him suspiciously. "Why should I love it?"

"Because it's set in South Africa — adventure, romance, animals..."

"Why would J.D. go along with that? Has he some blocked funds in South Africa?"

John shook his head. "His wife Dinah found the subject, and thinks you're the only director to make it!"

Dinah Sheridan had worked with me nearly every day for a year when we were making *The Huggett* series. I adored her, but not necessarily her choice of subject. This one proved to be pure women's magazine stuff — the adventures of an English girl who goes out to marry a game warden and finishes up with another game warden! When I showed the novel to my buddy, Guy Elmes, he said, "Well, the storyline's a bit thin, but I guess we can cook something up!"

"I don't want just any old picture," I moaned. "Listen," he said, "they're offering us both better money than we've had before, and it's a great chance for you to go off to a continent you've never seen. Maybe you'll come back with something wonderful." (I did, but not in the way he was thinking!)

At this period, both Guy and I believed we could turn almost any material into a viable screenplay, and the opportunity to travel again and make a movie with the easygoing John Stafford finally swept away any scruples I had. "It's really only just to give us time to hook Brando and make the big movie next," he assured me.

CHAPTER SEVEN *More Adventures... And Promise of a New Start*

Once again, I set off on a recce, flying South via Rhodesia (now Zimbabwe). We landed in Johannesburg and I was met by Alex Bryce, my second unit director from *Robin Hood* and *Sword and the Rose*. He was now living in the Union and said he would be only too happy to shoot animal material for me, if the picture went ahead.

We drove into the Kruger National Park, which is one of the best game reservations in the world, highly stocked with lions, elephants, gazelles, giraffes, monkeys of every type, and baboons. I clearly remember one morning, after sleeping soundly in a rondavel, we were driving out to watch the game come to a waterhole, when the car was surrounded by baboons, who climbed all over it, banging on the windscreen, clawing and grimacing at us... memorable and quite alarming.

We pushed on across the wide open spaces of the Transvaal into Swaziland, which was a small enclave, apparently run more or less by and for the natives, who were living quite well off timber and milling activities. One evening we watched native dancing which was almost as spirited and rhythmical as the Ukranian dances I had been fascinated with years ago in Prague. The main difference was that the ladies were topless, and their beautiful bosoms tended to bounce about most provocatively! I swore I would try to include a dance like this in the movie.

Pushing on into the old British colony of Natal, we came to the Valley of a Thousand Hills. I immediately fell for the scenery and life of the natives in this reserve. They were farmers and lived in kraals, run by a Head Man, who seemed to have complete autonomy. The women wore colourful skirts, but their breasts were bare — with often their babies feeding as they were carried gracefully on one hip.

Apparently, the Head Man could have as many as five wives, so as long as he could afford to build a separate rondavel for each wife. It was whispered that the rule of life in the Valley was survival of the fittest, which meant in practice that any babies born malformed were immediately buried under the midden where the cows grazed, and no one outside was any the wiser!

Midway between Johannesburg and Durban, on Cato Ridge, we found an excellent hotel capable of housing a whole film unit. So, now all we had to find was a trained lion — a vital part of Joy Packer's original novel. The lion was the constant companion of an old-time Boer tea planter. Near the end of the story, it turns on its master and mauls him. Although South Africa was full of lions we could only find one, in Bulawayo, which was allegedly trained. We drove miles to see the lion in its quarters behind a judge's house, and after sizing me up, it turned its back, lifted its tail, and shot a stream of yellow liquid all over my smart safari outfit!

Apart from the fact that Zorba obviously had not taken to me, I discovered he was twelve years old, and from everything the wardens had told us, old lions, even pets, were quite incalculable and potentially dangerous. Fortunately, back in England, Jane, my thirteen-year-old daughter, had become very excited about my having to work with a lion, and sent me a paperback entitled 'How To Tame A Tiger'. It had been written by a County Durham butcher who seemed to have the 'Androcles Complex'... in other words, his great love and hobby was to lie down with a baby tiger or lion cub and make it believe he was one of them. Then, as it grew up, it would remain his friend and playmate! If I could not find my lion in Africa, maybe I would check on what James Walton claimed to have in England!

Returning to the studio, I shared my experiences and observations with Guy Elmes, who attempted to 'flesh out' the screenplay. John Stafford and I set about finding a British cast, which should not have been difficult because there was no question then, of actors not wishing to go to South Africa for political reasons. The problem was that because of a generous subsidy, American productions were flooding into British studios, and many young actors did not want to put themselves out of 'the action' for at least three months. In the end, Michael Craig was cast as the game warden, and Patrick McGoohan, who had just had big TV acclaim playing *Danger Man* and *Secret Agent*. He accepted the role of the police inspector that we had manufactured, instead of having two game wardens as in the novel.

But our great coup was supposed to be Belinda Lee, a very beautiful model, who had been picked up by Rank and was now regarded, at least by John Davis, as their 'Big Attraction'. Nobody thought of her as a great actress, but she did look great, and I felt with careful direction, she could be adequate. My old Czech friend, Eric Pohlmann agreed to play the tough Boer farmer. He looked the part, but was really a pussycat, and secretly afraid of lions!

The final bit of casting was done in Paris. Maude Spector and I took a nostalgic trip over, and found a charming young French girl, Annie Gaylor, who had just had a success in *The Sound of Thunder* a hit throughout Europe. We wanted to her to play the role of the rather sweet animal-loving daughter of Eric Pohlmann. I liked her immediately, but it would be her first experience working out of France, with a foreign crew. She was shy and somewhat scared, but with my arm around her shoulder, and turning on all my charm, I assured her I would see she had a great time in Africa. But back in the Pinewood office, I found a new face... a dark-haired girl with a wonderful smile.

"Her name's Pauline," said Jack Martin. "The best production secretary in the business!"

I found her strangely simpatico, but she also was a little scared about going on a foreign location. Pauline had been married three or four years, but loved the movie business and the responsibilities which Jack and I were preparing to give her. However, six thousand miles was a long way from home, so once again I had to use all my charm to reassure her. "You'll love South Africa," I said with a smile. "And I'll look after you!"

My crew were the same loyal group who had been with me on *Across The Bridge* and other pictures... Bert Batt (who had started with me as a messenger-boy on *Miranda*), Nick Anson, Harry Edgar, Dudley Lovell, Dudley Messenger — all my old buddies, plus my favourite location cameraman from documentary days, Peter Henessey.

We now held an exciting event at Thamesfield — the audition of James Walton's lion! With my daughter Jane tightly clutching my hand, we watched Rikki, a magnificent four hundred pound lion, sit and roll over on the lawn. Then, on command, he strolled around the flowerbeds without any form of lead, and then James staged the fight, where it really looked as though he was being mauled and eaten! As he rolled out from under the lion, he grinned, "You see! No whips or chains — all done by love!" Rikki rolled over on his back and James tickled his tummy!

Over a buttered-scone tea provided by my long-suffering wife, Blanka, we struck a deal to fly James and the lion out to South Africa — which later, several newspapers pointed out was like 'carrying coals to Newcastle'... and some Jo'burg Journalists even found it insulting to their macho country's image!

Secretly hoping she would not accept, I invited my wife to come out on this chance-of-a-lifetime location. Blanka shook her head sadly. She was bored with film folk and the life of a director's wife, and being a normal and intelligent woman, I guess she was fed up with my affairs and refusal to be moulded into her ideal. So, with Jane looking from one to the other, with big and somewhat worried eyes, the three of us had a civilised farewell dinner at the 'Green Man' Shepperton, and the next morning I again caught the plane to Jo'burg, to experience the most topsy-turvy, yet fulfilling, six months of my life... up to then!

I drove straight into the Valley of a Thousand Hills where my Art Director, John Howell, another old friend, was building sets based on the stills I had taken on my recce. He had arranged for us to have powwows with the local Bantu Chiefs to get their co-operation. As soon as their agreements were obtained, I jumped in a car and drove back to Jo'burg, to meet the crew off the plane. The moment I saw Pauline, I knew she was the one I would try 'to woo' on this location. She was feisty, but had that sweet smile and very down-to-earth attitude to life, get on with the job, learn as much as you can, and savour every moment of new experience.

I can hear you saying, "Off he goes again — deliberately woman-chasing!" What is the film business??!! But, in my experience, the woman you are with — or not with — on location shooting, makes a hell of a difference to the quality and attitudes a director puts on the screen.

From the first day, troubles began to hit us — to start with — the Pinewood electricians! Despite my plea that it was essential to take only a crew of young men — because of the intense heat — the 'brothers' had got together in Pinewood and decided which one most deserved a holiday. We were lumbered with six 'sparks' who were all over sixty!

Rod, the gaffer, was around forty-five, and seemed to be efficient and willing, but as usual, a Communist shop steward was in charge. Visiting the rondavels where they had been accommodated, Pauline found on the back of each door a 'sickness roster' showing that the electricians had already agreed the number of days and the dates they planned to go sick!

Not more than two days after the start of shooting, several of these old sparks, nearly caused us to be thrown off the reservation, by trying to persuade every black girl they saw to pose topless for one pound sterling! A dozen or so of the Headmen controlling the Valley, took a very poor view of this, especially since many of the girls were their wives!

One day, the shooting in a rondavel was especially trying, because the moment we put an arc lamp inside to illuminate the scene, the branch-woven ceiling was seen to be alive with cockroaches which started to fall in a shower upon us. Poor Gladys, our rather large script clerk, had hysterics and had to be dragged out by her feet through the low doorway.

Before this happened, I had been fascinated to see in full light, a ledge full of broken eggshells, chicken feathers, half-lemons, gold buttons, and animal fur. These were obviously the stock-in-trade that the witch doctor used, always in dim mysterious light, to tell fortunes, forecast the weather, and lay spells on errant members of his tribe. Most of the people in the Valley believed in his powers which I put down to auto-suggestion, but I have to admit that when we were having atrocious weather, I casually appealed to him through the Headman, and we had two beautiful sunny days!

We were shooting a lot of good material showing our four characters travelling through the supposed game reserve, and pairing off in romantic settings. And, since we were miles away from any cinema and therefore unable to project our 'rushes' at the end of the day, I used to call in the production office and try to persuade Pauline to go off with me to a restaurant or night club. Quite often she made excuses which, of course, made me only the more eager.

Since I was quite experienced in dating, I could not understand her reluctance, until one night she told me how my good old buddies in the unit were constantly warning her against my advances, with lurid tales of my philanderings on other locations! But I love a challenge and seemed to be making out well both in work and winning Pauline, when suddenly we received a shattering cable from London!

Apparently, there was something radically wrong with Peter Henessey's photography. Arthur Alcott reported that it was either flat, washed out and often streaked with strange colours. The labs could do nothing to help. John Davis was so disgusted that he was sending out Harry Waxman, the top studio technical cameraman. We stopped shooting for two days while the camera crew pulled the cameras to pieces, and Peter made hand tests, but no obvious faults could be found. Peter resigned and Harry took over as Director of Photography.

As we began the retakes, the humidity increased and it became more of an effort to move about the Valley. Despite his efficient style, Bert Batt had a difficult time driving the cast and crew, and I felt puzzled and depressed as I watched Harry balance the glare of the sun with his 'brutes'. He seemed slow and overcautious, painstakingly reading the light from every lamp on his meter right up to the moment of the take. But in this, I found he was the tough professional, and as his stuff turned out perfect I caught a whisper of how Peter had been sabotaged. Three of the 'brothers' had been consistently putting the wrong filters on the arcs because Peter was 'from documentary' and had no time for unions in movie making! With Harry no one could get away with anything!

We were now coming into the rainy season, so had to be prepared to shoot exteriors or interiors. When the sun shone we established Eric Pohlmann and his screen-daughter Annie Gaylor as living together in a picturesque old planter's house. Eric was terrified every moment when he had to strut around with his whip, two steps *ahead* of the lion... But Annie, after being taken into Rikki's quarters by James Walton and introduced to the lion, was quite happy to treat him like the pussycat he was. But you never knew.

One day we had the camera set up on the floor. Jimmy Devis, the camera assistant was stretched out, shirtless, and concentrating on his focussing. Rikki was let loose, and did his usual stroll to a bowl of milk, then, licking his lips, he sniffed the chairs, then suddenly walked straight into the camera. He stopped right over Jimmy, and bent down, his mane touching his shoulder.

"Don't move," I whispered to Jimmy. He half-turned his head, and with terror in his eyes, mouthed, "You must be joking!" Rikki took four big licks of the salty sweat on his shoulders, then backed away, to squat down and stare contentedly at us!

We managed to shoot something every day, but a strange madness was creeping over this production. A black mamba was found to have made its nest under the Elson toilet which had been put up for the girls — you can imagine the screams and fuss. From then on, one of the black helpers had to go with the girls and inspect the toilet before they could use it — all very embarrassing, but necessary as a mamba bite can kill in five minutes!!

The unfortunate Gladys refused to wear socks and boots and was bitten by some insect, which caused her ankle and foot to swell to three times normal size. I brought Pauline out to replace her as script clerk. She loved the chance to work with the 'shooting unit' and the camera and sound crew did everything they could to help her.

However, on the third day, she set her typewriter up under a tree with long hanging vines, and a white spider dropped down and bit her! Within minutes, one eye was completely closed. In great pain, and heartbroken, she was whisked away to the local doctor who set her up in his spare bedroom.

Every evening for a week, I used to go and sit with Pauline... trying to ease her sorrow, and show that even miles away from home, somebody cared for her, which was more than true, because by this time I was falling genuinely in love with her. There was nothing much we could do but hold hands and talk about who was going out with who... because sex had undoubtedly raised its ugly head in the Cato Ridge Hotel!

As well as gossip and sweet-nothings, I started to confide in Pauline. She had a tidy, logical mind, and had been running the production office like clockwork, but directing a movie, with all its problems was something she knew very little about. I needed desperately to share my problems because, despite the efforts Guy Elmes and I had made, the screenplay had not escaped its 'women's magazine' origins. The situations were trite, and the relationships cliché, so that neither I nor the actors were making the dialogue real and convincing. "The whole crew are working their guts out for you," said Pauline, as a loyal crew member. "You can't let them down !" I heaved a deep sigh, as she continued, "They all think you're a marvellous director, what else have you got if the story's not working?"

I considered a moment, then blurted out, "I might salvage the movie by filling it with so many animals that the audience will become fascinated with them and not notice the weak story and characterisation!" Pauline frowned. "I would have thought it was obvious that you must show a lot of wild animals in this setting..." As we talked, I knew her common sense approach had helped me to a decision, so I kissed her good night and left feeling a little happier.

John Howell began erecting some large wire enclosures, and soon we collected quite a menagerie — three cheetahs; an eight-week-old lion cub, which had clearly been mauled at some time; a young baboon we had saved from vivisection in a Durban hospital; a porcupine; several giselles; some Mynah birds and parrots; two cobras and, of course, several ponies, and Rikki!

A local farmer, Robin Hart who had two very sturdy sons, was press-ganged into looking after our animals, but Mike Craig loved the young baboon so much that he would often come to the set with the inquisitive animal bouncing up and down on his shoulder. Sometimes in his exuberance, Jimmy would rip Mike's shirt — to the annoyance of Joan, our wardrobe lady. But, as the high-spirited animal bounced from Mike's shoulder to the top of his filing cabinet, the scenes in the game warden's office were definitely livened up!

The only problem was that whenever Gladys took her seat beside the camera to take continuity notes, Jimmy would begin to masturbate — embarrassing, and impossible to shoot, until we arranged that the second camera assistant would take the notes and Gladys stay off the set!

We had one scene with Belinda Lee on safari with Mike, and we needed her to rush out of her tent to find him in danger of drowning. I thought up the gag of using the porcupine as the excuse for her... So, we fixed up an invisible electric fence calculated to guide the animal into the tent. He charged straight in all right, and Belinda rushed out shrieking, but a second later, the porcupine came out from under the tent flap and made straight for the camera tripod, where he paused, his quills quivering right under Dudley's crotch! My normally unflappable operator yelled blue murder and ran into the river followed by the porcupine! I'm afraid the poor animal lost quite a few quills as Robin and a dozen members of the crew struggled to get him back into his box.

Attempting to make a scene with the actors constantly involved with animals, slowed down the shooting no end, and some of the unit began moaning that they would not get home for Christmas! Belinda became quite a pest. Squatting beside me whenever I relaxed, she produced a string of airmail letters written to her by a Prince in Rome. Apparently on her last movie, she had fallen desperately in love with this very important scion of the Vatican. Now, he was writing to her saying that he would kill himself if she did not come back to Rome by Christmas! All I could do was promise to do my best for her, but the shooting continued each day with an intermingling of the absurd and the macabre.

By this time, Jack Martin had proved to be a conniving, pompous production manager, unpopular with me because of his coarse behaviour in front of Pauline, but also he was thoroughly despised by the crew. We were lining up the last shot before lunch when he was seen coming officiously down a wooded trail from our canteen. Bert Batt nudged me and pointed to our baby lion lying on the branch of a tree right above Jack's path. We all knew that the Hart kids had encouraged the cub to jump on them as they passed under that tree, so everyone watched Jack's approach.

"It's not lunchtime yet!" he yelled. "God knows we're enough behind schedule..." Before he could finish, he was under the tree and the cub jumped! There was a scream and Jack departed faster than the proverbial Vicar chased by the devil! The unit killed themselves with laughter, but that night I found that Jack was in a hospital with a mild heart attack. I was genuinely sorry and felt we had been negligent in allowing the cub such liberty. All the crew would say was: "He deserves to dies, the mean bastard!"

Suddenly, Christmas was upon us and we had by no means finished shooting. It was agreed that the unit would have two days holiday and Belinda begged to be allowed to fly back to her lover in Rome. The soft-hearted John Stafford agreed. And, in his wonderful way, trying to make me happy, he arranged that he and his wife would move down to the Edward Hotel in Durban and they would chaperone Pauline in adjoining room, while I had another room. When we all got down there, Pauline found that her room was not much more than a closet, while I had a suite with a big double bed.

Although we had spent a great deal of time kissing and cuddling, Pauline was striving hard to be faithful to her husband, but as Christmas Eve drew to its close, full of 'bonhomie and champagne', I managed to persuade her to come for a good night kiss into my big room, where, of course, I made myself completely irresistible! It was quite unfair, and later she accused John Stafford of having connived in the whole plot. He merely smiled and said, "It's the producer's job to keep his director happy, and from the look in Ken's eyes, I think your fate was sealed weeks ago!"

At six am we were rudely awakened by John Stafford. He had just received a call from an indignant John Davis in London saying, "What the hell is Belinda Lee doing in Rome? She's just tried to commit suicide!"

Apparently, in desperation because she had to come back for more shooting, she and her prince had made a lover's pact, which she had taken seriously. She had slashed her wrists, losing a lot of blood before being taken to the hospital. The prince was at her bedside, having made only a token attempt to take his life!

John was ordered to fly to Rome and bring Belinda back, in whatever state! Misfortunes never come singly. That same night, Pat McGoohan, struggling to remain faithful to his new wife, had celebrated too well with a group of Rugby players, and turned his car over four times, in a drunken drive from Cato Ridge to Durban. He was now in a Little Sisters of Mercy Hospice, suffering from concussion. Pauline and I went immediately to visit him and were appalled to find his face covered with gravel abrasions. There was hardly a centimetre of skin that hadn't been scraped and torn. I left Pauline to find a plastic surgeon, while I rushed to find out what was left for us to shoot. Bert Batt and I studied the board...

"No good thinking of any scenes with Annie," he said. "She's down with a bug in the bowels — Doc thinks it's amoebic dysentery!"

"Poor kid," I said. "I feel kind of guilty about her..."

"You can't be expected to look after every bleeding female," he said in his brusque sergeant-major fashion. "Annie Gaylor's just another casualty on this spooked movie." We passed our fingers across the numbers of scenes still to be shot. Bert sighed, "With McGoohan in the hospital and Belinda, God knows where, all that's left to us is Mike Craig and the cobra!"

Guy had written a scary scene where the game warden is riding in his Land Rover through the reserve, while, unbeknown to him, a cobra has taken refuge under a tarpaulin. As he drives, the snake comes out and rises behind him to strike. Mike Craig was quite willing to drive the Land Rover for the front-on shots, but understandably was not prepared to sit with his back to the cobra while it swayed behind his head.

But there is always someone willing to take a risk for money! The stills man, a local from Durban, had lost heavily at poker over the holidays and needed money, so he dressed up in Mike's clothes, while Robin milked the cobra's poison sac. Since I was possibly risking someone's life and had handled a cobra in Ceylon, I lay down under the tarpaulin, holding the head of the cobra. On the cue that we were rolling satisfactorily, I pushed the snake up so that it appeared to rear behind the driver's head. It made several strikes, which I prayed would be harmless, since two wardens told us that a snake's poison sac could not refill or become lethal in less than fifteen minutes! We got the shot, but in the afternoon we had another close shave.

With Mike Craig apparently out of control when he discovers the snake, the Land Rover had to go over a bank and turn over. Since there were no trained stuntmen in South Africa, we hired a stock-car driver who had plenty of courage and skill, but no accurate sense of timing. The camera was set up low on baby legs, with Dudley lying beside it and Harry on the other side, insisting on taking constant meter readings because the clouds were changing all the time. Over a ridge, we had constructed a trip-rig so that the car would turn over about fifteen feet in front of the camera.

The first two takes the car stopped before the rig, but on the third, the speed was too great, and Harry Waxman was only saved by Ted, the dolly-pusher, dragging him feet first to safety. Dudley stuck behind the camera, but for the first time in our dozen movies together, he roundly cursed me for being careless. Thoroughly understanding,

Ken prepares the bathing beauties for the pageant in *Holiday Camp*. English film star Hazel Court is second from left. (1946)

Bob Westerby (screenwriter), Phyllis Calvert, Ken and Margot Graham in the studio fuselage of the wrecked Dakota in *Broken Journey* *(1947)*

Ken directs a scene including a young Petula Clark (left) for *Here Come the Huggetts* *(1948)*

Behind the scenes on *Miranda*. A bespectacled Ken is in the centre of the photo, with Director of Photography, Ray Elton just in front of him. Sitting on the left is Assistant Producer Roy Rich and the Producer, Betty Box. *(1948)*

Ken escorts Glynis Johns to the premiere of *Miranda* (1948)

The fabulous Glynis Johns as *Miranda* (1948)

Margaret Rutherford gives a sparkling performance in the necklace scene with Glynis Johns in *Miranda (*1948)

Ken explains the days work to Bert Batt (in profile on the left), Frank Green and Peter Manley (both on the right) on *Hotel Sahara (1951)*

Ken on the set of *The Planters Wife* with a young boy. *(1952)*

Claudette Colbert in a scene from *The Planters Wife* (1952)

Ken explains a scene to Richard Todd in *The Sword and the Rose(1952)*

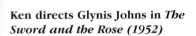

Ken directs Glynis Johns in *The Sword and the Rose (1952)*

Perce Pearce and Ken discuss a shot for *The Sword and the Rose* (1952)

Ken with Glynis Johns and Rosanno Brazzi are snapped by the press in Monte Carlo during the filming of *Loser Takes All* (1956)

Rod Steiger and Dolores put in a powerful performance at the conclusion of *Across the Bridge* (1957)

Ken and Walt Disney admire the Matterhorn, while filming *Third Man on the Mountain (1959)*

Ken (in the beret) supervises cinematographer Harry Waxman (in the white cap), for a very difficult setup on the slopes of the Matterhorn for *Third Man on the Mountain (1959)*

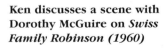

Ken discusses a scene with Dorothy McGuire on *Swiss Family Robinson (1960)*

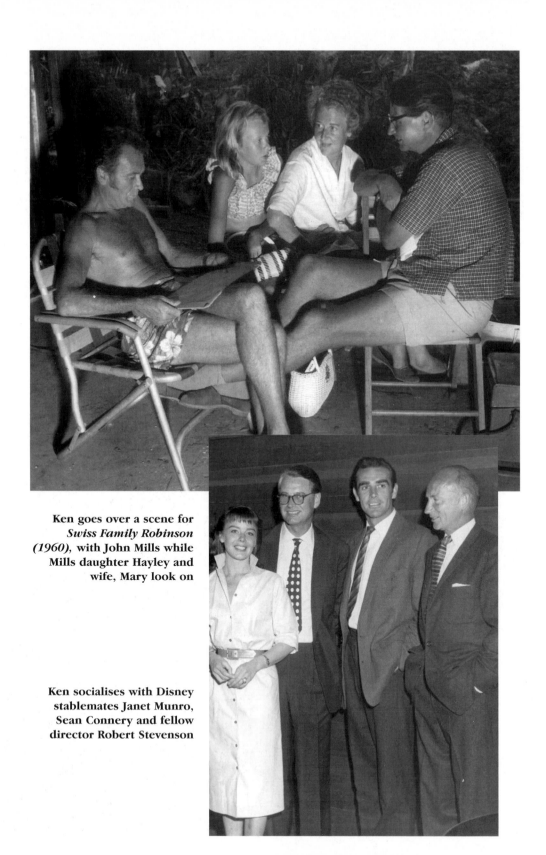

Ken goes over a scene for *Swiss Family Robinson (1960)*, with John Mills while Mills daughter Hayley and wife, Mary look on

Ken socialises with Disney stablemates Janet Munro, Sean Connery and fellow director Robert Stevenson

and somewhat ashamed that I had allowed this near-accident to happen, I ordered the camera moved back, and changed to a long focus lens. On the sixth attempt we got a thrilling shot.

But everything now was a problem. The electricians were completely ruling the roost, living all over the area with women they had found in Durban or distant Pietermaritzburg. They continued to apply strict union rules as to hours of shooting and tea breaks, even though we were well over schedule and everyone dying to get home. I recall an acrimonious meeting on top of a hill, up which we had steadily moved to try and catch the slanting rays of the winter sun. They demanded that we stop shooting because it was three-thirty pm and they had started the day at seven-thirty am. The Communist shop steward threatened that if we went on shooting with two willing local helpers (who were, in fact, moving all the heavy lamps), he would cable immediately back to Pinewood and have the picture 'blacked'!

Belinda returned looking pale and wan, but as luck would have it, the scene she had to play that afternoon was one where every word in the script seemed to fit her own sad situation. For once she sobbed genuine tears, but in order to get her to concentrate and stay with subsequent scenes, I had to use all my patience and accumulated knowledge of actresses, their foibles and tricks.

The next day we staged a brush fire. Everyone was on edge in case it should get out of control, and in the confusing, billowing smoke it seemed to take hours for Bert to get the actors on to the set. In my frustration, I started yelling at him. He yelled back, and with streaming red faces we almost came to blows. Saying he was through with me forever, Bert stormed off!

I struggled on for two more days, slave-driving the crew, till Bert came back and apologised for his behaviour. A lump came into my throat, because Bert could never be unprofessional — he was a loyal, hardworking guy who was as weary as we all were of working in that accursed bush.

Alex Bryce arrived back from the Nongoma National Park, having shot nothing but a few atmosphere shots of animals and some useless material of elephants. Kip Gowan, my second assistant, told me that Alex had completely lost his nerve and refused to risk close shots of passing elephants, which the script called for.

It became clear to me that I would personally have to go to Kenya to get the big elephant stuff I envisaged, and Kip was sent off to Nairobi to prepare the way. Meanwhile, we shot the Dance of the African Maidens — which I staged to match the almost naked dancing I had witnessed in Swaziland. Actually, our thirty Zulu maidens were not naked, but wore sweatshirts and tight brown jockey shorts under their grass skirts.

We had suffered for weeks under torrential downpours, and I had reckoned on staging this dance in real rain. But with our luck, we had to set up rain machines. As we turned on the taps, the girls' costumes became so wet and clinging that they were even more sexy and alluring than if they had been completely naked! We spent one whole afternoon on this dance, and it was reported next day that the males in our unit had been inspired that night to even greater sexual exploits!

Now all we had left was to polish up the sequence of the lion attacking Eric Pohlmann. We had completed the master shots of the mauling with James Walton and Rikki, as planned. The only surprise was that when James was wrestling with his face under the lion's mane, we heard a yell in broad North Country: "Get off me feet, you daft bugger!" and a moment later the lion fell back from him and rolled on the floor.

"What happened?" I said to James.

Ruffled and sweaty, he turned to me and smiled, "Forgot his manners, I guess, so I tweaked his balls!" Rikki was now on the floor licking himself. "Not to worry," said James with a grin, "He loved it, really!"

But now came our last indignity. I had long realised that for the close-ups needed to link Eric Pohlmann into the lion fight, I would have to dress up a man in a lion skin. Jack Martin had found both the skin and Terry, a midget from Durban. Wardrobe had fitted Terry so that the lion skin could be zipped up skin-tight, and he had been rehearsed by James to make a credible lion's leap. We were all set up in the plantation house and were just about to shoot in what I thought was a 'closed set', when I saw the face of a stranger at the window. Bert went chasing out, but the man had completely vanished. The next morning, however, on the front page of the *Durban Examiner* there was a photo of Terry being zipped into the lion skin, and a very snide article about the British director who claimed he had had to bring a trained lion from England while all the time he was using a South African midget in a lion skin!

We survived the laughter of the locals, and succeeded in finishing the film, but not without daily phone calls and cables from the studio ordering us to wrap and come home! Now, most of the unit was sad to be leaving and there were many tearful farewells and exchanged promises.

Pauline and I sat close together on the plane holding hands until I had to deplane in Nairobi... and there, in a fifteen minutes stopover, we embraced and looked deeply into each other's eyes, seeking proof that ours was true love, and that we would face up to our promises in the difficult days which must lie ahead, when we returned to our respective home and spouses.

The three days of safari which Kip and I now set out on was again a unique though saddening experience. Kip had gleaned that the best place to find herds of elephants was up north, near Lake Rudolf. So, we made a three hundred mile trip in a Land Rover, passing through areas teeming with wild life. We saw lions, rhino, giraffes, monkeys of every kind, masses of wildebeest, cheetahs, kudu and deer... some of which I filmed from a handheld Arriflex and hoped for the best!

We were met by Don Bredon, an ex-RAF settler, who, as a profitable sideline, arranged safaris for rich visitors from all over the world. That night, he and his wife regaled us with stories of the way men and women behave when they escape civilisation — human aberrations that would have given a Hemingway or a Maugham enough material for half a dozen novels!

At five the next morning we were in the air, and almost immediately spotted six groups of elephants. As we swooped low over them, they scattered into the bush. "Don't worry," said Don. "They won't go far. They like those yellow-barked acacias too much." We decided on a location which was accessible by Land Rover and which reasonably matched the terrain I had established in the Valley of a Thousand Hills... so, by eight o'clock we were on the trail.

Don noticed how the birds were flying up from a group of mawapani trees, and dropped three of his native boys to scout. They made signals and pointed to a line of high scrub. We dismounted and set up two Arriflexes. Suddenly, without any warning, an enormous tusker pushed his head through the bushes and flapped his vast ears at us! Kip and I stood our ground, as Don had briefed us, and after taking a long look, the elephant swung his trunk slowly backwards and forwards, then turned and trotted away. We both agreed we had secured great shots, but not the mass movement, looking like a charge — which I wanted.

For a couple of hours we trailed behind the native boys as they spread out to find the group of forty odd elephants we had spotted from the air. Around noon, we stopped for sandwiches and cold beers, when once again there was the sound of crashing branches, and the same massive elephant appeared, swinging his trunk, pawing the ground, and making loud bellows. For a terrifying moment he threw up his trunk and trumpeted, then again turned and vanished. We had no cameras ready for that appearance!

"What would we have done if he hadn't gone?" I asked Don.

He shrugged. "I had him covered and normally it's only a rogue who would attack humans. This one's a family man, just wanting to feed in peace."

The native trackers came back and indicated that they had found the whole group grazing on the veldt about a half mile away. They suggested we leave the vehicles and take our cameras into a fairly thick patch of bush to the leeward side of the elephants. We moved down the trail — as we thought — quietly, and saw our family complete with babies grazing in a tight group about a hundred fifty yards away. We set up the cameras on tripods, fully concealed (as we thought) by bushes.

On a signal that we were ready, the native boys came out to the side of the group banging tin cans. The family began to move en masse across the screen. Suddenly, I saw our big friend turn, and after a moment, began to jog-trot *straight towards camera!* I looked over my viewfinder and saw the whole herd swerving towards us. This was not at all what I had planned, but it looked sensational! Don fired a shot into the air, but they still came on, their feet pounding the ground till it made the camera shudder.

"Kip!" I yelled. "For Christ's sake, run!" and set off as fast as I could towards the tall trees. I remember thinking, "Unless they decide to stop, we've had it! Even if I can climb a tree fast enough, the big bugger will shake me down!" Suddenly, a shot rang out. I turned and for a moment the herd seemed to keep advancing... then suddenly, they stopped... and returned to where the big elephant was teetering... and now, in slow motion, collapsed on to its knees, and rolled over. Don came running forward with a face distraught: "I had to shoot the poor bugger or we'd all have had it!"

The big elephant had fallen some fifteen feet in front of the cameras and now all the other elephants, including about eight young 'babas' were gathered around, trying to touch him with their trunks and making pathetic moans. It was one of the most heart-rending and harrowing scenes I have ever seen on or off film. Our film had run out in both cameras and there was nothing more we could do. As we walked back to the vehicles, Don was almost in tears.

"I have a license to shoot two elephants a year, or if the odd rogue becomes a menace to life or property,' he said. "But that fine fellow was just minding his own business."

"You had to do it," said Kip. Don nodded, then looked me straight in the eye. "I'll never shoot another — not for you or anyone else!!" He broke away, tears in his eyes. My whole body seemed to be shaking. I looked at Kip. He made a shrugging gesture and put his arm around my shoulder.

The way the situation had gone, there had been no alternative but for Don to shoot the elephant. This was, of course, quite a few years before mass-poaching by ivory hunters threatened the extinction of the elephant population of Africa. But I had never had the instincts or desire to be a white hunter, and the memory and guilt of that killing has stayed to haunt me to this day.

On the way back, with little enthusiasm, we filmed a few more atmosphere and close shots of animals, but by the time darkness fell, we felt physically and emotionally whacked. Don's wife had fixed up a small safari camp about sixty miles south. We retired early, but I could not sleep. I listened to the sounds of the jungle, which changed every hour... Suddenly, there was a ghostly padding of feet. I looked out in the pre-dawn light, and saw a herd of perhaps five hundred giselles passing silently through the camp. Nearby, a lion roared — too close I thought, and sure enough, the ghostly hunter padded past, within a dozen feet of where I was peering through the tent flap.

After breakfast around the campfire, we said goodbye to the Bredons and their trackers, and set off in our Land Rover for Nairobi. It was a hazy morning, but for one glorious moment, the mists cleared and we saw the snow-capped peak of Kilimanjaro glistening above the clouds — perhaps a sign from God that life was indeed noble — and must go on!!

CHAPTER EIGHT
New Start — Back
again with Disney

Back in Pinewood, I found Ray , the editor, hard at work cutting the last shots into the picture. He said the Kenya material didn't pay off, and we might have to shoot some extra denouement scene to send the audience away feeling satisfied with the way the characters had developed and interacted. Suddenly the phone rang. It was Pauline. "Where are you?" I yelled.

"In the office" she yelled back. I rushed across the car park, and there she was... loving, wonderful, but a little tearful. We found we both had kept out promises, and revealed to our respective spouses our whole relationship. Burned our boats... LEFT HOME — not without bitter recriminations (which for my part, I had been deserving for years!) The die was cast and we set about making a life together — financially almost from scratch! But it didn't matter; we had each other and were head-over-heels in love.

As for *Nor The Moon By Night* — as I had always suspected, it could never make a great statement about Africa, but after shooting a new ending, the result was passable entertainment. But we had gone so far over budget that my honeymoon with John Davis was over. All the promises of my making *The Singer Not The Song* were broken. He had already put another director (Roy Ward Baker) to work on the project, and Dirk Bogarde was cast in the lead role in place of my more grandiose and correct casting of Marlon Brando.

Contract-wise, I could do nothing but accept the situation because my producer-friend John Stafford had stood by me through all our troubles, and now rather meekly — even humbly — was accepting the situation. Over the long haul, the movie recouped its budget in Europe, and made some profit in the U.S. under the title of *Elephant Gun* — but there were no bonuses or deferments for us — except that I had Pauline, and no bonus could have been greater.

We set up house in an unfurnished two-room flat in St. John's Wood, London and for three or four days went around blissfully happy, buying furniture and other basic essentials for our love nest. Suddenly, I got a call from Sydney Box. "Disney wants you again. A guy called Bill Anderson wants us to meet him at eight sharp at the Mirabelle, just the three of us".

During dinner I broached my tricky subject, saying how, because of Pauline, I was full of new energy and enthusiasm, and that I trusted she could work with us. Bill nodded and said he saw no reason why not. I chortled and said, "Fantastic! I'm going to make you and Walt the best film you've ever had!" We shook hands on the deal, but as Bill's taxi sped away, Sydney shook his head, "You nearly blew it, old boy. A lot of people don't like lady friends around a production, especially if they don't know them."

"That's how it's got to be, Sydney," I said. "Pauline and I have both jumped over a precipice hand in hand, so to speak, and it's got to stay that way or I know it will never last." I broke into a grin. "And it's going to be the great love story of all time." Sydney gave a slight shrug and grinned. "I hope so, for your sake, old boy... I made a good deal for you, I think." I shook his hand. "And the best directing fee I've ever had. You're always lucky for me, Sidney."

And so, a week later Pauline and I found ourselves with Bill Anderson and Basil Keys in Chamonix, that picturesque French ski village under Mont Blanc (which had seen the start of my 'Broken Journey' adventures). This time we were visiting Gaston Rebouffat, whom we were told was the bravest, luckiest son-of-a-gun in the Alps. He showed us two hours of sixteen-millimetre film that he had shot during his rock climbing exploits. It was hair-raising footage, different and tremendously exciting. We unanimously decided that Gaston could take care of all the second-unit shooting and the staging of dangerous shots with doubles on the famous Swiss peak known worldwide as 'The Matterhorn'.

For this movie, Walt had bought a new best seller called 'Banner in the Sky'. It told the story of the first conquest of the Matterhorn, in the early part of the twentieth century, by a British climber called Whymper. It was based on true fact, except that a young character called Rudy had been invented, whose father had been an expert guide and claimed to have found a secret route to the top of the mountain. Unfortunately, he had lost a party of climbers, and Rudy had now to retrieve his father's reputation and lead Whymper up a narrow rock chimney to the summit — one could easily see why such a story of youthful achievement had appealed to Walt.

After a couple of fairy-tale days in Zermatt and the slopes leading up to the unique 'crooked-peaked' Matterhorn, Pauline and I were flown to Burbank, for pre-production work with Walt. Since we were not married, we found ourselves booked into adjoining suites in the massive Roosevelt Hotel, overlooking Hollywood Boulevard. The suites were so enormous that even with the communicating door open, we had difficulty in hearing each other no matter how hard we yelled! Of course the situation was ridiculous, because we quickly moved into one bedroom! I would go to the studio each day, while Pauline sat by the pool, took riding lessons, or was introduced to Beverly Hills by Bill Anderson's wife, Jinny. Walt's wife, Lillian was also dutifully attentive, but Pauline had to spend long hours reading and watching television while I was closeted with Larry Watkins, the screenwriter, Bill Anderson and Walt.

This time Walt seemed to have such confidence in me that so long as he was convinced that I knew exactly his approach to the story and how he envisioned the characters and scenes, he was not demanding that the whole script should be storyboarded. He allocated three of his sketch artists to work with me, but we only sketched out the key scenes. Peter Ellenshaw, the matte painter, was now thoroughly established in Burbank and a key figure in Walt's organisation. Under Walt's guidance he had perfected his technique, and his skills were now used to the full so much so that I had to fight against his desire to paint almost the whole of the long shots in the Alps and eliminate completely the Swiss location!

After a couple of weeks in the studio, I was closer to Walt than I had ever been. In daily conferences I saw how his mind worked, constantly solving story glitches with a solution that was sheer entertainment. He had been raised in a small town in the Midwest, and had never lost the gut feeling as to what things and ideas appealed to his kind of folk who, of course, composed the heart of America.

Walt began offering Pauline and I the use of the Disney executive cottage in Palm Springs. Quite often, on a Saturday evening, we would be invited to his nearby ranch-style home where he would cook (personally!) and regale us with stories of his past or discuss his dreams and show-biz plans for the future. Lillian was a great support to him — not creatively, but she provided the atmosphere for him to work at maximum capacity and in a comfortable and relaxed attitude. Lillian and Pauline became great buddies and I know they often discussed the way film-crazy husbands should be handled. "Let him go off on location without you for a week," said Lillian. "Maybe even two. But if it's going to last three weeks, join him by hook or crook or your marriage will go on the rocks." We were both very receptive to this idea because we wanted desperately for our relationship to last and I, for one, did not have the greatest record of being faithful. When you are all keyed-up on a movie and try to unwind after a hard day's shoot, if you are alone, you are more than likely to sniff out a receptive female — and there are always plenty of them around a film unit!

Naturally, this being our first visit to California together, we tried to see as much of the life as possible. I had a few friends in Beverly Hills and Bel Air — like Bob Coryell, who from his Morris Office executive chair had helped me so much with the casting of *The Planter's Wife*; Eric Ambler, for whom as the Colonel heading the Army Film Unit, I had made two or three training films; Alfred Hitchcock and Alma, whom I knew through Cecil Bernstein of Granada Television; David Niven, from my earliest trip to California; and Peter Ustinov and his charming wife Suzanne... with whom I had a very special relationship.

When I first met Suzanne, she was a young French Canadian actress, crazy to play Juliet for Orson Welles. As Welles remembered me from that backstage visit with Graham Greene, he asked me to shoot a test of Suzanne in Pinewood. Unfortunately, that day she was doubled up with pain from 'the curse', but somehow I managed to baby her through the test pieces. She got the part and never forgot. Peter, of course, was an old friend from *Hotel Sahara* — so between them, they made sure we went to all their Beverly Hills parties and met everyone they knew.

'Hitch' was an expansive, larger-than-life character, and one day I checked with him the truth of a story told me by Dudley Lovell when we were shooting *Miranda*: Hitch was making *The 39 Steps* at the Islington Studios, London. His leading lady was Madeleine Carroll, a blonde beauty, but difficult to animate. Half an afternoon had been wasted trying to get her to register horror, when suddenly she shrieked and gave a fabulous reaction. Dudley operating the camera turned and caught sight of Hitchcock rising from his director's chair and buttoning up his flies! "I've always wondered whether that was true," I said to Hitch at one of his soirées. "Of course it was," he grinned. "And I've used the same technique quite a few times on some of the dumb blondes I've been lumbered with!"

I discovered that Hitch regarded actors as a necessary evil. For every set-up and sequence, he had his thumbnail sketches and knew exactly how every frame should look, and where the actors should be at any given moment. One day I witnessed Eva Marie-Saint asking the maestro how she should play the lines. With a sharp, cold look he turned to her and said, "It is my job to tell you when to move from here to that rock, but the lines are in the script and you're paid good money to say them right. Let's shoot!"

Although I was always a tremendous admirer of Hitch, at that moment I felt he was only doing half his job as a director. In television today, many directors behave in the same way, but they lack Hitch's genius in building suspense and I always feel they are missing half the delight of their profession which is 'creating' with actors.

At the studio I was introduced to James MacArthur, who was then eighteen, and starring in *The Light of the Forest*. I watched him working on the lot and agreed with Walt that he would be great as the young hero in, what was now called *The Third Man On The Mountain*. Jim was stocky, muscular, good-humoured — the adopted son of Helen Hayes —well educated and with an excellent sense of humour. We immediately struck up a great relationship that has lasted through the years. Jim loves adventure and whenever I have asked him to do something a little dangerous or out of the way, he has trained and mastered it, whether it required tough rock-climbing, or apparently fighting with a twenty-foot anaconda in a mangrove swamp!

The time came to return to England and find the rest of the cast. My old friend Maude Spector was engaged again and quickly lined up Michael Rennie to play Whymper. Mike had been shooting on the next stage to me at Gainsborough when I made *Holiday Camp*. We hadn't gotten together at that time because he was a top star and I a first-time director. Now we got along so well, that a few months later he served as best man for our wedding!

We ended up casting James Donald, a hot star from the London theatre; Lawrence Naismith, also with a great theatrical background, and Herbert Lom, who had come from Czechoslovakia just before the war and established himself in both theatre and movies.

The love interest for Jimmy was to be provided by Janet Munro, a perky Scots girl of eighteen who always said she had been born backstage in Glasgow — in a costume basket! Her father was a well-known Scottish Music Hall comic and, from the age of four, she had supported him in his act — as an acrobat, a magician's helper and feed for his often very bad jokes. At eighteen, Janet was the complete trouper, ready to try anything —little did she know the things I was going to ask her to do on *The Third Man* and *Swiss Family Robinson*!

We arrived in Zermatt in February to find it exactly like a picture postcard. Basically, it is a ski and climbing resort that, to this day, permits no automobiles on its streets, and is best reached by a small mountain railway. It is a 'gingerbread' village made up of picturesque Swiss chalets surrounded by high mountain ranges of snow-covered peaks, and dominated by the ever-glistening Matterhorn. After eighteen weeks this view made Pauline scream every time she looked out the window, especially because she had been cheated out of working.

The last day before we left Burbank, Bill broke the news that Walt had made an edict, that no wives should work on any of his productions. "Bad for morale — can look like nepotism," said Bill, trying to justify the decision. It was a shattering blow, and I expected an outburst from Pauline, but instead she went very quiet. "With this outfit," she said, "it was bound to come to this. The Disney wives are such prudes, and because they don't work, expect you to be available to join them in social activities." Pauline paused. "I'll just have to look for a job on someone else's movie."

"No!" I said. "That'll break us up! Impossible! I'll talk again to Bill." A compromise was reached. Pauline would supervise the movie for TV, showing the making of the *Third Man on the Mountain* — which she did with her usual efficiency.

At the outset of the filming, Bill and I decided that in order to make this mountaineering movie look real, we and the whole cast ought to have some instruction on the technique of rock-climbing. The Zermatt guides were accustomed to taking physically-fit tourists up several routes on the Matterhorn, and now skillfully hung us over one thousand foot drops; showed us how to use pitones; and how to rappel, and scale simple rock faces.

Walt had insisted that we must show the actors in full figure as they climbed. "We must see their feet — no faking," he had said. So, we developed a modus vivendi that if a guide could assure us that this actor could make the climb safely, we put them in the shot, and no doubling.

Even though our actors were not much used to physical action, they threw themselves into this new experience with the greatest enthusiasm and began to vie with each other to show who was the best climber — with one exception, Herbert Lom. He refused point-blank to train or to be put in any situation where he did not have a firm platform under his feet. He argued, "I am an actor. I assure you I can *act* climbing convincingly. If I am supposed to be the best guide on the Matterhorn, that's what you'll see in *the* finished film. I will play this character and be completely convincing, but I am not going to risk my neck in one single shot, no matter how much you or the other darned crazy actors may try to blackmail me into climbing".

So, three riggers had to be flown out from Pinewood, and all over the rock faces below the Matterhorn, platforms were erected out of tubular scaffolding. Sometimes this meant we had to wait several hours for a shot, but Herbert Lom just sat on a rock looking into space. Soon the crew and the rest of the cast began to ostracise and haze him for being chicken — letting down the side, and adding to the time they were going to be away from home. Herb stuck to his guns!

In order to work on glaciers at ten thousand feet, we would ride in the cabins of the telepherique. The trip would take about half an hour. Dressed in warm ski clothes and ready for a fun day in the invigorating air and fantastic glacial scenery, everybody would be laughing and joking, except Herbert, who would be left on his own at the back of the train. But when the movie came out, which actor looked the most convincing climber on the Matterhorn? Herbert Lom, just as he'd said!

We began shooting on a Wednesday in March, and at the weekend I could find no trace of Jimmy MacArthur, with whom we regularly played tennis and canasta. On the Monday morning I found him stretched out and yawning on our hillside location... clearly pretty exhausted. He admitted to me that he had secretly arranged (and paid) his guide to take him to the top of the Matterhorn. "But for God's sake don't tell Bill," he said. "He'd have kittens over my jeopardising his insurance cover."

I shook my head as Jim continued: "If I'm supposed to be the son of the greatest guide on the mountain, how can I give you a real performance if I don't know *exactly* how it feels up there?" He grinned, "Now I know, and it was fantastic!"

Janet Munro played Jimmy's girlfriend, the one who gives him the courage to lead Mike Rennie up the secret route to the top of the Matterhorn. She provided the rather sentimental, romantic interest for Jimmy, but we involved her in some pretty scary climbing. In one shot, she had to apparently slip and hang from a rock with a five hundred foot drop below her. I could have used a double, but she impressed me so much with her levelheaded judgment and acrobatic ability that we put a harness under her dress, wired her to the rope, and at the top end attached it to a winch operated by Eddie Fowlie, our Special Effects man. On camera, it looked for all the world as though Jimmy and Larry Naismith were hauling her up.

All Janet said when she stepped on to solid rock at the top was, "You might have padded the harness. I think I've lost both my boobs." She was a great trouper and not averse to drawing attention to her physical attractions.

One day we went higher up the glacier than ever before — to a crevasse where our construction manager and the riggers had prepared an ice platform anchored deep inside. Mike Rennie was lowered on a rope from a small ski plane and we shot most of the day with him imprisoned in green-blue ice, which could never have been reproduced in a studio. The only girl on this reduced crew was Kay Rawlings, our script clerk. And for the first time she had nowhere to hide when she needed to go to the bathroom. We guys would just stroll a short distance away and turn our backs. But poor Kay insisted on having a guide take her fifty yards away from the unit. Naturally, when we all caught on to what was happening we stopped work and cheered her slippery progress.

Suddenly, without warning the clouds descended on us. The little ski plane, which had taken us up, would no longer be able to land safely, and so we all had to follow the guides down a path that they made by cutting out steps with their ice picks. What had taken us ten minutes in the morning, took us four hours at the end of the day. We arrived back at the hotel in pitch-blackness, cold and somewhat shaken by our adventure. But this unit didn't complain — accepting it as part of the day's work, because Bill Anderson and Basil Keys were running the show with consideration, and good sense.

Every morning about this time, Eddie Fowlie used to make straight for a workshop in the town to check on his team who were cutting out and gluing big chunks of Styrofoam into what he called 'fuff rocks'. They were to be used hopefully with safety, to simulate an avalanche. I think he prepared over a thousand rocks, and then for three days we saw them being dragged from the top telepherique station, by sled end pack mules, along the snowy rim of a long slope. At last he said he was ready. Obviously, we had to try and get the shot in one, so we set up five cameras, rehearsed the cast, then let Eddie push over a half dozen fuff rocks. In free fall or rolling they looked great, but when a fuff rock hit a real one, it bounced high in the air end seemed to float — as in slow motion.

Harry Waxman, who was photographing for me again, had prepared for this and together with all his assistants had timed the bounces. After swift calculations and loud arguing, he called for another trial rock launch... It was decided we must reduce the speed of the cameras to around sixteen frames per second, and to generally confuse the scene, by blowing artificial snow with our three massive wind machines across the widest area possible. I rehearsed the actors again making them slow down their movement to almost half-speed... Suddenly, Eddie appeared on the rim, followed by his crew of twenty helpers. They began waving and dancing about like banshees.

Over the intercom, Eddie said, "For Chrissakes, shoot the bloody thing! We're frozen!" I looked to Harry, as always checking his meters and exposure tables.

"We gotta go, Harry," I said. He nodded, walked to every camera and personally checked the f-setting, the motor speed and the filter. He turned to me and threw out his arms in an "I can't do any more" gesture. With everyone set, I called "Okay! Cameras!" and over the intercom, "Okay, Eddie! Let 'em go!"

I don't know how he had rigged it, but we saw a thousand fuff rocks rolling over that rim, and the wind machines whirling the artificial snow across the slope. I waved to the actors who, for over a minute, reacted, dodged, rolled and fell. To the naked eye it looked impressive, but somehow unreal. Everything had gone as planned. We couldn't really know till we saw our rushes. I yelled congratulations to everyone and we wrapped for the day... but it was as though someone had died an anti-climax... which lasted really until eleven o'clock the next morning, when we saw Basil running toward us from the telepherique waving a sheet of paper. The labs had seen the stuff and phoned to say it all looked great. "Convincing?" I yelled to Basil.

"Sure," he gasped. "That was the first thing I asked them."

"What were they printing at?" asked Harry.

"Here's your bloody numbers, you miserable sod," said Basil, handing him the report. He turned to the crew with a glowing red face and yelled, "You did it! You worked the bloody miracle! Where's Eddie? Somehow Eddie had timed it to be beside us. He grinned from ear to ear. A cheer went up and a few of us hugged each other and then continued with the day's shooting.

Every day there were new physical and logistical problems to be solved. For Harry and I there was such a wealth of awe-inspiring backgrounds with their ever-changing moods, depending on what was happening in the thin air around the Matterhorn. I think for the most part the unit was as elated as I was. The air was pure, we felt completely free and in the evenings top French chefs prepared the food in the Zermatterhof, and despite hard physical days, we would often dance until midnight.

For Pauline and I it was almost like a honeymoon, except that in the daytime when she was not occupied with the little PR film, she was often bored to distraction. While it was still winter, she learned to be an expert skier and figure skater. She bought every type of winter gear, just for something to do, and as the snow melted, tennis courts and a swimming pool appeared where the skating rink used to be, so she played tennis, sunbathed and swam — an idyllic existence one might say, but to her at this period, Zermatt was like a mountain sanatorium to which she had been banished to cure some disease like TB. As the fifteenth week began, she suddenly announced, "I've had it! I have to go down to the flatlands, see ordinary people, a city!"

And so it was agreed that she would go to Venice for a few days with Netta Shannon, the equally bored wife of the Disney publicist. It was the first time we had been separated, and although every night both girls giggled into the phone and said they were having a ball, they came back fast enough when at the end of a week Basil grabbed the phone and said, "Pauline, dear, you gotta come back. He's like a bear with a sore head, blowing his top at the smallest things and making my job impossible!"

Pauline admitted that she had missed me like hell and surprise, surprise, the communal life of the film company (which is really something very special).

As the snow melted from the lowland pastures, and the 'Nestlé' milk-cows went out to graze, the cowbells giving us a constant tinkling background, the grassy slopes became confettied with wild flowers. Walt arrived on the location and approved everything we were shooting. He brought with him a portable projector, which was something new in those days. Henceforth, we were able to see our dailies within four days of shooting. Walt immediately had the idea of devising a romantic scene with Jimmy and Janet walking hand in hand through the flowers towards the Matterhorn, accompanied by a sentimental love song which he promised to have written by the Sherman brothers, a Hollywood song writing team he had just discovered (later they went on to write wonderful scores for *Mary Poppins*, *Jungle Book*, and a string of Disney favourites).

The very down-to-earth Janet Munro was somewhat blasé about the new love scene, so Jim rehearsed it with his childhood sweetheart, Joyce Bullifant, who had just arrived from New York, chaperoned by the great Helen Hayes. Never one to miss a trick, Walt immediately devised a small scene in the Alpine town so that Helen could be included in the movie.

A large crowd stood watching us all day as the chippies laid the longest camera track I have ever used, and with Walt whistling into a mike, the melody which he had just heard from Hollywood over the phone, we shot and reshot Jimmy and Janet's romantic walk under the shadow of the Matterhorn. Walt knew his audience in an uncanny way, because when the movie came out, they loved this idealised scene of young love, bringing out handkerchiefs, and moaning 'ooh's' and 'aah's' in cinemas across America.

Pauline and I used to be awakened about three in the morning, by a typical Tyrolean type who would sit on a hillside opposite our bedroom window and rehearse on his long Swiss alpenhorn. We hated him and his mournful notes, but Walt thought him unique and worked in a place for me to include him! He then went down into the valley and brought back the local choir to sing in our square. The Valais citizens appeared in picturesque folk costumes, and that was when I gave Pauline and Netta a little break, by including them in the second row of the choir. My camera operator Alan Hume slipped over to them and whispered, "See that little chalk cross above the lens? Well, make sure you can always see it, or it'll be the tintack for me when the Gov sees the rushes". (Tintack is Cockney rhyming slang for 'the sack'!)

George Pitcher, a sixty-five year old production manager, had been engaged to supervise Gaston Rebufat's small mountain unit. He took his duties so seriously that, despite his years, he insisted on going up with the climbers as far as he could, and then watched them all day through binoculars. One day he slipped and broke his collarbone. But that did not stop him from bringing over a wonderful new batch of climbing shots for us to project. Walt went crazy about them and immediately insisted on making the trip back to Chamonix with George, and sketching out a new sequence for Gaston to shoot with doubles for our actors. It turned out to be the most exciting sequence in the picture, and I learned that in the right clothes, you could match doubles with your actors even as close as a knee-length shot.

It was pure film trickery, which has always appealed to me ever since I studied the early work of the French wizard, George Méliès. Ideally for me, a film should always lean towards fantasy — the making of the impossible look believable. That is film magic, and of course the formula which George Lucas and Steven Spielberg have both latched on to so successfully.

After sixteen weeks of mountain shooting, I was as fit as the chamois, which we used to see jumping from rock to rock. And despite the long days on my feet, on the seventh day (Rest Day), Pauline and I challenged Mike Rennie and Jimmy MacArthur to a tennis doubles match. We were going great guns until, without warning, my leg folded beneath me! I was whisked to the first-aid post where they found I had ruptured an artery in my right calf.

Sudden abject misery — three weeks still to go — how could I finish the picture? Walt would be as mad as hell that I'd done this to him — and on a day off! My guide came to the rescue and said, "Don't worry, sir, I'll get you up to the locations. You'll walk to the train with a stick, and I'll have a pack-mule waiting at the top of the telepherique. You can ride up with the lunches and any spot too difficult, I'll drag you up by rope and stick."

And that is how I finished the last three weeks of the shoot — often in great pain and feeling most awkward and restricted, but it proved that one *could* direct from a rope-chair or sitting on a pack-mule! These remarkable animals are so sure-footed, capable of negotiating the narrowest track around a rocky spur. But the fifth morning I was clinging to my animal when the beast of burden in front of me slipped, spilling out knives, forks, and chicken sandwiches from its pannier bags, to tumble the thousand-foot drop below. I have to say I was greatly relieved when the necessity of riding to work on 'the canteen train' was over!

Walt returned from a holiday trip, completely enamoured by Swiss folk dancing, blue lakes, and the fairy-tale castles which he had visited and sketched — especially Chillon on Lake Geneva, around which Goethe wrote his famous poem. Walt re-ran our total dailies over a three-day period and met us coming back from work with the broadest smile. "I think you can wrap the location, Ken. Peter Ellenshaw can paint all the remaining down-angle shots far better than anything you can do." For some reason connected with perspective, this is a well-known photographic truth. The camera flattens out the most dangerous-looking down-shots. Eventually, Peter painted thirty-two of them so effectively than when the movie was shown in Kansas, half the audience suffered vertigo and covered their eyes!

After twenty weeks in Zermatt, I took the unit back to Pinewood Studios where John Howell had constructed matching sections of ice faces and rock. For the scenes where it would have been impossible to take our actors, we used the special sodium light process that had been developed for Matte shots in the Disney Studios. Feeling that every shot should be top quality, Walt loaned us Ub Iwerks, who had made all of Walt's dreams become technically possible in Burbank. I picked up several wonderful technical tricks from this old master, which have stood me in great stead ever since.

When we wrapped at Pinewood, I completed my rough-cut with Peter Boyter, the same editor with whom I had worked on *The Sword and The Rose*. When I was satisfied with the cut, he took all the material back to Burbank for Walt to approve, polish and add the music.

Third Man On The Mountain became his favourite real-life movie and still has not been equalled for its climbing shots combined with a good story and romance. But there are purists who might say Walt fell between two stools. Climbing buffs have no time for the sentimental scenes between Jim and Janet, and Walt's Swiss choirs and alpenhorns, which undoubtedly soften the impact of the movie. But you could never change Walt from his determination to make complete, all-around family entertainment.

Walt was deeply influenced by his stay in Switzerland and went on later to build the miniature Matterhorn in Disneyland. Pauline and I were invited for the opening and rode in a crazy buffeting car through its tunnels, ahead of Walt and Lillian, and Richard Nixon and family. Nixon opened this new attraction and we discovered, to our surprise, that Walt and he seemed to have a lot in common. They shared the same pride in their pioneer heritage and grandiose vision for the new America. By that time Walt believed passionately that the monorail, which he built all around Disneyland, was the best way of solving the growing traffic congestion in big cities. That afternoon he sold his ideas very hard, and Nixon seemed to be persuaded in his logic, but as we all know, when he became President he soon had other things on his mind!

Staying in Burbank again, I found that Walt's ever-restless mind was striking out into new fields. He was obsessed with the idea of everyone being happy, busy, and proud of their country. Apart from expanding Disneyland, he wanted to develop a big recreational centre in Squaw Valley, Northern California and had just endowed a college for young people to learn film techniques (both Lucas and Spielberg were later students and gained much from the treasury of film know-how Disney left behind).

Even with his brain increasingly occupied with outside problems, Walt still kept his finger on every creative activity in the studio. He was very lucky in that his brother Roy devoted his whole life to helping make Walt's fantasies and dreams come true, in down-to-earth and financially viable ways. In his personal daily life, Walt never carried any ready money. He had two secretaries with different chequebooks who dealt with his business affairs mainly on the instructions of Roy and Lillian. I once asked him how much he thought he was worth. He shrugged his shoulders and said, "Enough, I suppose. I've always believed money is for using and doing the things one wants to achieve — never for just hoarding or lying buried in a bank vault."

In these early days of Disneyland even Roy almost allowed Walt too much rein — the original Theme Park fell deeply into the red for over three years. The studio had to be mortgaged and even their two homes. But Walt knew he was onto something unique and persevered just as he had in the cartoon days. He had great taste, a showman's flair and a belief in top talent — even though he did keep everyone working in his shadow.

Walt's top art directors between pictures and cartooning designed all the attractions in the original Disneyland at Anaheim. They came from all over the world and felt they were the luckiest guys in the world to be developing the ideas of a genius. I felt the same.

CHAPTER NINE
Swiss Family... *From Its First Concept*

Before we left Burbank this time, Walt invited Pauline and myself to Palm Springs. After a meal at the Smoke House, where Walt ate all his barbecue steak like everyone else off a plain wooden table, we strolled onto the lawn and listened to coyotes, an owl and a fox. I began pumping him about his feelings for animals and birds and realised, to my surprise, that he really didn't have much time for them except insofar as they could provide him with characters for his fantasy world! He studied their behaviour and characteristic movements, but was by no means an animal lover! We drove back to his home and began talking about tropical islands.

"You know, Ken," Walt said, "the story I'd like to tell next is that old classic by J.R. Wyse, 'The Swiss Family Robinson'." My wife caught the gleam in my eye, and shook her head. "What's the matter?" asked Walt. "You think it's too old fashioned."

"I wouldn't know," said Pauline. Like all of us who had worked with Walt, she knew better than to oppose any idea Walt came up with. "It's years since I read 'Swiss Family'. It's just I can sense Ken drooling at the idea of a desert island. Since he's made a little money, he's been threatening to buy a yacht and sail off God knows where."

Walt fiddled with his moustache. "Well, this idea could save you both a lot of money and take you to some romantic places." He took a sip of wine and continued, "Just imagine, a whole family thrown together on a desert island, no help nearby, but everything they need is lying around if only they have the guts to use it."

"I love the idea," I said. "Especially if we could have the island full of interesting animals!"

"Sure thing," said Walt. "There are endless possibilities. What I'd like you to do is to start thinking of all the things you'd like to happen to that family if it were yours. Think of anything, no matter how crazy!"

Three weeks later, Pauline and I settled into a motel just outside the studio, where our neighbours were the young Sean Connery and Janet Munro, who were playing small parts in Walt's *Darby O'Gill and the Little People*.

Every morning I would go into the studio about nine and join Walt, Bill Anderson, his Production Chief, and Lowell Hawley, a rather stolid ex-radio writer whom Walt felt would faithfully translate our joint ideas onto paper.

We knew we had to start off with the family on a ship sailing to the New World to seek a free and independent life. This was in the book, and there had to be a storm and shipwreck close enough to a desert island so that after they had been washed ashore they could return to the wreck and salvage the things they needed to build a new home. Because of the wild animals they quickly discovered they had to build a tree-house. So far so good. Then what?

We tried to give interesting characteristics to the three sons, but as the family settled, adapted themselves to a daily routine, their life became boring, no matter what mad scenes we came up with. I arrived early one morning and was telling Walt about an evening we'd spent with Janet Munro, who had kept us in fits of laughter as she told us stories about her father — a famous Scottish comedian. At one time he ran out of gags and only saved his act by bringing Janet on as a six-year-old "straight man" dressed in a sailor suit.

"That's it," said Walt. "There's our solution. The boys need a girl. We'll have Janet dressed as a sailor boy, and have her captured with her uncle. He's an Admiral and will make a good hostage!" Bill and Lowell arrived and listened to the idea.

"But who will capture them?" asked Bill.

"Pirates, of course!" said Walt.

"But that will make a very different type of story," said Lowell. "In a family story, do you really want to get into old-time swashbuckling — compete with Burt Lancaster in *The Crimson Pirate*?

"And there was always quite a bit of sex in those movies," added Bill. "Is that what you really want, Walt?"

Walt drew a deep breath. "Pirates are okay in this story, because I remember in Chapter One of the book, the ship was driven into the storm trying to avoid a pirate ship. Wyse wrote that, so pirates can be quite legit in our story." He looked at our blank faces and grinned. "Just an idea from the top of my head, but I think it gives us something to play with."

In exploring Walt's new concept, we came up with the idea that the two eldest boys persuade their parents to let them explore the other side of the island. And so, travelling in a homemade canoe, they come upon two pirate ships.

On the beach, the 'horrid' pirate chief is being very nasty to Janet and has the Admiral on his knees begging for mercy. In a clever ruse, the boys rescue Janet, who, of course, is dressed in the sailor suit. The boys soon discover she's a girl, and start to fight over her. Their good relationship is completely broken up by jealousy, but upon returning to the tree-house, Pa and Ma Robinson sort them out, only to realise that the pirates now know there is someone else on the island and will obviously come to find them. This gives the whole family a chance to put up ingenious ways to defend themselves... then, the inevitable battle — which we agreed should be a mixture of real danger and comedy — and we still had to find out how to dispose of the pirates and create a happy, satisfactory, emotional ending!!!

Walt approved this general storyline, but said, "Now we need to use the animals more." He smiles at me. "Keep this in mind. You can bring in any animal you want so long as it adds colour and excitement!"

"If we take that route, how do we explain say a tiger, elephant, giraffe, and monkeys, all on one island?" asked the logically minded Anderson. Walt grinned. "Oh, somewhere, Lowell will drop the hint that there was once a land-bridge between the island and Africa!" Walt had an answer to everything if he was pushed.

Some days later we were still battling out a final storyline. Walt was gazing out of the window. "We're going okay, but we've still got to find things to do with the animals, not just look at them — and the pirate attack needs a dramatic or comic lead-in." He began pacing the room, while we waited for what might be a good idea or a terribly impractical one. "I remember the book says that after they'd been a year on the island, they had a Thanksgiving Celebration. Why don't we have a kind of gala race with animals they've adopted?

"And the pirates might arrive in the middle of it," I put in.

"And wonder what the hell is going on," added Walt triumphantly.

As everyone knows, we devised the race between an ostrich, a baby elephant, a zebra, a tiny pony, and a monkey riding a Great Dane... Now, everyone knew the shape and essential elements of our movie.

Walt now made what to my mind was the judgment of Solomon. He set me loose with John Jensen, a top sketch artist, who had been discovered by Cecil B. DeMille years back when he made *The Ten Commandments*. With, as yet, no written script, John and I were able to visually develop the whole second half of the movie in sketches, while Lowell wrote the first half with its appropriate dialogue.

"The first half is obvious," said Walt. "All it needs are down-to-earth lines in character to fit the scenes we're all agreed on. But the second half is mostly action. Every set up needs imagination and the practical knowledge that the shot can be achieved."

John used his pencil like a writer's pen. I would describe the nature of the scene I was aiming at, and his pencil would start doodling on the paper making thumbnail impressions. He was a thwarted adventurer, I would say, and loved pirates and any trick he could devise to make them squirm! He also adored animals and the funny things one could do with them.

I would say, "What if the tiger could..." and this would set him off on a new inventive sketch, which I would embellish. So, every day we created storybook scenes that made us laugh and laugh even at the drawing board. One great plus, also; John would never design anything unless it was practical and would work. The tree-house, with its waterwheel and homemade buckets to lift water from the stream to the first-level kitchen — how would they work? John's solution was so perfect that the tree-house showpiece now in Disneyland was built exactly as conceived for the movie.

As the walls of our big drawing office became covered with sketches, Walt used to drop in before lunch to view each sequence, shot by shot — the race, the pirate landing, and their attack on the family fort. He invariably had a contribution to make, either to increase the fun or make the action clearer.

As a director, I discovered that there is nothing, no matter how way-out it may seem, that cannot be broken down in sketches to its essential elements. Then, you and everyone, the camera crew, the special effects, stunt people — everyone in the team can SEE the magic they are going to achieve, before a foot of film is exposed.

Walt had decided that the youngest Robinson was to be 'Moochie' Corcoran, who at that time was only twelve years old, but had already made sixteen movies for Walt. He was a remarkable boy, very much in the style of the 'Our Gang' two-reelers — resourceful, streetwise and prepared to have a go at anything. He was wonderfully coordinated and had hung around so many animal trainers and stuntmen, that he knew exactly what was called for and how much of the action he could handle. I never had to use a double with 'Moochie', so that when the ostrich had to be captured in the movie, it was 'Moochie' who clung onto him and was dragged unceremoniously all over the field. It was 'Moochie' himself who swung like Tarzan across the mountain pool. The only thing he hated was playing scenes with the pet monkey. During the Christmas scene he suddenly said, "Mister Annakin, that little bastard bit me again. Why can't we use a dummy in his scenes with me, and prove it is him in close-ups?" He was right, in a way, but I wanted to show a relationship between them, and so persisted my way.

But I'm jumping ahead. We had reached the stage where Lowell was turning in his four to five pages a day of the script, fully dialogued, and John Jenson was polishing up the storyboard sketches. Walt suddenly said, "Roy is pressing me to know what all this is going to cost."

"It's not going to be cheap, I can tell you," said Bill Anderson. "Collecting and shipping all those animals will be a monster headache!"

Walt drew in a deep breath. "I agree. *Swiss* has its problems, but so has everything worthwhile, and that is why I'm bringing over Basil and John, who served us so well on *Third Man On The Mountain*." Basil Keys and John Howell were my British Production Manager and Art Director — old and trusted buddies.

"We need a budget based on definitely chosen shooting sites, construction designs to fit those sites, housing costs and transport for a big crew. I suggest you start looking in Jamaica."

"Why Jamaica?" I asked.

"It worked well for the exterior shoot in *20,000 Leagues Under The Sea*. It might work for this one, too."

And so, I found myself again in the Constant Springs Hotel that had seemed to me like paradise on my first trip round the world. It was still as I remembered it, and I found it very pleasant to show Pauline, Basil and John where the adventurous part of my life had really begun.

We found Walt's beaches at Negril were miles away along a rugged coastal road. The palm fringed sands were beautiful, but as Basil said, "They may have been okay for a small second unit shooting from a boat, but where in hell could I house two units for sixteen to eighteen weeks?"

And John said, "How do I get all my materials and workers here for the building of the wreck...? And there's no kind of forest for a tree-house."

So, we explored the more accessible Ochos Rios Coast, where Noel Coward and Peter Fleming had built beautiful homes, but as John Howell pointed out, none of these beaches would work for us, because we could never get rid of the villas and signs of the modern world.

The world-famous rapids on White River could have provided an exciting sequence for us, but when we became enthusiastic about a huge cotton tree, ideal for building a tree-house in, Basil put on his sternest Production Manager face and said,

"It's too deep in the forest. We'd have to spend a week bulldozing a track, and any cameraman would demand at least six brutes to boost up the light. It's just not on, fellas!" He was right. The site was beautiful but impractical, unless we were to go crazy cost-wise.

I phoned Walt and explained why we couldn't use the Negril beaches or anything else in Jamaica. "But we've been tipped off that Trinidad may be ideal — much more choice," I told him.

"That's fine with me," said Walt, "so long as you find places where the scenes we've created can be staged." He paused. "And I guess you want to catch Carnival in Trinidad. I've always heard it's the best in the world. Enjoy it and bring me back a stack of pictures."

We did indeed fit Carnival into our schedule of daily trips round the coast. The parades and streets filled with revellers were an experience never to be forgotten, but Trinidad, with its big oil fields and militant sugar and wharf-side workers, did not seem the place for us. However, during a crazy night learning how to do the 'Jump-Up' at the Country Club, I learned from the barman that there was an island paradise just twenty-five miles north of Trinidad, where Robinson Crusoe was supposed to have been shipwrecked! This sounded like the answer to our prayers, so with clear consciences that we had not wasted Walt's money, the next morning we crowded into the small plane which touched down each day in Tobago.

Here everything miraculously fell into place. By pure chance, or Disney luck, we hired one of the less-battered taxis driven by a smart, ever-smiling black gentleman called McEuen. We told him the kind of places we were looking for and in twenty-four hours he had led us to every location we needed — six completely different beaches, some with breakers and one, at Pigeon Point, with translucent green water.

We found the one giant tree, just asking to accommodate a tree-house under its theatrical spreading branches. At the northern end there was a mountain ridge ideal for the boys' journey across the island. Halfway along the coast road, a group of rocks just perfect for drilling and erecting our tubular scaffolding to hold 'the set' of the wreck, backgrounded by a hundred-and-eighty degree seascape. And near the biggest hotel, a cone-shaped hill for our family fort and the pirate assault.

Fourteen miles of road, which ran all the way up the East Coast, connected every location, and there were four hotels to house whatever size unit we might need! They had, in fact, already serviced a recent John Huston production, *Heaven Knows, Mr. Allison* with Robert Mitchum and Deborah Kerr. If the island and its facilities were good enough for such stars, it must be okay for us! I reported back to Walt and he seemed vaguely pleased — a little worried that it required three plane changes from Los Angeles, but said he would send Bill Anderson down immediately.

While waiting for his arrival, we went snorkelling with Robbie, an enormous, jolly, black fellow with the largest feet I have ever seen. He was a great swimmer and knew every nook and cranny in the reefs, and in fact had guided three *National Geographic* underwater expeditions. He showed us the cave where Bertie the Barracuda lay in wait for unsuspecting fish. We saw sharks, which he even succeeded in assuring the dubious Pauline, were quite harmless. He would dive down and tickle their bellies and, like good Disney cartoon fish, they seemed to smile.

Bill Anderson arrived and was thrilled with the locations and the deals that Basil was making with the local planters, hotelkeepers, and transport people. In his thorough search of the island, he added a couple of extra locations. One in a mangrove swamp at Pigeon Point (where we eventully staged the fight with the anaconda) and the mountain pool over which the boys swung in their Tarzan act, while Pa and Ma Robinson watched contentedly and waxed romantic. Bill put on his producer's hat. "Our briefing is to include everything we would like to share with the family. If I had grown up in a place like this grotto, it would have been sheer heaven and I know it will be for our audiences."

Unfortunately, when we came to shoot both these locations, it turned out that they lay under some kind of cloud belt which formed daily around eleven o'clock and invariably blocked out the sunlight. At that time we were using rather slow film and Harry Waxman, the perfectionist cameraman, insisted on full sunshine for every shot, with the result that we went four or five weeks over schedule because of Bill Anderson's insistence on "sheer heaven." It was good for the movie, but didn't make either of us popular with Walt ... but that again is jumping ahead.

We left Tobago reluctantly, but highly elated. Pauline had found an idyllic bungalow for us to rent on Baccalet Point. We were told, "The soft trade winds will caress you day and night." This was true, and often made up for the worries and friction, which developed during the actual filming.

On returning to Burbank, Walt expressed satisfaction with the pictures and plans we brought back, but was still worried that Tobago was so far away, or at least difficult to reach, from Los Angeles. He was also under great pressures about the costs and overruns of his Big Dream — Disneyland, which was showing a massive loss in its first year. But, true to his determined character, Walt swallowed deeply when he was shown the budget for *Swiss* — amounting to just over three-and-a-half million dollars — which far exceeded the cost of any film he had made up to date. Under Roy's worried eye, we had meeting after meeting, and Walt made gestures of suggesting cuts, but in the end he gave me the go ahead to shoot the movie exactly as we had laid it out in sketches and script.

John Howell returned to work out exactly how his sets would be built and the labour necessary to achieve his designs. Already the island was abuzz with stories of the jobs that we were bringing — especially since we had decided to improvise a studio in a field near the tree-house. It would be one hundred feet by eighty feet, built on tubular scaffolding and covered with corrugated iron sheets. In the days ahead, this was to save our filmic asses and enabled us to shoot every foot of the movie without going into any studio, either in the US or the UK.

True to a private promise, Bill arranged for Pauline to work along with Bill Watherwax and his son John, the Disney Studio animal trainers, who were now teaching eight Great Danes to play and double for the two character dogs we had written into the movie. Pauline probably likes dogs even more than people and she was fascinated to learn the way these Disney old-timers could take completely strange dogs and in three weeks have them working to instruction without the use of any force or cruelty. Olympia was a remarkable swimmer; Snatch had hunted mountain lions in Colorado, but had to be trained to face up to our tiger; Baskin was a character dog capable of smiling, nodding and generally looking as though he understood the family conversation.

Pauline was thrown into a whole new world of animal handlers and training-farms dotted around California. She discovered a charming baby elephant whose mother had starred in fifty movies; chose three ostriches to be ridden and raced; two zebra raised as pets but capable of nasty back-kicks. A birdman in Orange County said he could provide thirty flamingos and sixty other tropical birds, *plus six hyenas,* if we wanted them! And, of course, I grabbed them!

One scorching day we visited the San Diego Zoo and met a giant tortoise, a hundred and fifty years old, who didn't object to us riding on his back! Yes, we had great fun choosing our animals which were gradually rounded up and housed in a specially built corral near the Disney lot. Walt talked MGM into loaning him a supervisor who had looked after that studio's animal pictures for years. But no one had ever had so many varieties in one movie, as we collected for *Swiss Family Robinson.*

Everything was coming together just fine, and Walt was smiling again. He had just talked to John Howell, in Tobago and learned that the key British construction crew, who had been building the sets for three months, were now practically ready. "We set them some difficult tasks" he said. "I admit, I was worried!" He grinned and added, "Before you go off, how would you and your wife like a Day at the Races? I keep a box at the Santa Anita track, so if you like, there'll be a limousine to pick you up, along with Sean Connery and Janet Munro, who've been doing a great job on *Darby O'Gill*. There will be a hundred dollars 'gambling money' for each of you. I reckon you've all earned it!"

It was an idyllic day. We saw Cary Grant, Burt Lancaster, Barbara Stanwyck and Lucille Ball in neighbouring boxes. We drank champagne and danced like kids as we backed winners, then made sure we lost it all just for the fun — all except Sean who scowled and said he didn't approve of gambling! I always wondered how he managed to change his image for 007!

All that was left now was to spend an evening with Philip Scheuer of the *LA Times,* talking about our plans and preparations for this big movie. Over dinner at Chasen's we hit it off so well that Philip insisted on taking us back home. I've often wondered why, because Phil lived in a small suburban house in the La Brea District. He had a permanently sick wife upstairs and a sitting room filled with ham radio equipment. It seemed a very strange background for a man who was feared by all Hollywood for his sweeping critiques and comments on the show-biz scene. Phil Scheuer could make or break you at this period, yet I remember thinking that if this is how he lives, how can he have the good taste and worldly experience to criticise our movies! The next morning in one-inch type, the LA *Times* emblazoned *"ANNAKIN'S ARK LEAVES FOR TOBAGO."* Pauline and I thought it was great fun and we were very proud.

The plane left early for Tobago, and so we missed Walt's reaction which apparently made him explode! "Annakin's Ark? Who the hell does he think he is? They're my animals and my picture, and I'm paying for them!" If I had known this reaction I probably would not have been surprised at what happened much later!

Our return to Tobago was like a homecoming. Everyone knew about us and wanted to help. The tree-house was complete and looked like something you'd expect to find in an enchanted forest — straight out of 'Swan Lake' I thought. The home was built on a platform thirty feet up in this giant tree, with an upstairs cabin and a loft for 'Moochie'. Lianas hung from every branch. It was really solid — capable of holding twenty crew and cast and constructed in sections so that it could be taken apart and rebuilt on film by the family.

Six miles up the coast, we found the wrecked ship stuck at a crazy angle into the rocks with rough seas breaking over it. John Howell had ensured that I could give the illusion of being at sea or play scenes on the deck after the barque had been wrecked.

At the weekend, Annakin's Ark arrived in two Dakota cargo planes. They had stopped in New Orleans to pick up Mel Coons with his tiger, and a three-month-old lion we were not going to use, but whose training he could not break. Also, there were two twenty-five foot anacondas, one of which proved later to be pregnant; twelve brilliantly coloured macaws; and forty-eight Rhesus monkeys. Led by the baby elephant, two ostriches and the zebra, ridden by Mitch, an ex-rodeo wrangler, the whole menagerie paraded through the little port of Scarborough and up the six miles of coast road to the zoo compound, which had been prepared beside our giant corrugated iron studio. Native kids and their parents turned out from their wooden cabins and gaped in amazement at the animals they had never dreamt of seeing on their island. Most of the hundred sixty-odd white residents visited us, too.

After church on Sunday, Pauline found herself acting as a guide to Lady Beetham, the wife of the British governor of Tobago and their two daughters. Everyone killed themselves with laughing when Pauline, showing off that she knew Bahloo, the baby elephant, was given a hearty swipe across her butt with its trunk!

The unit, mostly from England, began arriving and had to be housed in the four beachfront hotels. There were immediate complaints that some of the crew were housed nearer to the sea than the others! That was too bad! They were lucky to be in Tobago.

Yakima Canutt, the greatest second-unit director in the business — he had shot countless American Westerns and the chariot race from *Ben Hur* — arrived with fourteen American animal handlers. They had come for serious work and settled in without a single query, except how soon would I want their animals to work? "We'll get along fine," said Mitch, "if you can give us at least twenty-four hours notice of what you will require from our animals, sir."

The work atmosphere was completed by the arrival of our pirate junk from Port of Spain. A sixty-foot lighter had been converted with the super-structure of a two-masted barque. It was always top-heavy and 'yawed' in the slightest swell, but as we all piled onto it for a picnic that second Sunday, we enjoyed ourselves like a load of drunken tourists.

For the most part, I remember this movie as days after days on glaring white beaches and shooting fairy-tale scenes with animals and kids. James MacArthur and Tommy Kirk developed exactly the same rivalry in real life as they had in the story. Tommy, the bright but erratic second son, always wanted to show off and outstrip the muscular and beautifully coordinated Jimmy MacArthur. 'Moochie' Corcoran was like a well-built pixie, jumping onto the baby elephant whenever he came down to the sea for a morning dip. Bahloo loved to swish seawater onto his back, and then roll completely over in the waves. But Moochie always seemed to come up still hanging on.

Johnny Mills and Dorothy McGuire, playing the parents, began in real life to watch over the kids and sometimes from their long experience in movies, would question the athletic and potentially dangerous things I was asking the kids to do. But in truth, I would always consider carefully what each one was capable of and made my decisions accordingly. In this the wranglers and our British stunt men invariably helped me.

We had brought twenty stunt guys from England, many of whom I had worked with before. Their main job was to prepare for the pirate attack, rig spectacular falls from the cliff, and help the special effects men work out and rig all the comic traps for the pirates, which John Jansen and I had devised on our storyboards. My stunt buddies were a great help in controlling and rigging the raft with its flotilla of pigs, ducks, sheep and geese, as they floated from the wreck. This sequence was a veritable nightmare to set up. First, the raft had to be held in position in relation to our floating camera platform. Then, the animals and birds had to be tied individually to their floats and boxes, and strung out on separate floats behind the raft.

The script clerk would cry out, "Ken! Ken! The pig's on its back again! Stop everything. No film is worth the life of a poor animal! There's a sheep drowning! Ken, you're trying for the impossible. For God's sake, give up. How can you be so heartless?" All day long, these kind of moans would complicate my efforts! When all appeared to be perfect, we called for the actors to be rowed out to the raft and sure enough one of them would be on the toilet, or Tommy Kirk would be fooling around with some kids. By the time they were in costume and on the raft, the animals would be all tangled up again in their ropes, and *truly* near drowning!

For two whole weeks we struggled with this problem, complicated by tides and the trade winds, which brought up clouds over the sun every afternoon, causing Harry Waxman great lighting problems. In the end we got the shot with every stuntman and the extra crew of local divers, hanging onto each floating piece and diving out of sight the moment I yelled, "Action!" *But we got it,* exactly as Walt had described the scene originally!

I knew this was one sequence I had to get just right or I would hear him saying to me, as he had done on both *Robin Hood* and *Sword and the Rose,* "Why didn't you shoot the goddamn shot as we agreed?" I'd answer, "Well, it's taken us two weeks and Basil says we're going over-budget."

"Have I ever queried what you were spending?" he'd say, hardening his voice, and you would know you had boobed and somehow, with or without you, Walt would have that shot!

Now, as the first novelty of this tropical island and magical adventure wore off, there were murmurings from the crew, especially Harry Waxman, the director of photography. He was light-skinned and sandy-haired and his feet had gotten terribly blistered in the sun. Suddenly, I found he was spreading the word around that I was attempting the impossible and no one would ever get home for Christmas. I hardened my heart, closed ranks with my still-loyal technicians and became a dictator. Of course, when it came to the race, and the crew saw that I was *really* trying to get a true master-shot of the zebra racing the elephant, the ostrich, the mini-pony and the Great Dane ridden by the monkey, all in one shot with the actors riding around the paddock, they were perhaps justified in thinking I had gotten crazy! But I felt it was worth a try, and in this case I was lucky. Animals and cast performed the miracle.

Right up to this day, Dorothy McGuire tells the story in Hollywood of how I put them all onto the raft and made them sail through a real whirlpool past huge jagged rocks. The raft was, in fact, attached to steel cables and supported by oil drums, but the waves washed over it and soon soaked Dorothy's long dress. Suddenly, in the middle of a shot, she yelled, "Ken, Ken, we're sinking!"

I yelled back, "Don't panic. There's a swimmer standing by for each of you, ready to jump in and catch you if anything breaks."

Then Tommy Kirk piped up, "She's not kidding, Ken. This isn't funny! We're really going down!" And I must say it did seem the water was nearly up to their knees. But the shot was nearly complete and it was real with no doubles, so I jollied them on.

"I bet you never did anything like this in Hollywood, Dorothy, and John's getting some sensational stills." John was her husband, the famous *Life* photographer, John Swope.

"Who said I'm not worried?" he said just behind me. "Surely you got enough to make a good sequence now."

"Almost" I whispered out of the corner of my mouth. "I'm just going to pan away to the dogs and link them all together, then I'll cut. It's a fantastic shot with everything working and they're really all quite safe." Once again, courage had paid off and everyone was happy, especially when they were able to boast about their bravery to every new visitor who came to the island.

John and Mary Mills had brought their two children with them — Jonathan, who was preparing for Eton Public School, and Hayley, who was then about ten years old and had not yet made *Pollyanna* or become a famous star. The two kids were put into the local village school that was composed mostly of black students. The Mills kids were really shaken when they found that the Tobagoan kids were better at algebra than they were, and if they didn't do two hours homework every night they could not keep up with the class! But at lunchtime, if we were working nearby they could come and swim with their parents.

One day they were swimming around with Bahloo, when Mary came up sputtering, "How disgusting. I've just swallowed a mouthful of elephant turds!" The kids thought it sensationally funny, especially since they usually saw their mother sitting sedately at a typewriter working on some serious play.

The pirate attack, led by the famous Japanese actor, Sessue Hayakawa, intrigued everyone, because no director had ever been called upon to shoot such a fun kind of battle — with its mixture of drama and comedic defence by a normal peace-loving family.

In the script, after a family conference at the tree-house, where everyone contributes ideas on how to defend themselves with the resources at hand, Pa Robinson devises a series of land-mines; trip wires to allow hidden arrows to be fired from the trees; a bridge over the lagoon which collapses when the pirates cross it; stacks of logs which roll down and crush the assailants on the hill; and barrages of exploding coconut bombs! No one was ever more excited at throwing the coconut bombs than Dorothy McGuire, who had always played serious dramatic roles during her brilliant career at Twentieth Century-Fox.

The lunch break during this shoot held a unique fascination for all of us. Sessue had brought over a Japanese lady who looked after him like a geisha. As he reclined under a sunshade, she fed him with titbits, massaged his feet and shoulders, and pillowed his head on her lap when he felt like a snooze. The stunt boys were most envious of him and used to ask him how he got such service and feminine attention. He would just smile inscrutably, in the same way he used to do when watching them play their games of poker in the evening.

One evening, stuntman Ken Buckle said casually, "You ever played this game, Sessue?" Sessue smiled and shrugged.

"Like to sit in?" said Steve Dahl, another stuntman. "We'll soon teach you the rudiments." They planned to make a fool out of Sessue, and maybe punish him for his cruelty to the British prisoners of war in *The Bridge on the River Kwai*. But, of course, when it came to playing poker he beat the lot of them, because night by night he had been craftily studying their game.

There was another time when Ken Buckle asked him, "You ever done judo, Sess?" Now, Sessue was at least sixty-three, and *they* were all between twenty and forty. He raised his eyebrows and smiled, "Once I did try a few throws,'" he said. "Perhaps tomorrow on the beach?" And there, in front of the whole crew he threw all twenty stunt boys, one after the other. From that moment everyone loved him and begged him to tell the secret of his strength, and his way with the ladies!

Meanwhile, we continued to put impossible shots with animals and people onto film and, for the most part, were having fun in doing so. However, I discovered poor Yak was having a great struggle to achieve the shark attack shots to cut in with our material. The studio had allocated two Special Effects men who had worked at Disneyland but never on a movie. They were trying to tow a wooden log with a phoney metal fin through the water when I heard Yak cry, "For Christ's sake! Ken says he knows a guy who can tickle up a genuine grey nurse. Why don't we try the real thing?" So Clive Reed, one of my assistants, brought Robbie-of-the-Big-Feet to the Blue Haven Hotel and they threw a grey nurse shark into the pool *and tried to make it look aggressive.* For a whole week my unit came back all hot and sweaty after shooting and couldn't use the pool because the shark was in occupation! They listened to the sad tales of Yak and his crew. Suddenly, two of them said, "To hell with the shark!" and jumped into the pool. None of them were bitten or even scratched. So eventually Yak got a shot by fastening a cable to the shark and pulling it along the surface of the pool.

The scene where the boys and Janet Munro find the zebra stuck in a quicksand and surrounded by vultures was another problem for Yak. He had found an old quarry, almost a pit, with high rock walls and only a small gully spilling into it, which could easily be blocked. He had dug a shallow hole, filled it with liquefied bran, and stood the zebra in it. Vultures were wired to rocks nearby, then he released the six hyenas. While far from going *anywhere near* the zebra, two of them made straight for the camera crew while the other four tried to scale the cliffs. Yak was prepared. He had brought an old wooden chair, which wranglers often use to defend themselves with. He held off the two threatening hyenas while his four wranglers pulled lariats from their belts and expertly lassoed the rock-climbing beasts. I witnessed all this during a lunch break, when I came to visit. It was exciting stuff and Yak was in his element. "Don't worry about this one," he grinned. "I'll beat those sons-of-bitches." And a week later we saw some wonderful rushes establishing the scene.

Now I had to match the scene in close-ups with my actors. For this we only needed a couple of vultures, one hyena (tethered!) and the poor zebra, which now had to appear to make an effort to pull itself out of the bran 'quicksands'. It was scared and just stood in the hole. Mitch came up behind me and produced his 'hot rod' — a device capable of delivering small electrical shocks. "This is the only way you'll move her, sir," he said. So, we hid him behind a rock, fixed the hot rod (like a bicycle pump) to a pole and pushed it into the bran hole. As he switched the current on and off, the zebra jumped — very convincingly for the scene — and I proceeded to bring the kids beside the animal and in eight or ten different set-ups, shot the scene where they rescue it.

Unfortunately, during this time Pauline came for lunch carrying a bottle of cold Pouille Fuisse. She took one look at our shooting and said, "I'm afraid I can't stay for lunch, darling. I know you have to do it, but I can't bear to see that poor animal suffer." No amount of explanation or persuasion would convince her that the pain was minimal — I even went so far as to have the hot rod put on my own butt. She nodded and said, "Perhaps you're tougher than she is, poor thing," and departed. Kay, the script clerk, didn't like it either, but she had to stay because her notes were essential for the matching of the close-ups which we were putting into the can.

I don't remember the same fuss when Jimmy and Tommy Kirk fought the anaconda. I first shot this sequence with two American doubles, Chuck and Lauren Courtney. In discussion with Wesley, the snake handler, we decided there was really very little to it — the anaconda is a constricting water snake that has to come up for breath when it is in the water, just like humans. The trick of setting up a fight with it was for one of the boys always to hang onto the anaconda's head. When we saw the material assembled, the sequence roughed out by the doubles looked fine. But now Jimmy and Tommy had to study it closely so as to match the various parts of the action in close-ups — which would prove that it was they who really fought the snake. After several evenings of studying the material, they came to me individually and proposed in a secretive sort of way that I should let them redo the *whole* fight. They had been pumping the doubles about every reaction they had felt, just how difficult it was, and now they wanted to show they could do it all themselves. They put up arguments like, "It's unfair to try and cheat the audience."

"I'll never be able to live with myself if people begin to suspect it isn't really me," said Tommy, becoming all macho. I discussed the matter with Bill Anderson who didn't like it, especially from the insurance point of view, but he eventually agreed that if it would make them happy and get a better scene, let them try. The day came.

Joyce Bullifant, now Jimmy's wife, came to Pauline and said, "He didn't sleep at all last night — he was kicking and struggling — look, my legs are black and blue. Does Ken really insist on his going through with it?"

But now it was a contest between Jimmy and Tommy as to who was chicken. They gargled with disinfectant, jumped into the water, wrestled with the snake for five minutes while I covered the whole action, long shot, medium, and close-ups with three cameras. *They* would have gone on for hours but the snake got cold and had to be put in his box under an arc until his blood flowed normally again. At least that's what Wesley said!

While we were in the swamp, I had to put Janet Munro into breast-high murky water, and lay an ugly looking three foot iguana on an overhanging branch. She had to put her hand on to its tail. It turned and spit; she registered wonderful horror, dived into the water and came up with no complaints. In fact, the only moan Janet ever made to me was when she was thrown head first off the zebra during the race. She rose slowly from the sand, rubbing her butt and as she passed within afoot of me, she hissed from the corner of her mouth, "I don't know why I do all these crazy things for you."

In the last three reels of the picture, Janet was our romantic interest, and supposed to look very pretty, but her skin had coarsened in the constant sunshine and she was lonely. She was, in fact, twenty-seven playing sixteen, and did not have anything in common with the boys in the cast. Most of the crew had made various liaisons with local women or were being faithful to their wives in England — which seemed a long way away, and which some were beginning to doubt they'd ever see again!

Pauline and I visited Janet one Sunday and found her surrounded by press cuttings and two empty bottles of brandy — this was the extent of her loneliness — and though we put the word out that she be included in whatever social activities went on, she continued to hit the brandy so much that Harry Waxman complained that he could no longer cope with her in close-ups. As Ernie, the camera operator, and I looked at her through the lens and view-finder, I had a quick vision of a sad-faced Glynis Johns and how Rossano Brazzi had brought life back to her performance (in my movie *Loser Takes All*). Yes, I'll give you one guess!

Half-seriously, I whispered to Ernie, "Well, there's nothing else for it, someone in the crew will have to sacrifice himself. We've got to get some sparkle back into those eyes." Ernie took the hint, but the two of them were so circumspect in their affair that it was weeks before I knew, and all the time he was passing on to Janet my frustrated, derogatory comments about her appearance. It didn't help my relationship with an actress I was really very fond of, and it taught me a lesson never to discuss actors with a member of the crew.

One day in mid-December, Bill came over to me at lunch with a long face. "I have to tell you, Ken, this is becoming a nightmare. We're nearly three weeks over and from the calls I'm getting from Walt, something's really eating him! He seems to know everything that's going on and he's making noises about pulling the plug."

I shrugged. "As you know, for one reason or another, we've been shooting bits of everything but very few sequences are complete. He would have no picture if we stopped now, Bill."

"Well, we've got to think of something," he growled.

"I'm very willing to listen to any ideas you may come up with," I replied, "but until then I'm just going to put my head down and press on with what I know Walt really wants." And I walked off. Bill was really on my side, but as I have had to show producers on numerous occasions since, if you know that you are onto something really good, something which has a chance of success, you won't make a good movie unless you are really tough and dig in your heels.

It was only months later that we discovered what had been really getting to Walt. His favourite and most trusted talent was now the British Matte painter, Peter Ellenshaw. As usual, Peter was going to add scope and magic to some of our shots, but this time instead of painting them comfortably back at the studio, he had decided to actually paint on a glass screen fixed in front of our camera, while our live action was taking place. There were four such shots in which he was going to add a second pirate ship — to save the cost of building another.

Peter had arrived in Tobago all ready to get the shots painted and done with, but it was twenty-two days before we were able to arrange for him to complete them. Each night Basil and Bill had to consider the weather, the availability between three units, the provision of each unit with props, costumes and cast, without overlapping. And it often meant that the Matte painter, however important he was, would have to wait.

It was a bad tactical error. Peter felt slighted, and when he returned to the studio he poured poison into Walt's ear about our *Swiss Family* production, and the way it was being run. We were inefficient, having fun and not caring when we returned home. So naturally Walt was peeved and beginning to lose faith in us. And now the weather turned so foul that we wondered how we had ever swum and surfed or thought Tobago to be a paradise!

The skies opened and dropped two metres of rain in three days. Our studio, fortunately constructed on a big concrete slab, was an oasis in a sea of mud. It was our only place to go on shooting. We had the tree-house set moved inside and shot all the interior dialogue scenes. But the rain battered so hard against the studio's tin roof and iron panels, that I could hardly hear the words the actors were saying, It became a matter of lip-reading for them — quite ridiculous one might say! Why not wait for the storm to pass? But it did not pass, and we were behind schedule. Walt was angry! So we shot and because I had decided to post-synchronise the dialogue anyway, eventually it did not matter. A few days before Christmas the weather began to improve and we were able to complete sequence after sequence, rushing back into the studio whenever the 'liquid sunshine', as our smiling drivers used to call it, became too prolonged.

A shot with a tiger, which I had been putting off and off, had to be done. Walt had devised, in addition to the other hazards the pirates had to face, a tiger trap. We shot the exterior and got a wonderful thirty seconds of our three stuntmen leaping up in the air as the tiger jumped out of the pit. That had taken some courage and arranging, but now I had to build suspense — audience anticipation — by showing the tiger waiting angrily in the pit. Rather than digging a hole for the camera (and none of the camera crew were prepared to share the location pit with the tiger!), we built a pit upwards, in the studio. I asked Mel how high we should build it to be safe.

"Oh, twelve feet, I reckon," he replied. "Jacko couldn't jump more than that from a standing start." So we built a platform eighteen feet from the ground and pointed the camera down into the constructed hole. We watched Mel lead the tiger onto the stage, open a door into the hole, and push the tiger inside and lock the door. Jacko took one look at us standing beside the camera and without apparently making the slightest effort, leaped up and passed through the tripod legs without disturbing the camera — though I distinctly heard Ernie gasp as its fur passed by his crotch! The tiger landed gracefully on the stage floor, its tail switching and began to move around making low guttural murmurs. The part of the crew we unkindly call the 'lay-abouts"'— makeup, hairdresser, costume assistants, publicity, etc. — scattered as everyone shouted, "Mel!"

Like Daniel in the lion's den, Mel appeared holding the customary wooden chair, with bared legs. The tiger stopped in front of him, but instead of holding it with the chair, Mel punched it right on the nose. "You lousy son-of-a-bitch!" he yelled. "The moment I turn my back on you!" The tiger sat down meekly while he put the chain around its neck and led it back into the pit set. We could hear him talking to her, "Now you stay in there. And when I yell, look up, you look up! But if you jump again I'll belt the living daylights out of you!" He unhooked the chain, and backing out with his forefinger pointed as to a naughty child, he yelled to us, "Roll! For Christ's sake, roll the goddamn camera!" We rolled and got exactly the shot I needed. For me, all the tiger shots were a must no matter how long they took or whatever they cost, because the tiger was truly Walt's baby!

Back in the script-creating days Walt had said, "And 'Moochie' says why don't I catch that tiger that's been snooping around? We can dig a pit and put him inside, and then when the pirates come creeping up he'll wake him and say, Gosh, I'm hungry, a pirate is just what I fancy. His brothers will pooh-pooh the idea, but Pa Robinson will encourage him." This was the beginning of all my problems with the tiger. I remembered my experiences in Africa with the wild animals (*Nor the Moon by Night*). I suggested to Walt that perhaps a lion might be easier to work with, but Walt jumped back at me.

"Oh-ho," he said. "At last we've found something Ken's afraid of. If you're scared to film the tiger, I'll come out with a sixteen mili camera and shoot it myself!" And so throughout the scripting sessions, the jibbing went on and built up. Because I had opposed an idea "from the top" of his head, Walt was determined to milk the tiger sequences. This led to:

A)   we had to see a tiger wandering freely around the tree-house;

B)   we had to see the dogs attack it. Walt said, "I don't care how you do it, but we must see the two Great Danes make contact with the tiger and knock it into a net. You can build the sequence up in cuts but I gotta see those dogs hit the tiger — *in the same shot!*" This had led to us having to find the Great Dane who had hunted mountain lion, and the poor old tiger had to have her front claws out and her incisor teeth filed down, and God had to be with us when we tried to get the shot (which fortunately for me He was!).

C) No matter how carefully we rigged the pit shot with the stuntmen, no one could guarantee that they might not get mauled when the tiger sprung out of the pit and chased them. And no one could really forecast whether we could recapture the tiger before it could run amuck all over the island!

But there was Mel, hidden behind a tree and yelling instructions and obscenities at his animal, and she obeyed him. Mel, who had a string of animal scenes in Hollywood movies to his credit, was a remarkable man — tremendously courageous and tough with his animals, but always fair. Unfortunately, five years after *Swiss*, Nemesis caught up with him and he was mauled in MGM Studios by a tiger and died.

Whatever Walt might think, we had to take Christmas Day and New Year's Day as holidays. Pauline and Joyce had discovered that the local doctor was an exceptionally kind-hearted man who invariably filled the two hospitals on Tobago at Christmas with as many black kids as possible. This way they had a chance to have more comforts and attention than they otherwise would have had. The crew started a fund to buy toys and candies for Christmas stockings, and on Christmas morning, each member of the crew who wanted to feel the spirit of the day, trooped into the hospital, gave out presents and joined in the carol singing. The joy on most of those little faces was something we have never forgotten — because, although by no means were they starving, most of them had never seen or held a manufactured toy or doll.

New Year's Eve was something really special, too. Sir Edward Beetham was the last white governor of Tobago.

He had been representative of the Throne in Malaysia, South Africa, and America, and was now basking in his last easy posting, in a superb white mansion sitting on top of a tree-lined slope overlooking the harbour. We had provided free entertainment for his wife and two daughters on numerous occasions, and now to celebrate New Year, Johnny Mills and Mary, Dorothy McGuire and John Swope, Bill Anderson, Pauline and I were invited to join the Governor's party.

There was a great rushing around to press evening gowns and tuxedos (and to remove the mildew which had quickly formed on our clothes in our closets and suitcases). We arrived at Government House, looking as smart as we could and were served champagne. Each one of us had a white-gloved waiter standing at our shoulders, ready to replenish our glasses. Then, in two Rolls Royce limousines, and flying 'corps diplomatic' pennants, we swept past the rows of coconut trees and cabins we knew so well, to the Robinson Crusoe Hotel. This was the oldest building on the island, wooden and gaudily painted, and to me reminiscent of the stories of Robert Louis Stevenson and Somerset Maugham in the South Seas.

His Excellency held out his arm for Pauline, and I offered mine to Lady Beetham. To the strains of 'God Save The Queen', played by the champion steel band of the Caribbean, we marched up the steps. The whole island seemed to be present, certainly all the one hundred sixty-two British residents, plus a large contingent of well-to-do or politically important black people. They could not have sung the National Anthem with more loyal voices if the Queen herself had been present. The meal and conversation was stimulating, with everyone reminiscing about their lives and experiences quite different from the crazy lives we movie people live. I remarked on the fantastic diamond ring Lady Beetham was wearing. She flung her arm back in the most blasé way and said, "I got it for launching a battleship, young man."

On the stroke of twelve everyone rose, joined hands and spread out in a vast circle to sing 'Auld Lange Syne'. I have never kissed or been kissed by so many people ringing in the New Year. And the dancing that followed to the strains of a calypso band still brings goose pimples to my whole being.

As the New Year dawned, we staggered back to the tree-house to pick up close-ups for the race. The sun was suddenly so hot that our two ostriches started to wilt and had to shelter under the umbrellas put up for Dorothy McGuire and Johnny Mills. That day the animals were more important than the actors!

Meanwhile, high up in the branches of the big tree, Eddie Fowlie was laboriously securing our forty-odd monkeys in visible positions. On this movie, Eddie was officially our property master, but in reality was a jack-of-all-trades, doing everything no one else on the crew wanted to do. I had first met Eddie back in my documentary days in Merton Park Studios, just outside London. He was a shaggy-headed rough diamond who would do anything for me. When the pig tipped over and looked like it might drown, who would be the first to swim out and right it? Eddie! Who would jump first into the smelly mangrove swamp to clear the way for the actors? Eddie. Who would sneak up beside me and suggest how to improve a special effect? Eddie.

Now, I wanted monkeys — which had proved to have a nasty bite — sitting on the branches above the tree-house. Eddie had sat up nights making little leather belts attached to wires, which he was now securing to branches.

Without being tethered to the tree, we knew the whole troop would take off — as they did soon afterwards, never to be filmed again, and to father all the families of monkeys now infesting the forests of Tobago! Suddenly, Bill Anderson arrived on the set with Basil Keys. They seemed very distressed. I saw them call Eddie down, and a big argument began to develop. Eddie swung on his heel and strode over to me. He stuck out his hand. "Sorry, Gov. I gotta go."

"Go? Go where?" I frowned.

"Home, Gov. Back to Blighty." He nodded towards Bill and Basil. "They'll tell you about it."

"To hell with that," I cried. "Are the monkeys all fixed?"

Eddie shook his head. "No, Gov. I've only had time to fix about ten of the little buggers."

"Then, get back up in the tree and I'll sort things out."

I saw tears forming in Eddie's eyes. "No, Gov, not this time." He held out his hand. "Sorry, Gov, don't think too bad of me." And he loped away across the field.

Bill and Basil were walking toward me with long faces, and before I could really blow my top, they managed to explain that while we had been seeing-in the New Year, a high drama had been taking place on Blue Haven Beach. Eddie had been living in a caravan with a dark-haired, big busted, Gypsy-looking girl called Frieda, whom he adored. Sprucing himself up to see the New Year in, Eddie had gone into the Blue Haven Bar to find no sign of his girl. The stunt boys and everybody on the crew knew better than to tangle or to flirt with Frieda. "I think she went for a stroll on the beach," Ken Buckle told him.

"Alone?" yelled Eddie. Several of the stunt guys shook their heads.

"Who was it?" yelled Eddie.

"None of our boys," said Joe Wadham, leader of the stuntmen.

Eddie looked around. "Where's Gordon?' (Gordon was a newcomer to the Special Effects crew.) Everyone shrugged, but a voice piped up, "Said something about going for a skinny-dip, Eddie." Eddie rushed down the steps on to the beach, but now it was too dark to see anything. Beating his head like a wounded animal, Eddie dashed into the native boys' quarters and came out a few seconds later swinging a panga. He rushed to the water's edge and apparently found Frieda and Gordon prancing around naked. Eddie felled Frieda in a blow, then chased Gordon into the sea yelling that he was going to chop his balls off. They struggled under the big breakers until Ken Buckle and three other stunt guys separated them.

The crew and cast were getting restive as they saw us arguing, so Bill and Basil took my arms and led me into the tree-house kitchen. "You must understand," said Bill. "Walt could never tolerate such behaviour."

"But he's my Best Boy. Who else would fasten monkeys up in the tree?"

"Fuck the monkeys," said Basil. "With all these people around, someone is bound to leak this to the press."

"Let's wait 'til they do," I argued. "I'll sort Eddie out. He'd never break a promise made to me."

By this time, Len Shannon, the publicity man, had joined us "You've got to listen," yelled Len. "I'm here to protect Walt's image. Imagine what it would do to him if Variety comes out with a headline 'Near Murder On Disney's Swiss Family Set.'"

"But no one was killed", I yelled back. "It was just a drunken brawl. You can't just throw away twenty weeks of shooting for one stupidity on New Year's Eve!" Bill tried to pacify me. "Listen, Ken, I know how much Eddie means to you."

"He's like my brother," I gesticulated. "My right hand!"

"I know all that," said Bill. "And if it had been any other picture he'd have probably gotten away with it, but Walt is special to all of us." We argued for another hour, and of course I lost. Eddie was packed off with Frieda on the next plane to London. We never worked together again, but David Lean picked him up for *Lawrence of Arabia*. And since that time David never made a movie without Eddie. Over the years, he gave him two Rolls Royces and kept him on his payroll through long preparation periods, so much so that Eddie was never free to work on another movie for me — a constant regret. Every director of big movies needs a rugged, offbeat guy like Eddie — the salt of the earth. Without his kind of talent and devotion, we could never attempt many of the things we do.

The shooting finished on *Swiss*, and we had a wrap party in our tin shack studio. Five hundred black faces passed in front of Pauline and me, grabbing our hands, crying and saying, "God bless you and come back again soon." We swore that we would and then flew directly to London.

Walt had never visited us on location, though, of course, our dailies (rushes) had always been seen by him in the studio — even before we saw them. But now, to my surprise, he was *not* insisting on the picture being edited and finished in Burbank. So, I completed the visual editing in London and brought back the whole cast to work in the re-recording studio in Pinewood. For twenty-eight days I sweated in the theatre remaking every word *the actors had spoken.*

When all our post-synchronisation tracks had been edited, the resulting dialogue was clear and clean and occasionally improved on the original — supporting a theory of mine, that one should always concentrate on shooting the best possible visual — the sound can always be taken care of later, so long as you, the director, make sure that the original lines are mouthed absolutely correctly, and have the support of top sound editors and recordists.

I was already getting involved with another movie *(The Coming-Out Party),* so Bill Anderson flew home with the 'married print' and apparently ran headlong into Big Trouble. "How dare you take the *title* of producer!" flared Walt, as the credits went up on the first projection.

"Because I was there for every foot of the shooting," said Bill. "And every stage of post-production!"

"But it's my *baby.* I developed it from the first thought ...and you are still only my studio Head of Production!"

For once, Bill put up an argument against Walt, with the result that, for the first time, our movie went out under the banner of 'Walt Disney Presents'. I was told later that Walt ran the picture with Bill a half-dozen times, made a few small changes, tried it out on his usual test audience composed of studio employees, and finally said, "I can't see anything we can do better. It's what we set out to make. Let's see what the kids say."

Swiss Family Robinson was released and became the studio's greatest moneymaker for many years. And even in its second and third re-releases, at seven year intervals, it made much more than the picture cost. Apparently that always remained a sore point with Walt. The picture cost just over four million dollars, and he could never get out of his mind, the stories of waste and muddle brought back by the disgruntled Peter Ellenshaw.

In England, *Swiss Family* ran for two uninterrupted years at Studio One, the regular London cinema for Disney films, breaking all records. Suddenly, Walt came over again with Lillian. He sent a message that he wanted to talk to me about Sir Walter Scott's great classic 'Westward Ho'.

"Larry Watkins (who wrote the scripts for *Robin Hood and His Merrie Men* and *Sword and the Rose*)" said Walt "has been playing around with the adventures of your greatest pirate, Sir Francis Drake. He looted Spanish galleons in the Caribbean, sailed round Cape Horn and up the coast of California. There are bags of material, but we just don't seem to be able to get a handle on a good storyline. My hunch is that we should kick it around together, as we did with *Swiss*.

I was already smiling.

Pauline and I were now living in a pleasant but small apartment in Onslow Square, London, together with my oldest daughter, Jane. So, together, we decided to put on a very special dinner, with the best white and red wines, and before-dinner drinks. During our visits to the States, we had observed that Americans always seemed to need two or three double bourbons or vodkas before they partook of food. Over dinner Pauline talked mainly to Lillian, whose glass I seemed to be refilling more often than usual. Walt enjoyed telling Jane stories about his early efforts in cartoons. He even offered her a job in Disneyland, on our return to California.

Everything sounded good, and having quickly reread 'Westward Ho', I proceeded to talk about the scenes I would like to see in the movie. Walt still had a few worries about American kids and their changing tastes, but it began to look as though we were almost set to make the movie the following year in either California or Hawaii.

Around eleven o'clock Walt's limousine arrived. We shook hands, Walt kissed Pauline, and I kissed Lillian. She began descending the six stone steps into Onslow Square, teetered and fell, sprawling on the ground. I rushed down to help her and was raising her to her feet when Walt took over. Brusquely, he pushed me aside and led her limping to the car.

As we waved them away and closed the door, Pauline said, "You'll never work for Walt, again."

"Don't be ridiculous," I said. "We've practically made a deal on 'Westward Ho'."

She shook her head. "I know Walt, he'll never forgive you for witnessing that!"

Although it seemed absurd, she proved to be right. To my everlasting surprise and sorrow, I never did work for Walt again — nor did he ever make a movie out of 'Westward Ho'.

CHAPTER TEN
Striving With New Challenges...
Near Disaster In Pretoria...
Recover... And Back Again
To Comedies

When you finish a movie like *Swiss Family Robinson* you feel there must be some big offer just around the corner, but — of course — it is usually six to eight months before the picture is released, and you have become 'hot' — if you are lucky.

Sydney Box was now back producing small family films for his wife Muriel to direct. He was also putting together deals for his sister Betty — now making a successful series of 'Doctor' comedies; or for her husband Peter Rogers, making even wilder and lower comedies with his 'Carry On' series. They were all teamed up with directors and, in any case, I would not have wanted to be involved.

So, I decided to try another agent, Dennis Van Thal, who had been casting director during my period with Sir Alexander Korda. He had just formed London Management, and jumped at the chance of representing me. But still nothing exciting came on offer. Perhaps I had been spoiled by *Swiss Family Robinson*. I must admit that I secretly felt that I might have reached the peak of my career and would never have such a wonderful film experience again!

I decided to develop another adventurous subject my old friend Guy Elmes had been writing. This was set in Ethiopia, at that time another mysterious land. The theme of Guy's story was greed and what it does to three people when they are thrown together seeking a fortune in gold. As they get deeper and deeper into the desert they are plagued by unseen enemies with no chance of a plane finding them when they are lost. This time we had three great parts, an American flyer, a beautiful but spoiled heiress, and an Ethiopian doctor. Dorothy McGuire came over to London and became so enthused about Guy's script that Pauline and I decided to invest two thousand pounds for a trip to Ethiopia by Guy and John Howell — Guy to gather true atmosphere and John to find locations, costs, and bring back photos.

They did their job magnificently, and soon I was chasing stars to give me a solid basis for setting up our masterpiece. Through Peter Finch, who had worked with her (and made love to her) on *Bhowani Junction*, I met with Ava Gardner. She looked wonderful — the sexiest woman I have ever met. She seemed to like the idea, but hoped the film could be shot in Spain, and refused to even look at the script till her agent, Freddie Fields, had approved it. I knew from the experience with Brando, that Freddie wouldn't talk to me until I had a deal for the movie with a major studio, and that no studio would make a deal with me for a picture of this size until I had a star!!

Guy had met and married a beautiful Hungarian refugee who had set up beauty parlours in the fashionable Capri and Rome. Her clients included top stars like Elizabeth Taylor, Audrey Hepburn, Gina Lollobrigida and Sophia Loren. So, we made a trip to Rome and met Gina who took the same attitude as Ava — but was a bit more rude about it! Sophia was living with Carlo Ponti, who was an important producer and could actually finance movies..

Sophia read the script and loved the female role. It was indeed gutsy, sexy and appealed to her especially because she finished up with the Ethiopian — a daring thing in those days — after all, he was black, but not Negro! Sophia pointed out that she had made *Two Women* and *Legend of the Lost* in which she had endured tough location conditions. She would love to film in Ethiopia, where an uncle had lost his life in Mussolini's war against Haile Selassie. Carlo Ponti was more practical. "I don't want my girl having to carry the picture."

"There's a possibility I can get Omar Sharif for the Ethiopian doctor," I said. Carlo shook his head. "If you can get a bankable *American* star, then I think we could sell the project to MGM with whom I have a multi-picture deal."

So, we returned to London, where I met with Warren Beatty who was doing a publicity trip for *Splendor In The Grass*. He came to our flat and spent one whole Saturday afternoon talking but really saying nothing! Pauline was fascinated with his virile good looks, but I got the impression that he did not really want to be involved in a made-up adventure, no matter how well it was scripted. He was searching vaguely for something based on true characters known by the American public. Several years later he achieved this ambition magnificently in *Bonnie & Clyde*.

The most-likely candidate for my American was Robert Mitchum. He came to town to do some post-synchronising on *The Sundowners*, which he had just made in Australia. He was staying at the Savoy and my agent Dennis Van Thal set up a meeting. I arrived at his suite around five o'clock, as arranged, and found him sitting like a Buddha in a window alcove, backgrounded by the River Thames. His eyes seemed more hooded than usual and before we could have any discussions, he said, "Howdya like to smoke a few friendly joints with me?" At this time, in England we had heard about pot, but I had never been asked to smoke it before. I took a few puffs and then, politely, got rid of the joint.

Mitchum was morose but became lucid at intervals, telling me about the Irish film he was going to make. He never asked me what I had done or seemed at all interested. Around six o'clock a girl arrived and made straight for the bedroom, followed by three other women at approximately ten minute intervals. Beginning to feel I had not caught Mitchum at the right moment, I suggested that perhaps we should meet for dinner at another time.

"No, no, no," he replied. "Stick around. When they join us, you'll find this is gonna get very interesting." I stuck around, and the girls joined us in various states of relaxation and undress. I could see that very soon I was going to be tempted, but since I had come together with Pauline, I hoped that I had put this sort of thing behind me. Mitchum rose and went to the toilet. I followed him and there we held a five-minute discussion on *The Gold Lovers* and his role in it. So long as we shot the film in Italy, not too far from Rome, he said he could well be interested, in about eighteen months time, when his present commitments would be through.

"Keep in touch. Sorry you couldn't stay. These girls could make you feel like an Eastern potentate, which I thought would appeal to you after reading the sexy scenes in *Gold Lovers.*" We parted on good terms, but I felt he belonged to a very different world from the one I knew and felt comfortable in. Also, I really couldn't take 'all this crap!' I was a writer/*director* — a filmmaker — obviously not a true independent producer, prepared to wait and wait and court stars for years at a time. The great Sam Spiegel is reputed to have waited two years to hook Humphrey Bogart for *The African Queen* and had to create a special part for William Holden in *The Bridge on the River Kwai* because Guinness was not regarded as box-office alone for the U.S. market! I did not have all these years or patience for all I wanted to do!

Parallel with these efforts to woo stars, I had been exploring the possibilities of raising finance in the City of London — with merchant banks like Hill Samuel and the Baring Brothers (one of whom was actually a film producer). Here again, I found you went to endless meetings with enthusiastic executives, backed by so-called experts who spent hours making projections of potential profits out of figures taken from the air. If one was lucky enough to make a breakthrough, the head honcho would invariably come at you with a demand for impossible collateral!!

I was tossing around my experiences one day at Pinewood with my old friend and ally, Earl St. John. He knew that I knew he had been gradually castrated at Rank so far as the choice of subjects was concerned. John Davis, the financial wizard, had taken over. So, there was no question of my asking any favours of Earl.

As I poured out my frustrations, he leaned forward, put his hand over mine, and said, "The star system was fine for the big studios, but now with the stars taking over the store, chasing them is futile for someone like you. And as for seeking financial backing for your own subjects, that is a world for hustlers, liars, and gamblers — none of which you are." He leaned back and ordered another double gin and tonic. "I'll probably be plastered all afternoon — "cause, as you know, I can't drink." He shrugged, and then studied me.

"An actor you gave his first chance to, David Tomlinson, has brought me a script which I think could be commercial. J.D. won't go along with it because Tomlinson is on his hate-list. Do you know Jack Davies?"

I nodded vaguely. "I met him in the RAF in my pantomime days with Delderfield."

Earl nodded. "Jack is a very underestimated writer. He concocted *Doctor At Sea* for Betty Box, and quietly knocks out all the Norman Wisdom comedies."

"Knock-about comedy!" I said, rather impatiently. "But great box-office," smiled Earl. "Jack has an uncanny knowledge of the old music hall gags, and all the routines of Chaplin, Keaton, Harold Lloyd... He trots them out very successfully for our British *little man.*"

"So?" I asked.

"I have a hunch he's capable of much more — shall we say legitimate comedy — and you might be the one to organise and give his work substance."

"After *Across The Bridge* and *Swiss Family Robinson,* I don't think I want to do more comedies," I said.

Earl breathed deeply. "You like big audiences and success. The script I'm talking about is based on escapes by RAF guys during the war — Jack wrote it and I think still owns it. Why don't you let me set up a meeting between the two of you?"

"But what if Rank won't finance the bloody thing?" I said, making a useless gesture with my hands. Earl nodded wisely. "I've been nurturing a kind of subsidiary at Beaconsfield. If you can lick the subject into shape, they'll back it, I assure you."

And so Jack Davies came into my life and became my great collaborator. We shared the same sense of humour and creatively, we brought out the best in each other... until the monster Cancer got hold of him. We were writing a comedy called *Spooks Anonymous* in Palm Desert when he died in the mid-Nineties. I still miss him deeply.

In *Very Important Person*, Jack had taken a normally serious dramatic situation and made a very original comedy out of it. The action was set in a prisoner-of-war camp somewhere in Germany, and the story required a high-ranking British boffin to be helped escape. Professor Pease — eventually played by James Robertson Justice — had crash-landed on a mission designed to inform him whether some screwy secret weapon would, in fact, sabotage the German war effort. Now his whole future and patriotic usefulness lay in the hands of a group of British 'silly asses' — or so it seemed to him!!

British comedians like Leslie Phillips, Eric Sykes, and a new Scottish comedian Stanley Baxter, who was proving on television that he could be quite brilliant as a man of many faces and characters, would play our silly asses. Jack and I worked together on the structure of the film for a week or so, and I felt so relaxed and so enjoyed our sessions that, I agreed to make this low-budget British movie.

The shooting took place in mid-winter in and around the Beaconsfield Studios — which were not even a quarter the size of Pinewood. Apart from the short days when we had to stop shooting exteriors at two forty-five pm, everything went smoothly. The scenes played well, and I found myself a wonderful new first assistant, Clive Reed, who had been working with the second unit on *Swiss Family Robinson*. He was clearly going to be another Peter Bolton.

V.I.P or *A Coming-Out Party*, as it was called in America, was launched well by Rank — despite John Davis' original objections — and had enthusiastic notices. It was sufficiently successful that soon afterwards it was chosen to represent British films at the San Sebastian Film Festival. Pauline and I were invited and treated like royalty. I remember we entered the theatre under an arch of swords, held most inconsequentially by men dressed as Spanish peasants. We were led into the Royal Box and applauded by a very full house.

Unfortunately, the committee had insisted that as the show only started at ten pm we partake of a feast of fish at a supposedly top restaurant. Pauline, though not being partial to fish, had been persuaded to eat calamari (octopus legs) and halfway through my film, she began to have terrible stomach cramps. She leaned over to me and said she must leave.

I shook my head and said, "You can't! Everybody will think you hate my movie!" Terrible to admit, I made her stick it out to the bitter end! As everyone applauded and filed out, I arranged for her to be taken back to the hotel, while I went on to another party to gather acclaim — which seemed to be the order of the evening.

All very enjoyable, but not quite so enjoyable without my darling wife, whom at two am I found hallucinating in the bedroom. When dawn came, the flowers started to arrive: Twenty-six bouquets, mostly gladioli, which Pauline looked at and groaned. "Take them away! They're going to attack me! I can see it in their eyes." She screamed and continued through a nightmare of imaginary persecution throughout the day. I was as sympathetic as I could be and tried to slip away quietly to perform the minimum commitments I had as leader of the British delegation to the Festival.

The final day, Pauline was able to join the fun again and was rewarded by being introduced to the joys of peaches and champagne, by Billie Whitelaw, who had come out to add some glamour to the British contingent. We enjoyed every moment with her, and I've always regretted that I was never able to use her in a movie, because I think she has proved to be one of the most genuine working class actresses in Britain.

Dennis Van Thal now sent me along to meet with Irwin Allen and Cubby Broccoli at the headquarters of Warwick Films. This company had a multi-deal with Columbia and was perhaps the most important Independent making movies in the U.K. (Cubby went on to produce nearly all of the Bond movies.) Sitting opposite each other at an antique partner desk — and I understand they never made any deals without the other hearing every word — they offered me a Western to be made in South Africa. Since both Pauline and I had wonderful memories of that country, I decided to accept the assignment.

The script for *The Hellions* had been adapted from an American play by Jaime Uys, a young and very prolific maker of Boer films (and later actor/producer/director/writer of the very successful *The Gods Must Be Crazy)*. Jaime showed no signs of this wonderful sense of comedy, as we shot *The Hellions*. He was playing a small-time general storekeeper — a role that seemed to fit him to a T, since as co-producer he worried about every small detail of the production and the budget. Fortunately, Irwin had given me Richard Todd as the real star, plus three wonderful British character actors, Lionel Jeffries, James Booth and Colin Blakely — all to make big names for themselves in later years. Irwin's girlfriend played the female lead — the less said about her the better!!

The cast quickly latched on to my idea of making *The Hellions* as a spoof of the normal American Western. With many laughs and broad gags — such as were used so successfully years later in *Cat Ballou*. We proceeded to shoot the film this way, until the strangest things began to happen to me.

Working north of Pretoria, in a dirty, mainly East Indian township called Brits, the temperatures soared into the hundreds. We used to eat lunches from open-air tables where the flies would swarm on the salads. The crew developed dysentery and kept taking days off. I suffered too, but continued to work until one afternoon my legs gave way beneath me. Clive Reed, who was functioning brilliantly as my first assistant, to my great horror and shame, had to help me climb out of a ditch where we'd placed the camera.

Returning to the hotel, I found I could only reach the bathroom by walking on my knees. Reduced to this state, we called the doctor. Both Pauline and I were reluctant to do this since we had become very staunch believers in homeopathy. A Dr. Van Rohen, a Boer, and the late Prime Minister's doctor, was sent to examine me and declared that I was suffering from heat exhaustion. I found this hard to believe because I had worked twice in Ceylon, five degrees from the Equator, with no trouble.

He gave me several injections and said he would come back again in the morning.

After a night of tossing and turning, I had to tell Pauline that I could not go out and shoot. The first time in my life that this had happened. Harold Huth, the British co-producer, and the good Clive came to my bedside and I gave them detailed instructions as to the set-ups to shoot, until the next day when I was sure the doctor would have me on my feet again.

Far from it! Shipped into a hospital by lunchtime, I was completely paralysed by nightfall from the waist downwards — with a growing paralysis developing in my shoulders. Pauline fought back the tears as I was taken into the operating theatre to be thoroughly examined and given a spinal drain.

Only weeks later did she tell me that the brusque Dr. Rohan had told her to face facts and be strong, because the paralysis might well reach either my heart or throat during the night. This would, of course, kill me. I had been diagnosed as having poliomyelitis.

Apparently, Pauline cried desperately throughout the night in the home of a newly made Boer friend. But there was no sign of crying, or what she had been told, as I looked up at her from my bed the next morning and admitted that I could not even move a toe on either paralysed limb. Although my right shoulder was difficult to move, I could still turn on my elbow using my left arm. The crippling paralysis had stopped. No one knew how long it might be before I might move. Pauline was told that there were twenty-six other cases of this epidemic in the area. Two had died.

'The Little Sisters of Mary' ran the hospital and I was allocated a pretty Irish nun in a blue habit. Nurse Storey was the one who comforted me by saying that as long as the paralysis did not return, this type of polio (and we learned there were six main types) should gradually disperse. The muscles and nervous system inevitably suffered some damage, but could at least be partly restored by therapy.

It sounded bad, but I could have been dead! On the information gleaned from Nurse Storey (not from my doctor) I determined that it would be up to me to work for the best recovery possible, but I planned to return to the filming in a wheel chair soon. My head and brain and determination were completely unaffected, so every night I insisted that Harold Huth and Clive come to my bedside. I would then describe in detail each set-up I would like them to make the next day. The actors came too, and I gave them as full a briefing as I could. Pauline stayed with me every hour of the day trying to be cheerful, reading to me, playing canasta and gin — allowing me to win quite often because I am a very bad loser (and she was afraid that getting worked up might delay my recovery!) She was wonderful, and I used to admit privately to her that if I did not recover or if I made only a partial recovery, I would somehow keep us going by writing. She announced that she would cheerfully go back to work.

I said, "You are wonderful and beautiful, but knowing what a director is and his needs on a location, I hope I never have to ask you to do that." She nodded ruefully, and went out to buy materials to start painting (which has proved to be a saviour for her sanity many times throughout later years).

Suddenly, on exactly the third week after my hospitalisation, Pauline arrived and I told her to pull back the clothes at the bottom of the bed. With a grin, I wiggled my left toe and we went mad with excitement. From that time on there was a little improvement in all my limbs each day. And after five days of this progress, I announced that I was definitely going to work in a wheelchair. Nurse Storey, who had already on a number of occasions pronounced that I was obstinate, over-impatient and trying to run before I could walk, said, "Okay. I'll have a wheelchair here for you in the morning."

Pauline helped me get dressed and Nurse Storey assisted me to stand and slide into the chair. Suddenly, she said quite casually to Pauline, "How wonderful it is that Ken is making this effort. How much everyone will admire him, but isn't it a pity that he will always be a cripple, never be able to play tennis again or perhaps even swim!" I looked up at her for a long moment and said, "Okay, you win. Help me back into bed."

Three weeks later we flew back to England and for five months I had daily therapy under the supervision of Dr. Sharma, my homeopath. He had not been allowed to come to South Africa because he was an Indian, but he had sent various homeopathic remedies, which I had secretly taken in the hospital.

Now he really went to town on my treatment, insisting some days that I work with his assistants as long as seven or eight hours. The result was that almost six and a half months to the day, I played my first game of tennis at the Hurlingham Club in London.

Now I thanked God that He had brought me into contact with Jack Davies. Either Jack would come to my flat in Onslow Square, or Pauline would drop me at his apartment in Bryanston Square and we would create comedy. The result was a script called *Crooks Anonymous* based on the very simple idea that you could cure habitual crooks like alcoholics, by making them call in reformed fellow-crooks as soon as they felt the urge to steal.

We milked every gag that Jack could remember from his early days in Music Hall (his aunt used to be fired from a cannon) and finished up with seven ex-cons all dressed as Santa Claus, trying to save each other in the vaults of Harrods's Store on Christmas Eve. All seven succumb to temptation and exit carrying sacks of loot, only to be sent back to replace everything by 'a good woman'.

Leslie Parkyn, who was now running Beaconsfield Studios, was only too happy to give us a home to make the picture, but let us down tragically over the top cast we had written the picture for. Alistair Sim was to have been our arch crook, supported by Joyce Grenfell, who played in most of this wily old star's comedies. We finished up with Wilfred Hyde-White, a fine actor, but basically straight, and Pauline Jameson, a competent character-actress.

Terry-Thomas should have been the incorrigible crook — Parkin settled for Stanley Baxter... and Leslie Phillips played the part written for Kenneth More. What we called 'the first team' would have cost probably five hundred thousand pounds extra — we finished up with the *whole picture* costing a quarter of that amount!

The exciting element for me was a new girl suggested by my daughter, Jane. Jane was now nineteen and attending the Central School of Drama in London. She had no aspirations to become an actress, but was learning all the aspects of theatre production. She told me that there was an outstanding young actress who had just graduated. She was not the traditional English rose, but had a special magnetism, determination and a good sense of both drama and comedy. Her name was Julie Christie.

Pauline and I took Julie out to dinner and were very impressed, except for the fact that she went around everywhere with a string bag containing all her belongings, and seemed to have no financial background and no permanent home! I made tests.

Everybody liked her, and Pauline arranged with one of the London costume houses to supply Julie with clothes for every-day wear, as well as for the movie. In London, it was not quite the time of the Carnaby Street hippy scene and actresses were still expected to dress reasonably respectably if you took them out to a restaurant.

But Julie was a natural hippy and we had the greatest difficulty in making her conform, but the result was worthwhile. Each day she would travel in my chauffeur driven car to and from the studios, and I would instruct her in basic film technique and acting as I saw it as a director. She listened patiently, intelligently, and performed in the studio as though she had done several movies. For eight weeks I became her Svengali and loved every minute of it.

Apart from Leslie Phillips and Stanley Baxter, Julie had to stand up against old hands like Wilfred Hyde-White, who although he always looked genial, was a crafty old bugger and knew how to steal a scene. Robertson Hare had been a stage and screen star in all the old Ben Travers farces. I had always been an admirer of his and had to stop myself making the same mistake of letting him run wild, as I had done with Peter Lorre.

Despite all my directorial efforts, *Crooks Anonymous* remained a typical low-budget picture, making a small profit to the very insular producer and British distributors. Once again, I learned you may write the best script in the world, but if it is a comedy depending on certain type of offbeat characters, unless you cast them with the A-team, it is all a complete waste of time and effort.

We accepted the 'second team' casting because the set-up with Independent Artists was easy, the cast were our friends, and I was exasperated with going out to seek independent financing. It is one of the regrets of my life that I did not stick out for dear old Alistair Sim, Joyce Grenfell and Terry-Thomas. If we had, I believe we would have finished up with as big a critical and commercial success, even in America, as *A Fish Called Wanda*.

CHAPTER ELEVEN
Surprise 'Pick-up' by Darryl Zanuck... Wonderful Experiences On The Longest Day

When *The Hellions* premiered in London, I was away in New York. Most of the critics panned the film for being uneven — which was not surprising since I had directed big portions of the scenes tongue-in-cheek while Harold Huth and Clive Reed, God bless them, had loyally tried to complete them but somehow had allowed everything to be played straight. One critic was especially vicious, writing "Ken Annakin has perhaps seen his best days. His work is slipshod, without direction. What might have been a brilliant spoof turns out to be a dismal mishmash!"

Pauline was so indignant that she broke my dictum that one should never tangle with a critic. She called him up and pointed out that he of all people knew very well what had happened in South Africa because he had headlined my illness in his column months ago. Apparently, he apologised saying, "My dear lady, I had completely forgotten. Of course that explains the discrepancies in the movie. I promise you, I'll make it up to Ken next time." Which he did. On a film called *The Fast Lady* he gave me the best notice I'd ever had for comedy!

In my experience, the critics are generally a rather sad and frustrated breed. They would all like to be writing novels or film scripts — but rarely succeed when given the chance! Week in, week out, the poor creatures sit through hours of movies in unhealthy projection rooms. No wonder they become weary and cynical. In order to exist at all, they try and write controversial columns to bolster their egos and build up reputations. For the most part they do not think about the damage some 'clever-clever' remark may do to an actor or filmmaker who has perhaps worked months, even years to put out the best show he or she could with the money, time and conditions available.

But to continue...

Jack Davies and I had just begun writing another comedy together when I received an intriguing phone call from Dennis Van Thal. Darryl Zanuck had arrived in town and was considering me to direct the British section of the war picture to end all war pictures called *The Longest Day*. I was not certain whether I wanted to make a war picture. I had become fond of Jack and didn't want to leave him high and dry.

"Take it," said Jack. "You love big movies and we can always put this one on the shelf until you come back — which sounds as though it will not be more than five or six weeks."

I never met Zanuck in London, but Dennis showed him some clips from *The Planter's Wife* and *Swiss Family Robinson* and made a deal for me to go over to Normandy immediately. I was to prepare and shoot for three weeks, then return for another three weeks in November. I arrived at the Hotel Royale in Caen, to find nobody there except a rather long-faced assistant, Sam Iskovitch. He had been asked to give me my portion of the script.

"I've done a preliminary breakdown," he said. "And if you like I can take you out to show you the locations." We jumped into his little Deux Cheveaux, and speeded out to the bridge over the Orne River (Pegasus Bridge), which was exactly as it had been when the British Commandos made their glider and parachute descent on it in 1944. They had come under heavy German fire from the auberge on the far side, and had had to take and overrun foxholes and sandbagged strong points, before Lord Lovatt was able to lead his force of British Commandos across the bridge and continue a triumphant campaign.

It was all there, and because it was history and very accurately researched for his book by Cornelius Ryan, the action would have to follow the pattern that it had taken in reality. It seemed to me that all I could do was to make sure that the fighting was tough, as accurate as possible, and exciting.

When we came back to the hotel, the two French Units had returned from their day's work and were sitting together at two long dining tables, laughing and joking like a well-knit film company. Sam and I were clearly on the outside — sitting at a small table twenty feet away. Suddenly, Zanuck walked in, said a few words to people at the two main tables, then came across to me. He asked Sam to leave and sat down in front of me.

After shaking hands, he forced a kind of smile, saying, "Sorry I couldn't meet you in London, Ken, but the logistics of this movie are a bitch." He looked me straight in the eye. "I know your work and know you can handle the British actors. What I want from this film is absolute truth. It must be war as it really was, not Hollywood war. I'm giving you a military expert who was on the spot to guide you, and in five day's time, Lord Lovatt will be arriving to tell us exactly how it looked from his point of view." He stood up and I rose too, nodding my head several times. A blonde secretary had come over and was chatting to him in slow French. (I discovered later that she was one of a team of four who worked round the clock to service 'the Dynamo'.) Zanuck moved off with her and then turned back to me.

"Sam is a good assistant," he said, "and can work the French Army extras efficiently. Augie Loman has rigged the gliders and tested them, and you'll have six of my twenty-eight Special Effects guys for your explosives and guns."

I swallowed deeply and nodded again. He walked a few more steps, studying a cable, then turned again. "I suggest that tomorrow you come out to Point de Hoche and watch Andrew 'Bundy' Marton shoot the GI's storming the beach and cliffs." I raised my hand in acknowledgment, and he was gone.

The beach was alive with landing craft and GI's (French soldiers in costume) rehearsing their runs up the sand. Sam introduced me to Alex Weldon and Karley Baumgarten, American and German explosive experts, who were carefully showing the leaders of each group where to avoid the shell-hits. Hanging from ropes on the cliff, about thirty French stuntmen were rehearsing hand over hand climbs and telling other Special Effects men where *not* to lay explosives!

As I walked along with Sam I pointed out Sal Mineo, Paul Anka and Fabian — all young pop stars that Zanuck obviously thought would attract the teenagers.

Then, who else should we run into but my old friend Rod Steiger, dressed as a Colonel. We went into a bear hug and he hissed in my ear, "Neither of us, will have the freedom to express ourselves on this one like in Spain, but it's gonna be a movie you can't afford not to be in!"

We agreed to have dinner together, and Sam was duly impressed with my familiarity with American stars. For my part, I wasn't exactly sure how I felt about *him*, because he had revealed to me that he was brought up as a guerrilla fighter in the Haganah, and had killed many British in Israel... but then I thought of my documentary friend Jim Phelan, the old Sinn Fein executioner, who had also killed my countrymen a quarter of a century ago. I decided you had to forget the past and take people as you found them *now* — there was always a background that you would never know.

Just before lunch everything was set for the first shot of the day, and from a position between cameras one and two, I watched the shooting. It is actually very rare that you ever get to watch another director at work, and I was horrified to see that Zanuck was breathing down Marton's neck — in effect, directing the whole scene while Marton just used his expertise to set multi-cameras and use his explosives, smoke and men.

If this was how this job was going to be, I knew I wouldn't last long. I would be quite happy for a great filmmaker like Zanuck to make comments about the show and about the rushes afterwards, but the man in charge in front of cast and unit must clearly be Ken Annakin, otherwise I could not function.

I talked to Bundy at lunch and found that he really didn't care as long as he was paid well and kept in work. Whenever I could, I used to sneak away to watch him because he was quite masterful in filling a big screen with action. Darryl wanted the action, but also was concerned with story and the best use of actors like John Wayne, Bob Ryan, Red Buttons, Hank Fonda, and Richard Burton... all of whom he persuaded to work for a few days in the movie. This was one of the reasons he worked his secretaries twenty-four hours a day, constantly finding who was free and how they could be hooked into his Grand Effort.

Bob Mitchum appeared one day, looking quite different from when I had seen him last. Smart, alert, smiling — as he came up the hill, he grasped my hand and said, "Gee, Ken, when are we going to make *Gold Lovers?* I still think it is one of the best scripts I've read in years!" Since that abortive meeting in the Savoy, I had never really known whether he had bothered to read the script properly! I told him that I was still trying to find a backer and hoped perhaps I might interest Zanuck. He slapped me on the back. "Let's work on it, kid!"

I was now deep in the planning of my own sequence at the Orne River Bridge... walking the whole area with Sam, driving in numbered pegs for camera positions, drawing rough sketches. The art director, Ted Howarth, told me his ideas, which were helpful since he'd been attached to the picture for nearly a year. Augie Loman showed me how his gliders would slide in on their plaited 'shock cords', and I realised that here was a Hollywood old hand who really knew his business. The prop man, 'Nobother' Graham, insisted that I inspect all of the rifles, sten guns, webbing and hand-grenades.

"We ain't worked together before, Ken," he said, looking up me like some kind of elf. "They call me 'Nobother' because anything you want will be no bother to me, so long as I know about it twenty-four hours ahead." I realised that I had really been plonked down among a group of true professionals.

Pauline had arrived, bringing with her an English shooting stick, so that during the long days of shooting I could half-sit and relax my back, which still ached occasionally. We now sat at one of the long tables and were made to feel part of the French Unit who would be working with me. Bourgogne, a very down-to-earth French cameraman who had seen some of my movies, was especially friendly and helpful.

The day before shooting, who should turn up but Richard Todd, who said he had never expected to see me working again after the South African illness debacle. Most remarkably it turned out that during the war he had actually taken part in the assault on this bridge. His parachute had almost strangled him, but lying beneath its folds had saved him being mowed down in the first wave of British Commandos overrunning the Germans in foxholes around the bridge. Throughout the shooting, it was great to slip away and double-check with him details of the action.

During the night shooting I was never conscious of Zanuck's presence, though I knew he was around from time to time, dropping down in his helicopter to gather reports from a production assistant — whom I quickly realised was his 'spy'. He had one on each of the three units. He was now keeping an eye on me.

Zanuck was delighted with my first four day's rushes, so I prepared for the day sequences, and Lord Lovatt's arrival with every confidence. Shamus Lovatt, tall and blond-haired, was every inch a Scottish clan Chieftain accustomed to commanding people. He took one look at my set-up on the bridge and said, "We never came along that riverbank. We came straight down that road opposite."

I looked at him and gave him what I hoped was a disarming smile. "I'm afraid I have to say that filmically, that approach is not as good as the one where I can pan your commandos in from the right and connect them with the bridge." Lovatt turned away, saying, "Well, I'm here to tell you how it really was."

Zanuck suddenly came up and listened to both our points of view and to my surprise said, "I think we'll stick with Ken's set-up. It's gonna look much better and take far less time on the screen."

Fortunately for me Lovatt's attention and nitpicking, switched to criticisms of Peter Lawford, whom Zanuck had chosen to play Lovatt. As Peter led the troops in what seemed to me the perfect military fashion across the bridge, I heard Lovatt moaning, "Look how that idiot walks. I never sway like a sissy, and anyway, he's not tall enough!" But Lawford was great and so were the rushes, so much so that two days before I was due to finish my British section, the three crews were sitting in the theatre watching dailies when Zanuck raised his hand and called, "Ken, Irina and I want to talk to you after dailies."

Bourgogne gave me a nudge and said, "That's the end of you, Ken. Nice knowing you! Five guys have tried to put her on the screen to satisfy the two of them. They're all history! Gone!" It now turned out that Zanuck had been devising a new sequence with and for his French girlfriend, Irina Demick — playing a leader of the French Resistance.

"I want you to stay on," said Zanuck, puffing at his cigar. "And if you can get a good sequence with Irina while we're at the bridge, you can take over the whole French Resistance section."

As we walked back to the hotel, Pauline said, "What are you going to do?"

"Over-cover the sequence," I said. "I'll treat Irina exactly as I would a child." This is what I did and it worked. I was awarded the French Resistance sequence and not much more.

One of Zanuck's great film conceptions was an eight-minute helicopter shot showing the attack around the casino at Ouistreham. It was a very involved shot showing the Free French Troops in action. It involved nuns being rescued from a convent and the overcoming of the Germans on the casino roof. Every director who had been on the picture had tried to complete this sequence to Zanuck and his editorial advisor, Elmo Williams' satisfaction.

So, I found myself introduced to Gilbert Chomat, French helicopter wizard pilot, who could do anything with an Alouette and had an uncanny sense of swinging the camera exactly where you wanted it — so long as you gave him detailed instructions. I studied the shot as it had been previously made, listened to Zanuck and Elmo's criticisms, and went up with Gilbert to re-shoot it for the seventh time. The shot I'm still very proud of is the sequence which survived into the final edit of *The Longest Day*.

Irina Demick was a very pretty redhead, not the greatest actress, but very willing to take direction once she trusted you. That trust quickly developed in the next few weeks as we moved to the completely rebuilt Norman town of Evreux, where Zanuck insisted that Pauline and I dine with himself and Irina every evening. In deference to her, Zanuck spoke all the time in a very accented French, and Pauline had to try and tell jokes in her schoolgirl French. But we all got along fine.

Come rain or shine, Zanuck watched nearly every shot that I made with Irina, but always at a distance and it became a sort of competition as to whether he could ever think up a small change in the set-up or action before I discovered it myself. Our kind of rivalry gave an extra dimension to the shoot.

The derailing of a full-length French steam train was a challenge and a marvellous experience. I was allocated Bob McDonald and his son, two top-ranking American Special Effects men to prepare the stunt, which required undermining a section of the line and shoring it up with timbers which could be blown on my signal from the camera.

Because it was clearly a one-time shot, I insisted on setting up six cameras to cover the event. Everything went absolutely as planned, except for the engine, which slid straight towards number one camera, reminding me exactly of the charge of the elephants in Kenya! But this time the front of the engine stopped exactly two feet in front of the lens. No one was hurt and everyone said it was a remarkable shot.

There seemed to be no question now of Pauline and I returning to England and coming back in November. Zanuck seemed to like having me around, and Elmo Williams invited me into the cutting rooms to see where we could do with some extra shots. We had to decide how best to achieve them, now that all the major cast and big armaments had gone. We would, of course, still have troops and big equipment available for my British landing sequences, when the American Navy was scheduled to be making exercises off La Rochelle in Brittany.

Elmo was an excellent editor who claimed to have created the tension in that classic Western *High Noon,* by every now and again cutting in the ticking clock. On one of our trips to find suitable locations for some pick-up shots, Elmo confided in me that he would give his soul to be a director. He had made some shorts for Disney and directed TV stuff in Germany, but nothing out of the rut.

"Here I am coordinating this vast canvas for Zanuck and what then? You'll be offered big movies, and me? Shit, as usual!" In point of fact, he was rewarded for his faithful and excellent service to Zanuck by being appointed Head of Fox Productions in Europe. As often happens in this business, our paths crossed again most positively a few years later, and it was a constant embarrassment and stumbling block between us that, Elmo had revealed his inner feelings to me at this time.

In between doing some extra night shooting of the GI's landing by parachute around the little church of St. Mere Eglise (and the unfortunate soldier who got stuck on the steeple played by Red Buttons!), I picked up close shots of Gert Froebe – playing the first German soldier to spot the Allied armada approaching on D-Day; and a sequence with Bourvil, playing the Mayor of Caen, offering champagne to Allied troops as they began streaming across the countryside.

Both of these continental stars were to play important parts in future movies of mine, and I'm sure I would never had known about them, nor they about me, but for this unhurried working together on *The Longest Day*. Gert was the only German actor I ever met who had a sense of humour like the British, and Bourvil had a unique talent based on traditional French mime and the zany throw-away style of Jacques Tati... quite different from the classic American comedy players. But it doesn't always work out that because you have worked with an actor you can persuade him to work for you again.

Sean Connery had been sent over from London by Maude Spector (from my Disney casting days) to play a double-act cameo with a young English actor, Norman Rossington. Zanuck immediately took a dislike to Sean and said, "That Limey mumbles his lines and looks like a slob!"

I said, "Really, Darryl... Sean's done a lot of good work. Before I left London I saw him play Alexander the Great on TV. I'll talk to him and get him to lighten up."

Although we had met in Burbank when he was playing the gardener in *Darby O'Gill* and we had shared that day at the races (courtesy of Walt Disney), Sean did not really respond. I guess he hated being one of the crowd, and in the next scene we shot, he continued to glower while Norman was outgoing and funny. "Take the lines from that punk," shouted Darryl at the next showing of dailies. "Give them to the little guy!"

"But Norman's got to have a buddy to talk to," I objected. "And the lines are not all that funny!"

Zanuck glared at me. "The little guy's handling them like Cornelius wrote them. I'm not going to have my film ruined because..."

I interrupted, "Okay! Okay, Darryl! I'll deal with it." And so, I had to take the two actors aside and as tactfully as I could make Sean the straight man to Norman's comedy. Despite my explanations on the side, and apologies for Zanuck's attitude, Sean never forgave me and turned down every script I ever sent him. This was before he played 007 in the Bond movies, of course.

During this period of 'pick-up' shooting, Pauline and I went for long rides around Normandy. The most thought-provoking visit was to the U.S. cemetery at Avranches, where endless lines of white wooden crosses covered fields on a three mile stretch of cliff overlooking the Atlantic... a ghoulish reminder of the war we were filming. I wanted Zanuck to use this as the anti-war background for the credits and titles at the beginning of the picture, but he decided, it would set a film of achievement off on the wrong note. Spielberg has since used this idea in his film *Saving Private Ryan.*

The time had now come to prepare for my major shooting of the British landings. Thirty-six U.S. landing craft were taking part in an exercise off the Ile d'Ore — an oyster-breeding island off the French Naval Base of La Rochelle.

It was bitterly cold and foggy at 6 am when the two French multi-camera crews had to catch the ferryboat — if I was lucky, I would helicopter over with Zanuck in the Alouette. Apart from the landing craft, he had borrowed tanks, jeeps and all sorts of carriers from the French Army. For the big scene where Ken More stalks up the beach with his pet bulldog, three thousand troops were being bussed in from all over Brittany.

They arrived around eleven am 'Nobother' Graham and his helpers handed them dummy rifles, dummy grenades, a canteen, and a packet of sandwiches, while my assistants led them off in sections to strategic points along the three mile flat beach. This took approximately a couple of hours, which meant I only had them for another hour.

Alex Weldon came up to report that he and his assistants had laid all the charges in duplicate, and that Karley Baumgarten had set enough rubber tires and smokepots to last two takes. He was covered with black powder but smiling. "We can't do anything more, boss." I put my arm around his shoulder and gave him a final briefing on all the whistles, flags and hand-signals we would give.

Zanuck came up beside me, puffing his cigar a bit more furiously than normal (he smoked fourteen a day). "You know, Ken?" he said with a sweep of his hand. "I calculate you've got three million dollars of hardware on this beach today. I'm relying on you to make sure I see every dollar of it!" He looked at his watch. "And don't you think we should try one?"

I nodded my head, strode off to check all the cameras, while all my assistants except Sam, changed into uniform, and ran to join the various sections of troops. "I don't trust any of the bastards," said Sam, "except my boys!"

The rubber tires piled up at six different points, were set alight, and as soon as the smoke started drifting across the scene, I gave "Action" on my radio. The first take looked great, but since Alex could be ready again in thirty minutes, I moved four of the cameras, and we shot again.

As the three thousand troops were marched off, we shot the dialogue scenes and close-ups until darkness fell. It had been a great day, and that night, being Saturday, we piled into the cafés and stuffed ourselves with oysters, shrimp, lobsters — you name the crustaceans, we had them — washed down by ice cold Bordeaux white wine!

In the week that followed we had to shoot an even bigger action sequence — with fires raging in a castle set Ted Howarth had built on the cliffs; two Stukas dive-bombing and strafing the beach; and Lord Lovatt leading his commandos ashore beside his favourite Highlander playing the bagpipes. All this had to be covered in one master shot!!

Again, I set up six cameras to give me the establishing shots and cover details of the action. The question was, "Which camera shall I stay and work from to give my overall signals?'

I decided that the most important thing was 'to stick with the money' as I had been taught as a first principle in my early days at Gainsborough. That meant riding in the landing craft with Peter Lawford, our most expensive star. His barge was the pivot of the shot, so far as the general timing of the action was concerned, and Zanuck impressed on me that he wanted to see the British commandos jump off the ramp so that they landed in the sea *exactly waist-deep*.

"I wanna see Lawford quite clearly — *and* the Queen's Piper." He removed his cigar from his mouth. "You don't know how many strings I had to pull to bring *him* here today!"

So, I chose one of the landing craft and went out with the American Top Sergeant-In-Charge to rehearse with him exactly how long it would take to drop the ramp after I gave him the signal. I chose a point of reference on the cliff, and gave him the signal. In seven separate rehearsals, it took exactly sixteen seconds for the ramp to be fully lowered. After five hours of hard preparation everything was set and I went out with Lawford and our one hundred genuine British commandos.

Receiving signals from my assistants that everything was ready for their cameras, the Special Effects, and the Stukas, I fired a single flare into the air and all hell was let loose. My landing craft started to go in and came level with my point of reference. I gave the Top Sergeant his cue and, to my horror, the ramp went down with a loud clang in *only three seconds!* Before I could stop him, Peter raised his hand and the one hundred trusting commandos jumped into the water, only to vanish completely. I watched in dismay as these brave lads eventually surfaced, and with the Queen's Piper shaking water out of his bagpipes, he led them ashore, followed by a very bedraggled Peter Lawford.

A sense of survival made me decide not to return to shore for a full twenty minutes. I occupied that time arguing with and berating the US top sergeant whom I found had been hitting the bottle and was completely plastered. "What the fuck," he said. "They were only bloody Limeys!"

Arriving back at the beach, Zanuck strode up to me and I expected the worst. "What the hell happened, Ken?" he said. I explained as quickly as I could and added, "But surely that kind of thing must have happened in the real war. How did it look?"

He removed his very chewed cigar. "So far as I could see, everything else worked out fine — exactly as planned — and maybe it's a great shot, but I always saw it with Lord Lovatt and his Piper leading his men ashore majestically, and that is what I think I'll still require!"

The dailies were exciting to watch. The explosions and the strafing worked marvellously, but I was not at all unhappy when Zanuck gave me the opportunity to re-set up the shot two days later, so that apart from my landing craft camera, I could move the other five to different positions where I could collect more detailed coverage of the action.

For this second bite, Alex Weldon, now my friend and perhaps the brightest of the twenty-eight Special Effects men, took over the handing of the ramp from a different top sergeant. This time everything worked perfectly and the whole crew were thrilled with their achievement. But there was an extraordinary backlash to this shooting.

Peter Lawford threatened to sue the company and the wardrobe mistress whom he said had not bothered to completely zip up his wet suit because he was only going to be submerged waist deep! As it turned out on that first take, the suit filled with water and Peter was nearly drowned. She argued that it was at his insistence that the suit was not fully zipped, and knowing actors, I believed her.

Every one of the British Commandos lined up in front of the cashier and put in extra claims because they said they had "stowed their personal money" in their hats, and it had all been washed away when they were so rudely submerged. Who could argue with that kind of claim?

But the heaviest one came from the local oyster-bed cultivators, who argued that the explosives going off all over the beaches had ruined their crop! I never knew what happened to that obvious try-on, but Zanuck was not mad at the extra expense or the time needed to achieve perfection for his concept of the landings. In fact, his behaviour was exactly what I had experienced with Walt. At their best, they were both great men — geniuses.

Despite the fact that Christmas was approaching, we were still not able to return to London. The day we cleared up everything at Ile d'Ore, Darryl put his arm round my shoulder and said, "Ken, I've got a proposition to put to you. As you know, we have four weeks more, shooting at the Boulogne Studios in Paris, to wipe up the American sequences. This may be my Swan Song and it would give me a great kick to direct these sequences myself. Unfortunately, there is so much clearing up to be done on this most expensive and complicated production, and I have to tell you that I'm locked in daily struggles with the money boys to get the final funds we need to complete." I nodded understandingly and wondered what this was all leading up to.

He continued, "Would you be prepared to set up each of the remaining two hundred shots or so, and I'll slip down from the office and call *Action* and when I'm happy, you can set up the next one for me."

My face must have been 'a study', as they say, because he slapped me on the back saying, "And if I can't get away, you'll shoot the darned things anyway!"

My first reaction was "What the hell is he asking? I'm a good, established director, how will it look to stars like Wayne and Burton and Mitchum if I play ball with Zanuck in this way?" I discussed the situation at length with Pauline and she said, "Oh, do it. You've built up a great relationship with Zanuck, we've made a lot more money than we thought we would, don't let your dignity stand in the way of a new experience."

And so I moved into the Boulogne Studios and was reunited with my old designer friend, Vincent Korda. He had been quietly building set pieces for me, and big sets for the German director, Bernard Wicki. I had met Wicki on the Normandy cliffs where he had been shooting a few sequences in the big German gun-emplacements. But most of his scenes were in the underground bunkers or at various command headquarters, which had been built in the studio so that German actors could be brought over all at one time, for convenience and to save money.

Wicki was basically an actor, but had gathered a lot of kudos as a director with a very touching anti-war film called *The Bridge*. He had shown the tragedy of boys in their teens called up to fight a lost war for the Fatherland. I remember Ken More and

I drifting on to his set one day and being very intrigued by the constant German reference to 'Robber Dommies'.

"The British are dropping robber dommies!" an actor was yelling over the phone.

"Robber dommies?" queried Kenny, "I thought this was supposed to be the true story of D-Day."

I went across to Bernard and said with a frown, "Robber Dommies?" He nodded and pointed to the script. "Sure! It says so here." I looked at the script page which read, "The British are dropping rubber dummies!"

"Am I not correct?" said Bernard. I nodded. "Of course, but we say rubber *dummies.*" He smiled with relief, "But we are Germans! The audience will understand when they see them!"

My studio shooting went marvellously, and quite often Darryl was not able to slip down from the office to call "Action!" and "Cut!" So, I directed in my usual way, making new friends with stars like Bob Wagner, Stuart Whitman, Eddie Albert, and Richard Burton. We all loved the French studio hours — the crew call was for twelve noon. We would break for a meal around five or six, and continue shooting till around eight or nine in the evening. This meant we could go out to the theatre and nightspots, wake up late and generally enjoy life as well as shooting — which is very typically French!

As usual with big American productions, all the material we had shot was shipped back to Hollywood, and was finally edited and dubbed there, under the eagle eye of Elmo Williams. The next time I saw Zanuck was at the Royal Premiere in London, where we were presented to Queen Elizabeth and Prince Phillip at the Leicester Square Theatre. It was a fantastic evening and Darryl was all smiles and most gracious to myself and Pauline, whom he had always insisted on calling during the shooting "Your lovely bride!"

CHAPTER TWELVE
'Down To Earth Again' With two small British movies. Taking stock... And the birth of my biggest (and most successful) project

Returning to our home in London from the three months' labours on *The Longest Day* — labours, I must say, which had been highly enjoyable because I was under no stress or worries about the shape of the final movie — I suffered the usual let-down.

Jack Davies was busy finishing another of the 'Doctor' comedies for Betty Box and about to start another Norman Wisdom comedy. Dennis Van Thal had nothing definite on offer so Pauline and I decided to take ourselves off for some sunshine in the Caribbean.

We flew out to Barbados, where as luck would have it we found accommodations at the Coral Reef Club. It was a paradise. Self-contained bungalows were dotted around three acres of lawns and an old plantation house. Smiling Creole ladies brought us breakfasts of paw-paw and bacon and eggs, which we ate while idly watching coloured birds winging their way over endless blue sea. Sprightly yellow and green sugar birds vied with dopey doves for crumbs and sugar, which we spilled for them on the glass top table. We read, walked on beaches populated mostly with well-to-do British and Canadian visitors, plus the friendliest ever-smiling native Barbadians.

Refreshed and relaxed — as from a second honeymoon, Pauline and I returned to London where I again made an attempt to set up *The Gold Lovers*. Darryl had given me introductions to some of the studio heads in Hollywood and I felt that Dennis Van Thal and his American associate agents ought to be able to get some action. But, although everyone seemed to like the idea of Sophia Loren and Robert Mitchum, they hemmed and hawed over the idea of Belafonte. I felt he would be perfect in the role of the Ethiopian doctor, but no one could put together 'the package'. I might have taken a chance and gone over to America myself, but comments kept floating back that the day of the 'trek movie' was over. "The public don't wanna see a gal and a couple of guys struggling through wind and shit, even if they do screw half a dozen times!" Jack Warner was reported to have said. "On top of which, black screwing white, even with Belafonte, it is just not on!!"

Guy Elmes came over to London and I persuaded him that Cortez and his Conquest of Mexico, would make a great movie. For nearly two weeks we lived 'on a high' as we studied the original diaries of Fra Bernal, and reams of descriptions and illustrations, which we found in the wonderful library in St. James Street, London.

But it would take Guy months to produce a script. So impatient to direct again, I pushed Jack Davies into finishing our *Fast Lady* screenplay. In less than a week, Leslie Parkyn bought it and set a production date in Beaconsfield Studios — with our old repertory team — James Robertson Justice, Leslie Phillips, Stanley Baxter, and once again Julie Christie, because she had to work off a two picture contract he had given her. I say 'had to' because Julie was developing quickly. She had now gained more experience by working in Birmingham Repertory Theatre. Although responding obediently to all my directorial requirements, it was quite clear that this kind of comedy, where she really just had to be a pretty, trendy kind of girl, was just marking time for her. Julie's real ambition was to play big dramatic roles.

"I know I have it in me to be another Sarah Bernhardt," she said to me one day. "Or at least a Garbo!" I nodded and said that night to Pauline, "I think we've lost her."

"Why?" she frowned. *"You* could have made a big dramatic love story with her."

I shook my head. "Somehow, I don't think I'll ever be offered that kind of movie — and, as you've seen, I'm not too hot at setting up one for myself."

Julie made it, I would say, in *Dr. Zhivago*, but that was her apogee. Warren Beatty and the crowd that life threw her amongst, combined with her natural leaning towards the unconventional, caused her to make some 'way-out' choices. Inside, she was loving and generous, almost to excess. I remember the first thing she did with the pittance we paid her for the comedies was to buy a painting from a starving artist, and a brass bedstead. Her 'string-bag' existence was deeply ingrained, and her intense feelings about social injustices drove her eventually into living in a commune, and helping friends to deliver difficult babies rather than keeping faith with 'her calls' on the set. We all make mistakes in our choices — or to the outside world we appear to do so. On the other hand, that may be the way of life the inner-self really wanted, or was predestined by the genes to finish up with! I love Julie and feel *that* her less than frequent movie experiences are always interesting and full of warmth — but I think she could have chosen better.

As usual, I tried to introduce some glamour into *The Fast Lady*. We devised a sequence where Julie took a bet that she could get a job as a strip-teaser in a Soho club. As in everything she did, she was most anxious that her routine should be correct, so one night we went to the Windmill Club and studied several performances — even going backstage to discuss techniques with two of the strippers. The result was a very sexy, sensual sequence with Julie, but as happened in quite a few instances with me, the British censor took exception to some of her teasing gestures and butchered the scene. Julie was furious and neither of us could understand how other directors were getting away with far worse sexual innuendos and nudity. She took her revenge in Warren Beatty's *Shampoo*! I have still to be allowed to get away with a really saucy scene, and can only think that some heavenly censor is guarding my reputation as a 'maker of films for the whole family!'

CHAPTER TWELVE *The birth of my biggest (and most successful) project*

The Fast Lady was actually a vintage Bentley Continental — a beautiful green convertible — which the accident-prone Stanley Baxter was persuaded to acquire by Leslie Phillips, in order to impress Julie. Apart from some imaginative dream sequences, it was an easy picture to shoot — although in the last reel we did achieve a memorable fun chase. We roped in half a dozen of Britain's top music-hall comics — Fred Emney, 'Monsewer' Eddie Grey, Robertson Hare, and Frankie Howard — they all played guest spots, none of which took up more than half a day to shoot. Their well-honed skill at getting laughs gave me a new insight into handling broad comedy, which I was able to use with telling effect later in my production of *Those Magnificent Men In Their Flying Machines.* Perversely, when it began to look as though we had developed a successful formula for light comedies, I jibbed. I always enjoyed the six weeks or so of writing with Jack, but now he had the bright idea of making a comedy about all the disasters that could happen to a young couple building or remodelling a house (an idea exploited most successfully by Tom Hanks and Shelley Long in *The Money Pit*).

Leslie Parkyn loved the idea and rushed to contract our same team, but to me it smelled of the *Huggett* series all over again. I could feel the same gags coming up, and I hated the idea of repeating myself. I needed a new challenge.

Pauline and I kicked over the situation endlessly. She was quite willing to make the break, and try our luck in California where it was obvious all the big movies were now being hatched. However, I was very conscious that she was 100% British, had a tight circle of friends in London, and quite a large family she cared a lot about. I had none except my daughter Jane, who was now in training at the William Morris Agency in London. "What is it you really want to do?" asked Pauline after I had turned down two more small British film offers.

"I want to make movies like Carol Reed," I said.

"He's still your idol," she sighed. "But his great films like *Odd Man Out, Fallen Idol,* and *The Third Man* were made years ago. What has he done recently that was any good?"

It was true that Carol was having difficulties. I talked with him after he came back from Tahiti, where he suffered agonies trying to cope in his quiet manner with the insults and domineering behaviour of Marlon Brando. He had lost control of *Mutiny On The Bounty* and had been replaced. He would never go back to Hollywood.

Despite my self-assurance and even bossiness on the set, I recognised the fact that I also was a shy, private kind of man, and might well not be able to cope with Hollywood heavies — their tough uncaring attitudes and the domineering ways of stars. One had heard of Burt Lancaster, at this period, making it almost a principle to find some excuse to have the director fired within the first ten days of shooting — just to satisfy his ego it seemed, and to prove his power. Kirk Douglas had the same reputation. Was that kind of 'director-baiting' worth the move? I had enjoyed Disney, but now the studio was turning out movies like *Pollyanna, The Parent Trap,* and *Son of Flubber.* In their way these movies were just as parochial as the films the Box family were making in England. In any case, if Pauline's prophecy was true, Walt would never offer me another movie, even though we had actually been keeping in touch. Walt had indicated that if I could acquire the remake rights to *Jungle Book,* from Zoltan Korda, he might let me shoot a new version in India. I did get the rights for Walt, but after much deliberation, he decided a remake would not be as good as a Cartoon version.

As always he was proven right!

My third idol was David Lean, who was still making wonderful movies like *Bridge On The River Kwai*, and the magical *Lawrence of Arabia*. Fantastic! He had found a producer who, according to David, might be a pain in the backside many times over. But Sam Spiegel got the subjects financed and set-up solidly. I clearly needed a showman/businessman/producer — one who was literate enough to understand the quality of subjects like 'The Gold Lovers', 'Cortez', or even 'Elephant Bill'!

Sydney Box would have filled the bill to a tee, but he had tilted briefly at the windmills of Hollywood, and was now acting as coordinator for pictures made by his wife Muriel, Betty, his sister, and Peter Rogers, her husband. They were all making pots of money and were quite content to be small fish in the British pond. They had also one advantage over me, in that they all loved the social life — attending the premieres, being seen and photographed at star parties, never worrying about taking long lunches or dinners at 'Les Ambassador' or 'The White Elephant', to do business and meet stars. Actors and actresses do the same thing. I remember at Les Ambassador, the two Collins girls and the beautiful Shirley Ann Field would invariably arrive about eleven, stroll (very noticeably) through the room and join visiting celebrities like Frank Sinatra, Warren Beatty, Kirk Douglas, Jack Warner, or Mike Frankovich. They all made the grade and good luck to them!

This was one way of getting jobs and keeping in the mainstream — necessary for an actress — but somehow demeaning for a writer/director trying to create great movies. I had been conscious of this way of advancement from way back in my early days at Gainsborough. I had watched executives like Tony Darnborough, Frank Bundy and Vivian Cox rise to power in the Box stable, purely by socialising, but their careers always seemed to flop after three or four years, unless they had real talent.

Socialising, except with one's friends (who nine times out of ten were not in the film business), was such a bore — a waste of precious life and almost as whorish as directors and producers who climb the ladder on the backs of 'hot' stars. How degrading to enter a relationship with a star so that you can rise into the picture business! It may sound pompous, naive or foolish now, but I had chosen to build up a life with Pauline, sharing together fun and adventures, separating my professional life from our private life, so that we could indeed *have* a private life. It was a deliberate decision — namely, that I would climb the ladder by my talent and skill, and to hell with kowtowing to people in temporary positions of power.

But if I wouldn't sell my soul to the devil, how could I make great movies which needed power, money and influence — the acquisition of which needed time, patience and single-minded devotion? I slipped over to Paris to see Darryl Zanuck, but he was up to his neck in complicated problems..

Immediately after the success of *Longest Day*, Darryl was drawn into a struggle for the control of Twentieth Century-Fox. The disastrous *Cleopatra* had almost broken the studio and the money boys decided that Zanuck was the only man who might pull the company round. The very human problem was that Darryl was enjoying his life in Europe and making stars of his girlfriends — from Bella Darvi to Juliette Greco, now Irina Demick (and later Genevieve Gilles). He could not physically go back to Hollywood, because he had not officially broken with his wife, Virginia. So, at the time, he was running Fox through his son, Dick Zanuck, while remaining firmly anchored to his life in Paris. I tried to persuade him to produce for me. "You could set up 'The Gold Lovers' or 'Cortez' with a few phone calls, Darryl!" I said.

He shook his head. "It's not at all like that these days, Ken. I took a beating over *The Longest Day* — you'll never know how hard it was to get those last few dollars to finish it".

"What about Fox?" I said. "Aren't you the head of the studio now?"

He sucked on his cigar. "Not like in the old days. Now I have to convince Dick and a whole lot of other people to spend a dime. It's all too exhausting." He shot a loving glance at Irina, curled up on his sofa, and said in a low voice, "You know, Ken, I'm thirty years older than her. Anything I do has to include a starring role for Irina."

So, I was back again at square one!

Pauline was very sympathetic, but fed up with me going around like a bear with a sore head. "Go back and talk to Earl," she said. "He's at least American and a wise old owl about the business."

"You know, Ken, you're not using your assets as well as you could", Earl St. John said. "I teamed you up with Jack Davies because I thought with all your travelling and world outlook, you'd lift him out of the rut of these small comedies. Have you seen *Mad, Mad, Mad World* yet?"

I nodded. "I love it, but with all those gags it must have cost the earth. And it's very American!"

"Write something as crazy and fill it with comics from all over the world," he said.

"A kind of *Around The World In 80 Days*," I ventured, thinking aloud.

Earl rose to his feet and indicated he must go to the john — his favourite retreat when he felt stress. "That's for you to sort out with Jack," he said. "But for Chrissakes get off your asses and write a funny picture that's good for everyone!"

When I told Jack, he said, "Who's going to put up the money?"

"I don't know," I sighed. "But I think if we come up with something different, Earl would at least come up with the money to write a script."

"Different?" said Jack, stroking the nose of the Siamese cat that invariably sat on his desk. "We've got to have something to hang the gags on ... like a bicycle race."

"The Orient Express speeding across Europe!" I said.

"Fill it with comics from England, France, Italy!"

"Too static," said Jack. "What about a ship?"

"Or submarines?" I threw in, "There must have been some funny things happen when they were being invented."

Jack rose and went to a bookshelf. "I've got a book somewhere with some very funny contraptions in it." He dug out a book called 'Victorian Inventions'. It was full of illustrations showing inventors' efforts to power ships and submarines. To our eyes, they looked like cartoons, but someone had seriously thought they might work. I flipped through a few pages.

"What about dirigibles — zeppelins, balloons? There were some crazy pictures of airships with sails and oars — weird flying machines with flapping wings and powered by pedals!"

"I like these," said Jack. "But we can't make a documentary — just getting laughs out of funny machines.."

"A competition for inventors," I suggested.

"Or a race," said Jack.

It was several days before we hit on the idea of having a race for old airplanes. We could use zany contraptions, but old airplanes did actually fly and there must still be some around. "What we ought to do," said Jack, "is to have someone dig out old diaries and anecdotes of pioneer flyers as they tried out their machines. It's always best to build from things that really happened."

I saw he was getting steamed up on the idea and remembering some of the funny things that had happened during my flights in California with Loretta, the Busby Berkeley dancer, before the war, I knew we were on to a good thing. I sought out a girl in London who was working on a magazine called "Aeroplane."

"The basement is stacked with old copies giving accounts of hair-raising crashes and escapes," said the bright-eyed Ann Harrington. "I'll be happy to dig them out for you." I made a deal with her, while Jack contacted an old RAF buddy who came up with photos from the Royal Aero Club, which proved that the strangest looking planes *had really flown* in the early days.

Eighty pages of hairy escapes and accidents and mishaps came in from Ann. They were true accounts, told straight, but we found them excruciatingly funny, reading them fifty years later. "All we need now is a plot to hang these on," said Jack.

"How about a flight across the Atlantic?" I said, thinking of Alcock and Brown.

"Too lonely," said Jack. Then, several seconds later, "We could have a race across Africa — from Gibraltar to Capetown. A woman pilot crashes in the jungle and is chased by a lion ..."

"Great idea to have some women in it," I interjected, as Jack continued.

"... And she says, when asked by a reporter how she escaped, 'Oh, I just lay down and let him have me!'" We both laughed like drains...

The next morning I came in very excited. "D'you know, Jack, I've found there was an actual race in 1910 from Paris to Peking."

"Planes?' he said.

"No automobiles. But we could use the same route and quite legitimately bring in French, Germans, Russians, and others..."

I knew Jack began to feel uncomfortable thinking of 'furrin' parts, so I was not surprised when he turned round and said quite forcibly, "You know, Ken, it's not going to be any funnier by going off halfway round the globe. Why not keep the action much nearer home and devise a race between London and Paris?"

"Fine with me," I replied. "So long as the competitors don't just come from England. There's got to be a German, an Italian, a Frenchman..."

"You can even have the Japanese, if you want,' said Jack. "The Japanese are notorious as copyists. They can steal the plans for a plane and it can fall to pieces just when they take off!"

I thought that was a great idea and it formed the simple basis for our characterisation of the foreign competitors. We took the most commonly accepted national trait — like the Germans being stolid and doing everything by the book — and got our laughs from behaviour rising out of this. Building on all these ideas, we knocked out a treatment for a movie we called 'Flying Crazy,' and with an assortment of pictures, took it to Earl. He liked it, but said, "It looks expensive. The planes are cute and I don't think it's been done before." He shook his head and walked out of his office into his private toilet where from past experience, we knew he often made decisions. We looked at each other, shrugged and crossed our fingers.

Five minutes later he returned. "You think you can find a part for Peter Sellers?"

he said, sitting on his desk.

"Great idea," said Jack. "We'll make him the villain of the piece. Villains are always the best roles to play."

Earl picked up the treatment. "On these ten pages I don't think I could ever sell John Davis, but I've a suggestion. I'm allowed a small kitty to play with. If I give you both five thousand pounds, will you promise to get out of town? Keep the whole thing under your hats and bring me back a script that's funny, international, and which no one can turn down?"

"What does he mean 'get out of town'?" said Pauline as we celebrated with Jack's wife at the White Elephant.

"He thinks it's so original he doesn't want anyone to steal it," I ventured.

"More likely, he's afraid all the hangers-on in the Pinewood Bar will think he's Santa Claus,' said Jack.

"Earl's scared stiff of J.D.," said Dorothy. "His wife is always telling me that's why he gets so pissed..."

"Where are you going to write?" demanded Pauline. We both shrugged.

She suddenly grinned. "Why don't we all go to Barbados?" My eyes lit up. "The Caribbean's wonderful this time of the year,"

Pauline continued. "We'll get Budge and Cynthia at the Coral Reef Club to give us bungalows far removed from the crowd. You can write in the mornings and I'll type what you've done the next morning."

"And tell us where it's not funny," growled Jack. "I'm afraid I'm too busy," said Dorothy who ran a boutique. "It's the Milan Fair and then I go on to Munich..."

"What a shame," said Pauline, then looked back at us. "But he's made it a condition you get lost."

Jack looked dubious. "I've never worked away from my study. And my cats?"

"This time it's going to be different," I said, taking over. "The whole picture's going to be different from anything we've done. It'll be good to be among Americans, wealthy Canadians..."

"And delightful black people. They might laugh at your jokes," said Pauline.

"Won't it be expensive?" said Jack.

"Not too bad this time of year," I said.

"He's paying ten thousand pounds between you. What's wrong with investing two or three thousand in yourselves?" Pauline's eyes were gleaming, but Jack was still wavering.

"Come on, Jack," I said. "Let's get out of the rut and have fun." Jack turned appealingly to his wife.

"I think you should go," said Dorothy. "It's a wonderful opportunity."

Pauline threw her arms around Jack's shoulder. "Well look after you, darling." She turned to Dorothy and added, "I promise."

And so we flew out to Barbados and established ourselves in the Coral Reef Club. The day after we arrived we started to write in a little room with only a window, which did not look on to the beach. Jack had said, "You know, I'm a weak character. I mustn't see any pretty girls in bikinis or the jokes will be too sexy."

We agreed we would work on the Graham Greene schedule — writing eight hundred words or four or five pages of screenplay every single day. It was obvious that only by sticking to such a regime could we possibly work in a paradise like the

Caribbean. So, each day about twelve-thirty, we put the cover over the typewriter and walked onto the veranda where holidaymakers were knocking back their first, or perhaps second or third, Planter's Punches. Who should be the first person we run into but my old friend, Dinah Sheridan! She had been scuba diving. We exchanged a wet embrace and began chatting fifty to the dozen and laughing like happy kids.

Suddenly, a stern voice called out, "Annakin! Davies! Whatever are you doing here?"

We turned and there was Dinah's husband, John Davis! We quickly told him that we were writing a script about the old days of flying.

"Impossible to write here," said J.D. "I can't even study a balance sheet in this lazy atmosphere."

We told him about our schedule of work and our excitement about the subject.

"Who are you making it for?" he asked.

"You, sir," I replied proudly.

A frown came over his face. "You mean to say the Rank Organisation is paying you to fool around here?"

"No, sir," I said. "Jack and I are paying for ourselves out of a writing fee."

He opened his mouth and his face began to go red as Dinah took his arm.

"Come on, now. We're all old chums. Let's settle down to some serious drinking."

So, we chatted a half-hour and Pauline joined us, bringing out the latest clean typed pages.

"There, you see, John. We're all working," I said.

He grunted. "Huh. What page are you on?"

"Eighteen," she replied adding, "...and that Dick Van Dyke stuff is a riot." She sat down beside Jack.

"How did you get Van Dyke?" said J.D. "What's he going to cost?"

"Oh, a quarter of a million, I would say, but he'll be worth it," I said, winging it.

"We haven't actually signed him yet," said Jack, trying to avoid another outburst. "But we have to have someone to write for."

"And we'll get him, sir," I added.

J.D. drew a deep breath and got to his feet. "We must all have dinner some evening," he said, as though it would break his heart.

We found out quite a while later, that he had immediately cabled Earl St. John to make sure that we were not being paid expenses by the Rank Organisation.

Obviously, we used to run into each other from time to time, and he would ask politely about the scenes we had been writing — sometimes, even allowing his face to break into a smile — we felt that he, as a very successful executive, resented the fact that two guys who often had been on his payroll, should be able to share his rich man's playground.

Actually, we found it very productive to be away from the daily phone calls from friends and business matters, and despite the late nights of dancing to steel bands by the moonlit ocean, we felt we were creating with a freshness and originality. Scenes like the firemen's drill was pure Mack Sennett, but when the German officer puts the spike of his helmet through the balloon, we were sure that had never been done before. Nor the payoff of his 'walking on the water!'

It was great to be able to try out new scenes on American or Canadian visitors we would meet on the raft or in the bar. Everyone knew we were writing and used to

CHAPTER TWELVE *The birth of my biggest (and most successful) project*

insist that we use them as guinea pigs — it was very useful and stupidly, I've never tried the formula since!!

Without complaint, though the temptations were great, Pauline continued to type the previous day's roughs, and over lunch we would listen to her comments and ideas. Occasionally, she felt we were becoming too ambitious and that some of the routines were too far-fetched. Usually, we were able to point to Ann's research notes and assure her that something very similar — or enough to give us the germ of a gag — had, in fact, really happened in the old days.

Even Jack, having laughed himself sick at something we'd created, would look at me and say, "Can we really do that?"

And I would answer, "Disney taught me that everything is possible on film if you break it down into its simplest elements. Don't worry! If it's fun and original, we'll find a way to shoot it."

There was one true incident of a pilot who had made a forced landing in a convent. He had skidded to a stop just avoiding running over the Mother Superior's pet poodle.

Jack grinned over the typewriter. "Let's have some fun with Pauline."

So, we wrote that our villain deliberately lands his plane at a country house and runs over a Yorkshire terrier, crushing it completely! When we received the pages back the next lunchtime, we found that Pauline, the dog lover, had changed the action and made the plane run over two Siamese cats (like Jack's dear pets at home)!

As soon as we had completed our four pages, we would rush on to the beach. Pauline and I would go water-skiing with our two wonderful teachers, who now had us cutting through the waves very stylishly on mono-skis. Before we were through we were skiing hand in hand — and if anyone thinks I'm exaggerating, we still have a record on 8mm film! Jack, in the meantime, would sink a few Planter's Punches, more often than not with Myra and Cecil Bernstein, who, like J.D., vacationed every year in the Caribbean. Cecil, along with his brother, Sidney, owned and ran the Granada Cinema circuit and TV network in the U.K. He was fascinated with what we were doing and promised to give us every help and introductions in New York, should we run into troubles with John Davis back at Pinewood.

Jack used to complain to all the pretty ladies who chased him (being a man alone), that I was a slave driver who wouldn't even give him a Sunday off. That was quite true, but since we were only actually writing four hours a day and had really 'got into the groove', I insisted that we could not let up — with the result that we finished the screenplay, complete with the first revisions, all cleanly typed in exactly six weeks.

Exuding good health and looking an envious brown, we drove into Pinewood Studios and delivered our script to Earl. For ten days there was silence, but we guessed (correctly) that even though he was very pro-us, he dared not open his mouth this time without collecting an opinion from J.D. — which, considering the circumstances, could go either way!

CHAPTER THIRTEEN
Those Magnificent Men In Their Flying Machines
The Whole Story

While we awaited the decision from 'God' we began trying our screenplay out on our own contacts — our respective agents, plus Sydney Box, Cecil Bernstein, and even more important, Peter Sellers. Towards the end of our *Fast Lady* shooting, we had been pressured out of the Beaconsfield Studios because Peter was moving in with a picture called *Only Two Can Play*. He was a busy man, shooting *Waltz of the Toreadors* at the same time at Pinewood, but we had developed quite naturally a good relationship with him by lunching side by side in the canteen. Now we presented him with our script, offering him the choice of two parts — the villain, Sir Percy, or the German Officer. As the roles had developed, we had often rolled around with laughter at the idea of Peter playing the phoney English gentleman or the German — whom he would undoubtedly caricature. Peter read the script overnight and came back to us with the greatest enthusiasm to play *both* parts — and perhaps we would even consider him playing the Japanese, as well!!

Earl called us to his office and admitted that he adored the script and John Davis thought it was 'pretty good' — so long as we could cast it and find a partner to split the cost. They were ready to pay us in full for the script and press forward. The handshake-agreement with Peter Sellers undoubtedly tipped the scales, and I was sent off to New York again to try and hook United Artists into a fifty-fifty deal with Rank. The script was very difficult for anyone to make a budget estimate, but John said he would okay a three million dollars estimate if UA would come in for one million five. I bit my nails at the St. Regis Hotel while David Picker, who had now taken charge of UA, considered the project. John Hargreaves, head of the Rank Distribution Organisation in New York was highly enthusiastic about the project, too, but did not believe it could be made for three million dollars and secretly, neither did I.

The first snag came up.

Peter Sellers was also in the New York area, staying in a big rented mansion on the

New Jersey Coast. I spent a fortune driving out in a cab to see him, and could not understand why he kept me waiting a whole hour talking, to his very garrulous mother. Suddenly, he appeared and, with a well-rehearsed sweep of the arm, said the situation had changed and he might not be able to play either Sir Percy or the German.

"I've been offered the marvellous part of a French detective in a movie with a very hot American director, Blake Edwards."

(The movie was, of course, the first of the *Pink Panther* series!)

"If, for any reason, Blake's production falls through, I'll be happy to consider yours." He put an arm around my shoulder. "But, quite honestly, Ken, I'm determined to get my foot into the American scene, because what I do is really without frontiers!" As he showed me to the door, he added, "You know, I'm completely pissed off, as I'm sure you are, with the little British comedies we have to make in studios like Beaconsfield and Pinewood."

I returned to the St. Regis to find a message from David Picker asking me to call him. He also was going to pass on the project — mainly because UA was deeply involved with *The Great Race* and he did not believe it would be fair to the shareholders to saddle them with two big crazy movies.

All my bounce and cheerful optimism ran out of my body like the sand from an hourglass. I had arranged to meet a friend at the Plaza for a drink, and as we went up the steps, who should I meet but John Shepridge, whom I had known as one of Zanuck's right-hand men during the shooting of *Longest Day*. He asked me what I was doing and after five minutes explanation, he said, "Well, why are you holding out on us? Let me send a copy to Darryl and, at the same time, you ship a script to Elmo in London."

"Why Elmo?" I said.

"Because he's now running the show for Fox in Europe," Shepridge smiled. "It wouldn't be wise to offend him!" I told him quite honestly about my meeting with Sellers.

"Don't panic yet," he said, giving me even more of his twisted smile. "If Darryl takes a shine to the subject, I guess he would give Peter as big an international platform as Blake."

I returned to London and within a week Darryl called me and said he felt the project could be a world-beater, but we would have to find a better title. "*Flying Crazy* sounds like a Chaplin two-reeler! But if Elmo can make a deal with you and Jack Davies, he'll have my support!" Elmo smiled his half-Indian smile and showed mild enthusiasm. "Our paths cross again," he said. "But I don't think you'll have anything like the money we squandered on *Longest Day*.

He established me in the office of his budget guy, and for two whole weeks we broke down the script and made more or less accurate assessments of the true cost. The preliminary budget came out nearer to five million dollars — which was quite big in 1963. Darryl's reaction was "Let's go for it, as long as Annakin undertakes to plan and supervise the preparations in every department."

Elmo added, "We must own the screenplay completely." This was a very different proposition from what had been agreed with Earl and John Davis. Earl took a kindly view and was willing to help me. "John will never go for those kind of figures anyway," he said. "But you've been working up to this kind of project for years."

"With your help!" I interjected.

Ken celebrates completion of filming *Very Important Person*
with (left to right) John LeMesurier, Jeremy Lloyd, Stanley Baxter (in uniform) and
Leslie Phillips. *(1961)*

Ken, with wife Pauline, were
the honoured guests at the
San Sebastian Film Festival in
1961 for *Very Important
Person.*

Stanley Baxter cuddles
Julie Christie while Leslie
Phillips enjoys a drink in
The Fast Lady (1962)

Irina Demick listens to Ken's
directions, with Sam Iskovich
making notes for *The Longest
Day (1962)*

(left to right) Darryl F.
Zanuck, Ken with wife
Pauline, and Richard Todd
at the world premiere of
The Longest Day
in London (1962)

Ken (with beret) arranges the British assault on Normandy while Zanuck with trilby) looks on for *The Longest Day (1962)*

Ken (left with beret) directs the landings on Sword Beach for *The Longest Day (1962)*

The men who fly the 1910 aeroplanes in *Those Magnificent Men in Their Flying Machines (1964)*. Left to right: Stuart Whitman, Terry Thomas, Alberto Sordi, Jean Pierre Cassel, Gert Frobe, Associate Producer/writer Jack Davies, Ken, Karl Michael Vogler, James Fox, Yujiro Ishihara, Gordon Jackson and Jeremy Lloyd.

Ken runs through a scene with Sarah Miles in *Those Magnificent Men in Their Flying Machines (1964)*

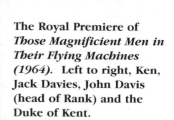

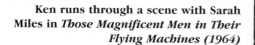

The Royal Premiere of *Those Magnificient Men in Their Flying Machines (1964)*. Left to right, Ken, Jack Davies, John Davis (head of Rank) and the Duke of Kent.

Baxter, the Annakin Yorkshire Terrier who should have been the first dog to fly with Jeremy Lloyd in *Those Magnificent Men in Their Flying Machines (1964)*

Ken looks on (extreme right) as (left to right) Sarah Miles, Stuart Whitman, James Fox and Willy Rushton go through their scene for *Those Magnificent Men in Their Flying Machines (1964)*. Dover Castle and the famous white cliffs provide the background.

Ken, Hans Christian Blech and Robert Shaw plan a scene. *Battle of the Bulge (1965)*

Ken explains what he wants to Henry Fonda. *Battle of the Bulge (1965)*

Ken helps Ty
Hardin out of
the river he had
enthusiastically
jumped into.
*Battle of the
Bulge (1965)*

Ken with James MacArthur on the Segovia location. *Battle of the Bulge (1965)*

Ken directs Henry Fonda, Robert Ryan and Dana Andrews. *Battle of the Bulge (1965)*

Ken discusses a scene with Robert Ryan. *Battle of the Bulge (1965)*

Telly Savalas
and Ken plan
the next
scene in the
Segovia
location.
*Battle of the
Bulge (1965)*

"That's true," he said, "but I've always known I'd never be able to produce this show." He put his arm round my shoulder. "You'd better turn your charms on John, who can be a true dog in the manger!"

It was summer and J.D. was busy harvesting on his farm in Kent. He refused to take phone calls, so I got in the car and drove down to his estate, where I found him on a tractor ploughing a square of corn. He claimed that he was afraid the weather was going to close in on him, so I ran beside the tractor and pleaded the case for him to let me have the subject back. He began by asking why should he give it back? — and suggested that I was getting too big for my boots, anyway. J.D. reached the centre of the field and turned off the tractor. I saw his wife, Dinah Sheridan, coming across the field with a tray of tea, so I quickly went to meet her, told her about the situation, so as John took his cup of tea, she smiled up to him. She said, "I do hope you're not going to be a shit over Ken's script, darling. He's been one of your most loyal and profit-making directors, despite *Nor The Moon By Night*, which was *my* choice. Give him the break he's been waiting for, if only to make it up to him for my error!"

John argued and shuffled, but clearly felt inhibited with Dinah now standing with her arm around his shoulder. Eventually, he said, "Okay, damn you, but I'll want double what we've laid out on the subject up to date — including your expenses in New York."

I breathed a big sigh, gave Dinah a kiss and left the field floating at least six inches above the stubble.

Sometimes in the fall, Elmo, Jack and I flew to Paris for a meeting with Zanuck at the Plaza Athenae. As I might have expected, Irina Demick was there beside him. She greeted me effusively, and quite soon we were informed that she would be in the movie. Darryl said, "You need more female interest than the Limey girl you've created, Jack. We've worked out some great scenes for Irina — a kind of fantasy running gag throughout the picture."

Jack shot a dark look at me, but I signalled him to be quiet — it seemed to me a small price to pay for the final go-ahead. It was clear now that Darryl was behind us for a truly international movie. John Shepridge came in and gave me a sharp wink. "I've already told Darryl that Peter Sellers might not be free, but we've come up with Gert Froebe for the German and Alberto Sordi for the Italian."

I could not complain about Gert because I had worked with him on *The Longest Day* and knew his undiscovered potential for comedy. Alberto Sordi, I knew, was the top-paid actor/comedian in Italy, and from the two films Shepridge later projected for us, both Jack and I saw he would fit our Italian Count like a glove.

Zanuck agreed that Susannah York, whom we had been talking to for the English girl, would be good and acceptable. He suggested we should test Michael Caine for the English aristocrat. Jack bridled, "But Michael Caine's a Cockney barrow boy. He could never play a *stuffed-shirt Englishman!*" Zanuck took out his cigar. "All I can say, Jack, is that he's convinced me that he can be an English aristocrat from his performance in Stanley Baker's *Zulu*. Test him and drop your goddamn British class prejudices!"

Jack was put in his place and felt very unhappy. But I was top of the world because at a later meeting Darryl agreed to put up fifty thousand pounds if I could come up with six old planes 'to fly' for that figure. I said that I did not think we could find genuine antiques to fly, but saw no reason why old planes should not be built for an average of five to six thousand pounds each, providing one chose the right supervisor and small-scale constructors.

"I'm sure you'll do it," said Zanuck, putting his arm around my shoulder. "But if you take my advice, keep Jack to his writing and gags. Don't have him anywhere near the logistics of the picture. If we work this way, I'll see that Elmo gives you all the support and finance you need. Good luck."

As I left, I blessed Pauline for having advised me to pamper Darryl's wish to appear to be the director for those last four weeks we had shot in the Boulogne Studios. Had I not had such a good relationship with Darryl on *The Longest Day*, I would never have made *Flying Machines*. Just imagine, what executive in the world today would have given me an almost blank check to build six old aeroplanes that nobody really knew whether they would fly?

It was now October 1963 and since we wanted to start shooting around the first of May of the next year, taking advantage of the full English summer (whatever the weather might *be),* there was no time to lose. The first job was to get the planes started.

I had already visited the Shuttleworth Museum just north of London, where the original plane in which Bleriot flew the English Channel was kept, together with several other veteran planes. Although the curator, Air Commodore Wheeler, was in the habit of 'showing off' the Bleriot once a year over the fields of Oxford, he told me that it was too valuable a relic to be loaned to a film company.

So, now the sixty-four thousand dollar question had to be asked. Would it be possible to build six planes of the 1910 period for an average of five thousand pounds each? "After all, they were very elementary," I said. "Made with wood, canvas and wire, with a small engine?" Allen Wheeler looked at me for a long moment. "I suppose you're thinking of that garage man at Slough who's built a Bleriot with his son?"

I nodded. "That's where I got the idea." I could not tell whether Allen was looking at me scathingly or not. After all, he had only recently been a test pilot flying Britain's latest jet, the Comet.

"Give me twenty-four hours to think about it?" he said finally.

The next day, Allen came with a bulging briefcase. "Number one," he said, "it can only work if you choose planes which have a definite record of having flown. Number two. You must promise not to muddle things up by bringing in any of your highfalutin Special Effects people, with their notions of lightweight materials and film ways of cutting corners."

"Why?" I asked. "Surely, in this day and age it would make sense..."

Allen was shaking his head vigorously. "It would mean redesigning the planes from scratch and I'm not prepared to do that!"

We went through all the old books and the photos we'd gathered together, and eventually settled on a cute little monoplane called the Demoiselle; a heavy monoplane known as the Antoinette; a couple of biplanes like the Wright Brothers used to fly; a plane with three wings, and the Bleriot. We made a deal for Allen to farm out the contracts to whatever small firms or individuals he felt could do the job.

Both Jack and I had been fascinated by various flying oddities of that period. One was a little plane that flapped its wings, called an Ornithopter. Another looked like a biplane but had completely round wings with a hole in the middle. Another one was like the Bleriot but was reputed to have flown backwards! Yet another looked like a bicycle or tricycle with fifteen or twenty parallel wings like a venetian blind. A big French plane had semicircular wings, and a British monstrosity called the Walton Edwards Rhomboid, had square 'sails'.

"You can have all those, as well," said Allen Wheeler. "But they never actually flew and if you want to see them make attempts, then pass them over to your Special Effects guys. Let them use all the trickery they like — it could be amusing!"

So, now I had to search for a very talented Special Effects man. Among the twenty-eight American experts with whom I had worked and made the most friendly contacts on *The Longest Day*, Alex Weldon seemed the most likely. I went over to Spain where I found him tipping a liner over with a thousand people on it — for Samuel Bronston.

To my surprise, he said, "Flying planes and the carefully calculated hydraulics you'll need are not my bag. I know of only one guy in the world who's dead right for your job. His name is Dick Parker. He flies his own plane, and for years he's been installing crazy side-shows for theme parks like Disneyland — you know, things like giving the illusion of being underwater... wire rigs for witches on broomsticks — that kind of magic."

After endless phone calls to California and weeks of haggling, I persuaded Dick Parker to join us — and began an association that has lasted right through to my last children's film *The New Adventures of Pippi Longstocking*.

During the months of preparation, Dick Parker built what he called a flying rig which consisted of two high construction cranes with three hundred feet of cable between them, on which we could hang any of our planes. With him operating what we called the organ, which was really the panel controlling a special hydraulic machine, he could make a plane appear to fly for a distance of a hundred and fifty feet at a height of twenty to twenty-five feet. He could make it rise and fall, dip or waggle its wings. Without this rig which Dick perfected, there could have been no *Flying Machines*. Dick also built us a hydraulic ramp on which we could mount any plane and tip it or waggle it in any direction. This was invaluable for process shots — back projection and blue screen — which were very complicated and occupied at least six weeks of our total twenty-four week schedule.

But I am jumping far ahead...

During the months of November and December, while Allen Wheeler was making contacts and contracts with the people who would build the planes, Jack and I ran thousands of feet of old films to find pictures of early planes and funny accidents in 'Man's First Efforts To Fly'. We decided also, that since all our planes were going to look, as the Americans say, 'cute', it would be marvellous to have a top cartoonist working throughout the picture, sketching and even exaggerating the funniness and cuteness of the planes. These could inspire the actors and we could use them for opening titles, perhaps several books and certainly for publicity. We were lucky enough to find Ronald Searle, the British artist who specialised in monster cats, but was just as happy to make characters of old planes. The pictures and caricatures he drew during the making of the movie are still valued collector's pieces.

My daily occupation throughout the next six months was working with Tom Morahan, the designer and art director whom Elmo pressed upon me. Tom had many big films under his belt, and had a brother who was a construction manager — something that appealed to Elmo in his plan to keep me on the straight and narrow!

Apart from constructing the planes, we found that we were going to have to build a scaled-down section of the Brooklands Racetrack. Most of the early British flyers had operated from this track, which was now completely changed and had no hangars — but figured quite large in our story.

We also needed an old windmill with a restaurant underneath; two large grandstands; and what could appear to be a dirty old sewage plant — which had existed next to the old Brooklands, and now provided the setting for several of our crashes. A big composite set was the only answer to all these requirements and Tom designed it brilliantly, guaranteeing to Elmo that he could bring it in for not more than one hundred thousand pounds, which was remarkable even for 1963.

Obviously, there were going to be so many tricks in this movie, plus a considerable amount of second unit shooting (which would mean a director working separately from me) that it was essential we use the storyboard techniques I had learned from Disney. To my surprise, Tom decided that he would like to do the hundreds of sketches, as well as designing the sets and overseeing their construction. This seemed to be a great idea because it meant that no third person was introduced between us and Tom turned out to be a master at sketching comic action. His only problem was that he lived a most Bohemian existence and spent all his evenings in pubs. As you may have gathered, when working I am a very disciplined person who demands good timekeeping. Hardly a day passed without Tom failing to arrive in our Soho office until around eleven o'clock. Sometimes he was limping, sometimes he had a black eye and was always full of excuses! But we ploughed on and everyone could see how the film was taking shape, what scenes would look like, and how the time and money would be spent to achieve our funny gags.

Elmo kept a close eye on costs and occasionally persuaded us to either cut or modify gags, usually on the pretext that Zanuck felt we were relying too heavily on gags and he preferred to build up and spend money on the romantic interest. Our 'Limey romantic interest' was becoming a problem. I had been sweethearting Susannah York for the role of Patricia, even to the extent of taking her into the Victoria and Albert Museum and showing her the cute little Pussmoth in which James Mollison had flown to Australia. She seemed intrigued and perfect for the role until her agent, Maggie Parker, persuaded her that a girl would never become a star in a picture surrounded by funny planes and comics.

Science Museum

We had a great difficulty in finding a replacement until we hit on Sarah Miles, who had just made a critical success in Losey's *The Servant*. I had, of course, approached Julie Christie, but she had registered big in John Schlesinger's *Billy Liar*. "I'm through with making gag comedies, Ken, and you know why!" Julie gave me a hug. I whispered, "Sarah Bernhardt?" She nodded and added, "Your Sarah will be okay — but not so easy to work with as me!" And she was right!

Other casting had gone well. Peter Sellers had, of course, stayed in America, but we cast the villainous Sir Percy with Terry-Thomas, who couldn't have been better. Eric Sykes, who had worked with us so effectively in *V.I.P.*, willingly joined him as the obsequious but hard-done-by manservant, Courtney. They began a double-act which ran through several later British movies.

As Darryl had insisted, I set up a very elaborate set of tests for Michael Caine, playing the young guard's officer, Richard. But in the opinion of Jack Davies and myself, he could not hold a candle to the genuine Public Schoolboy, James Fox, who was a handsome, sexy, up-and-coming British actor. We all agreed that Michael was very talented with probably a great future (we little realised how great!) but he was not our young snob.

I have to add that as a result of the turn down in these tests, in his heart, Michael has never forgiven me. When you combine this with a similar attitude from Sean Connery (the slighting of whom was not my fault), their lack of enthusiasm for me has been, to say the least —- ''bloody annoying'. But in a long life as a director, these misunderstandings occur — actors are thin-skinned, very insecure and have long memories!!

Robert Morley was happy to join my cast as Lord Rawnsley, the newspaper owner who finances the race from London to Paris, and Jack's connections in the music-hall field hooked us Benny Hill and Tony Hancock — in small parts that paid off handsomely.

The remaining gap in the cast was the American flyer, Orville. We had written the part for Dick Van Dyke, a bumbling kind of western barnstormer, whose double-takes and comedy reactions should have brought the house down. We naturally assumed that with Darryl behind us, Fox in Los Angeles would be able to persuade him and pay whatever fee he was commanding at the time. However, we had not reckoned with Dick Zanuck, who was looking after his own interests at Fox and trying to persuade Stuart Whitman to star in a Western called *Rio Conchos*. It was a lousy script and he only signed Stu by offering him a two-picture deal with our *Flying Machines*.

Three or four years later we met Dick Van Dyke while he was making *Chitty Chitty Bang Bang* in the south of France. He told Pauline how much he would love to have played Orville. I overheard this and said, "But you were offered the part. The script was sent to your agent."

He shook his head. "I never saw it, I promise you. If that's true, I will carry regrets to my grave!"

Once again, all I can say is these small tragedies happen. In this case, we were 'presented' with Stu Whitman — a very personable and hardworking actor, but not a natural comedian. He brought a feet-on-the-ground quality to the part of Orville and all I could do was to make him the pan-faced kind of guy whom nothing would fluster — not even when his trousers fell down as he walked the wings of the box-kite! Stu threw himself wholeheartedly into all the outrageous pieces of action we had devised, and made his own classic version of the American flyer... so in the long run, who were we to complain?

Throughout March and April, preparations went feverishly ahead. Suddenly I was presented with a super production manager who kept track of the day by day shooting, kept the work on schedule and within cost, and liaised between the set and the front office executives.

Darryl had insisted that I put the whole production together and supervised the logistics, but now we were near the shooting he called me into the London office. He said, "It's all come together just great, but now you've got to let go of the producing side. The two jobs don't mix and I want you one hundred percent directing."

My first reaction was anger, resentment and a feeling of letdown. I had everything at my fingertips, but when Darryl laid down his edict, Elmo, who had been a director (even if they were only small shows), was sympathetic and brought over a very mild-mannered guy whom he had known in Hollywood.

Nobody in the crew was ever aware that Stan Margulies had never produced before. All I was informed was that he had been a publicist for Tony Curtis and a manager for Kirk Douglas — both hard taskmasters. He said he wanted to make 'our movie'; went around cheerfully, never throwing his weight around, and latched on remarkably quickly to everything that was going on. Jack took care to stick close beside him to "Keep him on our side!"

Stan did a great job as Producer, taking the weight off my shoulders and handling me so well that everything worked out just as Darryl had planned — so much so that when the movie was finished, Stan had undoubtedly *earned* the title of producer (and went on to produce great shows like *Roots* and *Thornbirds* and many more).

But to come back to our time warp — Allen Wheeler kept reporting the progress on the planes. A problem had developed on the Demoiselle. This little plane had been originally built and flown by a Brazilian pioneer aviator called Santos Dumont. All the records showed that it had flown in many events over France, but when Bianci (who built the plane in his garage) tried to take it up, it wouldn't do anything but hop. It had been built exactly to the original specifications and materials but had a slightly more powerful Volkswagen engine. We assembled to watch Allen, the jet test-pilot, take it up, but again it just made twenty metre hops.

We began to tear our hair as Allen went to the phone and called his opposite number in the Paris Aviation Museum. The Curator said, "I suppose you realise Santos weighed only a hundred twelve pounds?'

"Of course!" said Allen. "That could be the answer."

So, he dashed off to the White Waltham Aerodrome and dug out a young lady named Joan Hughes. She was chief instructor of the flying club and had much experience with light planes — and she weighed exactly a hundred twenty pounds! Very dubiously she sat in the so-called cockpit of the Demoiselle, took the joystick, revved the engine and it rose into the air like a bird. The result was that for the next five months she became its regular pilot and double for the flirtatious Frenchman, Jean-Pierre Cassel. She was called upon to do hairy stunts such as swooping down over Gert Froebe's head — not more than six feet above it! But like all top-rank stunt persons, she calculated exactly what she could do with her machine and never accepted any order from me without full conviction that she could achieve the shot safely.

Allen recruited pilots from the most diverse sources. Peter Hilliard was a jet pilot; George Miles, an ex-Spitfire hero; Tom Clutterbuck came from Rhodesia where he had been a crop-duster; while Derek Piggot and Taffy Rich were both helicopter pilots and had taken part in air circuses.

But again, pulling back to April '64:

Only four of the planes had successfully passed their flying tests when Darryl announced he was bringing over eighty American journalists to give the movie its proper send-off.

A tent was erected beside our giant Brooklands set at Booker, twenty miles outside London. The champagne flowed and the planes were put through their paces. The four good ones flew! Fortunately, grey clouds came up from the West, accompanied by a big wind, so that when it came to the turn of the monster Antoinette monoplane to fly, we were able to explain that it would only taxi along the runway since it was now too dangerous to take it up!

None of the press and TV people seemed to mind once they started mingling with the cast — having their photos taken with Sarah Miles and Irina Demick — and sharing jokes with our multinational comics. Jack and I felt that this was truly big-time and that Darryl had really done us proud. We forgot the long hours we had spent trying to satisfy him with twenty different openings for the movie, and the subterfuges we had had to devise to defend our really funny gags which he was always somewhat nervous about.

The weather cleared and for five months we were able to shoot through a summer which was remarkable for Southern England. Sometimes it rained, but generally, we were always able to shoot — even if it meant going inside a hangar or a tent. One always has to cope with the varying sun in England — going in and out of billowy cumulus clouds — but on this movie we had to consider 'turbulence' — surges of wind currents which could even make our little planes appear to be flying backwards!

The best time for flying turned out to be between the hours of seven-thirty and ten, and five until seven pm. During these times the planes got priority over the stars. At times, we had as many as fourteen actors sitting in their chairs on the airfield, while planes flew overhead because Allen Wheeler declared, "Perfect flying conditions!"

There was hardly a day in three months when one plane or another was not up in the sky, and we looked up at them in wonder and admiration, as the enthusiasts must have done in 1910. Often, I would go up in the Alouette helicopter with Gilbert Chomat (whom I had brought over from France) and we would fly beside the planes as near as we dared, without giving away the doubles, filming take-offs and landings over the airfield.

The flights in formation — two or three planes in the air at the same time — or higher shots which showed the planes flying over the green fields of England, were the province of my second-unit director, Don Sharp, who took the storyboards out with him and tried generally to reproduce what had been sketched (as I used to do for Disney on *Robin Hood*). He was doing so much good work that Elmo persuaded me that to save time I should let him 'shape in' some of the comedy chases with the fire engine. But it soon became obvious that Don was a fine technician but had no real eye for comedy. The shtick we had written for Benny Hill and his firemen didn't get laughs. So, after a week the first unit took these sequences back and tried to catch up time by doubling our camera crew.

Clive Reed was now a full-fledged and brilliant first assistant, who came into his own on this movie. He anticipated my needs quite uncannily, and would set crowds of up to a thousand so correctly and cleverly, that I could rarely improve on his work. He continued to have fun with Pauline in the way it had started on the *Fast Lady*. I remember one day when she was bringing a woman journalist onto the set, Clive picked up the megaphone and yelled across the airfield, "Would those two ladies please get out of the goddamn shot?! You're holding up ten aeroplanes and a thousand people." Pauline looked around and scuttled away, swearing that no camera was pointing in her direction — and she was right!!

On another occasion, as a treat, she brought her dressmaker onto the location. We were engaged in a very involved crane shot, in which we were tracking close beside each of our actor-pilots, 'proving' that they were really flying the plane. We had built a quarter of a mile of curved track around a hillside. Dick Parker mounted the planes on his hydraulic ramp and tracked them beside our crane, keeping an equal distance, while we moved slightly up and down showing the horizon level change across a narrow valley. The shots really gave the impression of flying, but needed the greatest care so that we did not reveal our trick.

I had just finished shooting Alberto Sordi, in his small monoplane singing his Italian ballad. Out of the corner of my eye I saw Pauline arrive and came down off the crane some fifteen minutes later, knowing that I wanted to go and greet her. But, instead of giving her a kiss, I kissed the dressmaker on both cheeks and shook hands with Pauline — showing how deeply a director may get involved with his thoughts and plans for the next shot!

Sarah Miles was giving remarkably good performances and bringing a certain originality into the part of Lord Rawnsley's daughter. But as the weeks went by, she held us up more and more. One afternoon we had fourteen planes lined up on the airfield (we had cheated by adding in the background a few 1930 DeHaviland Moths and other light planes). The whole cast was stationed beside their planes for takeoff, and a crowd of nearly a thousand was standing or milling around the grandstands.

"Where the hell is Sarah?" I shouted to Clive.

"Still fiddling with her hair and makeup," he replied.

I put the finishing touches to one or two other pieces of business, then jumped into a jeep and sped across the airfield to the makeup tent. There I found Sarah sitting in front of a mirror with her hair all pulled down.

"She wasn't happy with what I had done," said the hairdresser.

"For Christ's sake, Sarah," I yelled, "Don't you know what you're doing?!" I explained how many people were being held up by her petty-mindedness.

"You want me to look my best," she said dreamily. "But you're wearing a hat and veil," I pointed out. I then ordered the hairdresser to pile her hair on top of her head, then physically pulled Sarah by the arm into the jeep. She yelled at me and fought and screamed, but in the end she realised that if she wished to keep any kind of respect and relationship with the rest of the cast, she could not hold things up any longer.

Both the makeup men and hairdresser told me later what her problem was — she would look in the mirror, decide she was utterly ugly, then struggle to achieve some impossible visual dream. Just another example of the basic insecurity of actors. Her performances were always so assured and inclined to be aggressive that no one would ever think that she had this secret problem. Although I had to be tough with her, as I had in the past with dear Glynis Johns, I tried to baby Sarah along and allow for her problems by doubling the time we allowed for her preparations.

Then, poor Sarah found herself in the midst of another problem. Either Stu Whitman was taking his part too seriously or he had genuinely fallen for her, but as the whole company drove down to Dover for the beach scenes and the big takeoff across the English Channel, Stu trailed her in his car and manoeuvred her into a field where he tried to corner and 'make' her. Sarah managed to defend herself by the old-fashioned methods of kneeing him in the crotch.

From that time on, these two who were supposed to be in love, were at daggers drawn. In filming a kiss, they refused to make contact, and in the end sequence where they embrace under the wing of the box-kite, I had to set up the over-shoulder shots with a double, and play the big close-ups with me just off-screen pretending to kiss and embrace them. Due to the magic of film, it worked and the scenes were believable!

On the Dover location, our two units had very different problems. Don had to cover the fourteen planes flying out over Dover Castle and clearing the white cliffs to head across the Channel to France. Somehow, the solid stone castle caused dangerous up-currents, and regularly as clockwork, a morning fog would climb up the cliffs. It took three weeks to get perfect conditions for the fly-out, and even then several of the planes started to drop towards the waves. They would probably have crashed if Don hadn't cut the shot!

But the eventual fly-out was thrilling — a magnificent culmination of all the struggles to build the planes. Pauline was not so thrilled because of one stupid logistic muddle. Jack and I had written a scene based on a true incident, where a silly looking young Englishman (played by Jeremy Lloyd) takes his dog on the trip. Naturally, the idea was to have our own Yorkie, Baxter, play the dog role, and he was all set with a tie-on placard saying, 'I am the first dog to fly!' The plane had to come down, float in the water, and both pilot and dog had to be rescued in a comedic but heart-warming way. Unfortunately, when the moment for shooting arrived and the weather was perfect for the planes, Baxter had not received his 'call!'

Don grabbed hold of the first dog he saw, which was a black mongrel setter, shoved her in the plane with an improvised placard, and went on with the shooting all day long. It was a perfect day and he achieved both long shots and all his close shots — which eliminated our poor Baxter! Pauline saw the rushes and she was heartbroken, because right from our days in Barbados we had planned this as a funny ongoing sequence, with our star dog continuing his career. Again, all I can say is that these screw-ups do happen!

Meanwhile, the first unit was shooting bathing belles in amusing costumes on the beach. While waiting for the weather to fly, our gallant aviators were having fun on the beach with the girls — as we had written in our script. The scenes were playing so well that Jack Davies had time on his hands and, in his charming way, began to 'chat up' the bathing belles.

Two beautiful showgirls, Alita and Sue, who had worked for me in *You Know What Sailors Are*, came to me and said, "Jack is making himself out to be such a lady-killer, we'd like to take him down a peg or two." "Fine with me," I said. "Go ahead."

So, they cooked up a plan with Clive. That evening, about seven o'clock, Jack got a call in his hotel bedroom from Alita saying that a few of them would be getting together to drink champagne, and would he like to join them? Jack immediately accepted, combed his hair very carefully, put on a clean shirt, and trotted down to the room number she gave him. Alita opened the door and Jack's eyes nearly popped out as he saw her in her tightest bikini shorts and bra, with only a thin cotton wrap covering them — revealing her superb figure to perfection! All smiles, she poured him a glass of champagne and a moment later Sue came out of the bathroom wearing a towelling wrap and brushing out her hair.

Jack sat down on the bed and began to chat them up in his usual fashion — but a little more nervously than he'd been doing on the beach. Alita excused herself and Sue sat on the bed beside Jack, still brushing her hair. Alita appeared again, holding up a mini-dress. She asked Jack for his opinion of it and, removing her wrap, started to climb into the dress. Jack's eyes were getting bigger when the phone rang.

A man's voice asked, "Is Mr. Davies there?' Sue reached over the bed and handed the phone to Jack, who was now getting very excited. The voice on the phone said, "Mr. Davies, your wife is down here in the lobby and wants to know whether she should come up and join the party." Jack went white as a sheet, staggered off the bed, and backed away to the door. The girls followed him, using all their wiles to persuade him to stay.

Suddenly, losing his cool, Jack fell to his knees and begged them to let him out of the room, shouting in a husky voice, "Please! For God's sake, my wife's on the way up!" The girls gave him a peck on the cheek and pushed him out. They listened at the door and then peeped out to see Jack's progress down the corridor, blocked by Clive and his two assistants. Clive had a script in his hand and started to ask him about a scene for the next day's shoot. Jack stammered and stuttered that he'll talk to them later, but at that moment Alita and Sue came out of their bedroom wearing nothing but bra and panties. The three assistants stared and looked at Jack accusingly.

"Oh, Jack, what have you been up to?" said Clive.

"Nothing, nothing, I swear. I've done nothing and I must go because my wife's on her way up!" John, our third assistant, now ran to the bannister, looked down and said, "Yes, there *is* a lady coming up the stairs." Jack pushed them aside and ran, only to be followed by laughter that built and built. Suddenly, he realised that he'd been set up and peered around the corner. "You bastards," he said. 'You dirty, rotten bastards!"

Harmless fun on location!

Back at Booker, Jack moved with us into a period cottage we had rented near the airfield. Almost nightly we went over the scenes to see if we can make last minute improvements to the gags and routines. Benny Hill and Tony Hancock were working out funnier than ever and were clearly prepared to do anything we asked. Unfortunately, Hancock had hit the bottle too hard on his first weekend, and the report came back that he had broken his foot. We rewrote his part, cashing in on "the brave flyer with his foot in plaster!"

Altogether, we seemed to be getting good stuff and often managed to add a few laughs from ideas we had picked up on rehearsals. I remember the scene where Gert Froebe had to try to fly the German plane 'by the book.' Jack suddenly climbed up beside me and said, "As he stands in the cockpit and opens the book of instructions, try letting him say, Number One. Sit down!'" It proved to be one of the biggest laughs in the picture.

Darryl Zanuck, although he never came to the location, was still trying to help us make a big, big movie. Suddenly, Red Skelton arrived from Hollywood. Darryl had persuaded him to play the legendary Greek who threw himself off a cliff wearing a pair of birdlike wings. Red was a joy to work with — inventive, willing — and helped us add broad comedy to the newsreel shots which open the movie. I have never worked with anyone who gagged and told jokes to the camera crew right up to the moment of shooting, yet switched into the take with complete aplomb.

The dive his character had to make was done by a stuntman, jumping from a tubular scaffold into a tank only twelve feet wide and not more than seven feet deep! I was very worried about the stunt, especially since it seemed possible that the wings might divert the flight and make the diver miss the tank. However, I was assured by both the stunt arranger, John Sullivan, and by Dinny Powell that there would be no problem. The cameras were turning and I gave the signal to dive.

Dinny came hurtling down to the tank, where John stood and broke the water just before he hit the surface. The wings had made Dinny turn over slightly and his thighs were a flaming red, but we had the shot! Then, I heard the second camera assistant calling behind me, "Please, Gov! Listen! We've got to do it again."

Absolutely livid, I strode back to Jerry, the focus-puller, who admitted he had made the mistake in adjusting the speed of the camera — speeding up the action rather than slowing it down. He apologised, "Can't think where my brain was, sir!" I felt like firing him on the spot, but went back to Dinny and John to explain the situation.

"Not to worry," said Dinny, "it'll only cost you another two hundred quid." He winked. "And for me, it's a piece of cake 'cuz now I know exactly how the jump feels." The shot worked perfectly the second time.

One might imagine that we must have had many accidents in more than three months of taking up these planes which were made of wire, wood and canvas. Almost every day there were problems and adjustments to the rigging or wing settings. It seemed to me the conversations and arguments among the fourteen flight mechanics we carried and the six pilots at the end of each day, must be mirroring almost exactly how it must have been in the pioneer times at Brooklands.

Once we had proved the planes would really fly, Elmo in his wisdom had ordered Allen Wheeler to have two duplicates made of each model. Now, almost every week we were cannibalising them — taking a piece from one duplicate to keep the other in the air. The only near accident we ever had was with the Bleriot — our most reliable plane and also Taffy, the best pilot. One morning he was passing over the field, when we saw the plane jerk up and turn on its side. Obviously, struggling and losing height, Taffy disappeared over the treetops to the West.

Clive jumped into the jeep along with a couple of mechanics, and drove to where Taffy had miraculously landed. They found the whole fuselage had twisted ninety degrees and the tail rudder was useless. But somehow, Taffy Rich had landed the plane and now Allen agreed with Dick Parker that the fuselage should be rebuilt — this time in duralumin, for extra strength. Everyone worked through the night and the next day the Bleriot was in the air again.

Dick Parker was a tower of strength. Because he was a flyer himself and a fully qualified engineer, he was always on hand with expert advice for every mechanical problem. His 'flying rig' with its cables strung between a hundred and fifty feet high construction cranes, took four days to move each time I needed a change of background. Whenever Dick suspended a plane, we had to paint the give-away holding wires the colour of the sky at *that particular moment!* — a very tricky chore, but it worked!

Scenes such as Alberto Sordi jumping from his burning plane on to the undercarriage of Stu Whitman's box-kite, could never have attempted without 'Dick's rig', plus a truck carrying the other 'plane' on its roof, running underneath.

I nearly killed Ken Buckle, my great stuntman-friend from *Swiss Family* days. He was doubling for Gert Froebe, steering the Harley-Davidson motorbike from the sidecar. He had to just miss a landing plane, and skid up the slope of the racetrack. To my horror, as he began up the track, I heard the bike rev-up instead of cutting back, and we had to stand helplessly by, as Ken shot up over the slope to disappear over the rim of the track. I knew that on the other side was our imitation sewage-farm, consisting of not more than a foot of dirty water held in black plastic sheets spread over low tubular framing!

As I ran to look over the edge of the racetrack, I imagined Ken lying there with his head smashed in against the tubular. By a miracle, he had escaped this fate. The

Harley-Davidson was on its side revving away like mad, and Ken was crawling out of the sidecar. He must have flown thirty feet through the air and although he was white as a sheet, it turned out that his only injury was a broken collarbone. He staggered over to me and apologised for ruining the shot!! (What a trouper!) He explained that somehow the twist control had stuck and, in his efforts to free it, he had increased the acceleration rather than decreasing it.

"Sorry, Gov," he said, "won't happen again." And three days later, he gallantly redid the shot.

Elmo was now getting anxious, and almost daily called Stan Margulies into the Soho office to discuss how the shooting could be sped up or scenes omitted. Stan, now hooked completely on our movie, was incredibly loyal to Jack and me. He told Elmo that the only cuts that could be made would be the sequences with Irina Demick, which we were going to shoot mainly in the studio. "We can't cut her scenes because of Darryl," wailed Elmo, "but maybe Ken could lose some of the gags, with those non-flying planes."

"But we've already spent a fortune building them," argued Stan. "It would be criminal not to show their crazy efforts to fly!"

"Every time Dick Parker moves that rig, it ruins the schedule," said Elmo. "We've just got to find ways to economise, otherwise my neck is on the block." Most executives get to feel like this unless they are top showmen, such as Jack Warner, or Michael Eisner at Disney in more recent years.

We continued to shoot, and even made a trip to Paris for the establishing shots of our three planes flying around the Eiffel Tower. The economies on which Elmo had insisted, resulted in the planes having to be achieved with models on 'blue screen' later. I shot all the basic material with tied-down cameras and again the composite shots worked acceptably.

It was now September, and I was still picking up material at Booker Airfield. When it rained, we improvised close-ups in a tent, but it all became very grim. Even though each day Elmo was issuing ultimatums that we had to close down, I went on shooting for ten more days, completing every sequence I knew the picture needed. Relations became so strained that when the usual 'wrap party' was discussed, Elmo said that the company had no money to pay for such frivolities. The result was that Stan, Jack and I had to cough up over two thousand pounds to put on the party. Every crew and cast throughout the world expect such an acknowledgement of their efforts — and if ever there was a time when they deserved recognition and 'a bit of fun' together, *it was this shoot!*

The rough-cut was coming along excellently — a bit too long, but obviously cuttable. On Friday night I had left my editor assembling the final day's work, knowing exactly how I wanted to edit. At two o'clock I was awakened by a call from the hospital at Slough to say that our editor, 'Rocky' (Gordon Stone) was dead! Either he had been working too long hours or had had a stroke. The fact is that he had lost control of his Jaguar, and hit a telegraph pole at speed and was killed almost instantly.

This gave Elmo the chance he had been waiting for. Even though he was the managing director of a big company involved in four big movies at this time, he couldn't resist plying his trade as an editor. He moved several movieolas (editing machines) into an adjoining office in Soho, and now ordered all our material to be shipped into that office. I resisted this most vehemently because I knew Elmo was now not in sympathy with the movie, and that on the pretext of following Zanuck's predilection for romance instead of comedy, he would start to massacre our gags and comedy sequences.

I was lucky enough to find that Anne Coates, who had been my editor on *The Sword and The Rose* was free, and I immediately established her in our cutting room at Pinewood. I called Zanuck directly to explain that, in any case, I would now need to work side by side with any editor, at least until they got familiar with the material. The ploy worked. Anne and I completed the final cut of just over two and a half hours, in five weeks. Darryl had ruled that the picture was going to go 'road show' — which meant the movie should run about two hours twenty minutes, with an interval somewhere in the middle.

Zanuck was still living and operating from Paris, so on a wet November day, Stan Margulies, Elmo and I took the rough cut across the Channel and locked ourselves away in Darryl's projection room in the Rue de Boiete for nearly ten hours.

The Maestro's verdict was that a couple of gag-routines should be cut, two new scenes should be written to expand the love story between Stuart Whitman and Sarah Miles... and he would like me to sit in with him and Irina Demick, to go in detail through her sequences on the morrow! In all, it looked as though we might have scraped through with a very good movie.

Jack wrote the extra scenes while I went ahead, post-synchronising some of the actors, and trying to find a suitable composer. In the end it was Elmo who found Ron Goodwin. He came up with a tape of his good-natured martial tune, complete with lyrics. I remember listening to it with Jack and feeling that this was not at all the kind of music that we had vaguely envisioned. But we had more tapes run off and, playing the tune over and over again, we soon decided that the 'oompah music' gave an added sense of the ridiculous, and the lyrics paid due homage and tribute to the early aviators.

I think *Those Magnificent Men in their Flying Machines* is the most perfect theme tune I have ever been given in any of my movies, and of course, it has become a standard with military bands and whenever the Queen reviews the troops outside Buckingham Palace.

I remember in my early days at Gainsborough, another piece of advice the old veteran Maurice Elvey gave me. It was, "Always try and have your next picture set before you go on the floor with your new movie!"

With the writing, pre-production, shooting and post-production, *Flying Machines* had occupied my whole existence. For over two years, I had not had a moment to think seriously about or prepare for any next picture. During that period, it is true I had brought an English classic, 'High Wind In Jamaica' to Elmo's notice, also a fascinating Australian subject with the title 'Call Me When The Cross Turns Over' — in which the lead character was called 'Fascinatin'!

Possibly to pay me back for our bad relations, Elmo had quietly prepared *High Wind In Jamaica* and given it to another director, Alex McKendrick. I had an option on "Call Me When The Cross Turns Over" and the two stars who had agreed to play in it. They were Diane Cilento and — surprise, surprise — none other than her husband, Sean Connery! He loved the name "Fascinatin'!

It was not an easy book to script and so, in the good old days, I had passed it to Elmo to develop. He had four versions written, but when the last one was in shape,

Sean Connery flatly refused to work with Elmo or Zanuck, because of their shabby treatment and scorn of his acting on *The Longest Day*. Things do tend to go in circles in this business — if you make an enemy, no matter who you are, it will catch up with you somewhere!

Elmo was making no special effort to offer me the picture with another cast. Suddenly when I was about the start dubbing the music, dialogue and effects on *Flying Machines*, an offer came to me out of left field. It was to make, what eventually became *The Battle of the Bulge*.

After much heart-searching, I decided I could safely leave the finishing of *Flying Machines* to Stan Margulies, who had proved to be a most expert and loyal producer. And Jack would be always available to represent our joint opinion about the comedy elements of the film. Also, to be truthful, since Zanuck had given his blessing to the rough-cut, Elmo's attitude had changed, and I knew that since he was such a pro, he would no longer try to sabotage the picture, despite our many disagreements during the production. In truth, the poor guy was simply eaten up with jealousy.

At a party thrown by the British end of Fox, Jack and I happened to overhear Elmo saying to a visiting producer, "Those two Limeys are going to gather all the kudos and residuals from this movie. My contributions as the active executive-in-charge will be forgotten!" He had a point! But, after all, it *was* our picture!

The British premiere was at the Odeon, Leicester Square, in the summer of '65. Pauline and I came back from Spain. She had a very special evening gown made in Madrid for the occasion, but when the moment came for Jack and I to stand in line and be presented to the Queen, some stupid Fox publicist pushed her out of the line of vision so that she never saw the great moment! But a few minutes later she was squeezing my hand, as the screen changed from the postage-stamp frame of the old-time movie shots for the 'Man's Early Attempts To Fly' prologue, and opened, apparently endlessly, into a wide CinemaScope shape to reveal Ronnie Searle's flamboyant title backgrounds. The audience gasped.

In the interval, Darryl came across to us and took both our hands, shook them, thanked us, and said he felt we had a well-deserved winner. I'll swear there were tears of joy in his eyes! John Davis passed me in the foyer with a beaming Dinah. He gave me one of his wry smiles and said, "An excellent job, Annakin. Should make a fortune!"

Jack and Earl St. John were already 'floating', as we went on to dine and dance in what was probably the greatest night of our lives. Pauline and I never got to bed, because we had to catch the first plane out to Madrid to shoot *The Battle of the Bulge*.

CHAPTER FOURTEEN
The Battle of the Bulge
Working and Playing With Big Hollywood Stars (And Their Ladies); An Unworthy Script Becomes A Memorable War Movie

The first I heard of *The Battle of the Bulge* project was from my agent, Dennis Van Thal. One of the American producers, Milton Sperling, had come over to London specifically to "meet with the director of *The Longest Day*." I learned later that for years Milton had been Zanuck's assistant and line producer. Over tea at the Ritz, I found him to be a very civilised and literate man, and after a brief outline of how and when the production would go (in Spain), he gave me the script.

It seemed quite a good narrative account of the German surprise onslaught against the American forces in the Ardennes and how the allied advance was nearly turned at this point, but the dialogue was not remarkable, the character relationships nothing special — it seemed to me just another war picture. As once before, I sought out the advice of my old friend Cecil Bernstein, who said, "Make it, dear boy! You don't know how *Magnificent Men* will be received, and war films go on and on forever..."

"How can you say that?" I said. "There must be an end to them sometime. Surely, people have had enough of war?"

Cecil shook his head. "Wearing my distributor's hat, war is big box-office. If the film is big and *real* war, and if Hank Fonda, Bob Ryan and Dana Andrews are already booked to play in it, you should not hesitate to accept!"

Sydney Box gave me the same advice, saying, "This is big time, old boy."

"But, surely, I should be able to make any subject I want with Darryl, after *Magnificent Men* comes out and is a success," I objected.

"You never know," said Sydney. "Take the bird in the hand."

"But what about the post-production of *Flying Machines* and my dubbing?" I asked.

"As you very well know, dubbing is strictly a technical process and so long as Stan Margulies and Jack are there to keep an eye on your concept of the picture, don't worry about it."

CHAPTER FOURTEEN The Battle of the Bulge

Milton had told me that *The Battle of the Bulge* was to be made in Cinerama, which was the latest wide-screen process — supposed to bring the action 'right on to the audience's laps'. I began to think how I might use it. The producers had already secured the use of eighty tanks from the Spanish Army — which was still using Shermans... a lot of toys to play with! Toys? Pauline had been making me watch a new TV series called *Doctor Who*, which featured the 'Daleks'. In this programme, humans had to find ways to thwart the apparently irrevocable onslaught of metal monsters. So, I decided I would try and use Cinerama as a kind of 3-D, shooting in such a way that the tanks would loom up like monsters against the humans, whom I would make small and puny, but their tenacity and courage would make them beat the machines! This would be my theme... something worthwhile and obviously never done before in this way.

With this concept I salved my conscience and accepted the assignment, even though I would apparently have only three weeks to prepare! Pauline and I set off for Madrid in early January '65. Despite what Milton had told me, I was pleasantly surprised to find all the locations had already been chosen; the sets built by Gene Lourié, a Russian born art director working in the US; the guns and props were ready, and my old friend Alex Weldon in charge of Special Effects — explosions, snow, fire, smoke — all the many visual aids that would be necessary to make war look real.

I discovered that Dick Fleischer had been originally set to direct the movie, but had walked off due to differences with the producers! I didn't like the sound of that, but I'd accepted the job, and now set about casting the many minor roles. We scoured Spain to find all the young American actors living there. It turned out there were quite a few — though I suspected some of them were not really actors. I felt I could work with *them,* but I had not reckoned with Bernie Glasser, the production controller — a small, rat-faced man who turned out to be mean, ignorant and an arch cheese-parer!!

During the first week of shooting, I found a number of small-part actors appearing on the set whom I had never seen before. When I questioned Leon Chooluck, the production manager, he said, "You'd better talk to Bernie."

Bernie wouldn't look me in the eye, but said, "The guys you chose didn't fit the costumes. It's too late to change them again, you'll just have to make do with the guys I've found!"

I had never come across that attitude before and was fuming! But Phil Yordan, Milton's co-producer, came over to me and whispered, "I've just got you Charlie Bronson and Telly Savalas!" He made it sound very personal! New names were turning up every day... Robert Shaw as the German tank commander; my old friend, James MacArthur; and Ty Hardin, who had starred in a slew of very successful beach boy/surfing TV shows.

Among the Germans, there were several old friends from *The Longest Day:* Hans Christian Blech, who was to play Robert Shaw's adjutant, and Werner Peters as Commandant of the German onslaught. Phil Yordan had written a very touching scene for a girl caught up in the war, and now he announced that he was bringing over the wonderful Italian actress, Pier Angeli. How could I complain?

Phil Yordan was a fascinating character. Like Harold Robbins, he had come from a tough Chicago background, and had made his way up in New York and Hollywood as a playwright and screenwriter. He was very talented, but over the years had discovered that there were always young men around eager to write, and he had gotten into the habit of employing them as a stable of ghostwriters. If any of them succeeded in getting their names on the credits along with Phil's name, they were very lucky! But without Phil's drive and producing ability, they would probably never have succeeded in getting any of their writing on screen, and he always paid them quite well. After a good career in Hollywood, where he had written such pictures as *The Naked Jungle*, *Johnny Guitar*, *God's Little Acre*, *Anna Lucasta*, Phil had moved to Spain and provided the screenplays for the big epic pictures, which that remarkable showman-cum-financial wizard, Samuel Bronston, was producing.

We could not help but hear the stories floating around — that in the 'good old days' of *El Cid*, *55 Days To Peking*, and *The Fall of the Roman Empire*, the "gravy train" had left Madrid once a month with loot for Switzerland, spirited away from the epic budgets by Samuel and his half-dozen associates, which included Velensky, the Italian designer, and Phil. Of course, this was an exaggeration, but undoubtedly symptomatic of what had been going on. Now, Bronston was broke — owing countless millions to banks, insurance companies, Arabs and God knows who else. But that did not stop him throwing a final lavish party in his Madrid mansion to which Pauline and I were invited.

Sam shook my hand and I immediately felt the magnetism, the silky charm — like that I had known with Sir Alexander Korda. Although they were undoubtedly rascals of the same ilk, they were great showmen with unlimited visions for entertaining the world and making the masses happier. The movie industry is no better off with the present po-faced take-over merchants, with their lawyers and accountants calling the shots!!

Presumably having studied Bronston's methods and sources, Phil had raised the money for *Battle*, and Milton had brought the guarantee of world distribution through his connection with Jack Warner (he was married to Jack's daughter). This was the 'unreal' set-up we found ourselves in.

In late January, the whole company moved north to the beautiful old town of Segovia — to shoot the main winter scenes with the tanks. Pauline and I were lucky enough to rent a small chateau with three-foot thick stone walls and many fireplaces, which had been occupied until fairly recently by Alec Guinness, when he had played Marcus Aurelius in *The Fall of the Roman Empire*. We could look from our front windows, up to the historic castle of Segovia, standing gaunt and grim on the skyline.

The first day's shoot required forty tanks to come out of a grove of pine trees in heavy snow. Alex Weldon had spent a week spreading marble dust all over the ground the tanks were to cross. He was now ready with four big wind machines and many sacks of artificial snow. Sitting beside the operator on the big Chapman crane, I gave the signal for the snow to start. The tanks sneaked out from amongst the trees. I turned to Alex and gave a thumbs-up sign and he pointed to the sky and shook his head, mouthing, "Not me, but *him!*" It was true. The heavens opened, and real snow was falling — and continued to fall in contradiction to all past weather records, for the *next five weeks!*

That part of Spain was not prepared with snowploughs or even salt to throw on the roads to make them passable. For days Jack Hillyard — who had been my operator on *Hotel Sahara* and was now established as a top cameraman — and my Spanish assistant, Pepe Lopez, who had been trained by Peter Bolton on *Across The Bridge* — set an example to the rest of the company, by striding up a three mile hill in order to reach our tanks.

Gradually, tracks were cleared and army vehicles were able to bring up the rest of the unit. But every day was a challenge — even to the point of being able to get one camera in position by ten am! Whenever the tanks approached, they threw up masses of mud and churned up the battlefield. We usually managed to shoot the major action with three or four cameras. The conditions were tough but we had to press on, because this was what real war must have been like. The actors had rarely, if ever, been asked to work in such cold and confusion. I remember one day when we were due to go down the hill to a bunker outside which Hank Fonda was to play his first scene in the picture. There had been many problems and delays. Suddenly, I turned to Pepe and yelled, 'Where's Hank?"

"My God!" he cried. "I forgot to tell him we would be late."

So, I jumped into a jeep, drove swiftly down the hill and found that Hank had been standing outside the bunker, keeping warm under a blanket and stamping his feet like any soldier *for five hours!* I apologised profusely. He merely said, "Don't worry, Ken. You don't need to tell *me* what filmmaking is like."

Hank was a remarkable professional. He was always on time, patient, eager to make the best of every situation, and always knew his lines. He wanted to give his best to the director, but could be very short with front-office types. The same could be said of most of the Americans in the cast.

Charlie Bronson arrived on the cold mountain set looking grim and formidable — at least that was the report that came up from my third assistant. We went ahead laying a track in the snow, past foxholes where the shivering GI's were entrenched to try and stop the advance of the panzers. Charlie's first shot in the picture was to arrive just as the GI's were panicking as the lumbering monsters appeared through the trees. Explosives had been set, guns fixed to fire blanks, smoke — it always helps the visual effect in a battle! But there was no sign of Charlie.

"He's fiddling about in wardrobe," said the third assistant over the intercom. "Can't move him!"

"He glares at you," said our rather mild second assistant, hurrying up to Pepe. "And fiddles worse than any woman," he added. "We're gonna have trouble with that one!"

So, I sent Pepe down to fetch him, in whatever state of dress he happened to be. When Charlie arrived, I told him quite firmly of the hardships the crew were going through — the days were short, the weather highly variable and it was my intention to shoot as much footage as possible each day, which meant I couldn't be kept waiting by actors fiddling with their costumes. Charlie's face broke into that very attractive, rare grin of his, and he took my hand. "Keep your shirt on, Ken," he said. "I won't keep you waiting again."

He never did! We developed a friendly relationship that has lasted to this day, and he gave, to my mind, a performance that showed what a truly fine actor he can be. The fact that he has often settled for movies he has just walked through, is another matter altogether.

James MacArthur, as the GI who loses his nerve, gave a very moving performance and was a joy to work with.

But another young actor of his generation, Ty Hardin, was a different cup of tea. Because of his good looks, fine physique and willingness to do *anything,* he had worked without stop in the States, but he was not great on dialogue and was accident-prone. His role was that of leader of Nazi infiltrators posing as Americans. The action called for him to take his column across a frozen river. Without hesitation, and almost before I had finished briefing him, he dived straight in with his full pack and steel helmet. The helmet saved him, but he could have broken his neck, because as yet no one had checked the depth of the water! We also had to wait twenty minutes while wardrobe put him into a dry costume!

Ty claimed to be an expert at any sport you might mention, and during his days off, he used to take Pauline up the snow slopes to teach her speed turns. The day we were shooting a German tank blowing up as it crossed a bridge, Pauline came to visit. Ty Hardin, trying to be gallant, bent to kiss her hand, rose too quickly and gave her a knockout blow under the chin with his steel helmet. This was the sort of thing that was always happening to him. He made up for it with profuse apologies or one of his surprise treats.

Sensing that the unit had little respect for him and was beginning to treat him as a laughing stock, Ty arranged to throw a big party and imported twenty-six girls from the dance halls in Madrid. He brought them up to Segovia by bus and the whole unit had a fantastic evening, contributed to by ever-flowing goblets of special punch.

The next morning on the set, Jimmy MacArthur and myself were both yawning our heads off, and exchanging notes, found that our respective wives had been insatiable in bed. Pepe, overhearing this, told how he and his two assistants had been mobbed by six of the girls, who at two in the morning had banged on their doors and insisted on sharing beds, because Ty had not provided a bus for them to go back to Madrid. They also had been sex mad and we found this was the story with most of the unit. Unknown to everybody, and believing it to be a great joke, Ty had filled the punch bowls with Spanish Fly – a notorious aphrodisiac! Although in retrospect the results were funny, at the end of each long day and battles with snow and ice, the last thing most of us wanted was rampant sex!

I pressed ahead with two units, often setting up vast panoramic shots employing the whole eighty tanks. It was a director's feast, but no joke for Alex Weldon and his twenty assistants. They were forever laying tubes of explosives or burning rubber tires to make the black smoke of war. Some days we had the whole landscape filled with tanks, armoured vehicles, jeeps, with the sound camera moving in to close dialogue shots of Hank Fonda, Bob Ryan and Dana Andrews, who never missed a beat or fluffed their lines.

This was quite something for Dana because, like Trevor Howard, he liked to hit the bottle. He seemed to have some professional sixth sense, which made him not get sloshed during big scenes, but only in close linking shots like negotiating the steps down from the Ambleve Headquarters. More often than not, he would have to be supported surreptitiously by Hank Fonda and Bob Ryan.

We had now fallen into a routine where I was sometimes shooting as many as thirty or forty set-ups a day, by working two units not more than a hundred yards apart. I would leapfrog from one to another with a verve and determination that caused the more lethargic Spaniards to gasp.

It was probably about this time that I got the reputation of being a slave driver, or 'Panicky Annakin'!

The director of photography of the second unit was my old friend, Johnny Cabrera, who had been a loader on the big three-strip Technicolor camera when we shot *Robin Hood*. He was the one who had led me to the wonderful locations on

Across The Bridge... and now he was working his butt off to achieve photography equal to that of Jack Hildyard, who was D.P. on the first unit. Fortunately for me, they were the closest of buddies and used to spend every evening comparing notes as to what filters they had found most effective, and how to match each other's shots.

One of our most effective sets was an old grey-stone town that had already been shelled and ruined in the Spanish Civil War. This also gave a great realism to many of our shots, and may have contributed to Jack Warner sending a cable to Milton and Phil saying that the rushes were some of the most impressive war material that he had ever seen.

When Milton came onto the set and showed me this cable, I must have been very heartened and thrilled, but Milton tells me that all I did was to nod and continue with the scene I was shooting, which was the massacre of the American troops at Malmedy. To me, this was one of the most poignant and important scenes in the script. S.S. officers had trucked in over one hundred sixty GI prisoners, lined them up in the centre of a forest clearing, dropped the tail-flaps of four trucks to reveal machine guns, and then mowed down all hundred and sixty — save one, who escaped miraculously through the trees to tell his tale.

I knew I had been shooting great battle material, but this sequence called for great sensibility, and meticulous positioning of where each soldier would fall on that white snowfield. It was a matter of life and death that I should stage this to achieve the maximum audience shock. I have always felt that I really pulled this one off, and that I was very privileged to shoot it.

The sequence, with Robert Shaw as the Commandant of the Panzer Brigade, was not quite so successful, at least the first time around. The massive German tanks had been repulsed by the courage of the American forces, but Robert Shaw had to be indomitable — determined to continue the assault. He gathered his commanders together and harangued them into regaining courage for the Fatherland and the glory of war — giving such an uncanny imitation of Hitler that I fell into the trap of allowing him to play the scene in this manner. When we saw the rushes, both Milton and Phil turned to me.

"This doesn't quite work!" they said.

"I know he's a monster," said Phil, "but he's a man leading a very special brigade. He has to be one of them."

"There has to be some light and shade in the character," said Milton, "or you'd never believe they would follow him." He turned to Robert. "Can't you see, you're throwing away a peach of a role?"

Robert rose from his seat and walked towards the screen. Suddenly, he turned on me, his eyes blazing, "You were the one who encouraged me to shout and yell like a maniac!" He leaned towards the producers. "If I had followed my instincts, I would have played the speech like this ..." And he proceeded to give a completely different reading — quiet, but with light and shade. He was so intense that it was quite intimidating.

"I'll buy that," said Phil. "Exactly what I intended when I wrote the scene."

"You'd better go back and re-shoot," said Milton.

As we walked out of the theatre, Robert looked at me with narrowed eyes and the suspicion of a grin. The thought flashed through my brain, "He's got his revenge!" Here was another actor whom I had tested and rejected — for the part of the police inspector in *The Informer*. Like Mike Caine and Sean Connery, he had never inwardly forgiven me.

As we re-shot and worked together, I discovered that Robert was a strangely dark character, really needing psychiatric help. When not on call he used to challenge Phil at golf, or play tennis with Milton, but they soon had to make excuses because he became so obstreperous if he did not win, that the games ceased to be fun. Robert was married to Mary Ure, a gentle, sensitive actress whom I used to adore. They would always attend each other's 'first nights', but according to a story Robert used to tell (with no compunction), Mary had broken their agreement on one of his plays, and coming home around two am he found her asleep on the sofa.

"I looked down at her sleeping peacefully as if nothing had happened," he said, "and I went into the kitchen, filled a bucket of water, and threw it all over the bitch!"

Once I had felt my way into Robert's psyche, I found ways to release a lot of his pent-up fury in the role of the Panzer commandant, with the result that he became immortalised as one of the most fascinating Nazi characters in World War II movies.

One weekend before we left Segovia, I received a message that Milton and Phil wanted to have a long chat with me. Having heard rumours through Leon Chooluck and the despicable Bernie Glasser, that I was going over budget, I thought they must be coming to discuss cuts and even perhaps a change in director!

But no, after an excellent meal that Pauline had prepared for them, Phil leaned across the big log fire and said, "Tell us, Ken, what sort of a film are you making?"

I said, "Well, I'm trying to make a movie about war, at least as true as *The Longest Day*, but of course the story is not quite as good, so I'm trying to make up for this by impressive shots of tanks against puny human beings."

"That's what we thought," said Milton.

"What we need is a theme," said Phil.

I had been brought up during my days of studying writing, that one should always settle your theme first, and *then* write a play or script to support that theme. Here it looked as though we were tackling the matter back to front, and I began to be alarmed that after all, I was perhaps not going to make the great movie I had begun to hope for. However, we spent several hours kicking around possible themes.

Phil said, "I'm going to write new scenes for you, Ken, feed them to you each day and you can say whether you feel they are achieving our new objective". This objective was to show that on the German side, a most efficient commander like Robert Shaw could lead his troops into dangerous situations and arouse tremendous loyalty, but unless he had a consideration for human dignity and the individual, he would lead them to Hell's Gates.

We returned to Madrid and, true to his word, Phil produced new scenes every day. From this experience I can vouch for the fact that Phil could be a top screenwriter without his 'stable' (which many people had come to doubt).

One way or another, a main theme and worthwhile side plots were developed *during* the making of this movie, which eventually succeeded and raised it into the top ranks of war movies. I've always felt it remarkable that we were able to break the rules and develop the 'raison d'etre' of the film as we went along.

There were quite a number of dialogue scenes in the script that were not top quality to start with. I remember going into rehearsal with Hank Fonda, Bob Ryan and Dana Andrews in the American H.Q. Office at Ambleve. I held a first rehearsal with the three stars whose reaction at the end of the reading was an almost identical grunt.

They looked at me for my reaction, but I shrugged and looked *back* at my script to gain time. "Well," said Hank, "let's try it. Jump straight in, play it straight and see how it sounds."

They did, and it was immediately quite a lot better. Hank began to make one or two variations, the others joined in. They were improvising, giving me a chance to pick out the way the scene might be improved, and I realised these three great actors could literally take a page of the telephone book and make it sound interesting!

Their strong acting instincts and long theatre experience made them able to give me hints and lead me into changes in the scene, to make it more plausible. Phil never remarked about the changes and Milton said he had never expected the scene to play so well.

About this time a new player arrived in this production by the name of Bill Foreman. It turned out that he owned the Cinerama process, and all the Cinerama theatres in the United States. He had seen some of the rushes with Jack Warner, discussed a pattern of release, but raised a point to which the producers had never really given much attention. Cinerama was really a projection trick to try and give a three-dimensional effect and make the audience feel they were participating in the action. I had been consciously attempting to use the process to make the tanks seem more monstrous, but this was only effective in close-up. Bill was anxious to introduce some fast downhill jeep rides so that the audience could experience the thrill and danger. Similarly, in the air, he wanted plane shots — diving and spinning. These were not strictly storytelling points, but they certainly indicated Bill's sense of showmanship. He had brought with him George Willoughby, a young American cameraman, who had been working on exactly these kinds of shots for demonstration reels to sell the system.

Milton and Phil thrashed out with Glasser how much the extra shooting of this kind of material would cost, and got an assurance from Foreman that he would provide the extra dollars. Willoughby was let loose with Leon Chooluck, trying to ensure that the vehicles or the extras he needed for the next two weeks would be available.

Naturally, this operation caused some confusion and limited what was available for my units. In the finished movie, not more than three or four of Willoughby's shots were used. Incredible though it may seem, it was more possible to invent a new theme for our movie than to try and incorporate the roller-coaster shots into a screenplay that had never provided situations to use them!

The other element Bill Foreman introduced was his girlfriend, a would-be actress called Barbara Werle. Phil was asked to write two new scenes for her with Robert Shaw. When they came into our hands, both Robert and I said they were absolute nonsense and had no real connection to the main storyline. When we came to rehearse with Barbara, we found she was an absolute dog — willing, but completely dumb. Together, we told our producers that we had been hired to make a serious movie, and that we were not prepared to play the game of pandering to an exhibitor or financier's girlfriend. Robert refused flatly to play the scenes with her. They were flabbergasted! They called us obstinate, stupid limeys with no sense of self-preservation.

"If you worked in Hollywood you'd know this kind of thing is always cropping up," said Phil.

"You had the same situation with Zanuck," said Milton. "And you made it work!"

I had to agree, but Zanuck's girlfriend was quite beautiful and did have some talent. With Barbara it was as though you had picked a girl straight from the cash desk of a supermarket — and her scenes were quite superfluous anyway. In the end, Bill Foreman was brought into the act. He took us aside and told us a story:

"I know you two guys are old pros, apparently with strong artistic principles, but I have to ask you a favour. Two years ago I spent quite a few months in jail for tax evasion. I could say I was framed but that would only be a half-truth. But I can assure you it was not the most pleasant time of my life. Barbara, whom I had met in the 48 Club, out of the goodness of her heart, used to come and console me every day of the week, for at least a couple of hours. She's a very ambitious girl. I made her promises. Now, I have to deliver."

Robert and I exchanged looks.

Bill continued, "I think we have a great movie here — one that will do us all a lot of good, but I could not live with myself if Barbara does not appear in it. Please shoot the scenes. If they're no good, we'll try and shorten them, but she must make an appearance."

Bob and I both drew a deep breath, gave a slight nod to each other and walked back onto the set. We played the game as well as we could, and I covered every line in close-ups, so the material could be edited. In the end, Barbara made the briefest appearance, yet at the gala premiere at the Cinerama Theatre on Sunset in Los Angeles, she came down the boulevard leading a hundred U.S. servicemen into the theatre. A showman-like publicity stunt. And she got the same billing as Hank Fonda!

In the stone mansion we rented from the Marquesa de Quintina in Segovia, Pauline and I were forced to keep four big log fires burning. When I returned home from the shoot, half-frozen despite my thermal underwear, I could not bear to strip and jump into the bath, unless two paraffin-heaters were wheeled in close! Sometimes before going to bed, we filled wine bottles with hot water and laid them under the sheets — electric blankets were unheard of in Spain at that time. Now we moved from these stark conditions to the sunshine and scorching heat of Madrid. Here, we rented a large villa owned by Ava Gardner. Mirrors lined the bedroom walls — and the ceiling above the bed! It was fun, but it took a little getting used to!

One night Pauline awoke and shook me vigorously. "Look," she whispered, pointing to the fireplace — where a little animal not unlike a gopher or marmoset was sitting upright. Naturally, I chased him out and tried to calm Pauline.

"Ah," said the gardener the next morning, "you must have seen a ratto — the whole street is inundated with them. But they never hurt Ava or any of her admirers!!"

We blocked the chimney and laid battens of wood against the bedroom door, because we found the rattos were quite capable of chewing a way under a closed door! But the villa was charming, and two wonderful Alsatian dogs went with it, so Pauline reluctantly accepted the ratto situation. We had a luxurious pool around which Pauline often entertained the wives and girlfriends of the producers — and some of the stars. One day, the blue water and lawns disappeared under a blanket of white fluff, falling like snow from surrounding cotton trees.

"No problem," said Julio, my driver, as he lit a match and threw it onto the floating white raft. It sizzled away immediately and the pool became quite clear.

Unfortunately, one afternoon when he was not on call, James MacArthur was fooling around with his wife, Joyce, and they began to sneeze uncontrollably. Pauline told him of the magical way to dispose of the cotton. He struck a match and tossed it into the fluff *on the lawn*. Immediately, a sheet of flame spread in all directions!

At that moment I was on top of the Chapman crane shooting a scene with Charlie Bronson, as American tanks and troops made their retreat through the street set of Ambleve. I heard a voice below and looked down. Phil Yordan was shielding the sun from his eyes. "I don't want to alarm you, Ken, but your house is on fire," he called up.

"What do you mean?" I cried. "The house is on fire?"

"Well, Pauline's just called in that message, but you don't have to worry. I sent three of our Spanish Special Effects guys up in the truck and the fire engine's on its way."

I gave the signal for the crane grip to lower me down, but as I came level with Phil, he patted me on the back and said, "I'd go back up again, if I were you. The sun will be down in half an hour and it's a big shot. I just thought you ought to know."

I took a deep breath, continued the shot, and as soon as it was through, came down and phoned Pauline.

Of course, there was no reply, but the message came back that everything was under control. That night I heard the whole story. A lot of the bushes in the garden had burned and three trees were scorched, but the villa was unharmed due to the gallant efforts of the Special Effects guys supported by Pauline and her friends. The local fire truck had eventually turned up, but the Spanish firemen had apparently behaved like a crew from a Mack Sennett comedy. "For all the world like Benny Hill and his men in *Flying Machines*." said Pauline. "They stuck the wrong end of the hose into the pool and all the water came back and soaked them. And when the fire had been put out — mostly by us — they insisted on posing beside the pool to have their photos taken!" Quite an afternoon, it would seem!

I have referred to the wives and girlfriends of the actors and producers. In fact, there were only two wives on the location — Joyce MacArthur and Pauline. The six others were girlfriends *hoping to become wives*. I have to say, that many evenings after twelve hours of shooting, I would return home to be regaled by the most amusing and way-out stories. In fact, it could be that I would never have been able to endure the rigours of this film if it had not been for Pauline's tales of the girlfriends!

Two of them kept asking advice as to what they should do in certain intimate situations with their difficult partners. I was amazed how frankly these ladies would talk about matters of the bedroom, but I had to allow for the fact that both Joyce and Pauline could be very wicked and highly skilled at leading people on!

A story came out about one of the girls never taking off her long false eyelashes. She said she kept them on in bed, because her man became aroused if she flicked them in his ears, on his chest, and other intimate parts.

This couple would also keep a tape recorder under the bed and whenever the stimulation failed, they'd playback recordings of previously successful couplings.

Another of the girls was seen to have nipples with mascara circles drawn around them. "Oh, I forgot to remove them. "G" is so short-sighted, he likes me to make a target for him when we're about to make whoopee!"

I pride myself that in two of the cases where the girls succeeded in marrying their guys after this film location, it was due to the advice that I kept leaking back to them through Pauline — at least, that is what I like to think!

The shooting days were now becoming hot and tense, with daily visits from Bernie

Glasser trying to save dimes, and Milton suggesting scenes that might be cut because of budgetary problems. About this time, David Lean was shooting the station scenes for *Dr. Zhivago* in Madrid. One evening over dinner I told him of my troubles.

"Don't take any notice of the buggers," said David. "We're no longer working for the gentlemanly J. Arthur Rank, Mickey Balcon or Alex Korda — real showmen who kept money worries away from us."

"Absolutely right," I replied. "For my first twenty-odd movies I never knew where the finance was coming from. I was conscious of the budget, but producers and all concerned seemed devoted to making the best film possible."

"That's the way it should still be for us," said David. "The whole system of film financing is changing, especially with all these independent producers and accountants taking over. But our job is to make outstanding movies, both for their sakes and ours. My advice is keep shooting. Put your head down and get all you need on film. Arguments can follow during editing and post-production, when somehow the buggers will just have to find the overages."

So, I continued as though the producers had no problems, and concentrated on mine as a filmmaker — which were huge.

It was now summer and the big tank battle was still to be shot. On the rolling hills of the Campo where the Spanish army tanks were allowed to chew up the ground and do their manoeuvres, the terrain was scorched, and was devoid of the pine trees we established in the Segovia location. I decided that the only way to stage my battle was to shoot downwards, which meant Gilbert Chomat and his Alouette. He flew down from Paris, and we worked out a system of controlling my eighty tanks by radio instructions from the helicopter and relaying them through assistants on the ground, concealed in disabled tanks.

For four days the tanks lumbered around like toys beneath us, as I made aerial tracking shots above them, keeping as close as possible so as not to reveal what the terrain really looked like. This shooting was a thrilling challenge. We pulled it off, mainly due to the uncanny cooperation between Chomat and my regular operator, Dudley Lovell.

On the ground we used our two camera units to shoot any close incidents with the tanks, and now the art director, Gene Lourié came into his own. He was a gnome-like Russian who had worked in Hollywood for George Pal — the highly imaginative producer-director who won five Oscars for his early science-fiction movies. Gene had widened his experience, designing sets for the Bronston epics, and now he was working for me.

He made model tanks in various sizes — Johnny Cabrera shot them against backgrounds showing a few of the trees we were lacking — and Alex Weldon made miniature explosions. In all, they achieved thirty or forty shots which were invaluable in boosting up my battle shots.

Telly Savalas and Charlie Bronson spent several sweaty days doing close-ups in tanks, and in the evenings they would often stay in the studio playing poker with various Spaniards who had picked up the game from American crews. We would arrive in the morning to find them both bleary-eyed — which they argued did not matter.

"We're giving you battle fatigue for free," grinned Telly. Since these were their last shots, I didn't care.

The stars had gone home by the time Pauline and I made our overnight dash to

London for the premiere of *Flying Machines*. When I returned, Phil called me into his office.

"I appreciate all you've done," he said, "and I've tried to support you, because you were helping me out of a serious writing hole. But we're truly out of money. Bill Foreman hasn't come up with the cash for the extra shooting, but he's demanding a delivery date for his Cinerama theatres in ten weeks time!"

I wondered what was coming. Did he want me to get off the post-production? Did he want me to finish the picture for free?

He continued, "We have four editors working on the material under Milton's supervision. We wondered whether you'd take over the editing of the battle."

I thought for a moment. "It's twenty years since I've worked on a movieola alone," I said. "Not since my documentary days."

Phil smiled and put his arm round my shoulder. "No one knows the battle material better than you. I'll give you a Spanish assistant and two weeks to do the job — for no extra money!!"

Of course I agreed, and for two and a half weeks had fun in a way I'd never experienced before in my feature career. Matching my location footage with Gene Lourié's miniature shots; four feet of a helicopter shot, cut with a couple of feet of a US tank rounding a rock and facing a Panzer; a shot of Telly Savalas at his gun site yelling, "Fire!", intercut with a miniature tank blowing up. This was just like my compilation of the newsreel material during the war for *Pacific Thrust* — but much better. *I had a ball!*

"Fantastic!" said Phil as we ran about ten minutes of battle sequence in the viewing theatre.

"You've done us proud," said Milton, clapping me on the back.

Phil began to walk out, saying as he passed, "Unfortunately, we can't afford to keep you here."

"But don't worry," said Milton, "I'm going to coordinate the whole show with a post-production crew working day and night laying the soundtracks, recording music, etcetera."

Phil turned in the doorway, "With luck, we'll just make Bill Foreman's deadline."

"Wait a minute," I called. "Having got so deeply involved in the editing, I'd like at least to be here for the dubbing." They exchanged glances. "I'm willing to stay on without any per diems," I added.

"I know how you feel," drawled Phil walking back. "But apart from the dough, we're having a little trouble with the Pentagon. The slant you and I have given to the movie deviates quite a bit from the script they approved. Now I'm sure we're going to get it okayed, but..." he began to grin, "... it may be that I'm going to blame you a little — maybe saying, 'Well, you see what happens when you get a limey director playing around with one of our big moments in history!!'"

What a double-crossing shit, I thought, but said, "Surely they can't stop the picture."

Milton shook his head. "No, no, of course not! But we'd like to get as much cooperation as we can from them. I guess Phil will feel less inhibited in any arguments with them if you're not around."

I could see there was little chance of my winning any arguments with Phil, whom I had now come to know as a plausible rogue, so Pauline and I went back to London where we started getting deeply involved in trying to adopt a child.

Pauline had decided since we had not succeeded in making a baby, despite our most pleasant and assiduous efforts under Ava Gardner's mirrors, we must start a family in the only way left to us. While in Segovia, Pauline had visited an orphanage, which was obviously desperate for money, but the Spanish nuns would not part with a single Catholic child to a Protestant couple. We now tried England with its many adoption societies, but all to no avail, since they said I was above the prescribed age for an adoptive father.

The news came through that *The Battle of the Bulge* would indeed premiere in Los Angeles around the 20th of September. As usual, I had been kicking around some story ideas with Jack Davies. We had almost decided that in order to keep up with the growing trend for youthful sex movies, we would devise a script about 'Debutantes'.

Suddenly, Pauline said, "Why don't we all three drive across America? It would be fun and might give you ideas for an American movie, instead of all this British stuff!"

"Bit revolutionary," isn't it?" said Jack, then after a pause, "Although Dorothy is going away buying for the shop..."

"We might catch up with some of the showings of *Flying Machines* in New York, Chicago, the Midwest," I said, never needing much pushing into a trip.

"We'd look after you," said Pauline, taking Jack's arm.

He began to smile. "I haven't been back to New York since I had that column in 'The Express'"." He picked up a copy of 'Variety'. "Let's see if our movie's still running at Loew's..."

CHAPTER FIFTEEN
Quandary? What to do now?
'Showing the flag' in America...
Basking in fame, offers,
temptations in Hollywood...
Back to Europe...
New movie in Italy, new
home in France

Flying Machines had been running successfully for weeks at Loew's Theatre on Broadway. With his great gift for showmanship, Darryl Zanuck had shipped three of our old planes to the US for publicity. We were told they had caused quite a stir flying over Manhattan (though not near the skyscrapers, of course!). Vintage plane clubs in Connecticut had snapped two of them up, and one had been trucked out West — I felt a pang of jealousy that they had fallen into 'foreign hands'.

But it was a thrill for all three of us to stand in Times Square and see our movie billed in ever-flashing lights. We didn't go into the theatre to watch it, feeling we had seen it too many times already — today I find that difficult to believe! Instead, we took in a couple of musicals and met up with a few old friends —then took the train to Chicago, because I was eager to press on and show Pauline and Jack the awe-inspiring landscapes of the West, and the people of the Heartlands, as I had got to know them on my hobo-wanderings across America before World War II. Riding in comfort across Pennsylvania and northern Ohio, the green countryside sped by the large Amtrak windows — not much different from the panorama from London to Edinburgh.

"Apart from those neat white wooden farmsteads," said Jack Davies.

"And those batteries of neon signs and hoardings, spoiling the towns," added Pauline.

The cinema where we were showing in Chicago was smaller than Loew's, but the billing and display of our names looked great! "This is what it's all about," said Jack. "Our names plastered all over America!"

"Giving pleasure to millions who've never heard of us!" I added.

"Fame and fortune, at last," yelled Jack, grabbing my hands and leading me into a little jig.

"Let's hope the fortune follows," said the practical Pauline. "Don't you think the real reward has been your fun in creating, picking on a dumb idea and turning it into all of this?"

"She's right as always," I said putting my arm around her. "But there sure is a kick in seeing our names in lights ..."

"And all the publicity!' added Jack.

I nodded and continued, "But we should use all the fame to get more chances to make other movies."

I was bubbling inside and couldn't resist taking the stage. "We should be like the Impressionists, being carried away in the sheer joy of expressing themselves on canvas... Van Gogh and Gaugin clearly revelled in what they were doing, even though life was hard and they never made fortunes."

I saw Jack nudging Pauline. "Hark at him!" He spluttered, "The other day he was Rembrandt, now he's Van Gogh! That's going a bit far, isn't it?"

"You know what I mean," I said taking both their arms and leading them away. "Van Gogh and Gaugin were achievers, and in that, happy men. If we can say that too, we are truly making our lives count!"

We took six days to drive from Chicago to Los Angeles, all three of us taking turns in driving. We made no plans — stayed in motels wherever we happened to arrive as darkness was falling, and enjoying 'getting the feel' of the real America — at least that is what we believed we were doing.

Somewhere between Des Moines and Omaha we drifted into a bowling hall and let the locals teach us how to knock down the maximum number of skittles (as we call them in England). In return, over jars of ale, we told them of the intricacies of our pub-game of darts, which hadn't as yet reached Nebraska. After seemingly endless hours of driving across corn-covered plains, we drove into a motel at North Platte where they had vibrating beds! They were a boon for our aching backs, but made us so light-headed that we 'gushed' about the entire string of boring places we'd passed through — as though they were enchanted villages!!

Denver was like a city in an oasis, but after a check up that our 'masterpiece' was indeed playing there, we pressed on south, along the East side of the Rockies — past Colorado Springs and Pueblo... with the scenery beginning to take on that bold Western sweep that we had set out to discover. Cutting across the Sangres de Christo Range we climbed laboriously over a pass and ran into a snowstorm. A Volkswagen driven by a crazy group of students cut across my track, throwing slush all over my windshield, causing us to skid and half turn over. Within a couple of minutes no less than sixteen cars had pulled up, and nearly everyone was giving us a hand to get the car back on the road — something we agreed would have been most unlikely in England or France.

Staggering into Santa Fe, we fortified ourselves with so many brandies that we had to stay the night... and I missed the opportunity to show them the wonderful artists' village of Taos, and the adobe houses and the Hopi cave-dwellings which I remembered from my pre-war wanderings. Breakfast in Albuquerque amazed us all — everyone sitting at counters or tables, still wearing their enormous ten-gallon hats and discussing all the local happenings in loud gritty voices.

We made a diversion into the Petrified Forest and took pictures of each other sitting on fossilised trees. Then we travelled across the Painted Desert, with stops to watch Navajo women weaving outside their hogans. The Grand Canyon caused us to gasp like everyone does, and for the moment made us realise how insignificant we are in planet Earth's story.

I insisted on making a little diversion to the Indian Store at Cameron. I remembered that glorious sunset evening in 1938, sitting with the young Navajo musician and discussing the possibility of bringing his Indian orchestra to London's Albert Hall. The store was still there among the tumbleweed, but it was now no more than a tourist trap, full of city-made knick-knacks.

We crossed the Colorado River where it passes through a rocky gulch no more than a few yards across, and filled with impressions of Western Wonders, we pulled into the neat desert township of Kanab. Two film units were shooting in the area. I ran into three guys whom I had met on *Longest Day*, and in our delightful white clapboard motel, we found two British actors — Bill Travers and Virginia McKenna. They were having a quiet dinner but we soon changed that! Though we were not the closest of friends at home, we embraced and laughed together for three hours — we wanted to know all about their experiences in working on a 'genuine Western', while *they* were fascinated with our trip.

Onwards we went, through another memorable day in Zion National Park — gasping at the wonders of nature... until we reached the greatest peak of artificiality — Las Vegas! Even in the 60's it was a garish oasis of bad taste — but an eye-opener for a European. I remember entering the foyer of the Desert Inn and being enveloped in a cacophony of sound, like I'd never heard before. Of course it was the slot machines — row upon row — batteries of them as far as the eye could see, manned by expressionless robot-like gamblers. For thirty-six hours we joined their arm pulling routine and tried our luck at the roulette and blackjack tables, punctuating our gluttony with short sessions at the luxury swimming pools and glamour shows. In a somewhat swoony state we arrived in Los Angeles just in time for the premiere of *Battle of the Bulge* — which, as I have said earlier, was a big evening and a heart-warming reception for the movie.

Phil Yordan came across the foyer smiling and holding out both hands — but I thought he looked a little guilty. "I know! I know!" he said. "Your tank battle! Milton started to play around with it, believing he could improve it, but he never did, and because we never made a dupe of *your* version, we could never get it back. I'm sorry!"

"Well," I smiled, "what you have is not too bad and so long as the audience doesn't know what they might have seen, I suppose I can't grumble." But it was a lesson every director should learn —always keep a copy of your Director's Cut.

The day after the premiere, Milton Sperling took me to the studio to meet Jack Warner. He was charming and insisted I sit beside him at lunch in his private dining room. Apparently, it was a daily routine to have about sixteen Warner producers and directors gathered around a long table, and I witnessed how Jack punished anyone who had fallen out of favour. He would pass a snide comment about the poor guy, and extract critical support from everyone present. I had the feeling that if one didn't join the game, that person would be the next victim. Naturally, I was *happy* to be the guest of honour, but hated to discover this kind of crucifixion was possible from a showman I had admired for years.

Jack Davies settled down as a guest of Pamela Mason, but for several days Pauline and I were lodged in the luxurious Beverly Hills Hotel — to be available for press and radio interviews – which, since we were a success, were a joy to give! After a few days we moved into the nearby home of Dorothy McGuire and John Swope, where we relaxed round the pool and met famous stars like Gregory Peck, Walter Pidgeon,

CHAPTER FIFTEEN *Quandary? What to do now?*

Deborah Kerr, Jane Wyman and Teresa Wright — all of whom had worked with Dorothy in her heyday at Fox.

Hank Fonda, with his new wife Shirley, joined in giving us a most attractive impression of how pleasant and civilised life could be in Hollywood... and this impression continued when we moved into the Valley to stay at the Tarzana ranch-house of Jimmy and Joyce MacArthur. They also put on a big party for us. Telly Savalas greeted us with his big smile; Charlie Bronson and Jill Ireland couldn't wait to tell us they were now married (she had been a camp-follower on *Battle*); George Peppard said he would love to make a picture with me, and Connie Stevens flirted outrageously with a group of up-and-coming stars — some of whom I had met on *The Longest Day*.

Jimmy MacArthur insisted I should talk to his publicity agent, Guy McIllwaine. I liked him immediately, and agreed to pay him one thousand dollars a month, to let people know I was in Hollywood. Guy was an imaginative hustler who somehow arranged for me to be mentioned in the trade papers every second or third day, as about to direct or consider some movie project. In one of his handouts I was supposed to be teamed up with Sir Laurence Olivier. "Who cares?" Guy said when I told him I'd never even met Larry. "Variety printed it and now everyone knows that Ken Annakin is around!"

My English agent, Dennis Van Thal, had links with a big agency called Ashley-Famous. Ted Ashley, a very smooth New York operator, came into town and welcomed me with ten of his colleagues. They were asked to arrange meetings for the new Limey with studio executives — which over the next eight weeks they did, but not one of them even asked what kind of movie I felt I was best at or would like to make!!

Out of the blue, we got a call from Harry Bernsen, a young agent we'd met at Jimmy's party. He pressed us to have dinner with him at Chasen's — one of the most 'in' restaurants of Hollywood at that time. Pauline and I arrived a little early and we were shown to a small table in the central section of the restaurant. Ten minutes later there was a big commotion and we were practically carried on our chairs into the front section where Harry was awaiting us. Apparently, we had not been spotted as important people and had been relegated to the tourist section!

Halfway through a delicious dinner, Harry produced a check. It was blank except for the signature at the bottom and what looked like 'Caesar's Pa...' at the top.

"Could be yours", said Harry. "No limits!"

He went on to explain, "You once made a movie called *Holiday Camp* in which you showed families spending a week's vacation at an organised camp with a lot of entertainment. Caesar's Palace, in Vegas, would like you to do the same for them. They don't want anything shown of the gambling — just swimming pools, the shows, the country around. Create half a dozen interlocking stories on the lines of *Grand Hotel*, calculated to make families clamour for a holiday in Vegas."

It sounded very interesting. Pauline and I lay in bed discussing the strange offer. "You think it could be Mafia money?" queried Pauline.

"Could be," I replied. "'Time' Magazine is always suggesting Vegas is run by the godfathers!"

"In that case, we should lay off," said Pauline.

"And miss the chance of making ourselves safe for the rest of our lives?" I blustered.

She snuggled up close to me. "You remember that book 'The Professor'?"

I thought a moment. "The one where the New York teacher was persuaded into giving a couple of kids extra tuition at weekends?" Pauline nodded as I continued, "The neighbours were so pleased with him that they paid him big money to give up his job and teach all their kids full time."

"And when he discovered who all these families were and they wanted to quit, what happened?" said Pauline softly.

"They turned nasty, threatened his wife and daughter, and eventually made his life a misery — ruined him!!"

She looked at me with big eyes. "We don't really need their money, do we?"

I gave her a kiss, and turned over murmuring, "I'll call Dennis tomorrow ..."

My agent in London reacted most positively. "You don't touch that offer with a bargepole! It's time you came home... I think we have a set-up for *Gold Lovers*... with Vittorio Gassman, Anita Ekberg and Tony Steele."

"Tony's not right!" I cried. "He's a wimp. It's throwing the part away!"

"Anita is the hottest thing in Europe," yelled Dennis. "And they've just got married! That's how we can get the deal!"

"Forget it," I said and hung up — because with all the hoo-ha and meetings in Hollywood, I was sure I was going to get offers with much more exciting casts.

Two offers intrigued me. I had a meeting with Ray Stark, who was then just an agent, but branching out into production. He had found a young writer named Francis Ford Coppola and had backed him to write a thriller set in Hong Kong. It was called 'The Fifth Coin' and George Segal was interested in starring. George and I had three meetings in his Beverly Wilshire suite. We liked each other and thought the subject had great potential, but needed character development and an original style of shooting. Coppola joined us and we became even more excited as this slim, black-bearded, young man latched onto our hints of ideas. "I'll rewrite it however you want," he said, "but only after that tight-ass Stark forks out more cash."

Ray asked me to meet with his production manager, Phil Feldman, and for one whole Saturday we sat at a table by the Beverly Hills Hotel pool arguing costs and the time it would take to shoot our new concept of the script.

As the sun began to set, I knew I was dealing with a tough, cutthroat accountant-type, who reminded me very much of the cheapskate I had had to endure on *Battle of the Bulge*. So, drawing from my experience of foreign locations, I laid down certain minimal demands regarding crew and equipment, and the number of days I would need to shoot. I never heard from them again!

'The Fifth Coin' was never made and years later, Ray agreed we should have found some way of compromising. Looking back I know I was naive and opinionated and that Phil Feldman, who became President of First Artists, probably knew much better what could and could not be done in Hollywood.

But in late '65 I was still being courted — the great Swifty Lazar who was to become the hottest setter-upper in Hollywood, sent an emissary to ask if he could represent me. Unfortunately, Dennis Van Thal said, "You don't need that fly-by-night," and being a loyal sort of chap, I obeyed him!

The most solid studio offer was from Universal who were going to make a Western called *Texas Across The River*. Dean Martin and Alain Delon had been signed, and the studio was negotiating for Catherine Deneuve and Shirley MacLaine. I couldn't complain at that cast and I would have loved to shoot a Western in Arizona — I think

CHAPTER FIFTEEN *Quandary? What to do now?*

I saw myself trying to outdo John Ford!!

Once again the production office came up with a schedule of only thirty-six days. Even with a marvellous second unit, I could not see myself and the actors having time for in-depth performances. In fact, the plan was for the first unit to shoot *everything*, including six big-action sequences with horses, wagons, Indians and shootouts.

Being me, I argued about the schedule and the budget — little realising that the general practice in Hollywood was to accept the budget after a token fight, then if you exceeded it, you cried crocodile tears and the studio coughed up the extra money. So long as the film succeeded at the box-office, no one cared! I didn't learn this till it was much too late! Ashley-Famous were getting a little fed up with my 'pickiness', but Guy McIllwaine came up with what appeared to be a great idea.

He said, "I think you're having a problem because you don't know the ways of Hollywood — how efficient they are, how fast they can shoot. My wife Pam is going to star in a new — and what I think is a very funny —off-the-wall comedy called *Perils of Pauline*. I think it would be right up your street, and being television, no one in any studio is going to care a damn how you perform. Treat it as a tryout — a kind of refresher course.."

I read the script and loved it — Pam turned out to be a bright and perfect 'dumb blonde' — and how could I resist a show with that title? Ashley-Famous were a little surprised, but made a nice deal for me with Herb Leonard, who appeared to be highly honoured that a big moviemaker would direct his two hour pilot. On the strength of my name, Terry-Thomas was signed to play the villain and Pat Boone the innocent stooge.

The first day we shot a seven minute sequence in the jungles on the MGM studio lot, and who should I find handing out a rifle to White Hunter Terry, but 'No bother' Graham (from *The Longest Day*). He gave me a feeling of 'belonging' and I immediately hit it off with the camera crew. The first assistant and production manager, I had a suspicion, were snakes — boss's men.

Herb Leonard and his wife Eleanora, who was editing the picture, claimed to be thrilled with the dailies, and the unit in general were excited by the way I kept the camera moving. But the schedule seemed to be getting tighter every day, with the result that we shot for fourteen hours one day at Long Beach; fifteen hours downtown the next; followed by days of fourteen hours, sixteen and eighteen. I remember staggering into the Chateau Marmont where we were now staying, and confessed to Pauline that I was whacked!

"It gets so that you can't think straight," I told her. "I've no time for discussion with the actors — no time to bring out the niceties in their characters. Terry can look after himself and Pat Boone just has to be told his moves, but Pam is a beginner needing a lot of work and experimentation." I shook my head and continued, "Believe it or not, some of the crew have to travel three or four hours on top of these ridiculous hours!"

"I thought the Americans had strong unions," said Pauline.

"I think they have," I replied. "But when I ask how they put up with this slavery, they say that if a producer is prepared to pay 'golden hours' they can't do anything about it!"

"Are they more efficient than our boys?" she asked.

"How can they be when they're absolutely shagged," I said. "The only guy who is fantastic is 'No bother'. I've never met a prop man like him."

Nearly every member of the crew complained to me and tried to egg me on to revolt, but I was determined to prove that I was a tough Limey and could cope. However, by the fifteenth day, I found myself really disgusted and bloody-minded. We had been driven out to the edge of the Mojave Desert where an old Foreign Legion fort from another movie was still standing. I had mistakenly thought the sun always shone in California, but on this January day it was pouring with rain.

"I'm going broke," wailed Leonard. "You gotta shoot somehow."

So, I was forced into shooting: 'They cross the burning desert' in drizzle; an attack on 'the glaring white fort'; a night sequence by a Bedouin campfire; a sequence in the Sultan's harem; and Pam doing a belly-dance in front of the Sheik!

At eleven pm I saw Herb Leonard and his production manager helping the art director prepare thirty yards of blue painted canvas against which I found they were expecting me to shoot Pam and a dozen Legionnaires riding camels across the desert in sunlight!

I have to admit that in desperation I went into Pam's motor trailer and suggested that for both our sakes, she should tell me she was too exhausted to stay on a camel. The poor girl was scared, but husband Guy arrived in the middle of our discussion and appeared to support our joint decision. So much so that *he* was the one who carried the message to Herb Leonard. After twenty minutes conference during which it began to rain cats and dogs again, the production manager opened the door and announced that Pam and I could 'wrap' for the day, but that Herb was going to stay and pick up a few more shots of camels, etcetera.

I left muttering, "Good luck to Herb. What time's the call for tomorrow?" I shouted from the car.

"Don't worry. We'll phone you," said the production manager.

Pauline and I were sitting having a late breakfast when the phone rang and a woman's voice said, "Mr. Leonard wishes me to tell you that your services will no longer be needed on *Perils of Pauline*."

Somewhat shattered I yelled, "Have you called my agent?"

Feeling completely justified with the position I had taken, I think I expected Ashley-Famous to sort out the situation, but I had not reckoned with the fact that Herb Leonard was a big-shot in TV, having been involved for years in the prestigious series *Naked City*. What I also didn't know was that he had just been waiting for me to step aside and let him take over as director, having quietly gotten himself a director's ticket with the Guild!

By the end of a day of feverish phone calls, the position was:

a) Guy McIllwaine had told me Pam had reported back to work with Leonard directing her because they had decided that if she refused, her career would be ended in Hollywood.

b) Ashley-Famous had informed me that they had dispatched a certified letter demanding immediate settlement of my contract, and they suggested that it might be a good idea to get out of town for a month or two!

"How can they do this to me?" I argued. "I've shot over half the picture!"

"Credits can be sorted out later," they replied. "But I was getting good stuff despite everything," I wailed. "I put up with all his shit, surely I'm due to damages or something!"

"In this town, if a producer wishes to change a director in mid-picture, he can do so provided he pays up according to contract," was the reply.

Seeing my frustration and unhappiness, Pauline put her arms around me and said, "Let's go home..."

It seemed like a great idea. I had clearly made a mess of things — expecting too much too quickly, and in my impatience had allowed myself to be put in a degrading situation where I was not in control. Herb Leonard, of course, immediately put an announcement in the trades that I had been replaced, and I could imagine all Hollywood reading it. Time to beat a retreat — definitely!

I received a call from Sydney Box saying that he had just been talking to Swifty Lazar. "He tells me you turned him down." I confirmed this.

"You must be out of your mind, Ken! That hustler could take you to all the places you've been waiting to go ever since I met you — and, for that matter, groomed you for!!"

I muttered some excuses about loyalty and reasons for turning away from Hollywood. Sydney had an idea. "Well, I know you haven't been interested in the small domestic stuff Muriel and I have been doing of late, but I think I'm putting together a big one. It's an action picture set in India. I already have a commitment from Trevor Howard and I hope to get a big American star, possibly Yul Brynner. Vivian Cox is putting the whole thing together with the Maharajah of Baroda. Rank has promised to match the frozen funds which Vivian succeeds in releasing in India."

"Sounds great, Sydney", I said. "As soon as you have a script and the finance put together, let me know and I'll most likely come running."

We returned to our flat in London, and suddenly an offer came out of the blue, which changed our whole way of life. 'The Italian Caper' did not seem a world-shattering movie, but I found "the caper" fascinating and the cast irresistible. Already set were Edward G. Robinson, Bob Wagner, Vittorio DeSica, Raquel Welch and Godfrey Cambridge, and the picture was to be shot in Rome, Naples and the South of France.

I met the producer, Joe Shaftel, in the Dorchester. He was a rather unprepossessing individual, but had produced about seventy episodes of *The Untouchables* for US television, and seemed to show a sensibility and intelligence that was unusual in the younger-run of American producers at this time. I was quite impressed when he told me that he had been a 'wonder-boy-violinist', performing in classical concertos from the age of ten. The script had apparently been written by a professional called Rod Amateau and was full of good comedy situations. It concerned a group of well intentioned, but unworldly Americans, who decide to kidnap an old Mafia godfather from his home in Naples. Unfortunately, having seized De Sica — who was to play the godfather — they were completely baffled as to what to do with him. They call for the help of Edward G. Robinson, an ex-Capone counsellor from Chicago, who leads them into incredible adventures.

So, in the spring of 1966, Pauline and I set off for Rome, full of optimism and high spirits. We were set up in a large new hotel called the Parco de Principe on the fringes of the beautiful Borghese Gardens. My old friend, Basil Keys, had been hired as the production manager, and once again Pauline was not allowed to work, but we had fun seeing all the sites of Rome and checking locations in Naples.

Everything seemed to be going perfectly on the preparations, when suddenly Joe was called for a conference with MGM, who were going to distribute the picture.

Messages came back that we must delay production for a couple of weeks while he sorted out some problems. Meanwhile, we had a great time watching the world go by in the sunny pavement cafés of the Via Veneto and the Corso. Almost every day someone turned up whom we had met in some part of the world.

Joe came back after ten days, looking a very worried and distraught character. Apparently, some reader in the MGM Studios in Culver City, remembering an old script, had turned it up in the archives, and found that it was basically the same story as we were about to make! What is more, a version based on the original was already in production in Florida, under the aegis of the great Sam Spiegel — with Anthony Quinn as the star!!

Unfortunately for us, they had paid for the rights for the original material, while now Joe claimed that he must have 'remembered' the old script submitted to him in his TV days, and now 'developed' by Rod Amateau. His memory must have been very vivid, because our script resembled the original so closely that Joe was ordered by Metro to come up with some arrangement with Sam Spiegel or drop the picture.

Apparently, the Maestro received Joe in the George V Hotel in Paris, lying in his bath! The interview was most painful and embarrassing — resulting in Joe being forced to give up his 15% producer's share of the profits (if any), and having to agree that our film would not be released till six months after *The Happening* — the title of Spiegel's movie. In addition, Spiegel had insisted that *he* should initial every page of *our script* and we must make no deviations from the version he had now vetted and agreed.

Completely chagrined, Joe insisted that we must start shooting *immediately* since our stars were 'on the clock' so far as their contracts were concerned. Unfortunately, during the sunny but treacherous days of March in Rome, while having lunch in an open-air café, I had removed my jacket, ignored the cool breeze on my back, and caught pneumonia!

Chandra Sharma, my Indian homeopathic doctor, flew over to Rome and treated me with amazing remedies, so that in two weeks I was on my feet. In the meantime, the company had moved down to Naples and Joe had, for five days, tried to shoot several sequences of the movie. Both actors and crew intimated to me on my arrival, that he had been absolutely hopeless as a director, and I would have to re-shoot everything (which, on seeing the rushes, I did).

For me, the shooting went smoothly and almost enjoyably. The lines played well, the actors were cooperative and created good characters, especially Robinson and De Sica. Robinson was like putty in my hands, completely trusting. To my mind, it was impossible to go wrong with him. Directing Vittorio De Sica was a different matter, however. He was always polite and full of charm, but I was somewhat overawed, knowing that he had directed classics like *Bicycle Thieves*, *Two Women*, and *The Gold Of Naples* — the latter two movies with Sophia Loren. He tried to make each set-up as easy as possible for me by saying, "Just walk through the movements you want me to make, Ken and I'll deliver the rest!" Though a little embarrassing, this method worked out excellently with DeSica, who was always adding amusing touches to the character of the godfather.

Quite often, Victor Meranda, my excellent French assistant, used to agonise about Vittorio because the moment a shot would finish, Vittorio would fall asleep, no matter where he might be on the set — even sometimes while leaning against a pillar! We discovered that this was because he kept two homes. His wife and sons lived in Rome, but he also had a mistress — the Spanish actress, Maria Mercada. Each evening he would make sure that he saw the kids into their beds, and then would slip away to Maria. But at dawn he would slip back home so that the boys would see him before going off to school! Apparently, the two women were quite happy — or accepted this arrangement, but throughout the day, it meant De Sica was always sleepy.

After the short Naples location — where all the streets were closed and shooting brought to a complete halt if there was a football match — we moved back to Rome and alternated between studio sets in the famous Cinecitta Studios and locations in the Coliseum, the Baths of Marcello and beaches just outside Rome. A developing problem was Raquel Welch.

There was no doubt that she was a very beautiful girl — though Robert Wagner always used to say that embracing her was like hugging two bags of cement! She had only made one movie in Europe — *One Million Years B.C.* — which had not required much acting ability, but she tried hard and was very much aware of the importance of still photos and publicity. In fact, she was married to Patrick Curtis, a very slick P.R. man, who never missed an opportunity to build up Raquel's reputation.

I was trying to catch up on the schedule for my producer, Joe, and did not wish to see top stars like Robinson, De Sica and Bob Wagner insulted by Raquel not knowing her lines, or by keeping them waiting while she posed for stills or fixed her makeup. I began to get peeved, as this happened several times. There was one afternoon on the beach where I felt she was behaving impossibly, so I issued an ultimatum that if she wasn't on the set ready to shoot within five minutes, I would cease to give her any more close-ups. Raquel rushed out from her caravan, faced up to me like a boxer, and let out a string of foul language that even a Mexican fishwife would have hesitated to use. Patrick appeared and pulled her away.

For fifteen minutes we watched them arguing on the beach. I explained matters to the rest of the cast and we waited with bated breath to see what would happen. Suddenly, Raquel rose to her feet, walked back on to the set and said, "Sorry, guys, to have kept you waiting. Let's make the scene."

And from that moment on I never had any more trouble with her timekeeping. I even spent a great deal of extra time trying to coach her just as I had with Irina Demick. On the whole, I was quite pleased with the results, because she really applied herself, and so long as one broke up the scenes into a couple of lines at a time, she became able to handle them quite adequately.

Godfrey Cambridge was a two hundred and fifty pound comedic black performer, who tried to fool around and be a fun character with everyone. But unfortunately, he carried an ethnic chip on his shoulder, which sometimes he could not hide. We had been shooting for a whole day in the beautiful Borghese Palace, when Victor called wrap. The usual string of artists' cars rolled up to the marble steps. Edward G. Robinson, DeSica, Bob Wagner, and Raquel all hurried down. Suddenly, Godfrey blew his top, "Why the fuck am I always last? This would never happen to me Stateside!"

Always quick with a reply, Victor winked at me and said, "We have a surprise for you today, Godfrey," and, sending a secret message out over his radio, two minutes later a limousine appeared, much larger than any of those serving the other stars. "There you are," said Vic. "You can have a red carpet, too, if you want."

Already wondering whether he should have made this outburst, Godfrey tried to walk with dignity down the stairs, tripped at the bottom, and grabbed the door handle. He obviously gave it his full two hundred and fifty pounds, because it came off his in hand. Opening the door from the inside he climbed in. Long pause... then his head appeared in the window. He smiled his usual broad grin. He called out, "Guess they don't know how to build cars for heavyweights in Europe!" With that, he vanished, giving a regal wave.

Joe claimed to be delighted with the rushes and said he was getting good vibes from MGM, but they wanted me to "give the picture more scope." So, although I didn't feel it was really necessary, I called Gilbert Chomat in Paris and within a day he joined us with his Alouette. We spent three days setting up scenes for him — with cars speeding along the Apian Way, flying low over the Coliseum, swooping down on to the Spanish Steps, and circling the Borghese Park.

Joe was delighted and wanted two aerial shots in Naples, but since they could be achieved with doubles, I persuaded Basil Keys and Joe to let Pauline set them up and supervise the shooting. Her reward on the way South was to be flown by Chomat into the mouth of the smoking volcano of Vesuvius. It was an experience she has never forgotten!

In the South of France we shot in three marvellous locations, and for the most part lived in luxury at the Metropole Hotel in Beaulieu. The most pleasant shooting was in the villa and gardens of the Rothschild Villa on Cap Ferrat. It was now summer and the Mediterranean sun was becoming unmerciful, but Portalupi, our Italian cameraman, often circled our stars with as many as six very hot lights, saying he needed their intensity to balance the strong sunlight. This made it impossible for the actors to open their eyes, but he insisted the lights were necessary. After a day of misery, I persuaded Joe to have the electrical truck opened up at night, and four of the brutes removed. There was much waving of hands and threats of resignation by Portalupi, but with a straight face, Joe explained to him that we were running out of money.

"You're an Italian," he said. "Your pictures are always running out of money. So, you must understand we've come to the point where we all have to make sacrifices!" For once, I agreed with the producer!

It was under the glare of these lights that Bob Wagner started to wear false eyelashes. Shooting was often held up as much as five minutes while he had the make-up man curl these bloody lashes and adjust them. Despite ribbing that he had turned gay, and was worse than Raquel in fiddling with his face, Bob insisted on keeping up this procedure. I thought I recognised the beginnings of a phobia, which artists sometimes develop through nerves or an inability to cope with difficulties, but years later I asked Bob about this eyelash curling.

He flashed me his broad grin and said, "Portalupi drove me to it. The whole situation was getting so ridiculous, I felt I had to make some gesture and establish my individuality." He put his arm round my shoulder and added, "I also wanted to gave everybody a laugh and take the pressure off you, old chap."

Strange 'non-sequitur' pieces of business kept cropping up in the script, now called *The Biggest Bundle of Them All*. At one point we had a tank drive on to a railway line and stop the train while our characters tried to rob it. We then moved to an airfield in Provence — right in the middle of Van Gogh country. By coincidence, it was near Salon where I bought the crashed Dakota for *Broken Journey* twenty years ago!

Now, I had another old plane to play with — making it slalom around a dozen parked cars. The car carrying 'our gang' had to slalom, too, then chase the runaway plane, with our 'would-be gangsters' climbing on the wings and into the open baggage compartment, to stack millions of fake lira notes. Needless to say, the film ended with the hatch opening and all the money showering down over the countryside to the dismay of our loveable villains. It seemed to me this ending had been used a number of times before, but I tried to make it more credible and funny.

In Provence, our way of life continued to be luxurious. Pauline and I were housed at Beaumaniere, one of the most exclusive hotels in France — near the old medieval village of Les Baux. The restaurant was Michelin 5-Star, but over the course of three weeks we became completely fed up with gourmet food, and would have given anything for simple English bacon and eggs!!

Throughout the picture De Sica had been kept away from his usual problem of compulsive gambling. He was known throughout the casinos of Italy and the Cote d'Azur as 'the gentleman loser'. On this picture, his wife had arranged that Vittorio would not be allowed into any of the casinos of Monte Carlo, Beaulieu, Nice or Cannes, but one night he managed to slip back over the border to San Remo, and lost half the fee he was being paid for the movie!

Now as we approached the end of filming, Pauline and I wanted to give Vittorio a fabulous evening so we invited him for dinner at our personal expense in Beaumaniere. He turned up with his wife, two sons and nine other close relatives — or so he said. The evening cost us the whole of our weekly allowance on the *whole* movie — but De Sica was such a dear and amusing character, we swallowed deeply and gave each other a knowing look that meant, 'We should have known better." Believing in some way that the world owes them a living, film stars invariably 'take you for a ride' in matters of food and drink!

Because of our action shots with tanks, trains and airplanes, Chomat and his Alouette helicopter were still with us. Three times during the location shooting, Pauline had flown with him to the 'environs' of Nice to look at houses — because 'mirabile dictu she had suddenly announced, "I think if we found the right house, I could forget London and live on the Cote d'Azur." So now, with the help of Bob Wagner, when he was not on call, Pauline started to look at possible properties. Suddenly, they came on a most exciting 'constructeur', building in the foothills of Vence. Eilif Gisselback was a brilliant Dane who was building his dream house on a small plateau right opposite the Chateau St. Martin, where Churchill used to come and paint.

The style in which he was building could have been called 'Arizona-Provencal.' The eight-bedroomed house was only half built, but they all pronounced it as "Sensational!" At the weekend, Chomat was prevailed upon to fly me over from Salon. After an exciting hedgehopping trip, we landed on the lawn of the new house. I was immediately enchanted, and like most developers, Gisselback was prepared to sell, if I could raise a mere one hundred thousand pounds!!! (I was getting a mere $250,000 for this movie). Absolutely out of character for the canny Yorkshireman that I am, I made an 'on the spot' decision to buy it... causing Pauline to pass right out!

Bob Wagner flew back with me to Salon, and could not stop talking about the 'Bastide de la Foux' — which he said would change our whole life. "That house in its setting will knock anything Beverly Hills has to offer right into the Pacific Ocean!"

"Really," I yelled over the noise of the 'copter.

"When it's finished you'll be able to invite Zanuck, Walt Disney, Ray Stark — all the top people. They'll be so impressed and responsive to your *obvious* success that they'll offer you more and more movies!"

This was a way of wheeling and dealing and getting work that I had never pursued, and even then, neither believed in nor wished to practice. If it were fun to have parties at the Bastide and I could afford to entertain lavishly, I would be only too happy to do so... but I still didn't believe that you had to keep up with 'the rich and famous' to make good movies.

We shot the final scenes of *Biggest Bundle* in one of the big dust storms which every summer sweep across this part of Provence. I was getting along excellently now with Raquel and really liked her — even to the extent of trying to find another picture with her. The rest of the cast, especially Bob, regarded her as a pinup girl on the make. Apart from the fact that Patrick never let her out of his sight, none of them thought she was especially sexy at this time — which is surprising since she became one of America's biggest sex symbols. I guess it all goes to show that if a pretty girl is determined enough and has great PR, she can probably make it!

CHAPTER SIXTEEN
The Saga of The Long Duel

Back in London, Pauline was put on the trail of a due-to-be-born baby we might be able to adopt, while I went off each day to Pinewood to work on the editing of *Biggest Bundle.*

Joe Shaftel, who had been an excellent line producer throughout the shooting, now became a nuisance — wanting to see each sequence as we finished cutting it, and generally trying to interfere before I had time to experiment and get the best out of the material I'd shot. This 'first cut' is every director's right, and in America is now sanctified by the Director's Guild.

So, when Sydney Box called me up to say that the finance was all in place for his Indian movie, now called *The Long Duel*, and that an advance unit made up of 'my people' had already been sent to India, I could not resist the most serious consideration of his offer. The script had been finalised and turned out to be a very acceptable adventure story set in the late days of the British Raj. Yul Brynner had been contracted to play the leader of a group of Dacoits (bandits) who were pillaging villages in the hills of Northern India. In fact, his character was a kind of Robin Hood, who would be pursued in the story by an indomitable Trevor Howard, backed by his boss, my old friend, Harry Andrews. The money Sydney was offering me was the most I had ever had for directing, and I needed most of it to close the deal on the 'Bastide', our new house in Vence, France.

Joe was only too happy to take *Bundle* back to MGM Studios. We agreed a final cut, (or so I thought) and since the baby was not due to be born for another three weeks, I begged Pauline to come with me into the Himalayas. She knew I never missed a chance to see new places. Pauline had learned to take chances and follow that principle with me, but now she was far too occupied with fitting-up a nursery, etcetera. I took the plane to New Delhi, promising that I would send for her, even if only for three or four days, if the location was exciting and really worth the trip.

Vivian Cox, Sydney's associate met me at the airport. He said that the Indian half of the money was 'not quite' in place yet, but he was sure the rupees would be in the bank within a week, A sixth sense told me that I should go see the 'tenth wonder of the world' while I had the chance! I made the side trip to Agra and found the Taj Mahal was everything it was cracked up to be. Shah Jehan's memorial temple to his wife was indeed a seventeenth century Muslim masterpiece — a vision in slender lines and white perfection — a lover's dream palace.

There followed a mad taxi drive north, past grubby villages and temples where every moment one had a view of the typical Indian priests in yellow saffron robes, beggars by roadside shrines, and cows wandering freely down the main streets with the traffic having to pick its way around them, since the cow is a sacred animal and has the right of way.

After a ten-hour drive, I met the unit in Dehra Dun — in a very small, but quite clean, Indian hotel. There, old chums were waiting for me in a small bar-restaurant — Frank Green, who had been production manager on *The Seekers*; Vetchinsky, my old art director from *The Informers*; Dick Parker, who proudly showed me Polaroids of the rope bridge he was building across a chasm. Quite remarkable! For the life of me, I could not see how he had been able to make such progress in no more than ten days.

"A bottomless pit of labour," he said. "As long as you have the money to pay them."

The accountant, George Davis, looked at me and shook his head, "That's the big problem. Vivian gave me a small float, but we've already got to the end of it and have to get out of this hotel tomorrow."

"Where are we going then?" I said.

"There's a big old hotel up in the mountains at Mussourie, which used to be a summer retreat for the wives of British Colonial officers when the weather got too hot and sticky in Delhi. The guy who runs it is an Anglophile and only too happy to think he may have the whole unit staying there."

The production co-ordinator was an attractive, tall blonde called Valerie Rawlings. She was a very down-to-earth girl and as we drove along a narrow road to Mussourie the next morning, she filled me in on everything that had happened and the broken promises of Vivian. She had picked up a rumour that fourteen Indian businessmen involved in a tax-shelter deal, which was to provide the finance for this picture, had all been put in jail on the allegations that they had never paid taxes on their incomes — our *rupees!* Vivian was now apparently relying on the Maharaja of Baroda in whose palace he was at present staying.

"You know Vivian," she said, "I've always thought he was gay."

"I've had suspicions for years," I said, "But it was none of my business."

"Well," said Valerie, "Baroda is one of those, and I think they're just playing games."

The locations that Vetch and Gil Taylor, the cameraman, had found around Mussourie were breathtaking. We walked around a plateau under the shadow of a range of snow-capped mountains. Vetch had driven in pegs to indicate where he would build the walls of the fort. "I've ordered the timber but they won't deliver 'til we've paid cash," he said. "But with over a hundred labourers, I can put this set up in ten days. No problem!"

We visited the barracks where a local section of the Indian Army was housed. It was a big compound, built to last in brick. It had been taken over lock, stock and barrel from the British when they left the country. The Indians appeared to drill, salute and behave exactly like their ex-British officers, and were only too willing to provide two hundred riders and horses as and when we might require them. They would serve as both Dacoits and the British troops who would be pursuing them.

The hotel in Mussourie was dirty white and rambling, with servants looking not much better than beggars. I was allotted an enormous bedroom with a fireplace and a sparse white-painted bathroom such as the British might have been used to in their barracks. No doubt this is all they expected when on leave!

My beggar-servant was most polite and attentive as he carried a large bundle of firewood to the fireplace, and lit a roaring fire. Unfortunately, he had trachoma in one eye, which made him look something of a desperado. Possibly, I could use him as a Dacoit!

That evening, eight of us partook of watery soup, roast lamb, boiled potatoes and watery cabbage, and discussed our plans and plight, dropping our voices to a whisper whenever the manager or his wife came near. No doubt the locations were most promising and we could probably make a fabulous and unusual movie *providing the money arrived!*

Gil Taylor told me that he had made a trip round the studios in New Delhi and we could certainly find the lights and electricians we needed, but there was not one adequate location generator. In his opinion we would have to ship one from England. God only knew how long that might take! Valerie and I devised a long cable to send to Sydney Box telling him of our problems and requirements, but when we went down to Dehra Dun where there was a post office, we found that the cost was going to be far more than we could rake up between us.

"Maybe the restaurant would lend us something," said Valerie.

"Even though we are owing them for two days of meals?" I queried.

Sure enough, with a bit of persuasion, the restaurant helped us out.

I called Vivian, laying into him for having misrepresented the whole situation. It was bad enough to find that the unit were living almost like paupers and stranded here, but the lack of full financing and a generator was unforgivable after the promises he had made both to me and to Sydney. "I'm dealing with it," said Vivian. "Just give me another forty-eight hours. Baroda is behind us one hundred percent and his name really means something in this country."

As we drove up the hill to Mussourie, the clouds suddenly cleared and there before us stood Mount Kemet, one of the group of peaks around Everest, and over twenty-five thousand feet high. It was an awesome sight, and lasted only a minute or two before the glistening white pyramid was enveloped again in cloud.

Apparently, here at Mussourie, we were only sixty miles from the Tibetan border and the next morning I couldn't resist taking a ride up the mountain track as far as the frontier, where I found fierce-looking sepoys facing heavily armed and aggressive looking Chinese. This was the site of a border dispute, which erupted every few weeks in local shootouts between the Indians and Chinese.

I drove back, and after a quick snack, *rode an elephant into the jungle,* accompanied by twenty beaters. This is what they used to do when the British were there — adventuring into the jungle to show the boss a tiger! Climbing trees and banging on wooden boxes, they succeeded in bringing out one of those majestic creatures. It paced slowly across a green clearing, stared at us, and then continued on its way towards a stream. I paid the beaters the equivalent of two English pounds and they felt they had been most generously rewarded — as I had certainly been!

We called Vivian the next day telling him that he must cable at least five thousand pounds worth of rupees, otherwise we would have to wrap. He pleaded with me to stay, hold the fort, keep up the morale, and he would do his best to cable *two* thousand pounds worth of rupees.

Having now seen all the locations and with no one able to advance their jobs without money, I agreed to sit down with Valerie and draw up a long memo, setting out everything that had happened since they first arrived. She said, "However much you may be accepting what Vivian says, I am certain you're going to need this document very shortly. We should set down the facts while we remember them."

Valerie typed twelve full sheets of a diary, with comments as to what had transpired since the project began. It made very disturbing reading — full of promises, betrayals and lies spread by Vivian before I arrived.

It began to rain in torrents and the hotel-keeper, who had been all smiles and bowed greetings, had apparently overheard one of our telephone conversations and was now hard-faced and almost threatening. In fact, that night he made it clear to Frank Green that he was determined to have his money. "No one will leave my hotel until the bill is paid in full," he said, drawing himself up aggressively.

In a whispered conference in my bedroom, it was decided that I must drive back to Delhi and sort out Vivian. The next morning, carrying no baggage, Valerie and I went for a walk down the little main street, where a car into which my suitcase had been sneaked out by the back door, was waiting for me. I kissed her goodbye and set off on the hundred sixty mile drive. Reaching Delhi, I found no Vivian. He had departed with his Maharaja friend to a destination unknown. There was nothing for it but to telephone Sydney. He said the Rank Organisation was giving him hell because they were already committed for nearly a million pounds on their side of the deal. "I think you should call Freddie Thomas yourself and tell him what is happening before you come flying back." A long reverse charge conversation with Freddie Thomas, who had now taken over from Earl St. John, resulted in my jumping the first plane back to London.

At Heathrow, I was met by Frank Bromhead, a VP of the company, who filled me in with the seriousness of the whole operation for the Rank Organisation. John Davis was giving everyone hell, saying that he'd never before been screwed out of a million bucks without a single foot of film being shot. He was fucked if he was going to allow it to happen now!

Bromhead was completely shocked by the diary-report, which I felt I had to give him in the car. On arriving at the Victoria Street Headquarters, we went straight up to Freddie Thomas' office and sat down to discuss the whole situation.

"We went into this situation in good faith," said Freddie, "mostly because of the cast and you!" I swallowed deeply as he continued.

"We committed three million pounds, but five million, or the equivalent of five million in rupees, was guaranteed by Sydney Box — through the release of blocked rupees, he said, or a group of Indian investors guaranteed by the Maharaja at Baroda."

"The rupees may still turn up," I said soberly, "but not in time to start shooting on the dates you have committed with Yul Brynner, Howard and Andrews."

"That's what we thought," said Freddie.

"Surely, Sydney with all his connections, has other sources of finance," I suggested. Freddie looked grim and turned to Bromhead who had just put down the phone.

"Muriel has just called to say Sydney has had a heart attack!"

I jumped up. "I must go see him at once."

Bromhead eased me back in my seat. "She refuses to tell us which hospital he's been taken to," he said quietly.

Freddie stood up and started pacing. "J.D. will have my guts for garters," he wailed.

Bromhead looked at me with spaniel eyes. "Something has to be done to save us all — *and* your crew held hostage."

I walked over to the window. After a few minutes I turned to face the two frightened executives. "Sydney brought me into this in good faith. He's been my guardian angel for twenty years. What can I do?" I said.

"If he's really in the hospital and his partner can't provide the money, the kindest thing you can do is to save his ass — and ours, if you know a way!!" said Freddie, now suddenly bull-like.

Bromhead turned me round to face him. "You've got an idea — I know you have."

"I know Spain quite well," I said, speaking slowly and thoughtfully. "Having made two movies there, I have good connections and friends. The terrain is not dissimilar to what I've been seeing in India. I believe we could make Spain into India, so long as our crowds are dressed as Indians, which will cost quite a lot more because it means providing *all* the costumes whereas in India they already exist."

"How long would it take to switch the picture there?" said Bromhead.

"Three or four weeks, I guess."

Freddie came round his desk to me. "Brynner and the other actors come on the clock three weeks from today. As a personal favour to me, I would like you to fly out to Spain immediately and do your best to make the switch."

Bromhead put his hand on my shoulder. "We all know John Davis has the greatest respect for you."

"And, in a way, you owe it to Rank for all the chances and backing they've given you in the past," added Freddie, smiling persuasively.

"I'm not sure about that," I replied with a wry smile, "there have been times when J.D. was no help to me at all!" I paused, looking at the two anxious faces. "I see what is involved. It's a challenge. All things considered, I'm prepared to try!"

I drove to Onslow Square and told Pauline the situation. How ironic! Here I am, in complete charge of a movie on which Pauline could have worked and been the greatest help to me, yet she can't leave London because the baby we are adopting may be born in three or four day's time!

"You have to be here, too," she said. "I can't choose and accept the baby on my own."

"I know and realise this is what we've been aiming for in the last two years, but here is the biggest challenge of my life. A whole lot of people are depending on me." I gave her a pleading look. "And we need the picture to go ahead, in order to buy The Bastide! I've got to go!"

"Okay," she said after a pause. "But promise you'll try and get back as soon as the baby is born."

"We'll talk every night," I said, embracing her and feeling terribly torn.

Spain has always been a lucky country for me. Johnny Cabrera was available to find locations with me; Julio Molina all ready to build sets; and Julio Mercado to drive us knowledgeably around, just as when we scouted for *Across The Bridge*. From the photos I had brought back from India, we all decided that the area around Grenada would be the most suitable for the fort and the main action. The snow-capped Sierra Nevada Ranges could serve as the Himalayas. The location for the rope bridge could be one of the ravines around Ronda.

The Dacoit country and, in fact, the Dacoits themselves, could be found to the East, around Gaudix, which was still occupied by Spanish Gypsies. It turned out to be a fascinating area where the modern 'gitane' lived in caves luxuriously furnished — like modern wealthy homes, and quite large. And, of course, they had masses of horses and crazy riders, which we needed.

After our London meeting, the Rank Organisation had cabled money to secure the release of my poor colleagues in India, and now with cables and telephone calls burning up the lines, Vetchinsky and Dick Parker arrived in Madrid to get construction started with Julio Molina. Johnny took Dick Parker to the site we've chosen for the rope bridge, while I spent a day with Gregorio Sacristan, my old Spanish factotum, fixing up a crew, lights, generators — everything which I knew he could so well provide.

Gregorio himself was dark-haired and half-Gypsy, something of a rogue — liable to be taking ten percent off everyone he hired and everything he provided — but he had proved on my previous two movies that he was absolutely reliable, knowledgeable, professional and a good friend to me. In this crisis situation there was nothing else I could do but put the logistics part of the production as much as possible into his hands.

I flew back to England and saw the baby with Pauline in a Hampstead nursing home. She was four days old, healthy, pretty and available. Our hearts missed a beat when we picked her up — we loved her immediately, named her Deborah Mary, and took her back with us to the flat. Legal papers were signed almost immediately.

Pauline was blissfully happy — though I was sure half of her was wishing she could be involved in the movie. What a cruel turn of fate, that for nearly ten years she had been dying to work with me, and now the way was wide open, she was tied up with a baby. Ever-helpful, Pauline found me an associate producer in the person of Aida Young — with whom she had worked in her production-secretary days. Since then, Aida had been making a number of low-budget movies and had proved to be very efficient in controlling crews and keeping down costs. I felt that by teaming her up with Frank Green and Sacristan, I would be able nominally to carry the responsibilities of producer, whilst ninety-five percent doing my job as director.

While in London I cried to get hold of Sydney Box. There was only a secretary in his office who said that the rest of the staff had been laid off. She understood he was recuperating slowly, but when I tried to speak to Muriel, she was never available to take my call. I didn't like the sound of that, but the film had to go on!

After casting the supporting roles, I fixed my old buddies, Jack Hildyard and Dudley Lovell, to look after the camera side. Then, I embraced Pauline, who promised that if she could find a nanny she could trust, she would try and slip away for a weekend or two during the shoot.

Yul Brynner arrived in Grenada with the largest motor home I have ever seen. It was luxuriously equipped with dining room, bar and private makeup room. Somehow,

Yul persuaded Dick Parker to be responsible for the moving around of it, and many times I would upbraid Dick because he seemed to be spending more time transporting Yul's caravan along narrow roads and difficult locations, rather than concentrating on his rope bridge and special effects!

My old friend Ken Buckle came out as horse master — ministering over three hundred horses and riders, which had to be corralled and transported in horse boxes to the locations as and when we needed them. Often, because we would be shooting right until sunset, the moves had to be made after darkness fell. Poor Ken had a hell of a job and lost several horses through falls in the dark, which upset us all.

Yul was a most amusing character, a hundred percent professional and, rather like Rossano Brazzi, claimed to be an expert at everything you could mention. We all knew he came from New York, but in the evenings he would amuse a table full of crew, telling stories of his youth in Mongolia, India and the Gobi Desert.

In the movie he was the leader of the Dacoits, and insisted on riding a tall white horse. He also insisted in bringing Doug, his special stand-in and double from Hollywood. Doug would do all the difficult riding scenes (very efficiently). Whenever Yul was required to do close-ups on the horse, Doug had to be very supportive — so much so that we began to doubt that Yul had ever ridden with the Mongols! In the film, he appears as a ruthless and efficient leader, and great on a horse — which was all I cared about.

We had winds that nearly blew everything away when we shot in the High Sierras, and many problems due to Jack Hildyard requiring six brutes to light the big scenes. Gregario, who had provided for all of our electrical need on *Battle of the Bulge,* was able to provide us with the lights Jack required, but at exorbitant cost.

One of my most harrowing memories is a sequence in a small tribal camp. The story required me to show a loveable peaceful tribe, the kind one would root for. So, in their mountain retreat, we established them weaving and planting and in the evenings making music and dancing with a tame black bear. The bear had been brought over from the Chipperfield Zoo near Windsor, England. The Chipperfield family were accustomed to providing animals for movies, and Mary Chipperfield was most attentive to our bear's needs and comfort. Unfortunately, in a raid where the tribe is massacred, we also had to show the bear being killed — the object being to get sympathy for the tribe and hatred for the marauders. I was surprised that Mary had not brought along the adequate dose of knockout dope herself, but she seemed quite happy relying on a Spanish vet. Under her supervision he gave the animal an injection. The bear went to sleep, and we filmed Yul's Dacoits wiping out the camp and riding away, but *the bear never woke up*! I just could not believe it... but as the minutes ticked away, it was clear he had died. I turned away heartbroken, tears welling into my eyes. I thought of the elephant in Kenya, and now this.

What should I do? It was three in the afternoon and we were fighting to keep up to schedule. But, I just did not have the heart to carry on. We wrapped for the rest of the day, with most of the unit leaving the set as downcast as myself. No matter how careful you try to be, tragedies like this do occur. Maybe one day, some place, I will have to answer for these two deaths, but as in all show business, the next day, filming had to continue.

The costumes we had shipped over from London, made the village scenes set against the background of dusty, sun-baked, Andalusian hamlets, believable for India.

CHAPTER SIXTEEN *The Saga of* The Long Duel

And I found an old steam train which was exactly like the one I would have used in Mussourie. The famous Arab-built Alhambra served magnificently as a portion of an Indian palace. The substitute locations were working out fine. Trevor Howard and Harry Andrews were great troupers, and marvellous to work with. However, every night, Trevor hit the bottle far too heavily.

During the day, Harry quite willingly became his keeper. However, in the evenings, when most of us liked to go out and dine in typical Spanish restaurants, Trevor was always a problem. The big scene was coming up where Trevor and Harry Andrews, bringing up a train full of soldiers, are attacked by the galloping Dacoits led by Yul. Bert Batt, my old first assistant, took his job very seriously and was not a drinker. That night, seeing that Pauline had arrived from London on one of her rare visits, Bert said, "Don't worry, Gov. I'll look after Trev."

We had a marvellous evening on the town, and returned to find Bert lying prostrate on the floor and Trevor quite happily propping up the bar. "Don't know what happened to your assistant, Ken," said Trevor. "Just couldn't hold a few beers — and a whisky or two!!" He grinned and collared me to talk boozily about his great desire to play General Wingate!

The next day, despite Harry Andrews' efforts to support him, Trev was in a very bad state. He was slurring his words so badly that I told the continuity girl to note that we would have to cover all his scenes with close-ups at some later date. The same kind of thing occurred in the night attack on the fort. Trevor had to come out of his office, walk down some steps, and find Yul and his Dacoits setting fire to the wooden gates of the fort and coming over the walls. In the state Trev was in, he would, in reality, have been shot to pieces and his men massacred! Again, because fire and special effects and sixty horsemen were all ready to go, I went ahead and shot, making notes that Trevor's close-ups would have to be redone.

One evening I spent an hour showing him all his scenes strung together. He was shattered, and promised that for the next three weeks he would guarantee to stay off the bottle and do all the retakes I wished. "You'll have to save me, Ken. I'm desperately sorry and ashamed."

He kept his word and I must say I still think of him as one of the most loveable and sensitive of British stars. He made over seventy movies, an amazing number of them memorable — especially *Brief Encounter,* which will always remain a classic.

Some of our days in Spain were brightened up by the fact that we had three very pretty girls in the cast: Virginia North (a top model); Laura Piper (daughter of John Piper, the famous painter); and Charlotte Rampling — a newcomer, not unlike Julie Christie, and equally eager to give of her best. I had a feeling she would make a very fine actress, but on this movie she was cast as the daughter of Harry Andrews, who had to fall in love with Trevor. Unfortunately, she was in her mid-twenties, while Trevor was in his late fifties. I felt they played their love scenes well, but I had a secret reservation that the scenes were not well motivated or credible.

In fact, the three girls did not really belong in this movie, but as often happens, Sydney Box, as the original producer, and Freddie Thomas, as the distributor, had decided that a big expensive epic must have a love interest, and pretty girls to relieve all that male 'derring-do'. This was basically the purpose our 'three little darlings' served — somewhat inadequately, but through no fault of theirs!!

The location shooting continued, with growing problems for me. As the line-producer as well as the director, I had to spend an hour or two each evening with George Davis, the accountant, going over the budget and the monies we were spending. It is a very difficult thing to wear *two hats* and initiate economies that will affect you as a director!

One glaring problem was transport. It appeared that because our locations matching India were spread out over a much wider area than normal, we had acquired a caravanserai of a hundred twenty vehicles. I questioned Aida Young and Frank Green and gave them instructions that they must find some way of cutting down the cars, but they seemed to be quite incapable of doing so. In addition, they were being very British and making no effort to coordinate with Sacristan. "The Spanish are all crooks," they moaned.

Due very much to our shared hardships in Mussourie, Valerie Rawlings had become my most loyal and trusted supporter. She now tipped me off to the fact that Aida and Frank were so involved in a passionate affair, that when I thought they were busy backstage organising the production, they were most likely, as we coarsely say in Yorkshire, 'having it off!'

I complained and threatened, but when you are out in the field all day, how can you keep your finger on what is going on in the office — or prove your suspicions? Only 'my second self' could have done this! The strain on a director, trying to think of everything; dealing with everyone's problems; and squeezing the best out of actors and crew is normal — but when the day to day organisational problems are added, your position becomes intolerable.

Pauline tells me that one night in desperation I yelled over the phone, "This adoption business is never going to work out. I need you here tomorrow — and to hell with the consequences!!" She was torn — even about to book a flight — when my daughter Jane, now twenty, put her arms around her and said, "If you lose Debbie — if they take her away after all this effort, you'll hate Ken for the rest of your life!!" And so, Pauline 'stuck it out in London'... visiting me three or four brief weekends, when Jane was free to hold the fort.

I survived the location shoot — with the backstage organisation more sloppy that it should have been. We clung on to Debbie, and Pauline and I are still in love and having fun together after forty-one years!!

Back in Pinewood I was not as popular with the Rank big-shots as when I'd set out to save their asses. It appeared from George's figures — which were not as up-to-the-minute as I had been led to believe — that we might well be around two hundred thousand pounds over-budget. They were very pleased with the material, and if I was over-budget what could they have expected after the quick and, I felt, brilliant switch that I had made from India to Spain.

However, this is the nature of the movie business and the people in charge. We finished three weeks shooting with daily front office visits and complaints. Much as I would have liked, I could not speed up the studio shooting, since Jack Hillyard, rightly felt that he had obtained fantastic photographic material in Spain and was determined to maintain his quality in the studio. As a professional and having 'come-up' on the camera, I sympathised with his problems and could not throw him to the wolves.

At the wrap party everyone was all smiles, including Freddy Thomas and Frank Bromhead. My only regret was that my ex-guardian angel, Sydney Box, could not be present. Rumour had it that following his heart attack he had retired to Western

Australia with his nurse, to start a completely new life!

With the pressure off, and my editor trying to make sense of all the footage we had shot in Spain, I was able to devote some time to Pauline and our beautiful Deborah Mary, whom we both felt enormously lucky to have successfully adopted.

Suddenly it was announced that the screenplay of *Those Magnificent Men in their Flying Machines* had been nominated for an Oscar. Jack Davies and I were thrilled, but in those days there was no indication to Europeans that they should dash off to Hollywood, give interviews, and hire publicity people in order to get a chance of winning! Neither was there an invitation to the Oscar evening by the Academy as there is today.

So I pushed on with other projects zooming through my brain, and Jack joined up with a Hollywood producer/promoter called Bernie Schwartz, who had the idea of making a movie, set around the Tour de France cycle race. Poor old Jack had to tag along with him in a car through rain and sunshine for twenty days, following the cyclists all around France. He was now expected to turn out a comedy script on the lines of *Flying Machines*. Every day he would read me out some of the funny sequences he was developing and said he hoped I would direct the movie if it was ever made.

He had created an important role for Brigitte Bardot, who was a most sought-after international star at that time. I could see the whole thing might work out very well, though I had reservations as to how many people in America were interested in cycling!

My agent had also gotten me involved with an American producer, Charles Kasher and Bill Foreman, a Canadian theatre owner — two very opposite but interesting characters. They had bought a book with a marvellous title 'The Flight of the Dancing Bear'. It was a charming and very clever comedic allegory on life in Soviet Russia. They had paid for a script by Julian Slade, a young Englishman who had written and produced 'Salad Days', a very successful nostalgic musical comedy. I felt the script was lightweight and that they would have difficulty in setting it up. However, I was most intrigued by Kamak, a loveable clown and his remarkable brown bear, Katinka. Zappotin the pompous Police Chief of Leningrad, who felt the bear had caused him to lose dignity by embracing him in the main city square, chases Kamak and Katinka halfway across Russia!

But first things first. I was determined to see *The Long Duel* through personally, especially because I had heard that Joe Shaftel had re-edited *The Biggest Bundle*, made some very bad cuts, and that the film was nowhere like the one I had handed over to him. Through contacts at MGM, I heard that the movie had no chance of being released soon because Sam Spiegel had not been able to get *The Happening* shown!

It could be another eighteen months before *Bundle* was in the theatres, and in my experience, somehow even though a film may be a period piece, it loses its momentum in delays — the audience gets a feeling of 'déja-vu'. Since I couldn't hope for much kudos from that film — especially if Shaftel had indeed butchered my cut, it was most important for me to turn out the very best film possible with *The Long Duel* material, and use my producer status to see it *safely* into world cinemas.

CHAPTER SEVENTEEN
Selling The Long Duel in New York...
I become Charlie Bludhorn's 'Blue-eyed boy'...
Adventures of a contract director inside Paramount

W e managed to put *The Long Duel* to bed just before Christmas. Freddie Thomas was delighted with it, and John Davis even allowed himself one of his rare smiles and put his arm around my shoulder. "I think you saved our bacon, Ken. In the new year I want you to go over to New York and show the picture to Charlie Bludhorn, a new guy who has taken over Paramount. We've had talks with them and they're looking for a product to distribute in the States. Hopefully, I may be able to get two million dollar negative pickup from them, which would ease our loan position at the bank!'

All over Christmas I was trying to persuade Pauline to take a chance and come with me to New York. "You've found her a marvellous nanny who seems quite capable of handling Debbie," I pleaded. "If there's any problem, all she has to do is call us in New York and you could be back in twelve hours." And so, we crossed the Atlantic in style and checked into the Regency Hotel, which we have always found to be smart, convenient and most comfortable.

At three pm we put the eleven reels of film into a cab and made our way to Paramount. Charlie Bludhorn turned out to be a short, rather toothy young man in his early forties, who had originally come from Vienna, having made a fortune in coffee. Brusque and businesslike, he led us into the projection room where an audience of forty-five executives and salespeople awaited us. The picture was received in silence. When Charlie, who was sitting beside us, began to applaud, the lights went up and everyone followed suit. Seeing the boss-man liked the movie, everyone began discussing how and where they could deal with it.

"You've done a good job," said Charlie, giving us his most pleasant grin. "I don't know how American audiences are going to respond to a story of British Colonialism, but I like your style. The picture is polished, smart — an easy-to-watch adventure on the lines of that classic *Gunga Din*." He turned to his guys appealing, "And Yul Brynner is still a star!" Collecting nods all round, Charlie moved to Pauline and without lowering his voice said, "I hope you two guys will have dinner with me tonight.'

Without thinking I blurted, "I'm sorry, Charlie, but we're going to a party at six-thirty."

His face fell. "Oh! I wanted to introduce you to my wife Françoise and Jimmy Coburn." He turned away and whispered to a colleague. I looked around the faces of his subordinates. They registered shock. What kind of a shmuck must I be to have turned down the invitation of the boss!

Charlie swung around. "Who's giving this goddamn party that's more important than my invitation?"

"Charles Brackett and his wife," I replied. "We're going along with our old friends, Cecil and Myra Bernstein."

Charlie frowned until a salesman leaned forward and whispered, "Granada Cinemas and TV."

Charlie grunted, then added, "Well, at least let my chauffeur take you to wherever it is."

As we went down in the elevator, Pauline squeezed my hand and whispered, "You've made a big boo-boo, but what else can we do?" I hunched my shoulders and threw a glance heavenwards.

Not only did Charlie lend us his chauffeur, but he also decided to ride with us to Riverside Drive. When we reached the Brackett's apartment, a group of smartly dressed people were going inside.

"Huh," said Charlie, "I see the party's for real. Who the fuck are these Bracketts anyway?"

"They've only written twenty or thirty winners like *Ninotchka*, *The King and I*, *Wayward Bus*, *Ten North Frederick*, and *State Fair*," I said.

"Huh," grunted Charlie. "Well, I hope you have a good evening and I'd like to see you in my office at ten o'clock in the morning." Pauline and I went into the party and reported what had happened to Cecil Bernstein.

"You did quite right to come to the party," grinned Cecil. "If Bludhorn wants to do business with you, he'll appreciate you even more for having shown your independence."

"I don't think he'll ever forget you turned him down in front of his forty yes-men," said Pauline. She shrugged and smiled at me. "Still, you can't help being you, darling, and I love you."

Charlie agreed to take *The Long Duel* at John Davis' price and was all over me the next morning.

"I'm the new boy in Paramount," he said. "I need to surround myself with good, honest filmmakers. I feel you and I can do great things together. Bring me all your ideas and, for my part, I'd like to think I can call you anytime about the things and people I take a shine to." Within a week, I got an invitation from Bud Ornstein, who was head of Paramount in London. Over lunch at The White Elephant, he made me an offer to direct 'Tour De France'.

"I'm sold on the idea," said Bud, 'but you're gonna have to fly out to Hollywood to sell yourself to Bob Evans, Bernie Donnenfeld and Marty Davis — the guys who are really calling the shots in this company."

"Fill me in about them," I said.

Bud drew a deep breath. "Well, Bob Evans is a personable young guy from the

New York rag trade. He made a fortune selling his shares to Revlon. The story is that in searching for a good investment, he stumbled across the fact that Paramount was sitting on a gold mine. A cemetery next door was bursting at the seams and the city was after the land. The whole caboodle was too big for Evans, so he took it to Bludhorn who knew how to handle bankers and parlay a situation like this into millions."

"I still can't see why I've got to be vetted by Evans and Company," I said frowning.

Bud leaned forward, "Charlie owes him one! And he wants to be the big cheese in Hollywood. The trio are not at all happy about Charlie picking up properties and stars."

I drew a deep breath. "Smack in the middle of politics again," I said. "I'm not too good at that!"

Bud smiled. "Fortunately for you, it seems a natural that you should direct a subject which Jack Davies has written. Bernie Schwartz, who brought the subject to us, jumped at the idea when Charlie suggested it to him. So, go in and pitch, but keep a wary eye on Evans, Donnenfeld and Davis. Try and get along with them, as I do!" Once again, I was on my travels.

To my surprise, I found that Bernie Schwartz was not terribly keen on Jack's screenplay. He said it was very European and the dialogue very British. I could see what he meant about some of the dialogue, but pointed out that the whole "Tour De France' takes place in Europe with European competitors and sponsors.

"Apart from the American competitor, which you have introduced — incidentally, there have never been American winners in the race — Jack's work should be quite simple to adjust."

"Bob wants me to hire the two guys who wrote *Revolution*," said Bernie, giving me a sly look.

"I don't think I saw that picture," I said.

"It isn't out yet," smiled Bernie. "They're new guys, but Bob loves their style of comedy and thinks they can give the script a shot in the arm!"

"I don't think it needs it," I ventured to say. "But if Paramount is paying, why not take them on to do a polish for a couple of weeks?"

Schwartz grinned. "You've got to make compromises in this business, Ken, and I'm glad you realise it. Some of the British we've had out here are very stiff-necked."

I met Bob Evans for five minutes. He was smooth, dark and handsome — quite different from the great moguls like Jack Warner, Harry Cohn, Zanuck or Disney.

He told me that he hoped we could get the script right and would appreciate my sitting in with Schwartz and the production manager to the get the budget reduced. It began to sound like a previous visit! But this time I was going to try and be the 'good boy'. I could see that I was going to be in Hollywood for several weeks, so I called Pauline and persuaded her to come out and share my bed at the Beverly Hills Hotel.

Charlie came out to the Coast and took us to dinner at Chasen's, but Donnenfeld, who listened in most carefully while Charlie discussed subjects and people with me on a very confidential basis, accompanied him this time. Very quickly latching onto the situation, Pauline tried to occupy Donnenfeld's attention and seemed to be succeeding pretty well while I laid out my personal hopes and ideas to Charlie.

"Tell me, Ken, what two subjects would you really like to make best?" he said.

I talked about 'The Dancing Bear' and told him the direction in which I thought the movie might go.

"I would like to take the story out of the present day and move it back to the Russia of the Czars. Folk dancing, big colourful fairs, and a sail sledge race across the ice with the bear steering. Have you ever seen English pantomime?" Charlie shook his head.

"Next Christmas, we must take you and your wife to the London Palladium." He nodded eagerly.

I pressed on, "If we keep it non-political, the Russians might even be persuaded to go into a co-production and lend us the Bolshoi!"

"I like the sound of that," Charlie beamed. "Something like Armand Hammer might be involved in —internationally important!!" He paused for a moment. "Why don't we see if we can make a deal with these two guys who own the property?"

Donnenfeld was brought into the act and promised to take the matter up with Bud Ornstein in London.

"What I really want out of you," said Charlie, "is another epic like *Those Magnificent Men In Their Flying Machines*."

"Nothing would please me more," I said, now flying! "Jack Davies and I have played with a comedy around old cars." More or less off the top of my head, I laid out the idea of a big international movie set around the Monte Carlo Rally. Again, we would make it period, say in the Twenties, with a cast of popular comedic stars like Jerry Lewis, Gert Froebe, Terry-Thomas ...

"Keep thinking about that one," said Charlie, patting my shoulder. "I know we're going to do a lot of business together."

As usually happens with writers, the new guys working on 'Tour De France' were going in their own direction and tearing Jack's comedy sequences apart. In daily sessions, I tried to keep the subject from falling apart, retaining Jack's comedy and latching onto more genuine American dialogue. There had been lots of arguments as to who should play the American cyclist. George Segal had been offered the part, but turned it down. The agents for James Caan, Dick Van Dyke and Ty Hardin were reading the material, but both Jack and I wanted James Garner from *Maverick*. For some reason, he seemed unattainable, too — even with a big offer from Paramount.

In the fourth week we were told we must fly for a meeting with Charlie and Marty Davis in New York. Throwing our things together, Pauline and I rushed to catch the 'red eye' which was due to leave Los Angeles at eleven pm The clock registered eleven-thirty, but there was no Bob Evans. Apparently, they were holding the plane for him! He had been to a premiere and arrived with a mohair coat slung fashionably over his shoulders. He nodded briefly to Schwartz, and as his glance flipped past me, he caught sight of Pauline and for a moment there was a smile. Then, his eyes glazed over and he flopped out — dead to the world. Pauline nudged me. "That's your Bob Evans?" I nodded.

She frowned. "Your boss?" she queried.

"Sort of."

She began to laugh and told me the funniest story. On a day during our 1965 trip to LA, she had been lying around the Beverly Hills pool and became intrigued by continual calls coming over the loudspeaker, "Mr. Bob Evans wanted on the telephone!" She looked around and saw a very handsome, slim, young guy who took great pains to see that everyone noticed him taking the phone.

"Wanting to know who this important guy might be... he might have been useful to you," she said, "I moved closer to him and almost killed myself with laughing when

I discovered the way he was operating. He would take a call from Twentieth Century-Fox and say he was sorry he could not come over for a meeting because he was deep in budget discussions with Universal. Then, he would call Universal and tell them Fox was clamouring for his subject. The same routine would follow with calls to and from top executives at Warners and Paramount. He would always say he was deep in meetings, when I could see him flirting with the latest girl to sashay past him ... punctuating his hard day with cool drinks and graceful dives into the pool. But, at the end of the day, starting from scratch he had fixed six top-ranking meetings with the guys who must have been falling over themselves to do business with him!"

"You're sure it's the same guy?" I said.

"Of course I'm sure. He's a great operator!"

The plane landed around six am in New York, and we all piled into a limo... Donnenfeld, Schwartz, Evans and the two of us. Driving into Manhattan, Bob suddenly started throwing out revolutionary ideas for the American cyclist in 'Tour'. "I think he should be a priest, attached to a university," he said from behind his ultra-dark glasses. He rambled on and the whole concept sounded ludicrous. I caught Pauline and Bernie Schwartz exchanging glances of disgust. If this was the tack Bob was going to follow — we were all 'up the creek!'

At eleven am I was sitting in Charlie's office with Evans, Donnenfeld, Schwartz and Marty Davis — whom I had at last met, and judged to be even slicker and more snide than Evans. It appeared he was in charge of publicity and advertising, but being in the New York office he was able to exert a strong influence on the irrepressible Charlie.

Everyone was thrown for six when Bob expounded his new ideas for the American cyclist, and it seemed to unleash secret doubts which Donnenfeld and Davis must have been harbouring about 'Tour De France'.

"Does this company really want to make a movie about sweaty asses moving up and down on bicycle seats?" said Donnenfeld.

"The American audiences don't care a fuck about cycling in Europe," grumbled Marty Davis.

"The script's not in shape and the Tour has to be shot in June," said Evans.

"I don't believe there's time to get it all set up," said Donnenfeld.

"But we have a deal," wailed Schwartz. "And I can bring in three million dollars worth of publicity from the guys who sponsor the race. I tell you, this is the biggest thing in Europe!"

"Fuck Europe,' said Marty. "We make our money from American movies."

For three hours Charlie made calls to Europe. He threw 'fucks' across the Atlantic to Bud Ornstein. He grilled his associate Luigi Luraski in Rome. The Paramount office in Paris seemed to be the only one eagerly welcoming the picture. Sweating and in shirt sleeves, Charlie drew me aside, "If I could get you this 'bear picture', would you switch?"

"Sure," I said, "providing you look after Jack Davies and I can be left alone to develop a script along the lines laid out to you."

He shook my hand. "We'll bring Jack out over here. He and Schwartz can struggle with Bob over the characters in 'Tour De France'. It's obvious we won't be able to catch the race this year and I don't want to have you wasting your time." He winked. "Get out of town with your bride before things get all screwed up!" Once again, that phrase "Get out of town!" I discussed the meeting with Pauline who felt that I should tell Jack everything that had happened, and leave it to him to try and salvage his script.

Leaving this cutthroat atmosphere of wheeling, dealing and double-crossing, we were glad to get back to London, Debbie, and the prospect of moving to our new home in France. As a result of payments for *The Biggest Bundle* and *Long Duel*, we had been able to buy our new French home, and in six weeks' time, we planned to leave London and begin life in a luxurious new setting.

Within a week Bud Ornstein called me to say that Kasher and Foreman had been bought out of the 'Bear Project'. "Charlie wants me to hire a writer to rush a script through on the lines you discussed with him."

Jack Davies was out. Fully briefed about the pitfalls, he had flown out to Hollywood to try and defend his script against the weak Bernie Schwartz, the powerful Bob Evans, and God only knew who else! I felt very sorry for him.

I phoned around and found that Guy Elmes had just broken up with his Beautician-wife in Rome and was back again in London. He was only too happy to work with me again, so for the next five weeks we 'created' in my fast-emptying study, while Pauline took care of all the preparations for the move. A crazy time... but perseverance paid off and on a beautiful spring day with my Jaguar and Pauline's Mini stuffed to the top with portable possessions, we set out along the famous Brighton Road from London to the Calais Ferry.

In two days, driving quite leisurely through some of the most beautiful regions of France, we arrived in Vence. Our property developer, Eilif Gisselback greeted us with smiles and champagne — but said he needed another two days to get his workers out of our new home.

The only thing we could do was to drive down to St Paul de Vence and book into the Columb d'Or — annoying, but quite honestly no great hardship because this 'hostellerie' has always been one of the most favourite 'watering-holes' for the top people who flock into Cannes for the Film Festival every May.

The dining room, bar and passages were filled with paintings by Picasso, Chagall, Miro and other famous Impressionists, whom it is alleged paid for their dinners with canvasses, in the old days when they were impoverished. Across the road Yves Montand, was playing boules with the locals, watched by his wife, Simone Signoret. It couldn't be bad!

But the respite was short. With our help, the Bastide was cleared up in five days — sufficiently for us to take possession, we dashed down to Nice Airport to meet Miggy, our faithful nanny, with Debbie. Her nursery was the first room decorated, and the Gisselbacks had rented basic furniture for us. Life in the South of France had begun!!

Guy Elmes joined us within the week and in the mornings we wrote 'Dancing Bear' in my empty but large study. Leaving him to polish the pages in the afternoons, Pauline and I went looking for antique furniture and all the odds and ends one needs to run a big house.

We sent off the script of the 'Dancing Bear' to Bud Ornstein around the end of May. For ten wonderful days and nights Guy shared with us the idyllic Cote d'Azur way of life, until a phone call shattered our joy. Bud said he liked the shape and overall plot line, but didn't find the script funny. Whether this was just his view or a combination of the opinions of Charlie Bludhorn and Bob Evans, I never knew, but the concrete fact was that 'Tour de France' had been dropped! Paramount still had their deal with Jack Davies and now decided they could save money if they could switch Jack on to the 'Bear' and pay off Guy!

What a quandary! Naturally, Guy was heartbroken, but he could do with the money. He had found a tiny old house he wanted desperately to buy in nearby Hautes de Cagnes. So, by mutual agreement, we accepted fate, and I softened the blow by promising to pay him out of my own pocket to write 'The Forbidden' — an original story about a diamond theft, set in the Namibia Desert of South Africa.

Jack was delighted for the chance of working with me again — at big money. More specifically, he was overjoyed because he and Dorothy had decided to move to France and settle close to us. Dorothy, like myself, had always dreamed of living in the South of France and now took this as an opportunity not to be missed.

We found another Gisselback house right below the Bastide. They settled in and Jack and I began to 'fun up' the 'Bear' script. I had to admit that Guy had been great on flowery descriptions of Russian life in 1912 and had faithfully adapted the characters in the book, but he was a serious-minded fellow and had never written an extravaganza. Jack immediately began to find comedic solutions for all kinds of scenes in the 'Bear'. In six weeks we had revised the script sufficiently for Bud to say: "Charlie wants me to give you the go-ahead, but there's a special condition attached. If it is at all possible, he wants the movie made in Rumania."

"Why Rumania?" I asked.

"Because it's next door to Russia and the countryside, we are told, looks similar. Believe it or not, it has a film industry with large studios, and Charlie has brought a guy on to the Paramount Board who is involved in big 'wheat deals' in Rumania. It means that Paramount will have a lot of blocked funds available which can be used for your movie!"

Although I wanted to get into production again, I was 'pissed off' with this development — to say the least. I felt I had proved I could make box-office movies, and now, why should I be shoved off into a remote Iron Curtain country to save Paramount a few million dollars??

It was in this negative mood that I set off for Rumania, where Luigi Luraski, an old film salesman from Rome, joined me. The studios were, undoubtedly, palatial with a marble column facade, but the sets we saw on the stages looked very primitive and the workshops lacked modern machine tools.

We drove around the Northern parts of Rumania, where we found a lake that the locals guaranteed would be frozen in winter — a very important factor for this movie. But most of the villages we passed through were filled with sad looking people and were generally depressing.

As we sat in the best hotel in Bucharest waiting to be served a very basic dinner, I said to Luraski, "I don't want to make the movie here. Our lines of communication will be terrible, practically everything will have to be imported, the crew will be miserable, and the comedy will suffer."

He said, "I can see your point, but Charlie will be very disappointed."

He came around to my way of thinking, however, when I passed him over to Dick Parker on the telephone. As in *Flying Machines*, nearly every scene that Jack and I had written needed complicated mechanical special effects, and I was relying on Dick Parker to provide them. "I'm not coming to work in any Commie country," yelled Dick from his new home in Spain. "Absolutely not! Unless you can go to some civilised industrialised country, count me out."

"I think we should take a look at Bavaria," I said to Luraski later that night.

He nodded, but I could not understand why he looked depressed. He knew, but dare not tell me, that Rumania was Charlie's way of guaranteeing that I should make the movie despite his enemies in New York and Hollywood!

Full of confidence, we flew to Munich. Within sixty miles of the city, we found all the locations we needed — a wonderful old railway line, a lake that was frozen over for two months in the winter. Bavaria Studios were large and almost the best in Europe. All the equipment we needed was available — and what is more they had a large lot with a cyclorama already standing where we could stage the close-ups for the frozen lake sequence.

Luigi talked at length to Bud Ornstein and apparently Charlie okayed him making a deal with Bavaria Studios, so long as I would agree to make the movie for not more than eight million dollars. Once again, I was to produce and direct with Luigi acting as watchdog for Paramount.

Within a couple of days Dick Parker arrived from Spain, driving his newly equipped special effects truck. Harry Horner, an American art director who had made a lot of pictures for Paramount, arrived to coordinate the building work with Bavaria's own art director and construction staff. Harry turned out to be a very co-operative guy with great taste and artistic ability. He very quickly made some key sketches of the sets we would need.

I wrote to Pauline, "Harry's enthusiasm is boundless, and the Germans are inspired to great efforts, despite the fact that they are accustomed since the war to work only forty hours in a five day week."

Basil Keys took over as the production controller acceptable to both Bud Ornstein and myself — and I went back to the Bastide for a few days with Pauline and Debbie. In the mornings I toiled with Jack on the revisions necessary for the script to fit the locations we had found. Amazingly, the town of Bamberg, a hundred miles to the north of Munich, matched the architecture of the old St. Petersburg to perfection.

It was now September, and we needed to start shooting in six weeks time if we were going to catch a little of the Fall and use the cold weather where people's breath registers, plus the snow and ice we need at the lake near the Finnish border.

Casting became the number one problem. Pauline tore herself away from Deborah for a trip to London, where we went into casting sessions with my old buddy, Maude Spector. Gert Froebe agreed to play Zappotin, the pompous Police Chief, and most of the smaller parts fell into place very quickly through our joint knowledge of actors in Britain, France and Germany... but we had no Kamak — the lead and, as yet, no bear!!

Alec Guinness would have been perfect but, despite the persuasive efforts of Dennis Van Thal, who was agent for both Alec and myself, Guinness declined to work with a bear. Michael Crawford, a brilliant young British actor who had been playing a sympathetic character on British television for three full years, would have been ideal, but Bud was worried by the fact that he had never appeared before an American audience. Michael later made a big international name for himself in the musical, 'Phantom of the Opera', as we all know!

We suggested that perhaps we could get away with "this talented unknown" by casting Kamak's dark-haired girlfriend with an American star actress. I asked Charlie to try to obtain Natalie Wood for us. Meanwhile, Pauline flew to Amsterdam to a private zoo where we had heard there were three large performing bears. She watched them put through their paces and was amazed. She phoned me, "I think we can make a deal, but by golly, you'll have to take care. These people say that because a bear's face shows no expression, an actor could be at risk — even the handler. For safety, they say, he should be castrated."

"Can he work with his handler dressed as a double?" I asked.

"Sure," said Pauline. "It's the daughter of the owner who will handle him — and you remember what the baboon was like with Gladys! Male animals usually love women!!!"

"If he's right, in every other way, have the poor bugger castrated!" I yelled, hating the decision.

Back at the Bastide, we had a visit from Bob Wagner and his remarried wife, Natalie Wood. Naturally, he was excited about the house and the way it looked, but I noticed that Natalie was rather glum and raised some doubt about the film ever being made. It seemed that Bob Evans, who told her that we wanted her for the film, had approached her and hinted to her agent that there was some question about the production going ahead. She was exactly the actress I wanted, and before she left, both she and Bob promised that she would take the part.

Bud Ornstein in London confirmed privately to me that Charlie was having problems with Bob Evans and Donnenfeld, but he had given Luraski full power to make all the business deals that we needed in Munich.

In a couple more weeks we were off to Munich, complete with nanny and baby. We went out to check the locations and the half-built ice set in front of the cyclorama, which they were painting with a soft mist effect. Dick demonstrated to me the mechanical sail sledges he had been building, and also the mechanical bear. He was, in fact, building two bears: one to be partly radio-controlled, the other operated on wires. The fact that a bear does not change its facial expressions had simplified Dick's job tremendously. I felt that the models were going to work and be very convincing.

Everything was advancing amazingly well. We were comfortably housed in the Four Seasons Hotel, relaxing over a glass of champagne, when Luraski appears, his face ashen. He has just talked to Charlie and thinks they're going to drop the project. "But nearly a half a million dollars has been committed to Bavaria, plus cast commitments," I objected.

"I know," frowned Luigi. "Charlie has great problems."

"What about the poor old bear with no balls?" cried Pauline. "I told them to go ahead!" Luigi nodded.

"And the Ukrainian Folk Troop, who've been rehearsing?" I yelled.

Luigi made a calming gesture. "I know! I know! And Paramount will have to pay for everything, but you must try and understand what Charlie is up against."

Evans and Company were determined to hobble him. Bob said, "We don't have a commercial cast, and Donnenfeld thinks it's a bad image for Paramount to pour money into a German studio."

"Why?" I shouted. "Mercedes cars are the most popular in Hollywood!'

Luigi sighed. "Don't forget Paramount was founded by a Jew and many of the stockholders are Jewish. They had relatives die in the Holocaust"

Two days later, we folded. I promised Harry and Dick I would do my utmost to see they were paid, and hoped that we would work together again soon. Luraski stayed to clear up the financial mess, while Pauline and I, along with Debbie and the nanny, flew back to the Bastide — thanking God that we had at least a wonderful home to go back to... and surely, we would be paid *something!*

CHAPTER EIGHTEEN
Those Daring Young Men In Their Jaunty Jalopies *Or, the better title:* Monte Carlo or Bust *An exciting but heartbreaking two years*

Within a week of arriving home, Charlie Bludhorn was on the phone saying, "Don't worry, kid, I'm going to make it up to you. You remember that Monte Carlo thing you talked about? Old cars and all that jazz?"

"Sure," I replied. "What are you thinking?'

"You said you could make another *Flying Machines* out of it with the same sort of cast," he laughed maliciously. "Don't worry, I'm going to fuck those sons-of-bitches yet."

Within two days, Dennis Van Thal arranges for me to fly to London and a new deal is thrashed out with Bud Ornstein. In addition to my fee for the "Bear," which had been 'put into dispute', another two hundred thousand dollars is added to it for me to produce and co-write an original screenplay with Jack Davies.

Fortunately, we had already decided we would write a veteran-car subject on spec, and had commissioned Ann Harrington to do research on every funny event recorded since the Monte Carlo Rally was inaugurated in 1900. She had done a great job on *Flying Machines* and now produced over a hundred pages of anecdotes and history, together with masses of photos of old cars in various countries.

Each year the rally covered different courses. Sometimes a competitor started in the Balkans; in the far north of Sweden or Norway; with some brave souls even setting out from India or Africa. They had to pass various checkpoints before making a rendezvous at Chambery in the French Alps. From here onwards, they all drove the same route to Monte Carlo, often sabotaging each other on the way! Ideal stuff for a movie, we thought!

Each morning we would write in my new study, and since Jack was living immediately below, he had only a short walk up the hill each morning, making it no hardship to start work at nine sharp.

We decided that the most attractive period to set the film was 1927. Cars like the De Dion Bouton, Panhard-Levassor, De Dietrich, the Bugattis and Lancias... were objects of sheer beauty, and the clothes sported by the drivers were flamboyant — especially as worn by the odd lady competitor — very chic with short skirt, and known at that period as 'the Flapper style'.

We were smack in the middle of the Jazz Age, and following something which Charlie had said when he first reminded me of the subject... "You know that idea about Monte Carlo and all the jazz..." We decided that this was the perfect title to work from.

Each morning I would lay out the task ahead as it seemed to me — the action we had to cover and the location it would be set in. Then we would talk about everything else but the movie... what restaurant we had been to the evening before, whom we had met, girls we'd been involved with at various times in our lives, cars we had owned and more! Suddenly, Jack would come up with a funny idea around which we could write the scene.

I would rough out our lines on the typewriter, and later describe the scene and elaborate on what we had come up with. One of us would venture a funny line, the other would top it... then another and another, till we dried up on that theme.

We found it was no good forcing ideas, and so would often break off to discuss the actors we would like to play the scenes. Naturally, the characters of Terry-Thomas and Eric Sykes were easy because we had already created the 'master and man' relationship in *Flying Machines*. The same applied to Gert Froebe, whom we were determined should be our leading German competitor.

We were on new ground with our other British characters. Two competitors, we decided, should be typical British sahib types from the Colonial days in India, and they would start out from there. We vaguely hoped we might be able to hook two exciting new guys from a Varsity Review called 'On The Fringe' which had taken London by storm.

The young actors were Dudley Moore and Peter Cook, and in order to catch their style, we managed to pirate a live tape of their show.

Alberto Sordi was again our first choice for the Italian, but he was now so busy directing his own pictures that Luigi Luraski in Rome said he would never be able to persuade him to play in our movie. However, he did come up with a new Italian comedian — very popular with the masses — and called Bossanca. Tall, lanky, and slightly cross-eyed, he loved making a fool of himself in the old Mack Sennett way. We had great fun writing a screwball Roman policeman who fitted Bossanca's odd looks.

The American was, as usual, a problem. He needed to be good looking, sexy, and capable of selling the movie in the U.S. As before, we thought of Dick Van Dyke whom we still regarded as the best young comedic actor in America at the time. Failing him, we again thought of James Garner... but knew from past experience we would probably finish up with whomsoever Bob Evans and Company decided would suit Paramount's overall program!

For the British girl, we originally thought of Charlotte Rampling, but she, like Julie Christie, had decided she wanted to make dramatic films with a social message. We began to think of Susan Hampshire, a very pretty actress who had established herself in the popular British television series, *The Forsythe Saga*. She had married a Frenchman and made one or two small movies in France. She might help us with English and French box-office.

Once we were over the establishing of the characters and their various starts from India, Sweden, the North of Scotland and Spain, the shape of the picture began to

Yul Brynner and Ken relax between scenes on location for *The Long Duel* (1966)

Ken directs fellow director Vittorio De Sica on *The Biggest Bundle of them All* (1967)

Ken getting the best out of Raquel Welch on *The Biggest Bundle of Them All (1967)*

Ken prepares Bob Wagner and Raquel Welch for their next scene. *The Biggest Bundle of them All (1967)*

The whole Annakin family had parts to play in *Monte Carlo or Bust*. Pauline, Debbie and Baxter the Dog wait patiently as Ken checks the framing of the shot. *(1969)*

Prince Rainier takes great interest in the filming of *Monte Carlo or Bust,* as Ken explains the plot. *(1969)*

Ken celebrates the London premiere of *Monte Carlo or Bust* with (left to right) Peter Cook, Jack Warner, Jimmy Edwards and Dudley Moore. *(1969)*

Ken and Mireille Darc outside the Astor Cinema in New York for the American premiere of *Monte Carlo or Bust.* The film was titled *Those Daring Young Men in Their Jaunty Jalopies* in the States. *(1969)*

Ken used old favourites Eric Sykes and Terry-Thomas to supply laughs aplenty in *Monte Carlo or Bust (1969)*

Jack Davies (in the rear) supports Ken in explaining the dialogue to Tony Curtis and Susan Hampshire (back to us) on *Monte Carlo or Bust* (1969).

Ken playing in
the pool with
daughter
Debbie and
young Japanese
actor Ando
while filming
Paper Tiger
(1974)

David Niven and
Ando in a scene
from *Paper Tiger*
(1974)

Ken is re-united with veteran cinematographer Jack Cardiff (right) on *The Fifth Musketeer (1977)*

Ken relaxes on the set of *The New Adventures of Pippi Longstocking* with young actress Tami Erin. (1986)

dictate its own course. We decided to have a big comedy sequence about a quarter of the way through the picture — on a frozen lake in the Arctic, involving both the British and German cars: Crazy, skidding sequences on the ice; a mad helter-skelter down a bobsled run, and perhaps a funny incident with a ski jumper.

As sequences and characters became firm, I sent pages over to Harry Horner in London, asking him to make key sketches — not full storyboards, but sketches that would help us find locations and sell the picture to the people whom I knew would have to give us the okay, in Paramount. Harry turned out to be a fabulous illustrator and an inspiration to anyone who looked at his visualisation of our comedy highlights.

For French audiences, we had an additional attraction — Bourvil, the popular comedian with whom I had worked on *The Longest Day*. I suppose we were influenced by living in France and watching French TV and movies. Bourvil was 'very French' and not the competitive type, so we decided to make him the fussy official in charge of the Rally finale in Monte Carlo. The choice caused me troubles later!

For an international rally taking place fifty percent in France we still needed a French competitor, but I dare not risk more 'very French' for American audiences. Charlie Bludhorn kept calling us and asking for progress reports. Sometimes I would read a scene to him. Suddenly, he came up with a marvellous idea for the French contingent.

"Why not have three pretty girls competing against the men?"

Little did I know that Charlie would come to the casting sessions and make it very clear to the young actresses that he was the boss man at Paramount and if they were nice to him, he might be able to advance their careers! A very human foible. Evidently, the young moguls taking over the movie business were going to behave exactly like the old!

The introduction of the three girl characters lightened up the movie and our days of writing. We used to fantasise about the scrapes they might get into as they came in contact with men. Some of our 'dreams' got into the pictures; others were too risqué or downright smutty to be included. But having these girls in the picture did allow us to devise a true French farce type of sequence, where everybody was running about the corridors in the hotel at Chambery and changing bedrooms.

We breathed a sigh of relief as we finished our first draft in just over five weeks. We knew we would have to make lots of revisions but it gave us time to have second thoughts on what we had 'bashed out' — and expand our social activities and knowledge of the Cote d'Azur.

It was clear we were going to need great cooperation in Monte Carlo, so I made contact with the Director of the Casino, a charming and most efficient American called Wilfred Groote. He introduced me to the French Automobile Club officials, who said they would be only too happy to cooperate, if the palace was happy about our shooting around it, and in the streets of old Monaco.

"Do you know the Princess?" said Wilfred.

"I've met Prince Rainier," I replied, "but not the beautiful Grace Kelly..."

And so, a couple of afternoons later, I drove from Vence down to Monte Carlo and was shown into the palace.

Princess Grace received me in a kind of throne-room and was indeed as beautiful and radiant as one would have expected, and very gracious. She listened to my ideas and proposals as a Princess, rather than an actress.

"I think it would be very good for the principality," she said. "I'll explain to Rainier what you're going to need, and maybe on your next visit, he'll show you his collection of cars."

"I knew he was a car buff," I said. "Do you think he might lend us some of his collection?'

"You'll have to ask him nearer the day," she said, smiling.

I left feeling that we would be given all the facilities we needed in Monte Carlo, and indeed for all the shooting in and around that area. Grace became like a patron to us.

Jack and I finished the script and sent it Express to Bud. For two weeks there was absolute silence, until on Christmas Eve, Charlie called personally to say he loved the script, and was coming to stay with Dino De Laurentiis in his villa near Villefranche.

"Could we pop in to see you one day with Francoise and my son, Paul?"

"Of course, we'd be delighted," I gasped.

Pauline and I rushed around seeing that everything was in its place and polishing all the furniture! Charlie arrived and was obviously very impressed. By now, with its large pool, hillside garden and spectacular waterfall, the Bastide really did compare very well with the homes we'd seen in Beverly Hills.

Paul, just thirteen, went crazy about the sketches and wanted to know which of the elegant vintage cars we would be using.

"There, you see," said Charlie, "if the kids find the cars as cute as the old airplanes, we'll be home clear!"

Our staff excelled themselves with the dinner, and as the guests left, Pauline put her arm around me and I saw a very satisfied smile on her face.

"It won't do any harm," she said, "for him to see that we are a success, even before his movie — if he really makes it."

Now we were brought down to realities.

Bud Ornstein called, "Charlie wants to get *Monte Carlo* into production as soon as possible. What's it gonna cost?"

"Oh, I would say around seven or eight," I said.

"It had better not cost more or you'll blow my European budget," said Bud. "I'm sending Stanley O'Toole to check your plans and work out a provisional budget."

"A lot will depend on the locations and where we actually shoot," I said. "The Victorine Studios in Nice seem ideal to us — and are only twenty minutes away from home."

"Sorry to disappoint you, kid," he said. 'I've just heard from Charlie that he's made a deal with Dino, which requires you to use his brand new studios in Rome."

"That'll be a whole new ballgame," I said. "We hadn't planned on going into Italy at all. It may cost much more."

"If I were you, kid," said Bud, "I'd remember what happened over Rumania and the Bear! This time, don't argue, and just roll with it."

Stanley O'Toole and I met in the Laurentiis Studios and were very impressed. They were brand new, large stages, and the studio lot was quite extensive.

"The only thing we've got to watch," said Stanley, "is what Dino tries to charge for equipment and lamps. He's given Charlie no more than a 'wall-to-wall' deal."

We made as many estimates as we could, but I pointed out to Stanley that the picture was filled with complicated tricks, which combined all the special effects and experience I'd learned throughout my career. I would defy anyone to make a reasonable guess at figures until Dick Parker had really 'broken down' his work.

The script was rushed to Dick, while we set off for a reconnaissance trip to Sweden. It was the middle of winter, desperately cold and with only four hours of daylight. In Stockholm, we made contact with a small production company which had been recommended by the Paramount office. Stanley settled down to get an idea of costs in Sweden, while I was put on a four-seater plane to the frozen North!

Again, it was one of those wonderful, memorable experiences — flying over the Arctic above a landscape which was completely black, white, and towards skies almost permanently streaked with purple, orange and pinks.

We landed in Are, which we had seen from the air. It had a vast frozen lake and behind the little ski-hotel, there was a bob sleigh run! This, and the fact that the locals said we would be able to gather, without too much trouble, three or four teams of ice hockey players from the district, persuaded me that I need not waste any more time on the spotting trip.

That night I was back in Stockholm with more concrete facts for Stanley, and the next day I had an audience with Prince Berthold in the Royal Palace. He was also a great enthusiast for old cars and promised that not only would he arrange the full cooperation of the veteran car clubs of Sweden, but that we could stage our massed drive-away in the square outside the palace.

To top everything, I discovered in the local Paramount office, a most remarkable man in charge of publicity, Bjorn Ortenheim. He was a film buff, knew everyone, loved old cars, and assured me that he could find technicians, extras, actresses, actors and everything required outside the normal run of production equipment.

Stanley and I flew back to Vence completely satisfied that he could now make a budget — which turned out to be nearer ten million than eight! I received agonised calls from Bud telling me that the studio would never go for it and I'd better make cuts.

"This budget is based on the script that Charlie approved and loved," I said. "Until he tells me to make cuts, I'm leaving it exactly as it is because most of the extra cost is due to his partner, Dino and moving the main shoot into Italy."

A few days later, Charlie Bludhorn came on the phone telling me that the budget was ridiculous... but so long as I didn't go over ten million, and allowed Dino to try and help us make economies during the shooting in Italy, the picture was a goer! So, I decided to 'roll with' everything — and count my blessings!!

Next came a very personal problem. Up to now Jack had been included in every idea and decision for the movie and he was clearly hoping that he could be co-producer on the film. Bud Ornstein would not hear of it.

"Jack's a nice guy and a funny writer, but this production is full of difficult logistics, planning, special effects, and a foreign cast. You mention it, you got it. You have to forget loyalty to old pals and bring in the most experienced management guys we can find."

"What about Basil?" I said.

"Basil Keys? Fine with me. With Basil in charge, I can sleep nights."

In most respects, I could not complain, Basil and I had done a lot of movies together, he was a hundred percent professional and we were good friends. But Jack was deeply disappointed and felt I'd let him down — even though I arranged that when we started the shoot with the actors in Rome, both he and his wife would be brought there and given the same per diems and allowances as Pauline and I — he never in his heart forgave me. Very sad — but that is one of the hard realities which happen sometimes in show business.

Casting was complete, costumes fitted, with several extra sets made for the doubles. I went ahead checking locations and general pre-production with the local Swedish company. Suddenly, a new face appeared in Stockholm —Steve Previn.

Bud had decided that he needed an extra watchdog to save his ass. Steve was an amazing little guy who had done a bit of directing for Disney in Germany. He settled in very easily with Basil, checking equipment and logistics, while I went around with Bjorn, looking at old cars. We found some beauties, and their owners seemed only too eager to show them off for free — which I knew Bud would really appreciate!

A bunch of our rally-drivers were supposed to start off from John O'Groats, the northernmost point of Scotland. I had planned to send a third unit there, but stimulated by Previn saying, "Can't we avoid another location move?" Bjorn came up with some pictures of Gotland, an island a hundred miles across the Bay from Stockholm.

On learning that Gotland was the jumping-off place for the Vikings, who eight hundred years ago had pillaged the East Coast of Britain, right down to Beverley, where I was born, I could not wait to see the island.

We hired a small plane and six of us, including Pauline, made the forty-minute air trip. The Vikings obviously had made a good job of their pillaging, because we found fourteen medieval stone cathedrals in Visby, the capital, and the remains of castles and fine houses all over the island!

The northern area was bare and surrounded on three sides by sea, and since few people would know what John O'Groats had really been like forty years ago, I readily agreed that the location could work — providing the veteran car club would allow us to transport their treasures on the ferry.

Bjorn said, "No problem."

However, we nearly changed our minds when, as we returned to the airfield at Visby, it began to snow. On top of this, we found our pilot had been fortifying himself throughout the day with Schnaaps and God knows what other liquors.

We had a helluva time taking off. The wind howled and swung the plane around on the little runway and snow blotted out everything. Basil wanted to cancel the trip, but Pauline cried out that she had to get back because our little daughter was in the hotel with only a day-nanny looking after her.

The pilot seemed blissfully confident and somehow got the bucking bronco into the air, but the bumps and swift drops and howling of the wind were terrifying. Previn lived what was perhaps his 'finest hour', keeping up a running commentary on the variety of possible deaths we were going to suffer in the icy waters, the disintegrating plane and even fire. It was a macabre but hilarious act and got us through to Stockholm without going stark raving mad.

A day or two later, having shopped for winter woollies, long-johns, Arctic parkas and the best ski boots and furry hats (Debbie looked adorable in her little Arctic outfit), we flew by regular plane to Ostersund and drove on icy roads around the lake to the little ski resort of Are.

It was February, the lake was white and frozen as the locals said, "At least a metre in depth." I could not wait for the arrival of the location unit composed of Italians from Rome, and the six British stuntmen headed by Ken Buckle and Joe Wadham — my faithful gang who had done all the crazy driving for me on *The Fast Lady* and *Flying Machines.*

While we were waiting for cars and wardrobe to arrive, I drove off with the art director Ted Haworth, along the road to Trondheim to see a big waterfall he had found. It was enormous and the falls were completely frozen. There was Dick Parker already fixing up platforms and cables from which to hang Susan Hampshire's beautiful MG Midget so that it could 'teeter on the edge'.

"A difficult and dangerous place to work," said Dick.

"But look how fantastic it is," said Ted — whom I admired because he was always determined to give his director the best possible set — but even I was a little worried about the practicality and safety of this location.

As it turned out, we were lucky. After shooting for three days, a thaw set in and the artificial track which Dick had built beside the falls, collapsed completely. We had only wrapped the final shot of the sequence ten minutes before/ Someone up there loved me, thank God!

The thaw also affected our big sequence with the ice hockey players on the frozen lake. In our story, Dudley Moore and Peter Cook, having survived all the hardships of the drive across Eastern Europe, miss their way and arrive at the lake the same time as Gerte Froebe in his big Mercedes Sports. They tailgate each other on to the lake and cause havoc among the hockey players.

We were 'shaping-in' this sequence very successfully with the stuntmen doubling for the actors... when, after four days, the ice began to melt and we were sloshing in about two or three inches of water. I prayed it would not show on film!

Following this sequence, the Lea-Francis with all the gadgets fixed on to it by the Peter Cook character, had to break through a snow wall and race down the bob sleigh run. It was impossible to rig this, so Joe Wadham volunteered to actually drive down the run. We made sure that every corner was banked with a wall of snow and sent him down the course, covering his mad ride with six cameras. A specially picked Swedish bob sleigh team had to be on the run and see the car hurtling down after them. They escape by taking a flying leap over the snow wall.

Ken Buckle joined the team to make sure their timing was perfect and we achieved a sensational crazy shot, which I believe has never been done before or since.

In my experience, every director shooting daring car stunts has to take some risks, and you need to know your drivers intimately. If a driver is a conscientious professional who really uses his brain and calculates exactly what the dangers are and how he can cope with them, it is normally safe to rely on his judgement when he says, "Don't worry, Gov, I can do it."

Stunt car drivers are very similar to racetrack drivers, except they intend to live and go on doing stunts, whereas some racetrack drivers are brilliant but occasionally rely on sheer luck. They take that split-second risk which can be fatal. No professional stuntman wants to work with such types, however brave they may be. We had a guy like that on our team of six. In a much later scene, staging a near miss across a bridge in Italy, he almost killed two of his fellow stuntmen. They gave him hell and made his life so unbearable, that I had to replace him, even though he had great qualities in other ways, and was slight enough in build to double very effectively for Susan Hampshire.

CHAPTER EIGHTEEN Monte Carlo or Bust

We were almost on the Arctic Circle and the dark nights seemed interminable. After our evening meal there was little to do. The Italian crew seemed to be reasonably happy drinking wine, having their private spaghetti parties, and telling jokes. The British stunt guys tended to go out and find local girls in the village, and in doing so fell foul of the local Swedes. Fights began to occur quite regularly and one evening, Ken Buckle got involved in a wrestling match with a six foot six ski instructor. Locked in a half nelson, they fell through a big oriel window, and would have killed themselves but for the fact that the snow was piled ten feet deep below. After picking a few shards of glass out of various parts of their body, they came back into the hotel looking ashamed of themselves. Everyone heaved a sigh of relief, bought more drinks and agreed to contribute to the cost of window repairs.

Pauline and I occupied the best suite in the hotel, but it was really just two small ski rooms. In the daytime our nanny, a charming girl from the far north of Lapland, taught and played with Debbie. In the evenings we would play Canasta and darts. One Sunday we took a trip to Trondheim, a Norwegian fishing village in a fjord on the West Coast. The fisher folk welcomed us with open arms and took us into their brightly coloured homes. Inside they were much like a Scottish Highlander's snug abode, but outside, the whole street was painted in reds, yellows, greens, and blues. They had clearly found a way to counter-balance the grey dark days of winter.

Our most spectacular shot in Are was made on the snow slopes under a competition-style ski jump. The German car had to pass under it just as a skier was hurtling down. Our script called for him to land on the canvas roof of the Mercedes.

We hired an ex-Olympic ski jumper and Ken Buckle drove the car parallel to the skier's line of jump. Actually, he was two feet from the skier's apparent landing spot. Both objects were moving and it took tremendous skill and judgment for the skier to time his descent so that for a split second from our side angle, he appeared to make contact with the roof of the car.

After a whole afternoon's rehearsal, we achieved the master shot and several useable close shots... and no one had been hurt.

With the ice and snow shots completed, everyone was happy to return to the comparative warmth of Stockholm — which was still only four degrees above zero most of the day!!

True to his word, Prince Berthold assisted us in every way to stage forty veteran cars setting out from beside the Royal Palace. They would form the northern contingent making their way south to Monte Carlo from Sweden. Included in the group were the rival Dudley Moore car and Gert Froebe's Mercedes. The script called for them to be ready to fight at every encounter. All their scenes were 'shaped in' with their stunt doubles, and matched later in or around the studio in Rome.

The stunt boys took their acting very seriously and in the end resented the real actors taking over — or so they used to pretend! They really did a great job and I have never heard anyone who saw the movie, spot the changeovers from doubles to principals.

The final stunt before we left Scandinavia, was for the MG Midget (eventually driven by Tony Curtis) to arrive just as the ferryboat to Denmark was sailing, and to make a flying leap on to it. Joe Wadham and Dick Parker made the most careful (and scientific) calculations as to the distance the car would jump at various speeds. Then a bed of cardboard boxes were set out on the lower deck, behind the normal car ferry ramp, held together with shock-cords and lots of mattresses. This preparation and rehearsal took a whole afternoon, and a worrying problem remained in that an iron girder stuck up right in the centre of the hold — we could do nothing about it!!

Mark, the young Cockney driver attempting the stunt, studied the whole set-up with Joe, then took the MG back along the quay. Six cameras set-up ready to shoot. I gave the cue for the car to start and the ferry to pull away. I had memories of the landing craft in *The Longest Day* and how it behaved differently from rehearsal. If the pull away now by the ferry captain was faster than the rehearsals, Mark would finish in the drink and...!

Mark accelerated to the agreed forty miles an hour, rose from the end of the quay (where we had built a concealed ramp) and 'flew' eighteen metres to land on the ferryboat ramp — a magnificent performance!!

With tremendous relief, Mark rose and climbed out of the driving seat, then I saw him go straight around to the front of the car, point and shake his head. Despite all our precautions the bloody pillar had concertinaed the front of the car. But Mark was unscathed, and like a true racing-crew, our mechanics worked through the night and the car was on the road the next day.

When you come to think about it, how can any accountant or studio executive expect to budget to the dollar, this kind of undertaking. That is one reason why budgets soar and get out of hand — especially since stunts have become much more ambitious and dangerous as the years have rolled by.

While we were shooting in Sweden, Steve Previn had gone to Paris to keep an eye on the staging of the three French girls starting the rally from Paris. Jack Davies accompanied him to make sure that the sequence 'sketched in' with doubles, looked exactly as we had planned. The comedy business and dialogue would, of course, be shot with the principals in Rome.

The second unit shooting was in the hands of one of the camera crews I had used on *The Longest Day*, and my old Israeli assistant, Sam Iscovitch. He was, in effect, directing the sequence. Unfortunately, they seemed to have a load of troubles. One of the reasons was because there was not a strong hand like mine directing and making definite decisions. Even if you are only shooting with doubles you have to direct their movements as though they were for real, or the main cast will jib at the action they have established. Another problem was that we wanted to establish sections of Paris, as it had looked in 1927, using fifty veteran cars!

The second set of problems were photographic. Although I knew my director of photography to be first-class, his material always seemed to be slightly out of focus. We complained about this and they did retakes, but the problem was never solved. To this day I tend to believe that one of the camera assistants had been paid to make small sabotage by the group controlling the Victorine Studios in Nice. They had been furious when Charlie had decided that we must shoot our studio stuff in Rome, and I believe French national pride was also involved. Many of the French took it as an insult that a Rally which was known throughout the world to take part mostly in France, should be based studio-wise in Italy.

We now augmented our unit with extra Italian crew, and moved into the Rome area, where we staged scenes purporting to be in Italy, Germany, Yugoslavia and France, with the real actors. I shot the dialogue scenes, while a second crew tried to shoot at least a couple of stunts a day — nearby, so that I could keep an eye on them.

Stunts like tipping a car sixty degrees off vertical so it appeared to be running on only the two side wheels; cars catching fire; cars fording rivers, etcetera, etcetera.

By now, we were within reach of the studio every day, so if Dick fell behind with his stunt rigging or some car had to be repaired, or the weather went foul on us, we could always schedule studio shooting. The Italian crew were marvellous, working hard all day, and at least giving the impression that they were really interested in the sequences I was shooting.

Around lunch time, one or the other of the electricians would sidle up to me and say, "What time would you like us to work 'til tonight, senor?"

There was no question of the hard and fast rules I had been brought up with in England... and no demands for exorbitant 'golden hours' as in America. I tried not to take advantage of them, saying, "Well, how about seven o'clock? Would that be okay?"

The gaffer would grin and shake my hand. "Magnifico, senor. Even seven-thirty, if you need it."

The matching shots — principals replacing doubles, were endless. They were either shot against painted backings which Ted Haworth and his scenic painter matched to the skies we had shot in Sweden, or we used one of his interior snow sets, which for once were so skillfully made that one could not tell the difference from real snow — a very difficult effect to achieve.

Sometimes we had to fall back on using the 'blue screen' process... Because of the size of some of our shots, where we had to hold the full length of the car, we had imported a vast luminous screen which was lit evenly from the rear by banks of five hundred watt lamps.

Explained simply, in this process, the foreground people and machines are photographed in front of the translucent screen, and make a 'matte' which is then married optically to the background shots — made specially for the purpose on location. We had around two hundred fifty of these special matte shots, with the result that Technicolor in Rome set up a special department to produce them. The trick was to make sure that no slight halo, of spill light, surrounded the actor — a sure give-away that a shot is not 'real'.

Once again I have been carried away by the intricacies of actual filmmaking, and jumped ahead.

The real headache awaiting me when we arrived in Rome, was that Charlie announced that he wanted Tony Curtis to play the American lead. George Segal had been engaged six weeks before, with everyone's approval. I had been rehearsing with him for a week. Now, for the second time, I had to make a break with George after getting close to him on rehearsals (and this time he never forgave me, though I swore it was not my fault).

I called Bud Ornstein, who spoke to Donnenfeld in Hollywood — Evans was never available to take my call —and quite apart from correct casting, I argued the *ethics* of Paramount's action with Charlie.

"Leave that to the fucking legal department," he shouted. "Our distribution guys think Curtis is better box-office — after all, he was a big success in *The Great Race*, which was all about cars, so think yourself lucky!"

"But the whole thing is unethical," I argued.

"Fuck ethics," said Charlie.

And so, I had to accept Curtis, whom I had to admit was a star and had given brilliant comedic performances in *Some Like It Hot* and many other movies.

Fortunately, I had not yet established him with a double, because his role began in sunny Sicily, but I suspected he might not fit into our team — and he didn't!!

He was brittle, self-centred and a bully — after all, as he once confided to me, "I was just a poor Jewish kid from the Bronx who had to fight for years to avoid being pushed off the screen by tough, experienced infighters like Burt Lancaster and Kirk Douglas!"

The first time he came onto the set with Susan Hampshire, she smiled at him and reached out her hand, "Oh, Mr. Curtis, I am so happy to be working with you. I feel I will learn so much."

And from that moment, he gave her hell — shat on her, ridiculed her in rehearsals, so much so that the poor girl used to pull me aside and cry desperately.

"What shall I do, Ken?" she cried. "I've worked on the London stage, I know I'm a good, competent actress but this man rewrites the script, changes his lines and I'm left without a cue — looking a complete idiot!!"

I had to admit we both had problems. Once again, because I admired much of Tony's past work, I allowed him to paraphrase lines, often to see if he could improve them, and make them more idiomatic American. After all, he should know, better than me how a Yank should talk!

But it was brutal for Susan and first rehearsals were always a nightmare, until having heard and seen what Tony might contribute, I would decide what to keep and what to change.

Even Terry-Thomas, the hardened old pro that he was, would often look askance at some of Tony's antics, especially in one garage-scene where Tony went into a kind of belly-dance, then rushed over and planted a wet kiss on Terry's lips! Occasionally, he used to do the same to me. A few times Tony made useful contributions, but for the most part his was an embarrassing performance, utterly selfish, as I had feared, and not in key with the rest of the cast or story.

There was the added problem of drugs. Apparently, Tony had been on coke for years, and found it easy to obtain in Rome. Thus, in the mornings he was bright, exuberant, and apparently very eager to give me his best. But after lunch I would come back and find him sprawled in a chair, scowling and looking ten years older. At these times, as a conscientious director, I would have to decide whether he was genuinely depressed with the scene we had shot, or whether it was just that the drug had worn off.

One day, on the lot, his behaviour was inexcusable and vicious. In the shot he had to take over Susan's MG and reverse out of the mud. The moment he revved up the engine, I feared the worst. He shot back at breakneck speed and backed straight into a beautiful white Lancia (worth $50,000) which we had borrowed from a Countess in Turin. It was a deliberate, vicious action directed against me, or rather against David Watson, our chief mechanic and proud borrower of the veteran cars. I learned later that David had refused to take drugs with him the night previously.

In some twisted, strange way, I felt it was even possible that Tony was showing off in front of the crew. But from that moment on we never let him drive a car again. We made a great show in front of everyone; attaching cables to any car he had to drive, and ignominiously towed him for every subsequent close shot — using his double for everything else. He knew exactly what I was doing, and for the rest of the movie, tried to suck up to me with gifts of paintings or Italian pottery. Tony had an excellent 'feeling' for all the arts and was a very respectable painter — but in all, a sad and mixed-up character.

For our three pretty girl competitors, two had been cast quite legitimately in Paris with the help of my old friend and casting director, Maude Spector. Our chief French competitor, Mireille Darc, had established herself as a very popular leading lady in France with her offbeat but stylish tomboy charm. In real life she was the girlfriend of Alain Delon, therefore always in the news and good casting for an international movie like ours. Marie Dubois was pretty in a traditional French way and a regular actress in French farces on the Paris stage.

But the third girl had to be Charlie's choice. I tested at least a dozen Italian models 'discovered' by Charlie. He used to walk up and down the Via Veneto with a copy of Variety under his arm and, seeing a pretty girl, would sit down at her table even if she was with a boyfriend, and spin a pitch that he was a big Hollywood producer, etc, etc... The next day I'd get her in for a test.

Finally, he had a two-night stand with Isabella, and told me he had made her a definite promise that she'd be in the movie, test or no test. She was dumb, short and not really very pretty. I put my foot down, Charlie yelled and swore at me. I called Bud, and enrolled Steve Previn and Basil Keys to do the same. Luigi Luraski, who knew all the actors and actresses in Rome, was brought in to salvage Charlie's big mistake, and payoffs were discussed. Eventually, Luigi came up with a very different and striking Italian actress called Nicolletta Machiavelli... I don't know whether it was truly a Machiavellian solution and whether she had to sleep with Charlie too, but I liked her, and Jack Davies thought she was an excellent 'third girl with a difference', so we accepted her. The crisis was over.

Feeling that as producer/director and co-writer of this movie we must make 'a good image' in Rome, Pauline and I decided to rent a somewhat palatial villa just off the Appian Way. Our neighbours were the well-known Italian director Zefferelli, Princess Saroya of Egypt and the best-selling American author, Morris West. We saw them all from time to time, went to their parties and occasionally gave our own, but because we always had 'the dailies' to see in the evening, we had very little time for entertaining.

We had cast Bourvil as the pompous, fussy, French official in charge of the last lap of the rally in Monte Carlo. Jack and I planned to deflate the character's pomposity in front of the big society crowd gathered outside the elegant 'Hotel de Parks'. We hit on the idea that as Bourvil bossed the competitors around, a dog would sneak up without him noticing it, and lift his leg against his trousers. The crowd would roar with laughter and jeer at Bourvil — who would hopefully arouse hoots of laughter from 'our audiences' while he tried to discover what was happening.

Obviously, the scene was made for Baxter, our beautifully trained Yorkie — but Pauline wasn't at all sure she could train him to do this. She argued that even Baxter could not be made to lift his leg to order.

Dick Parker had other ideas. He borrowed a mannequin figure and dressed the legs in Bourvil's trousers, then he, Pauline and Baxter spent one whole afternoon trying to get the shot. But, despite a thin wire attached to his leg, and Dick giving it a jerk from above, Baxter would not oblige.

Another dog was found who performed immediately — and rather disgustingly —

with a full stream. That was too gross!

As we were going to sleep, the phone rang. It was Dick for Pauline. "Tell me, dear, what leg does Baxter usually lift when he goes to the bathroom?" he asked.

"Damned if I know," said Pauline. "But I'll watch in the morning."

That was the secret. They'd wired the wrong leg. The result was that Baxter was back in the movie, performed brilliantly and got his fifth credit!

Contrary to my experience on *Flying Machines,* when we were three-quarters of the way through 'Monte Carlo and All That Jazz', no one from Paramount seemed to be bothering us about costs. Steve Previn and Basil conscientiously reported the weekly budget position to London. We seemed to be going a little over-budget, but we heard our overage was nothing compared to what was happening on *The Adventurers* and *Darling Lily* — two other big Paramount productions in Italy.

Our big set piece in the studio, was the circular stairwell in the ski-hotel at Chamonix — where all the competitors came together and stayed for one night. Eight identical bedrooms led off the landing and we had written a ballet-like routine for our comics and girls, as they lost their way to and from the bathrooms, ending up in each other's beds.

Our idea was for belly laughs, not sex. To make our routines work we had to have a fierce thunderstorm outside, so that the lights would fail. Therefore, one only caught glimpses in the moonlight of what was happening under the bedclothes.

The fun was in anticipating what would happen when one found 'Him' or 'Her' in someone else's bed. The climax was when Terry and Eric found themselves lying in bed with Gert Froebe in between them!

The Italian crew laughed at practically every set-up in this five minute sequence, but although when edited it got good laughs from most audiences, I have always felt I did not really 'pull it off'. French farce is an art in itself — requiring the most skilled timing and panache. I have always had the suspicion that I did not allow my comics to go sufficiently 'over the top." I would say now that you either shoot in the style of 'light comedy' aiming for continuous chuckles, or you pull out all the stops and go for true farce, with the audience 'rolling in the aisles' if you're lucky!

In complete contrast to this nonsense, we hit an actual open-air extravaganza in Rome which I have never forgotten. Verdi's great opera 'Aida' was being performed against the real background of ruined columns and temples. Our whole company sat spellbound for nearly four hours, listening to the music and watching the spectacle of ancient Egypt unfold before our eyes — Pharaohs and slaves, golden warriors and war-captives, swordsmen and horsemen engaged in battle. Full-sized chariots raced across 'the stage' and four enormous elephants were choreographed into the ballet scenes.

As Zefferelli said to me, "This proves theatre can be as massive and open to imaginative creation as any cinema production!"

At the beginning of August, we wrapped up all the shooting in Italy and moved down to Monaco and Monte Carlo. In 1968 the modern city of Monte Carlo was much less built up than it is now, but even then it was not easy to stage the Rally Finish as in 1927. The only area which had not materially changed was the square outside the Hotel de Paris and the Casino.

Beside the terrace, as Bourvil flagged each competitor off with a roar, I looked up and found I had placed him right under the balcony where Graham Greene and I had worked and polished the scenario of *Loser Takes All.* It gave me quite a pang...

CHAPTER EIGHTEEN Monte Carlo or Bust

Continuing her public support for the movie, Princess Grace brought Prince Rainier and their three children to watch a stunt at a hairpin bend on the Upper Corniche. The kids (now Princess Caroline, Prince Albert and Princess Stephanie) applauded enthusiastically when Terry-Thomas' car speeded around the bend and skidded over the edge of a steep gully. Terry's double got out of the car quite unharmed, because we were holding the car on wires. Princess Grace was not so lucky, when she crashed at exactly the same spot many years later!!

Everywhere we set up a camera — whether it was in Monaco itself or up in the French mountains above the town — the holidaymakers found us and pressed forward to take snaps and begging for autographs. But they were good-humoured and easily managed by my old friend and assistant Victor Miranda. He cleared corridors through them and pressed them back with smiles and wisecracks —quite unlike some of the crowds that we had experienced in Rome. There, street gangs had organised fires, played radios and did everything they could to make shooting impossible — until we paid them off!

The only place where we really had to ban the holidaymakers was on the Esplanade, on the seaward side of the Casino. There, David Watson had gathered together over sixty beautifully preserved vintage cars, Bugattis, De Deions, Peugeots, Renaults, Rovers, Rolls 'White Clouds' — name any famous old car of the 1900's and that day we had it!!

The sequence cost a bomb, but gave the picture tremendous "verisimilitude", as James Robertson Justice used to say — and great kicks to car enthusiasts all over the world.

We were now only forty-five minutes drive from the Bastide, so Pauline put on a very special 'wrap party' on the last night of shooting, which resulted in people from all over the world meeting us for years afterward and saying, "Have you still got that wonderful home of yours in Vence?" it was indeed a dream house — a true status symbol, but I don't know whether it ever got me a movie job!!

The shooting finished, we spent a couple of weeks at home with Debbie and Baxter — relaxing in the garden, then I had to return to Rome for the editing, post-synchronising and music scoring. This took us right until Christmas and, not having to impress anyone, we took a charming flat beside the River Tiber, looking out each morning at the magnificent Palatinate opposite.

No sooner had we completed the very first rough assembly cut, which lasted more than three hours, we received a heavyweight visit consisting of Bob Evans, Donnenfeld, and 'the nine hoods' as Valerie, still my secretary, used to call them. They nosed around in the cutting rooms and offices — without unearthing any dark secrets.

At any rate, Bob Evans was the only one who stayed on. For a week or so we sat through each reel of rough cut and he made suggestions. Quite a few were good, and he seemed to want to help — but I quickly found that there was a basic difference between what a young American actor, brought up in the rag trade, thought as funny, and what I knew worked and would get big laughs from European audiences. But at this stage, Bob never threw his weight about and was pleasant to work with and show around Rome. Before he left I persuaded him to give me the okay to hire Ron Goodwin to write the music — hopefully, as successfully as he wrote the score for *Flying Machines*.

Ron came over, loved the film and said that he could certainly give us a rousing theme tune which he hoped would catch on as before. When it came to the actual recording, Ron showed quite brilliantly what he could do if a section of music didn't seem to work or fit. He was quick to improvise and, with his arranger beside him, they succeeded in helping to support the laughs and build up to them.

Over the years I have learned that it is most important for a director to attend the music sessions. He can make important last minute changes, quite apart from it being a great thrill to hear for the first time the full orchestration and what it means to your movie.

December in Rome was amazingly cold, but without the tourists, one was able to explore churches, old buildings and art galleries, which we had never seen before. I will never forget the Piazza de Navaronna, decorated for Christmas. There, at both ends, stood the great fountains and sculptures by Bellini, and flanking them were stalls filled with Italian handicrafts, Nativity carvings — decorations and lights of every style. With snow on the cobbled street, it was like a painting by Breughel.

The day after New Year, we were informed that the Studio had booked us 'Dubbing Space' at the Todd A-O Theatre in Hollywood — the best, they said!... and we were off once again to a completely different set of experiences...

CHAPTER NINETEEN
We receive the 'red carpet' treatment in Hollywood. Suspicious developments... A Fatal Error! Those Daring Young Men in their Jaunty Jalopies *brought to the Screen – come what may!*

Pauline and I flew to LA first-class, accompanied by Debbie and a nanny. Paramount established us in a luxury bungalow attached to the Beverly Hills Hotel — we couldn't have asked for anything more luxurious.

Basil Keys had come out with us too, and for three weeks he and I sat in the magnificently equipped Recording Theatre, helping the sound mixers make perfect dialogue tracks. Before leaving Rome, I had taken the utmost care to post-synchronise every doubtful word or phrase uttered by our foreign actors like Bourvil, Bossanca, Gert Froebe and the three French girls. "You're sure you can understand them?" I kept asking Mike, the dialogue mixer.

"Now we've cleaned up the tracks, every word is clear," he said. His colleague nodded, so Basil and I nodded too, and breathed a sigh of relief.

As in *Flying Machines,* Ron Goodwin had written the theme song:

Get out your jalopy and polish the wheels
It's got to be the smartest of the automobiles
Polish the paintwork and clean off the rust
They won't see our chassis for dust
And when we arrived miles ahead of the rest
Everyone will know our jalopy is best
They'll have to attest our car is the best
So, it's Monte Carlo or Bust.

I felt it was a somewhat corny lyric, but my ambition had always been to get Jimmy Durante with his well-known, gravelly, voice to sing it. Although one wouldn't see his cheery face with its bulbous nose, I felt the familiar rasp of his voice would set the picture off on its boisterous road. Bob Evans agreed, and at the end of the first week, brought the "Schnoz" down to the studio. The old pro listened to the playback, which we'd recorded with an English group, nodded, put the lyric sheet on the stand in front of him, and in two straight runs, Durante gave me everything I'd ever hoped for. The rest of the afternoon I led him into reminiscences of his tempestuous career on Broadway and in Hollywood.

Bob Evans at Paramount seemed very relaxed and happy with the way things were going, but the second Friday he came in and dropped a bombshell. "I know how married you all are to 'Monte Carlo And All That Jazz,' as a title but the boys in publicity and marketing are getting bad vibes. They say nobody understands 'and all that jazz'!"

"Charlie liked it from the beginning," I said, "and no one has raised any problems before." Charlie Bludhorn was the *owner* and President of Paramount Pictures. So I thought we were safe with the title.

Bob shrugged. "Well, it's in the hands of the professionals — they've got to sell it, and across the country they say they're coming up against a lot of resistance."

"Do they have anything better?" I asked.

Bob shrugged. "Not yet — but they're busting their asses on it!"

"Why not just call it 'The Monte Carlo Rally'?" suggested Basil.

Bob shook his head, "Sounds like some foreign documentary". He patted my arm and smiled. "Just carry on the good work and we'll come up with something!"

I glared after him as he left. 'How dare they!' I said to Basil.

"They have every right," he said, drawing me aside. "After all, it's their money, they've got to get it back."

"But do they *know?*" I muttered. "Just think of all those hours I spent with Bob Jenkins and his Oxbridge Optical Printer in London, slaving over that visual version of our title with its spinning wheel and all those flags. *Eighteen thousand exposures!*"

"You shouldn't have devised such elaborate titles without their okay," he said in his breezy manner "That's obvious now!"

"You know I wanted to have something as good as *Flying Machines*," I said. "It'll cost a bomb to remake those titles!"

Basil shrugged. "That's their lookout, old boy. All we can do is deliver the best movie we can!"

So, we pressed on — meticulously dubbing each reel — sometimes making little changes in the laying of a music track, and searching for just the right effect, which the mixers felt, might improve the visual effect. I would have lunch with old friends like Bill Anderson and Milton Sperling, and bring them back to see whatever reel we were working on. Almost without exception, they reacted as one would have hoped — guffawing at the big laughs and congratulating us on the polish and professionalism of our work.

"The music's just great," said Bill. "I'll have to give a thought to bringing Ron Goodwin over to Disney."

Milton nodded. "That theme could become as memorable as that umpah one in *Magnificent Men*."

Basil and I exchanged knowing looks and basked in a kind of smug satisfaction. The reaction of our American friends was encouraging.

Most days Pauline would drop in to Todd A-O and give us 'an unbiased opinion' as to whether the music was helping a sequence or whether effects carried it better.

No one had lived with the picture longer than she had! But most days her time was occupied helping me get 'treatments' (synopses) on paper for two future movies I was vaguely planning.

"Gold" would be the story of a Scottish family emigrating to New Zealand in the 1880s, and following their adventures through the great Gold Rushes... picking up nuggets on the West Coast beaches, mining in Australia, and 'panning' in the Klondike. The other was a pop science-fiction picture called 'The Atomic Race — full of Eastern mysticism and farfetched adventures in space, dreamed up by my friend Bjorn Ortenheim in Stockholm.

Most evenings, Pauline and I would dine with old friends — the Coryells, Dorothy McGuire, John Swope, Jimmy McArthur... who were happy we were "on a roll." One weekend we accepted an invitation to stay with Bob Wagner and Marion in their Palm Springs home.

After tennis at the famous Racquet Club, swims, saunas and massages, we met up with Hank Fonda, his wife Shirley, Milton Berle and other celebrities at a new Mexican restaurant that had just opened. Hank insisted on Pauline sitting next to him and surreptitiously sharing her Margueritas with him (Shirley was trying to keep him on a strict regime because he was due to play Clarence Darrow on Broadway). Amid a lot of laughs and good food, I saw a very smart woman come over to Marion and talk in long whispers, while her eyes roved eagerly over the guests. Marion continuously shook her head, and nothing more was said about the incident until about four on Sunday afternoon.

Marion came into the gazebo, and said, "Sixteen times I've turned that woman down, because I just can't stand her and the nouveau-riche set she represents." She heaved a deep sigh and looked at me. "She asks us to take you and the Fondas over this evening for a quiet dinner."

"Why us?" I queried.

"Well, if we accept, Hank would be a feather in her cap, and someone's told her you are the new 'in' director," said Marion.

"They might find it interesting," said Bob, carrying out a jug of Bloody Marys. "Frank Sinatra tells me they've built this enormous spread next to him."

And so, at seven-thirty that evening, we drove up to this sprawling new mansion, adjacent to the Sinatra residence. The first thing we noticed was the illuminated plastic palms.

"You see what I mean," said Marion. "Those are real palms, but they've stripped off all the bark and wrapped them in plastic veneer to make them shine! Just awful!"

The next shock was that the house seemed to be overflowing with youngish women in smart cocktail dresses, and sleek men in immaculate dark suits. We caught a glimpse of Milton Berle and Lucille Ball! "I don't believe it!" said Marion, but before she could say more we were steered on to the end of a group who were being given the Grand Tour.

Lounges and sitting rooms opened out on to 'fountained' courtyards and covered pools. A gallery was filled with books and reproductions of Corregio and Lunghi ... a floodlit tennis court, then more guest suites, and a sauna-gym fully-equipped. It was a good twenty minutes before we could get back to the foyer and main sitting room where we were overwhelmed with caviar and champagne.

Hank Fonda and Shirley arrived — we were able to sidetrack them away from 'the tour', and comparing notes and times of phone calls, confirmed the suspicion that our hostess had 'worked a fast one' — telling each celebrity that the other was attending this special surprise party. Lucille Ball and Shirley Fonda fumed at the way they had been caught. Marion was all for leaving immediately.

"Wait a minute," said Lucille, drawing the women aside. I thought I saw a malicious glint in her eyes. We were seated at four large round tables. My neighbours were pretty girls who said their husbands were 'investment bankers'. I learned that our host was a contractor from Las Vegas who was making millions from rebuilding casinos.

We had just been served a second helping of 'steak mignon' when I heard a voice wail, "Say! Can we have some doggie bags?" I looked round and there was Lucille and her friends suddenly forking meat off plates and sweeping steaks into the bags the waiters rushed to provide! Our hostess looked puzzled as three other well-known ladies took up the cue, crying, "Don't worry, honey. It'll all go to charity — bring a smile to some poor starving kids! We'll see it gets in the papers!"

Someone turned up the music and everyone was talking loud and over-heartily... Sinatra's bodyguard was pointed out, and an unseen voice said they wondered how many people he'd bumped off!

Lucille suddenly yelled, "Let's turn out the lights and play charades!" I heard Pauline say, "What a great idea," but she was immediately pounced on by Marion and Shirley and told in the powder room that no one plays charades with Lucy!

With lots of beckonings and gestures, Bob and I caught on that the idea was to slip away. He was killing himself with laughter and whispered as we made it out the exit, "Women! It doesn't do to cross 'em in this town!" He lapsed into a grin. "Still, it might give you an idea for a scene!"

The next day in the dubbing theatre, Bob Evans arrived with a grin all over his face. He raised a finger. "We want to attract the same audience as *Flying Machines*, right?" I nodded cautiously.

"I woke up this morning and knew I got it," Bob said excitedly.

"Do the boys think it'll sell?" asked Basil Keys.

"One hundred percent," nodded Bob. "The studio loves it and Charlie Bludhorn's quite agreeable, according to Marty Davis." he added, looking me straight in the eye. I put my hands in my pocket and clenched them.

"Let's have it then," said Basil.

Bob gave a glance round, including towards the dubbers.

"How about *Those Daring Young Men In Their Jaunty Jalopies*?"

I nearly died. It was so corny, such an obvious rip-off from my other picture.

Bob was so high on what must clearly have been an 'off the top of my head' idea, that I held myself back and tried to call Charlie Bludhorn in New York. His secretary told me, "He's somewhere in the Caribbean — on some island."

"There must be some number I can reach him at — *darling*," I said.

"Hold on a minute," she replied.

A couple of minutes later, Marty Davis came on to the line, blustering, "I hear you've been trying to get hold of Charlie. I have to tell you he's on to the biggest deal of his life. If it's about the change of title for your movie, you've gotta get this into your head. Bob Evans is in sole charge of production for this company. What he says goes!" I remained silent. Davis was Paramount's CEO, and no one got to Bludhorn except through him. He continued, a little more persuasively:

"If we're to make the date you'd better get on with remaking the titles!"

"What date?" I gasped.

"You're going out the first weekend in May," he said.

"But I thought we were promised Memorial Weekend — the beginning of June?" I said querulously. I could hear him breathe deeply.

"If it catches on, old sport, you'll be welcome to great holiday business!" He put down the phone.

Maybe I had been spoiled, or not used to studio ways, but to lose control — even consultation — on the 'Monte's destiny' at this point was a bitter pill to swallow.

I called Jack Davies in France. Jack, as a former critic, was even more disgusted and afraid of the new title than I was! Over the next week, we devised and put up twenty alternatives — eventually pressing for *Monte Carlo Or Bust*. Bud Ornstein in London and all the European big boys in Paramount seemed to like it a lot ... but we could not overcome Bob's obsession with the title he had dreamed up, and eventually, that is how it went out in America, much to my disappointment.

The cartoonist, Ronald Searle, who once again had given us cute and original designs for the titles and credits, hated *Those Daring Young Men* so much that he flatly refused to supply his decorative lettering. But, of course, there were plenty of people in Hollywood prepared to acquiesce, so, like us, he bowed to the studio, and hoped they knew what they were doing!

Three more weeks and we finished the dub — a masterpiece of sound mixing by the Todd A-O crew, who said it had been a pleasure and an honour to work with us on the picture. The day after the new titles were delivered, we set off again for New York to show the picture to Charlie Bludhorn and a select audience of Paramount executives and bookers. As we filed into Loews' Theatre on Broadway, at four in the afternoon, the publicist allotted to the picture announced — with a great sense of achievement and pride — that he had brought in three hundred school kids to fill the lower part of the theatre.

A very nervous Charlie sat between Pauline and his wife, Françoise, and I sat on the other side of her. About twenty minutes into the movie, she leaned close to me, patted my knee, and said, "Merveilleux!"

I looked across her to Charlie who was relaxing, beginning to smile, but secretly taking quick glances to see how Donnenfeld, Marty and the marketing boys were reacting. It was very much like that first showing of *The Long Duel*... with no executive or even a secretary, daring to commit themselves even by a gesture, until they knew how the others felt.

After an hour and ten minutes of warm response and laughs in the right places, I was settling back comfortably, when suddenly out of left field, *Shock! Disaster!* A great racket from below sounded like the tipping up of seats. The whole of our row leaned forward and looked down. *The kids were trooping out of the theatre en masse!* I looked at my watch. It was five-ten and we were barely halfway through. Charlie leaned over to me with a distraught face – "Even the kids don't like it!" he wailed, throwing up his arms.

I just couldn't understand this noisy exodus because there had been very good reactions and laughter up to that point, but it engraved in the minds of Charlie and most everyone else, that most likely we had a *flop!*

It was only three weeks later that Mort Hock, the publicist, admitted to me that he had known the kids would depart at five-fifteen because they had been bussed from school without the specific permission of their parents. "Why in hell did you never tell Charlie?" I asked.

"I didn't think it important at the time," he said. "But I agree with you, it has given us a bad send-off."

"Really the understatement of all time," I thought! That evening, after the showing, Françoise was as charming as usual, but there was no gushing invitation from Charlie to join them for dinner.

The next morning I had a session with Charles Boasberg — Paramount's chief sales executive. I had met him years ago when he was at United Artists and I was negotiating the deal for *Planter's Wife*. He was a friendly, no-nonsense old-timer who knew his business. "I liked your movie, but you should drop the road-show nonsense!" he said, taking me into his private office.

"What do you mean?" I gasped.

"*Those Daring Young Men* is a family movie of the old breed. On the grind circuit I could do great business," he said.

"What do you mean 'grind circuit'?"

He offered me a cigar. "Cut your picture to two hours and I'll get you out on Memorial Weekend as Bludhorn originally promised you. On the strength of that opening, I'll book you in six or seven hundred theatres across the country and the picture can 'grind' through the summer for the kids and families."

I was completely knocked for six, but the stout Boasberg oozed confidence. "I don't always agree with this new management, but I know my business. *Flying Machines* did good business as a road show, but times have changed. The public don't know what they want, but they don't want to miss out, and there's a whole new run of movies around: porn, open sex, anti-establishment violence... the floodgates are opening and there's no stopping whatever's coming. I tell you, I'm having one heck of a time keeping up with trends." He lifted up a big chart. "My only guide is the daily box-office receipts."

We had lived so long with *Monte Carlo* as a road show concept that I could not agree to losing over twenty minutes just because Boasberg said so. I felt I should talk to Charlie, Bob Evans, Pauline, Basil, Jack Davies —- *everyone!* I talked to Mort Hock, head of publicity, while Pauline grilled one or two friends we had sneaked into the Loews' showing — it was impossible to make an assessment.

Back in LA, I was told the studio, in general, was puzzled as to how to handle the picture. A secretary hinted that there was a buzz going round that perhaps there were too many foreigners in it. "Even that adorable Dudley Moore and his friend, spit their words out like machine-guns bullets and are a bit tricky to follow," she said.

Coming out of the Beverly Hills Hotel a couple of mornings later, I ran straight into Charlie Bludhorn and Marty Davis, walking down the covered way to their limo. I had just received some heartening news from a knowledgeable trade friend, so I rushed straight up to Charlie.

I said, "Isn't it marvellous that Goodman loves the picture and wants it for Radio City Music Hall in New York?" It was Goodman's call as to what went into America's most prestigious movie theatre.

"Who told you that?" snapped Marty.

As though picking at a straw, Charlie turned to Marty. "How come nobody told me about that? I thought Goodman had passed?"

"That's what I heard," muttered Marty, giving me his darkest, killing look. "I'll check into it."

Charlie grinned, nodded and gave me a small pat on the shoulder before disappearing into his limousine.

That afternoon while polishing up the treatment for 'Gold', the telephone rang. Pauline answered it.

"It's Marty Davis," she said handing me the phone. Before I could say more than "Hello," my ear was almost blasted out with "Fuck you, Annakin! Fuck you! Fuck you a million times over! You interfering son-of-a-bitch!"

I murmured, "Hey, wait a minute, Marty."

"How dare you push your long nose into things which don't concern you!" he yelled, adding, "And I'm telling you here and now. It's curtains for you in Hollywood. I'll fucking well see to that!" and the phone was slammed down.

Naturally, Pauline and I were flabbergasted — completely floored, never having experienced this kind of assassination before. We consulted our friends — Bill Anderson, the Coryells, and Milton Sperling, who said he would make some behind-the-scenes inquiries as to what was going on at Paramount.

It turned out that the in-fighting that I had seen signs of in my early meetings with Charlie, had now become real cut-throat. Bob Evans, Donnenfeld and Marty Davis were deep in their campaign to cut Charlie down to size. They had channelled his enormous energy and negotiating skills into the making of brilliant buy-outs and mergers as far away as the island of Dominica. Charlie's deals in chemicals, spare parts, cosmetics, bakeries, publishing, ball-bearings were all being thrown into the melting pot of a holding company called Gulf and Western, and a very powerful conglomerate was taking shape. But even side-tracked in this way, Charlie, because of his instinctive liking for creative people — directors, writers, actors (and, of course, actresses!), was a menace to the plans of Davis & Co.

He must be taught the lesson that he must not choose or influence subjects to be made under the Paramount banner, so the word had gone round that for every reason that could be cooked up, our movie was to be a flop. As part of the plot Charlie had deliberately not been told that Goodman would be very happy to open the picture at Radio City Music Hall — which would clearly have given it a real flying start.

Realising what we were up against, I appealed desperately to our friends for guidance — after all, the *movie was good* — on the proven pattern and with the same kind of actors as *Those Magnificent Men In Their Flying Machines*. The story line and dialogue were, in fact, much superior!

"Has the picture ever had a sneak?" asked my old agent-friend Bob Coryell.

"Only that disastrous showing in New York," I replied.

"That tells you nothing," said Bob. "The normal procedure for a studio is to have previews in cities like San Francisco, Cleveland, Kansas City... or even smaller places, if they want to keep it under wraps."

I brought this up with Evans.

"Too late," he said. "The picture's already booked in New York and twenty other cities."

Without further ado, I took the plunge. "Boasberg in New York says if I cut the show down to two hours, he'll give me a much wider release starting Memorial Day. Would you go for that?"

Bob paused and studied my face. "You'd cut your baby by twenty-three minutes?" I nodded.

He walked around the table. "If you're asking me, I think it would make a much better picture, and if Boasberg says he can handle that, I'll go along!"

We shook hands, and I went back to Todd A-O to lift eight sequences out of the picture, an experiment I'd been playing around with for the last twenty-four hours. Confusion reigned in the studio, but apparently Boasberg and Bob were strong enough allies to push through the new plan — which in my heart of hearts I had come to accept..

Since we had come back to California, Pauline and I had been content to live in a kind of dream world — seeing old friends, becoming 'part of the scene', taking what we felt was our 'rightful place' as the makers of an important road show. But one couldn't help but be aware that because of the Vietnam War, great changes were taking place in public taste. The fervent peace demos, the anti-war songs, the clear emergence of student power... Andy Warhol... and the drive to examine and change everything which had been accepted as moral in the past. All these crosscurrents I had been aware of, but had done nothing so far about the film, until Charles Boasberg flashed the light through my brain with his box-office mirror.

Eroticism and violent overturning of all that had been sacred *was* truly permeating the cinema. Russ Meyer and his ilk had been turning out skin flicks for years but they had been kept 'underground'. Now Meyer's movie *Vixens* was sweeping through America — a piece of ogling, violent shit that I had been ashamed to see — *alone!* Costing peanuts it had brought in over $6,000,000 at the box-office and there were more of the same type of movie. *I Am Curious Yellow* and *Deep Throat* were opening everywhere and, according to the trades, drawing packed houses in every city.

The moment he had delivered his lecture to me, I knew Boasberg was interpreting the signs correctly, but it had taken a few days for me to accept the remedy and try to save my comparatively prosaic family movie.

It didn't take me more than a day to make the two hour version, and it seemed to 'flow', if one was not aware of the scenes which had fallen to the cutting room floor. I showed it to Bob Coryell... who slapped me on the back. "Well done, Ken," he said, "that needed guts."

I didn't really know whether he was sending me down the path of destruction or whether he really felt the cuts were an improvement.

After a pause, he added "This job is not easy, Ken I can't tell you how many directions I'm being pulled in." He suddenly turned and came towards me. "I've learned a lot from watching the way you tackle things." He began to steer me towards the door. "But if I were you, I'd start finding a home for your next movie, because in all honesty I have to tell you it won't be here! You've made a bad enemy in Marty!"

I walked away with lead in my shoes. That unintentional goof was clearly going to follow me around, and how far would the poison spread?

Two days later Evans called to say that the studio was sending me off on a big coast-to-coast promotional trip. "The ball's in your court again, Ken. Boasberg believes in the new cut, so we're giving you a wide-open chance to sell it — and yourself — in fourteen of our most important markets!"

Basil had been sent back to Europe — and, in truth, would not have been an asset in trying to sell. He was essentially an administrator, with too sharp a tongue for a publicity man! So, Pauline and I picked out our most fetching wardrobe and set out for San Diego.

A small cinema had been taken over and a market research company had gathered together about sixty mothers and kids together with about twenty local media people. I went up on to the stage and talked about the picture, played the Jimmy Durante record and showed the two main action sequences. The kids yelled at the antics on the ice and snow, and the mums and press people chuckled at the chase scenes through the bedrooms.

We were bombarded with all kinds of questions which showed a lot of interest had been aroused about the cast, the cars, and European locations. After the kids left we were photographed, toasted in champagne, and while Pauline filled reporters in with anecdotes from our various travels, I slipped off to do three radio interviews. A very good start, we felt.

Our next stop was San Francisco. Paramount Publicity had now rushed out a full promotional kit, consisting of a trailer which I was to show on TV and closed-circuit whenever possible, an LP record, and lots of production stills. In a day and a half we did over twenty-two interviews despite the fact that John Lennon and Yoko Ono were holding court and preaching 'Flower Power' in the grand Fremont Hotel!

The movie was screened to an audience of students at the University of California in Berkeley. There were a lot of coughs and throat clearing — an occasional chuckle, but as the lights went up, gritty questions rolled in about the social purpose of the film, movies as a weapon against propaganda, the importance of presenting stark reality, equality for women, and justice for blacks. In fact, only a couple of girls seemed prepared to discuss *my* movie — and that they did after the showing, over coffee.

"We're taught that the movies with no message are out," they said. "Every aspect of the media should be turned to stopping the war." The one with her hair pulled back said, almost wistfully, "A few laughs help the day along, I suppose — I loved some bits of your movie."

"It may be a bit corny," said the other. "I suppose you have to get yourself in the mood and forget what's going on outside."

I could see that in some areas we were going to have trouble, but one couldn't please everyone. This was a year before *M*A*S*H* — where Robert Altman proved that you could get roars of laughter in a way quite removed from traditional comedy routines — *and make a strong, anti-war statement.* From the comfort of Europe, we had not felt this change in approach necessary!

Before leaving San Francisco I made time to show Pauline the Golden Gate Bridge, Fisherman's Wharf, and a trip on the legendary cable railway. Then, she flew back to LA (and Debbie) warning me not to accept more interviews than I could comfortably handle, because they were clearly very exhausting, and "You might say things you'd be sorry for later," she said, giving me a parting hug.

In Denver ten large parcels were delivered to my suite. Inside were large hand towels — each printed with the Ronnie Searle logo and the title of the movie. Mort Hock called me from New York to check that I had received them. He could not have sounded more excited if he had sent me ten gold Oscars. He explained that he had a conscience about the departure of those school kids at the New York showing, and he suddenly remembered a woman who ran a gift shop near Martha's Vineyard. She produced printed towels most economically, so he had lashed out for twelve dozen to be silk-screened and shipped to me.

"Hand them out to anyone who likes you or seems like they might help the picture," he said. 'Leave a trail of goodwill with *Those Daring Young Man With Their Jaunty Jalopies* towels!"

I accepted the offering and did what he asked, but really, were a few tea towels, an LP, a five minute reel of film clips and a few colour stills all that a big studio like Paramount should be doing for a ten million dollar movie?

One-night stands in Denver, Dallas, Fort Worth, Miami, St. Louis, Kansas, Chicago and Boston, kept me frenetically busy from the 19th to the 28th of May — so much so that I could hardly distinguish one place from another. I was coming out with the impression that the youth of America desperately wanted change, but that there was a solid majority who wanted normal life as we had known it — love, marriage, children, regular work with as many escapes into fantasy and fun as could be managed.

I was quoted in Boston as saying "Movie eroticism? — I think there is a tremendous feeling against movies like *Deep Throat*, especially when they're shown in main houses like the one in Boston. The picture is being insidiously inserted into our lives, offending people who don't want to be involved!"

The article continued: "Annakin was in town yesterday to plug his latest flick *Those Daring Young Men In Their Jaunty Jalopies*, a follow-up to *Those Magnificent Men In Their Flying Machines*. Call them cornball movies or family entertainment, but their success is measured in box-office, and this new one spells boffo B.O.!"

I had clearly recognised the danger of the new trends and was fighting on the family front... I hoped it was not a rear-guard action!

By intention or cumulative bad organisation by Paramount, I arrived in New York the evening after the press show. Pauline could have attended because she had arrived that morning, but no one had thought to invite her. She showed me a newspaper ad for the movie — an eight-inch double-column in the *Daily News.*

"Surely, they should be giving us a better spread than this," she said indignantly.

I shrugged rather wearily, "Maybe tomorrow. They must know what they are doing!"

The next day Howard Thompson in the *New York Times* wrote: "The new Paramount release *Those Daring Young Men In Their Jaunty Jalopies* is the four-wheeled follow-up to Ken Annakin's blockbuster *Those Magnificent Men In Their Flying Machines*." I knew that bloody title would start the critics off on the wrong foot, because how could cars ever have the magic of those cute old planes and truly heroic pilots?

Thompson continued: "Judged apart from *Flying Machines* this new picture is lively and often hilarious as the drivers hang on for dear life and the olds cars honk, collide and careen. There is hardly a turn without a bang-up (The stunt men *must* have been black and blue by the finish!)" I was quite pleased with that!

The *Hollywood Reporter* wrote a well-balanced whole page, describing characters, plot, locations, and praising special effects. It finished with: "*Jaunty Jalopies* by its technical complexity and hair-breath hilariousness comes in the tradition of the great silent comedies of Roach, Sennett and Clair — wonderfully inventive and absurd." We couldn't complain at being classed in that company!

In various mad moments, Jack Davies and I had dreamed that we might have had a parade of old cars and their be-goggled drivers all the way down Broadway. A few sweeping searchlights between the skyscrapers would have been nice, or even just a red carpet leading into the cinema, with stars blowing kisses to the crowds as they entered the foyer arm in arm. But all Paramount gave us for the opening of this ten million dollar effort, were three veteran cars with their chauffeurs carefully guarding them, outside the Astor Cinema for the six pm 'Gala Opening'.

We saw no smart people going in with their kids, only a motley group of the strange looking people who hung around Broadway and 42nd Street (even in those days!). They watched with tired, perplexed eyes as Mireille Darc, Pauline and I were photographed, pointing to the posters, and the *Jaunty Jalopies* title in lights over the cinema. Mireille was a French star completely unknown in the US, but she was the only one of our star-studded cast Paramount had thought to bring over. (Where, at least, was Tony Curtis?)

We gave quite a few more interviews. One of mine produced six controversial columns, which were syndicated coast-to-coast.

The popular Rebecca Moorhouse hotted up the teleprinters with:

NEW YORK IS SODOM & GOMORRAH, SAYS BRITISH FILMMAKER ANNAKIN

Annakin toured the country before he came to launch his new film "Those Daring Young Men In Their Jaunty Jalopies." He was cheered by what he saw.

"In Europe," he said, "one gets the impression the United States is falling apart. Newspapers and television report so much that is chaotic. But a sweep through this country has convinced me that the heartland is absolutely solid gold."

New York is different says this mild-mannered man who made four big family successes for Walt Disney. "Everyone is so busy chasing new goals and the almighty dollar, that friendliness has vanished from the streets. Instead, there is tension, hatred and filth. New York is fast becoming a Sodom and Gomorrah!"

This prestigious filmmaker is shocked by all the adult bookshops and the skin flicks currently gathering crowds.

"I hate to think of even eighteen-year-old kids seeing them," he added, "because sordid images once seen, stay in the mind for life. How can romance, beauty, and family life survive in a place like this?"

That was spring 1969! And Sodom and Gomorrah never did happen. We packed our bags and 'got out of town' returning to the peace and quiet of our home in France.

CHAPTER TWENTY
Dropping the pace a little...
but still pitching!

t was a wonderful summer. We relaxed, taught Debbie to swim in our large new pool, played tennis, and got to know many interesting people and places around the blue Mediterranean. Several new friends had yachts and began inviting us for trips... to Corsica and Sardinia... fantastic islands where the rich and famous vacation and idle the time away. We did a lot of that, and I kept calling my agent, Dennis Van Thal, about trying to rouse interest in *Gold* and *The Atomic Race*.

Gold he said was too broad a canvas, even though I had shaped the story around a family who followed the main 19th Century Gold Rushes through Australia, New Zealand and the USA. "If you are really set on making this," he added, "you'll have to go the documentary route, which will kill your feature career!"

The Atomic Race was a very different cup of tea. I had been giving time and thought to it ever since the location in Sweden, where I had met a man who claimed he had lived many lives and was now being guided by 'The Power of Light' to introduce new energy systems into the world!

Bjorn Ortenheim had a stack of 'dreamed information''about the past and future, from which we devised the fascinating 'Atomic Race' screenplay, and in order to rouse interest among 'common mortals', I wrote the following blurb, which gives some idea of the story line:

Have you ever thought there might have been people on Earth before us with a higher civilisation — say 12,000 years ago?

Do you half-believe there might be people up in space, watching and perhaps caring for us?

Are you prepared to believe that the Great Pyramid of Egypt might still hold valuable secrets?

Do you sometimes toy with the idea that you might have lived on Earth before — as someone else ... Reincarnation sort of...?

Have you ever thought there might be a place where Love and Sexual Pleasures might be different ... and even more pleasurable!!??

Do you have nightmares about Nuclear Missiles being launched accidentally, or by computers, or by some idiot ... and destroying the world?

If the answer to any of these questions is: YES, then you will want to see The Atomic Race.

Because the script was quite involved with its "way-out" story and descriptions of special effects, I spent hours with Harry Horner, the American Art Director, developing 12 very special illustrations, which showed key scenes from this big- screen adventure.

Dennis Van Thal fell for the project, and managed to make first base with the guy in charge of Cinerama in London. I made several trips to sweet-talk him, and we worked out a budget in the region of seven million dollars — a fortune in the Seventies. He appeared to become 100% enthusiastic, and promised to push the project with Bill Foreman in California.

Unfortunately, Cinerama started to economise. The London branch was closed down, and I suppose I was either too lazy or a little shy of Hollywood, that I did not jump a plane to remind Bill Foreman of the *Battle of the Bulge* winner I had recently made him. Another glaring mistake, I now believe.

However, a very persistent Voice started calling me daily from Geneva. The guy wanted to make a movie of a Balloon Race across the Sahara. He was so persistent (and Geneva such a short flight) that I decided to have a meeting. The guy had maps and photos of suggested stops between Fez and Timbuktu, but it was me who would have to write the script and pitch it to some studio.

On checking up, his financial resources did not seem guaranteed, so I 'passed' on that one, and returned to 'basking in the good-life' in Vence!

Reports kept coming in about *Those Daring Young Men*. It appeared that in the US it was not exactly a blockbuster, but we apparently were running all summer in the 'grind-cinemas' while the kids were out of school, as Boasberg had suggested,. In England and Europe generally the movie was released under the title of *Monte Carlo or Bust* and did so well with family audiences that it became a kind of classic, running every Christmastime for years on TV.

Suddenly I got a call from Van Thal. "We have an offer for you to make Jack London's 'Call of the Wild'. "'Gold!'" I yelled. "And a wonderful dog called Buck," shouted Pauline, who had picked up the other phone.

"The snag is," said Dennis, "the Producer is Harry Alan Towers, and his reputation is far from good."

"But it's about characters from all over the world, prospectors panning for Gold — which, as you know, was one of the highlights of my travels in New Zealand", I said excitedly.

"I'd forgotten that," said Dennis. "The film is to be shot in Norway, with actors from France, Germany, Italy and Spain."

"Who is the star?" I asked.

"Well, Harry says he's negotiating for Charlton Heston."

"Then why are we dragging our heels?" I gasped. "I can't wait to meet this guy Towers!"

"Okay," said my very cautious and responsible agent. "I'll set up a meeting... but I can't say where, because for some reason at this moment, Harry can't come back into the UK!"

We met in Madrid. Harry Alan Towers turned out to be a very personable guy in his mid-forties. I checked him out and found that he had made movies like *Sanders of the River*, *Dorian Grey* and *Black Beauty*, in South Africa, Spain and Iran, with actors like Oliver Reed, Omar Sharif and Kurt Jurgens.

"My main deal is with Norsk Films in Oslo," said Harry. "They will provide the sets, locations and the supporting cast. But I have Michele Mercier from France, Raymond Harmstorf from Germany, Sancho Garci from Spain."

I held up my hand. "And these countries are all partners with your company, Tower Films?" I queried. Harry nodded and gave a secretive kind of grin. "The labs here will provide the raw film and the processing, plus post-synching and post-production."

"Seems a very ingenious way to finance a movie," I said. Harry smiled. "In this business you gotta have a bunch of friends worldwide," he said. "And don't fret. In the deal I've discussed with your agent, I've given him a guarantee that your monies will be paid on the Thursday of each week into his office in London."

It was a strange set-up, but it seemed plausible. "And who pays for Heston?" I asked. "Paramount, I guess," shot back Harry. "I'm in the middle of a deal with them where, in exchange for Heston, they get worldwide distribution, apart from the territories I've pre-sold in Europe."

No point in telling him of my spat with Marty Davis, I thought. See what happens. As we were shaking hands, a rather striking blonde hurried down the stairway. Harry turned and threw an arm around her shoulder. "Meet Maria." She held out her hand to me and smiled.

"Maria Rohm. I'm playing Mercedes in the movie!"

I smiled and nodded without a word. Same old story. Producer's girlfriend has to be cast in every movie... and I guess it has always been a must! I clasped her hand. "I look forward to our rehearsing in Norway. Don't forget to bring some warm underwear. It gets kind of chilly near the Arctic Circle in January."

The script was pretty good. The writer, Peter Yeldam, visited the Bastide for three or four days and we made a few changes to increase the dog interest — in fact, the 'love story' was between the Heston character, Thornton, and the part dog/part wolf that was Buck. After all, apart from the incidents with the gold prospectors and the ever-throbbing life of Dawson City and the Yukon, the real guts of Jack London's story was the kind of courtship between Man and Dog, coming up against the pull on the dog by his distant wolf origins — hence 'Call of the Wild'. I was getting very excited, because these were all elements to which I could really respond.

Negotiations continued. Heston seemed to be set, and I was allowed to pick my own Cameraman (Johnny Cabrera); Camera Operator (Dudley Lovell); joint Production Manager (Peter Manley)... all of them going back with me as far as *The Huggetts* and *Hotel Sahara*!!! — Plus Cliff Reynolds, a great Prop Man I had discovered on the Monte Carlo movie. The rest of the crew would have to be Norwegian (whom Pauline would vet and try to keep working 'on our side').

We arrived in Oslo, where daylight only lasted a brief three to four hours. The Norsk Studios turned out to be small but adequate — and very clean! We were shown a location set about an hour's ride away, which would serve for Dawson City and the main street of Skagway. I think it was a permanent Nordic country street-set, but extra facades and tents were being added by the local Art Director working from reference photos taken during the Klondike Gold Rush. I was very happy with these backgrounds plus frozen lakes, snow trails up and down steep pine-clad slopes — plus a 'killer-climb' I would use for the infamous Chilcoot Pass.

Considering I had not been part of the planning of these basic locations, I felt very lucky... until we saw THE DOG. In this story, Buck was the joint-male star, and suddenly we were presented with a large but ordinary German Shepherd POLICE DOG! He was good-looking, but not a trained film-dog — nothing like the trained dogs we had had in *Swiss Family*, or the adorable Dolores in *Across the Bridge*. However you looked at him, this dog was just a plain Alsatian trained for police work!

Chuck Heston and the other international cast arrived, and we were 'on the clock' to begin shooting! I must say, Heston was remarkable. He took the problem with the dog in his stride, and for the first couple of weeks, found ways to hold Buck's head affectionately close to him if they were sitting, and somehow made the dog keep looking expressively at him if they were standing or walking.

Meanwhile, in every spare moment when Buck wasn't shooting, Pauline took over. She taught the dog to crawl on his belly by copying her in the snow and how to scrabble and make a sleeping bed in the snow — again by copying her! Somehow over a period of fourteen weeks, Pauline and Chuck turned Buck into a fully trained and loveable dog, who eventually howled like a wolf and scampered after his beloved she-wolf.

Chuck Heston turned out to be one of the most skilled, cooperative actors with whom I have ever worked. He threw himself into this part as though he had been waiting for years to play John Thornton. I had even the greatest difficulties in stopping him doing his own stunts — in one case, rolling down a snow-clad slope where rocks under the surface could have broken his back! We cleared it very carefully for our stuntman while Chuck looked on almost scathingly!

We had quite a few stunts, like Maria on her sled, falling through the ice, which needed careful preparation above shallow water. Chuck and Ray Harmstorf often had to drive the dog-sled teams themselves, because I needed to show their reactions to difficult situations. They never made a murmur, except at those times when Norsk Films were late with some prop or costume because they were too mean to provide adequate transport. As I recall, we shot this whole movie with six cars, one bus and four trucks servicing us!

To beat the short daylight hours in the first weeks, we often switched into the 'casino/dance hall set' in Dawson City or Michele Mercier's boudoir. Michele was a very attractive girl. I detected an occasional embarrassment in Chuck when he had to play scenes with Michele dressed in risqué lingerie. In one scene, he had to pull her with him into the tin bath where he was scrubbing himself down.

Chuck looked up at me after one splashy take and said "You know, Ken, I was only reluctantly persuaded to take this movie because I admired your handling of the dog in *Across the Bridge*, and your fine action stuff in *Battle of the Bulge.*"

I grinned and replied "And I reluctantly agreed to direct only because Towers told me you were already on board!"

As we exchanged notes of how we had been double-dealt with by Towers, Michele crawled out of the bath and began towelling her wet body.

"You two are impossible, ungrateful ginks," she yelled. "Here am I showing you all I've got, and you argue why you took the picture! Surely I am worth a petit morceau of attention... a small erection or something!" she smiled coquettishly. "Just a little sexy relaxation after all that ice and snow?" The two of us gaped at her, then burst into laughter, which lasted the rest of the day... and almost the rest of the picture!

I say almost, because we had a number of complications. Apart from the training of Buck, Pauline had to spend part of every day closeted with Sven, the Studio Manager — trying to make him keep his promises, which were invariably not kept because of a special labour situation in Norway.

Sven could never fire anyone for neglecting to do a job or make some prop on time. Sacking was completely 'Verboten', and the result was that people didn't turn up on time and jobs normally done by some crew member, often had to be done by my 'faithful five'! I remember the first day we were due to shoot in the dance hall — I had to personally decorate the walls with French posters and photos of prospectors and their girlfriends.

On top of all this, Sven flatly refused to let us dope the sled dogs for the scenes when the 'villains', driving them back to Skagway without a rest, wore them out. "You can kill any dog you like," said Sven. "Make out it died from exhaustion, but the studio would be shut down if we let you hurt an animal... or dope it!"

Eventually I had to leave several downward close shots to the end of the shoot, and send Dudley Lovell over the border into Sweden to quietly knock off these shots.

But the biggest God-Almighty problem arose through Harry Alan Towers' intrinsic character. We couldn't see any of our 'rush prints' from the Madrid laboratories, unless Harry went and collected them, personally, and brought them illegally through Customs in his suitcase!!!

"For your sake, all our sakes, I can't take the risk of the Spanish Customs seizing our footage," said Harry. "I don't have either the cash or the connections to pay off the bribes they are notorious for extracting!"

The fact was that Harry loved taking risks. Every time he went sneaking through Customs he got a high. Pauline once said to him, "You know, Harry, you have a great brain, a fabulous story sense and know the business standing on your head. If only you would play it straight, you could head a studio in England — like Sir Michael Balcon or Sir Alex Korda." Harry gave her a sly smile. "That 'Sir' stuff is not for me, dear girl. I get my jollies manipulating the world. No time for that pokey little home-grown England!"

What could you say to a producer who thought and acted on such a concept of life? Although I must admit I felt a glimmer of sympathy with him, until the time came to deliver the finished *Call of the Wild* and Paramount found he had quietly pre-sold the rights to South Africa and parts of South America! Paramount was so infuriated that they only gave us minimum distribution in America!

But, to return to the shooting of the movie — every day brought me new creative joys, playing with light and shade in a white world. When the thaw began we were almost resentful to see the brown rocks and crushed greenery, sprouting through bare patches. In looking at the movie again, I believe I truly caught the spirit of the Gold Rush days.

A few summers later I persuaded Pauline to sail with me to Alaska. We disembarked at Skagway and strolled down the main street; rode on the original train up White Pass; sailed up the Yukon River; and cheered the Can Can Girls in Diamond Tooth Gertie's original dance hall. It made me proud of what we had shot, and 'laid' my hankering after Gold subjects forever!

CHAPTER TWENTY *Dropping the pace a little... but still pitching!*

Back home for another South-of-France summer, Jack Davies and I kicked around a subject, which we thought might be suitable for David Niven, whom we saw quite often at his home on Cap Ferrat. The idea we hit on was for a Mr. Bradbury, who tutored foreigners' kids in English, to be caught by one of his young pupils in the most gigantic lie, and for him to have to experience a similar dangerous situation with the boy. After hair-raising adventures together, the boy gives him the guts to save both their lives, almost in the way he has always falsely boasted.

David encouraged the idea and suggested there was one remaining international star he would like to work with — Toshiro Mifune — of *Seven Samurai* fame. I loved the idea, because I could see another adventure coming up, and maybe this time in Asia! As luck would have it (and I cannot stress too strongly the part LUCK plays in this game!) Euan Lloyd, a British producer of Westerns in Spain, came to live nearby in Cagnes-sur-Mer. Both Jack and I knew him from London and respected him for having independently set up *Shalako*, an impressive film with Sean Connery and Brigitte Bardot, so we showed him our script. Euan fell for it hook, line and sinker, and from his recent experiences and, based on the names of Niven and Mifune (plus ours, we hoped!), he said he believed he could find the finance in Germany and Japan.

From this lead, Jack decided to make Mifune the Japanese Ambassador in Malaysia, with a ten-year-old son who needed an English tutor (because they were soon going to be transferred to London). I latched immediately on to the fact that the boy would be a star part too, and in order to achieve this, he should be traditional Japanese yet capable of speaking English.

Miracle of miracles, after confirming that Mifune could be available, Euan Lloyd managed to raise enough front-money for me to go searching for locations and this boy. Breaking my flight to Malaysia, I stopped in LA to check with my Hollywood contacts as to whether there were any outstanding Japanese boys who had played in movies or TV. It turned out I could count them on one hand, and all those who were produced by agents for me to see, were typically Little League baseball playing types — and much too American-Japanese.

So I continued on to Malaysia, which I knew from my scouting trip in the Fifties — for *The Planter's Wife* (or *Outpost in Malaya*). My oh my! What changes had taken place! Kuala Lumpur was now a metropolis, a city of skyscrapers and auto routes... but still with its old British colonial buildings and occasional temple, a perfect setting for Mifune to have his Consulate.

Further up the east coast, the old Portuguese town of Malacca excited me with its old harbour and fortified castle... and driving northward to Penang, the road climbed through mountain and jungles, which I knew I could use for the main chase and action-part of our story. Approaching Penang I came upon one of the most weird and eerie places I have ever experienced. The Snake Temple at Bayan Lepas. Here, you went inside from the glaring sunlight and found yourself surrounded by the misty shapes of snakes, twisting and turning on metal lamp stands all around you. To me it was very scary, even when one of the Buddhist priests called out "Please walk freely around. This is a house of refuge for the snakes. Have no fear because the incense keeps them happy and harmless."

Apparently no one had ever been bitten, even by new snakes crawling inside, but much as I was tempted to work this temple into the movie, I decided the risk was too great with David Niven and a ten-year-old boy. Yes, THE BOY. Finding him was still the problem because Malaysia was peopled almost entirely by East Indians, Chinese, and Malays.

So, I moved on to Japan, a country I had always wanted to see. I contacted Mifune, who was so highly regarded in Tokyo that he practically controlled all the studios! His English was not great and he would fall back on an interpreter quite often, but he willingly arranged some auditions. There, among a hundred other boys, I found Ando Kazuhito. He had come dressed in traditional kimono and flashed me a cherubic grin as he held out his hand and bowed. "Hello," he said as a dimple formed in his cheek. "Goodbye." As he bowed again then turned, I grabbed his arm. "Hey, wait a minute, I want to talk to you."

"Those are the only words he can speak," said a tall man, now standing beside me. "In your language, that is. He has been on the stage since he was four years old... but only in Japan."

"Then how can I use him?" I asked, my gaze fixed on Ando, who was eyeing me eagerly with a mischievous smile. I knew I wanted him, but...?

"I'm his agent and I guarantee he's a quick learner along with..." he turned and pointed to an older woman dressed in grey. "His grandmother and I will keep his head down to study." The lady-in-grey bowed several times, and then took a quick swig at a liquor flask. I stared at Ando. "Ask him if he'd like to learn English." As his agent explained in Japanese, Ando nodded vigorously and threw his arms round my legs.

"I'll see what I can do," I said, patting the boy on the shoulder. His eyes sparkled as he looked up. "Kan...do," he said, copying me, and with more bowings and "Hello-pleases," Ando was steered back to his grandmother.

Sifting quickly through the other applicants (there wasn't one who really interested me), I asked Mifune to check Ando's record.

"He's what I think you call in America, a good trouper!" said Mifune, throwing me a smile. "And, as for his English, I will have to have a coach myself!" He paused, considering, and then added, "I can definitely see that boy playing my son."

Naturally, Mifune was not au fait with English teachers in Tokyo, but his secretary came up with a list. I interviewed three or four, but all of them shook their heads. Either they didn't have the time, or they thought the problem too great unless they had a year to school Ando. "Have you tried Berlitz?" one suggested.

"I didn't even dream there was a Berlitz school in Tokyo," I replied.

"Oh yes, a lot of Japanese swear by Victor Kohn, the American who runs it." So off I went to see Mr. Kohn — a youngish man who listened to my problem. "How many lines will he have to speak?" he asked.

"Oh, about one hundred and fifty, I guess. No long speeches, but he will also have to understand the story situations, and what I'm asking him to do."

Kohn mooched over to the window. After what seemed an interminable time, gazing down over the wall of the Imperial Palace, he turned. "If you like I could prepare a paper to test the Ando-boy. If he's bright, and prepared to study after his normal school classes, I'll be able to give you an answer."

"It's a deal," I said. "How long?"

"Oh, two to three days, if everyone cooperates."

"I'll take a bet Ando will," I grinned. "Meanwhile I'll take myself off to Kyoto. I've always wanted to see the temples and sacred gardens there."

"A man after my own heart," Kohn said as we shook hands.

The train sped north past Mount Fuji at 130 mph, and dropped me off in Kyoto.

Apart from its traffic and modern streets, the town was clustered with pagodas and gardens with fancy bridges over artificial lakes. I learned what some of the special rock arrangements meant, watched Kabuki theatre, and participated in the tea ceremony. Much of this I have incorporated into *Redwing*, a screenplay I have just finished writing as my Millennium effort!

Back in Tokyo, Victor Kohn had tested Ando and pronounced him to be a remarkably bright pupil. "I believe I can achieve the required result if you can give me 60 days minimum."

Tremendously elated, I called Euan Lloyd and found that he had been signing contracts like crazy and because of another Niven commitment, we might have to start shooting in 60 days! "Only if you can collect your team, cast the smaller parts including a German star, and get through the pre-production necessary!" he pontificated over the phone.

My heart began beating madly as I made a deal acceptable to Victor, and tried to impress on Ando that we would have a wonderful time together in Malaysia, if only he would do as Victor instructed him to do during the next two months. Back in France, we finalised the budget. Jack Davies and I polished up the script, making small changes to fit the locations I had found.

Key members of my crew — Dudley Lovell, Johnny Cabrera; Kit West (Special Effects) and Bob Simmons (Stunt Arranger) looked as though they could be available, and I insisted on one of my old trusted assistants, David Anderson, to be put in charge of the production and dispatched immediately to Malaysia. It was a good thing I did, because Euan suddenly announced that we must start the shoot in 40 days time!!

"But Ando," I wailed. "You're cutting him short by almost two weeks!" I was receiving reports from Victor that the boy was trying, but a tape that he sent me suggested that progress was slow. Ando was often getting exhausted or mad with himself and Victor!

But the money was there and apparently must be used pronto. The weather was more or less right, and I would have some shooting to do in Germany (Niven's exaggerated war experiences) before winter came to Munich.

Fortunately for us, school holidays were fast approaching for Debbie. Now nine years old, we told her she could come with us to Malaysia if she would take over teaching Ando English and become his constant companion.

"What if I don't like him?" she said. "You won't be able to resist him," I replied, and Pauline added, with a grin, "You'll just have to make the best of it, like your father does."

This was Debbie's first introduction to 'the business', and although seemingly insignificant, her 'work' with Ando certainly helped to make his performance as good as it turned out to be.

In Kuala Lumpur, we and all the cast were housed in the luxurious Hilton Hotel. The first morning we had breakfast beside the pool and were joined by Ando and his manager. Ando was full of fun and showing off his English. Debbie was watching him closely as he tried to eat a fried egg the Western World way.

"Not that way," said Debbie, putting her hand on his, as he balanced the egg on the flat of his knife and tried to tip it into his mouth. He stared at her in amazement then turned to his agent. "Do I have to take orders from her?" The agent grinned. "It might be a good idea," he said. "But she's a girl," said Ando. "She's also your director's daughter," smiled the agent with a bow to me. A moment of agony on my part, then

Ando pushed his plate towards Debbie and she cut the egg and took a dainty bite.

From that moment on, they swam together, played ball together and became the greatest buddies. Every day he picked up idiomatic English phrases to augment the crash-course to which he had been submitted.

I always recall Pauline coming on to the set one day and killing herself with laughter.

"You'll never believe what I just witnessed in our room." The crew gathered round. "There's Debbie and Ando, playing a game of Dominoes. Suddenly she jumps up and yells "You (pointing to Ando) are driving (steering a driving wheel) me (pointing to herself) up the wall (jabbing the wall behind her)!" Big guffaws.

As you can see in the movie, Ando may have learnt his English in many different ways, but he won out with flying colours. When we were on location in Genting Heights, shooting the scenes where Niven and Ando are being held hostage, Ando has to discover that his idol has feet of clay and is a liar. David used to religiously set aside one hour each evening to play with Ando. "A wonderful gesture," I thought, "from a great star". It certainly paid off in their relationship on the screen.

When you are a star of David Niven's magnitude, this kind behaviour and consideration for a little boy could have been a great personal sacrifice, especially since there were two very attractive Australian air hostesses who pursued him most eagerly on their days off. Not that he seemed to mind; in fact, David loved women and they, without exception on this movie, adored him.

In order to film a party in Mifune's embassy, Pauline went around Kuala Lumpur enrolling all the bankers, lawyers and CEO's of British companies, and their wives. To rub shoulders and joke with David Niven, made a wonderful break in the lives of these women and David enjoyed every minute of the scenes in the mansion loaned to us by the ex-Prime Minister of Sabah.

For me, this movie once again made me feel like a painter going out every day to capture some quirk of human behaviour against magnificent tropical backgrounds. Apart from Niven's encounters with Mifune, we filmed him instructing and explaining his phoney war experiences to Ando, amid the battlements of a castle in Malacca. David and Ando are abducted by a band of guerrillas in order to gain the release of their imprisoned comrades. Then, David drives a car in a mad escape down five miles of hairpin bends we had been allowed to construct through a jungle. Finally egged on by Ando, Niven scrambles up riverbeds and rocky gullies, to eventually be rescued by a big Army helicopter at the top of a mountain.

I remember Johnny Cabrera, Dudley and I photographing that landing, and Ando being reunited with Mifune... in temperatures of 105 degrees. We were scorched but loved our conquest of a most difficult sequence.

After all this final action, David had to be flown home, lying flat on his back on a British Airways plane. He told his wife Yjordis that I had given him such tough climbs, that an old back injury had been revived. She never forgave me, but it seemed to me he was carrying on 'in the character of Mr. Bradbury'. From our observation, his collapsed back was much more likely to have been brought on by the Australian stewardesses, than any action I had given him!

I spoke earlier of Irene Tsu. She turned out to be a most interesting character playing Talah, leader of the young guerrillas who kidnap Niven and Ando, to gain the release of their imprisoned comrades. Singapore-born and Hong Kong educated,

Irene had worked on a TV show in England on which David Anderson had been assistant. She could be very physical yet alluring and her recommendation by Anderson just proved how a bright colleague can sometimes help in the casting of a movie.

On practically every location movie I can remember, there were certain events that stay in one's mind as very special or very scary. On *Paper Tiger* I had my 60th birthday and, since every minute of every day was taken up with the crew or cast, Pauline had suggested to me that we should celebrate quietly with a candlelight supper.

Suddenly around 8 pm, I was in the shower and I heard her answering the phone. "What is it this time?" I called. Looking like a dream in a new chic silk dress, she came into the bathroom and said, "Another crisis, darling! Apparently Niven and Mifune are arguing about the scene they have tomorrow, and David Anderson thinks you should go down to sort things out. It may need a re-write."

Apparently, I flung open the shower door and yelled blue murder! I wasn't going to upset OUR EVENING. I had been up since six-thirty, coping all day with problems. They could all go to hell. Bickering and moaning, Pauline got me dressed and led me down to Mifune's suite.

"Ten minutes maximum," I was saying as we knocked at his door.

Suddenly the door swung silently open and a blinding light was turned on to us... hands came from behind which steered us inside. Full lights! Big cheers! As Mifune and Niven came solemnly towards us bearing glasses of champagne. We saw the whole crew and cast raising their glasses and waving Happy Birthday banners.

It had been planned with Pauline knowing all about it, but even she was shattered by the extent and 'no-costs-spared', in their determination to give us a memorable evening. This is something that can only happen amid the deep camaraderie and relationships that develop while shooting a movie on location.

The scary event was a fire that could have wiped us out if it had happened a day sooner. The whole crew, including Euan Lloyd and his wife, had been housed on the 10th and 11th floor of a new Holiday Inn. The majority of the crew had travelled with us to the Genting Heights, but half a dozen were still to follow. Suddenly at about 2 am, fire broke out in the cashier's office. Bob Simmons, our stuntman, flung open his door to find an action scene for which he had not prepared! Grabbing a handful of clothes, he dashed bravely through the flames and smoke, and leapt down the stairs. Suddenly he remembered Euan's wife Pat was still in her room. Making a karate-style jump at the door, he broke it down, grabbed the sleepy Pat from her bed and ran out with her kicking in her nightie.

Unfortunately, as they raced down a corridor to the fire escape, they passed another room, which was thrown open by Tommy Raeburn, our Prop Man, who had just acquired two giant lizards for our coming shoot. He was carrying them struggling under his arms. Bob and Pat collided with them and were sent sprawling on the ground, with Rae yelling "For God's sake, save the lizards. Ken will go crazy if he doesn't have them!"

Obviously Euan and I learnt about this second-hand: Euan discovered that his wife was safe, and I got my lizards! The only serious loss in the fire was the double set of books the film's accountant had set up. This caused me to have a week nipped off my schedule, because it was said we were now over budget!

But that is another story altogether. After wrapping up in Malaysia with more or less all the material I needed, I flew to Bavaria to shoot with a German crew, Mr.

CHAPTER TWENTY *Dropping the pace a little... but still pitching!*

Bradbury's exaggerated war heroics. David Niven was with me, but now showing no sign of his 'old back injury'!

In all, *Paper Tiger* was another great experience and adventure for Pauline, Debbie, and myself. It was crowned by four great premieres: The first in Monte Carlo under the patronage of Princess Grace and Prince Rainier. The next was at Leicester Square in London with the Duke and Duchess of Kent, closely followed by a premiere in Tehran, attended by Princess Farah of Persia. Finally it opened in Tokyo, attended by a Prince of the Royal Family.

The film did excellently in Europe and Asia, but what happens to any Independent movie once it gets into the hands of Accountants and Distributors, the Director has little or no say.

I seem to recall that, in order to cover his original financial backers, Euan eventually did a deal with Joe Levine in New York, who wanted to take advantage of a tax shelter scheme that existed at that time. All Levine needed to do was give a limited showing of *Paper Tiger* in the US, and he gained whatever tax benefit (profit) he was seeking on a whole group of movies he'd acquired.

But whatever happens on the way, a movie today has a life on video, TV, cable/satellite and now DVD. An audience will still get pleasure from watching your work if it is quality entertainment, no matter how old the film is. In the final analysis, the important thing from a Director's point of view is whether you have achieved your original concept. Like a parent, are you proud of the child you raised, or are you not! In the case of *Paper Tiger* I think I am still proud of it — with small reservations!!!

I made one more movie in Europe, based on that old favourite, Alexander Dumas' 'Three Musketeers'. Ours was eventually called *The Fifth Musketeer*. This was the only movie that came to me through my daughter Jane, who was now a leading agent in London. Over the years we had remained close, but she had a duty to find work for her William Morris clients, while I was still represented by Dennis Van Thal at his London Management agency.

On one of my trips to London, Jane and I were having lunch in Soho, when a young writer called David Ambrose came to our table. "Won't you please introduce me to your father," he said. "I've always wanted to meet him." So began a conversation that led me to Paris the next day.

Hal Richmond, an ex-Hollywood Producer whom I had met at the Cannes Festival, had taken up residence in Paris. He said he admired my work, and that he had a deal with Sylvia Kristel, the highly talked about French star of *Emmanuelle* and *Emmanuelle II*. I told him porn — Sylvia's claim to fame — was not my bag.

"Don't be stupid," said Hal. "These days you have to deliver sex in every movie. Purely because of her sales value, I think I can hook Cornel Wilde, Rex Harrison, Olivia de Havilland, José Ferrer, plus Lloyd Bridges and his son Beau. I only need a director who they will accept!"

The cast sounded interesting, and Hal said the movie would be shot in and around Vienna — with the full cooperation (and finance) from the Austrian government. The famous palace of Schoenbrun would be available to us, as well as the Vienna woods, castles and lakes — and for a grand finale, the historic St. Stephens Cathedral.

"And the script," I queried, bringing the project down to earth. "'The Musketeers' have been done a few times... *The Man in the Iron Mask*, for example?"

"We've built upon that," said Hal. "David Ambrose, whom you've met, has come up with a fascinating plot twist for using the iron mask, with action and sex, driving the old story along. A guaranteed commercial hit! Right up your street," he grinned. "Pure entertainment!"

I read the screenplay and felt that Ambrose had indeed created a good story with interesting twists... and a challenge for me to use a lot of double exposure techniques. Beau Bridges was to play the young king Louis, but also his identical twin, who had been reared by Cornel and his musketeer pals. The script called for the two young guys to appear on the screen at the same time — even fight each other... interesting!!

I was tempted, hoping that I could make another historical/costume picture like the Disney *Robin Hood* or *The Sword and the Rose*. I flew to Vienna and was completely bowled over by the locations, especially Schoenbrun Castle. This treasure house of History and Art, had 10,000 visitors tramping daily through its decorated rooms, to gape at antique furniture and paintings, every day of the year: Royal boudoirs, chandeliered corridors, Great Halls, and the whole ornamental gardens. I was assured everything would be made available and the tourists diverted elsewhere.

HOW COULD I RESIST?

Hal was a most off-hands producer. Consequently, I was allowed to bring in my key crew, plus this time, Jack Cardiff, the great British Cinematographer, with whom I had last worked in documentary 30 years earlier. In the interim, he had become the acknowledged master of 'painting in colour' by the skillful use of various filters.

I brought in two actors to make the cast a little more appealing to young audiences. Ian McShane, an exciting, but brittle new British actor who had shined in *Battle of Britain*, and in a movie called *Villain* with Richard Burton. The other was Ursula Andress whom I had greatly admired since her famous appearance in *Dr No*.

I found Ursula shooting a picture in Rome, and after half an hour of discussion in her caravan, she agreed to play the young King Louis' mistress. I felt that between Ursula and Ian, a balance and challenge to Sylvia Kristel (whom I found rather amateurish and a bit of a know-all) would be supplied. Sylvia was difficult because she knew she was getting $250,000 for the movie and that the money was predicated on her box-office pull, so that even a great star like Rex Harrison was only being employed because she was in the picture!!

As the male cast arrived in Vienna, everyone except Rex were given two weeks training in swordsmanship, which they seemed to enjoy and at which they became very proficient, especially Lloyd Bridges.

Costumes, Royal barges, period coaches, fine horses and riders — they all appeared as we needed them... and we even shot in the famous sewers of Vienna, just as my mentor Carol Reed had done in *The Third Man*. So far as I could judge at the time, I had shot a good action/period movie, in my usual conscientious style... BUT IT NEVER TOOK OFF!

For years I blamed Hal Richmond, as the Producer, for not having 'sat on Columbia's doorstep' pushing and pestering them to give it good distribution (he just sat in his home in Paris never making even one trip to Hollywood!). But looking at *The Fifth Musketeer* today, I can see I made a poor movie and I think 'If You Wanna Be a Director' it is interesting to examine the reasons why:

First of all, the storyline is bitty. It doesn't take you along with it. My first thought is perhaps we should have had a narrator linking the action... but someone explaining the plot is an easy way out and rarely makes an emotionally satisfying picture.

Digging deeper, you watch some action with Beau as King Louis in the Royal Court, and then cut to a sequence with him as his twin brother and the Musketeers in some completely different setting. Yet, the central actor remains indistinguishable in either role.

Beau has become a most respected screen-actor these days, but back in 1975 he was a raw kid. In his off-time as I recall, he was a loner, wearing outlandish clothes and playing a guitar. In my movie, he tried his utmost to portray a polished decadent king, as well as a country-boy. John was brought up almost as a peasant, but you don't believe this difference... AND YOU ARE NOT ROOTING FOR EITHER CHARACTER!

The fault was clearly mine in not spending enough time with Beau, to impart to him 'some method' to create a different character as John. Beau's subsequent career clearly proves that he had the qualities within him, and I missed bringing them out.

Taking the picture as a whole, it strikes me that something else may have happened. Feeling that I had an all-star cast, I think I let them play in their own way, while I concentrated on the staging and dramatic set-ups. I know I was very impressed by having Jack Cardiff, the world acclaimed master of colour photography, beside me, and because I had worked beside him as a beginner in documentary, I wanted to prove to him indubitably in every set-up, that I was a master too, in the technical and visual art of picture making!

On reflection, perhaps that is an excuse for my neglect of good story telling and not getting better performances out of the actors. But one glaring fact stares out and which I am utterly ashamed of. Sylvia and Ursula are AWFUL... wooden, pouty, unsmiling. Why did I allow them to play scenes that way???

I suspect that Ursula had just had a facelift. For sure, only her mouth moved in most of her dialogue scenes. I recall that she was highly jealous of Sylvia (feeling that she had not earned the popular acclaim she was receiving) and I deliberately encouraged this jealousy to come through in the two girls' face-to-face scenes, because that was their relationship in the script. But since they were playing royal personages, they both tended to mouth their lines stuffily, unemotionally... and I allowed it! I did not show them alternative ways to put over the 'royal' attitude.

Without excusing myself in any way, I have to say that this movie had the most pervasive behind-the-scenes parallel 'real life' drama taking place, on any movie location I have experienced. Almost every day, when they discovered they would not be needed for an hour or so, two of the Musketeers would slip into Pauline's caravan and ask her to cover for them while they slipped away 'to have a little nooky'.

Believe it or not, Rex Harrison worked himself up into such a state for the sexy Sylvia, that he proposed marriage (at least that is what she 'leaked' on the set!) But Sylvia had her eyes set on Ian McShane, who fell for her so heavily that he left his wife, Ruth, on the spot. Day after day, as we trooped out to work, we would pass poor Ruth, waiting in the lobby for a chance to speak to Ian. The crew hoped that the couple would turn up from the secret place they had spent the night, in time for their call. Usually they did, but as we worked, our thoughts were often half-occupied with the tragedy and amorous developments of this passionate affair.

Suddenly Sylvia and Ian, who had now taken the Penthouse Suite in the Hilton, summoned Pauline, Jack Cardiff, Dudley Lovell and me to a party. We debated whether to accept, but for good relations, decided we had to attend. The strangest group of people immediately intimidated us. One was a young Dutch actor who cornered everyone as they passed him and tried to convince them that the peak moment of Life was Death!

When I ordered scotch-on-the-rocks, another 'young friend' took my glass straight onto the terrace garden, picked out four pebbles and poured the whisky onto them — without a smile! Meanwhile, Sylvia took Pauline's arm and led her into the kitchen where Ian was cooking. As she was chatting to him, she noticed that he was stirring something into the Spaghetti Bolognese. "That wouldn't be a new-fangled drug?" queried Pauline. "Marijuana," beamed Ian. "And tonight you're going to try it instead of always griping." Pauline shrugged. "Neither Ken nor I believe in what it does to you." "For God's sake!" yelled Ian. "Quit being such a prude and enjoy yourself!"

Obviously we had to eat the Spaghetti Bolognese (Pauline did not reveal to us what was in it) and the meal was a disaster. Screwball theories about Life and Death, politics and sex, were kicked around all evening, punctuated by bubbling champagne squirted at our heads. Finally everyone was throwing soufflés at each other, covering the walls and window with a yellow slime. No wonder in the underground tunnels next day, Jack, Dudley and I could hardly distinguish between the sewage flowing at our feet and the shimmering reflections made by our lights on the carved-out roof!

I do not blame these kind of things going on in the background, for my failure to make *The Fifth Musketeer* into the movie it promised to be. Nevertheless, it is a background a Director would do well to try and steer his Crew and Cast away from, if he wants to make good movies and have a lifetime career in directing.

EPILOGUE

In the mid-Eighties, Pauline, Debbie and I moved permanently to California. The crisis which caused our decision arose from my efforts to finance a program of three subjects I had acquired: 'A Villa in Summer by Penelope Mortimer; 'The Ballad of Peckham Rye' by Muriel Spark; and 'The Playroom by Olivia Manning. All were highly regarded English novelists, putting forward avant garde ideas on human behaviour which appealed to me and had a growing audience.

Following a zigzag trail, seeking financial backing, I got involved with a group of so-called international investors, led by a Mafia boss, who at this time was living in a mansion just outside Nice. To the horror of Pauline and myself, in order to gain control of these subjects and my services, this guy implicitly threatened my family by telling George Nicholson, a yachting-agent friend, that he "knew the school Debbie was attending."

"Sounds a perfectly innocuous statement," I said. Nicholson shook his head. "From my knowledge of this guy's associates, I would take it as a definite threat!"

But quite apart from this, I had proved that the French Riviera was not the place to find genuine or serious backing for a writer/director... or even an ambitious producer!!

Once a year at the Cannes Festival, you could have meetings with a score of studio reps and independent US finance guys, but as soon as the festival was over, all was forgotten.

I would make frequent trips to London, but the old companies founded by Rank and Alex Korda were a shadow of their old selves. No English bank or financier would consider a deal without the participation of an American company. SO WE MOVED.

From the point of view of continuing the good life, it was no great hardship. We found a charming little house on a promontory overlooking the blue Pacific. Phil

Kellogg, an old friend who was heading up the Morris Agency, quickly found me work in TV. I made five long-form productions, one of which was an adaptation of a Harold Robbins best seller, 'The Pirate'.

Warner Bros. supplied me with a first-class cast headed by Anne Archer and Franco Nero. *The Pirate* was produced by the legendary Howard Koch, who had both directed and produced many winners. We became great friends and had fun telling this story of deceit among the rich. Reproducing luxury Arab homes in California, he taught me that you could match almost anything or anywhere, in California!

All my TV shows were based on good stories, but it became clear to me that the established heads of the networks set the price and made the rules. The successful directors were the ones who didn't oppose the system in any way. If you wanted to stay in favour you must not say "Lay a track there" or "I want a crane here." You must be a tame technician, carrying out the plan for shooting which has been set up by the office, and guaranteed to be carried out faithfully by tame production managers and their assistants. If you wish to make a career as a TV Director in America, you must treat it as a job, be a smiling 'yes-man', and attend every social function frequented by your TV family of Stars and Executives. This was not my scene, so I decided I would continue to write and direct features when I was offered or could promote a script (or adventure) that appealed to me... and to Pauline!

My old writing chum, Jack Davies, followed me to California, and we wrote several scripts together and had the usual laughs as we created comedic situations. But what the British think is funny does not necessarily make American audiences laugh, perhaps because Americans come from so many different ethnic backgrounds.

For one reason or another, we were not getting our new scripts off the ground. Undoubtedly Hollywood was changing, and neither of us had any true connections (or for that matter sympathy) with the new powers in the studios, who seemed to be obsessed more with Profit and 'the Bottom Line' than good story entertainment.

Of course, there was no denying we were getting older and no matter how hard we might make the effort to keep up with the trends, the young were experiencing different ways of living and expressing challenging attitudes.

Still, my luck returned when I was invited to take over the direction of a wonderful musical in Australia — a take-off of 'The Pirates of Penzance'. We shot in and around Melbourne and for four days we sailed and filmed on an ancient three-masted schooner up and down Sydney Harbour. It took me back to my sailing days on the 'Cap Pilar' some fifty years before!

The Pirate Movie was okay, but looking at it now, I clearly fell in love with some of my musical/dance routines, and allowed them to go on too long in the final cut. This can often be an error a Director falls into, if he does not have a strong producer or collaborator nagging him or her to cut tightly. It can also happen when an Editor has too much respect for a Director's past work to suggest they do the obvious!

The New Adventures of Pippi Longstocking occupied me for two whole years, converting Astrid Lindgrens' imaginative Pippi stories into a screenplay and movie. Here again the music of Misha Segal and the lyrics of Harriet Schock were terribly important to the film's success. For eight weeks in Florida I had a ball, creating Pippi's 'way-out' and undisciplined adventures — including flying across streets on a motorcycle and sidecar, and 'shooting the rapids' in a tub — all made possible by my old Special Effects wizard, Dick Parker.

CHAPTER TWENTY *Dropping the pace a little... but still pitching!*

Believe it or not, to find the right elfin-like Pippi, I auditioned over 8000 kids — in Los Angeles, Chicago, London and Miami. Here I found Tami Erin, who clearly had the gamin-traits, which could 'make every dream possible'.

The three other principal kids were found in these auditions too. Fay Masterton, a Cockney girl who played Head-Girl in the orphanage, has become quite a star, performing in movies with Morgan Freeman, Mel Gibson, Chevy Chase and Tom Cruise (*Eyes Wide Shut*).

But when we made *Pippi*, the kids were all under twelve. After a week or two rehearsing, we became a family, working in the closest unison — with me setting the shape of the actions, and the children making contributions and suggestions coming from their hearts.

Shooting *Pippi* was a joy, and a unique day-by-day creative experience. Even now I find it a heaven-sent reward when I meet a mother and she tells me her kids have run the *Pippi* video so often that they quote every line and sing 'Pippi Longstocking is coming to Town' so often that she could scream!

But perhaps the adventure, to top all the adventures that Pauline and I have ever had, was to be transported to Kurdistan, Kazakhstan, Uzbekistan and China — a 28-week shoot of a new version of *Genghis Khan*. The main cast was made up of 14 American actors, including Chuck Heston, Pat Morita, Julia Nickson and John Saxon, plus 52 Russians and 15 Chinese.

How did this project come to me when I was in my late seventies? Remember Harry Bernsen, who years ago offered me a blank cheque to do a remake of *Holiday Camp* in Vegas, and I turned it down because it might have been Mafia money? (Now, of course, scores of movies have been and are made with money from dubious sources!!!) We met Harry again at a party following some Disney film premiere. I was talking to Jeffrey Katzenberg about my years with Walt, when Harry came up, slapped me on the back and said "Ken Annakin! Are you still in this goddam business?"

"I would hope so," I replied. "What else is there as fascinating? Can't you see I'm trying to talk myself into a job at Disney?"

They both chortled, and a few minutes later I was listening to Harry saying excitedly, "This is Fate, Ken! I've just been asked to solve a problem for some old friends in Italy. A fabulous project which needs someone with your unique experience."

And so it began. I read all the books about Genghis Khan, went to Rome met the producer, Enzo Rispoli; and then rewrote three two-hour scripts with James Carrington, an Englishman, who had just written the brilliant screenplay of *Children of a Lesser God*. Before we knew it, Pauline and I were in Bistek, the capital of Kurdistan.

We shot battles with real Mongolian horsemen and 400 borrowed Red Army cavalry, and reproduced life in the yourt (tent) encampments, with genuine Mongol families with their children, goats and nomadic herds. Amazingly we never heard a child cry during work hours!

But what was the real fascination to me, was to tell the story of a carefree peasant lad from an outcast tribe, thrown into dangerous situations and picking up hints and guidance from chance meetings... until by sheer perseverance he became the all-conquering Genghis Khan.

This project, and our personal lives became closely entwined. Here we were in Far

Eastern regions hitherto banned from Western eyes, working and travelling through areas where the Soviets had built their nuclear missile sites — most of which were still there. Daily we drove past the remnants of ramshackle communal farms, down the wide main streets of Bistek and Alma Ata, which were almost as well laid out and maintained as Parisian boulevards.

In the midst of our shoot, Yeltsin arrived for a conference, and the whole unit were turned out of the old State Hotel where we had been housed, and made to find other accommodation. Pauline, Johnny Cabrera (Director of Photography again) and Peter Murton (one of my former Art Directors) were accepted to live with a small Russian family — an eye opening yet endearing experience.

Eight weeks in China were also eye opening, and an experience quite irreplaceable by any form of normal travel. In the old Beijing studios where we were based, locals were allowed to shack down in every vacant space. I will never forget lining up a morning shot of Genghis Khan riding down a leafy lane, expounding his philosophy for treating conquered people, when six doors opened and these 'night tenants' threw out their excrements under the trees!

Eventually we wrapped and 'got home for Christmas'.

Since the Editor and I both lived in LA, it had been agreed from the beginning that we would edit the material in Hollywood — cutting a six-hour TV mini-version first, then later reducing it to feature length. Apart from money always arriving ten days or more late, we worked on happily, and had just shown the visiting Enzo Rispoli my Director's Cut, when I received a panic call: "The flames are just coming over the top of the canyon, and your house is in danger!"

Explaining to Mr. Rispoli that I could not discuss changes at this moment, I jumped into my car and raced along the Pacific Coast Highway to Malibu, arriving at the exact same moment as Pauline, who had been attending an Art class. A helicopter flew low over the house, with a guy leaning out holding a loudhailer. "You gotta get out – IMMEDIATELY! The wind is blowing flames down the canyon and you're in the line of fire!"

I wanted to stay and fight. After all, we had a fire pump and a big pool. "I can always jump into it if it gets too hot," I argued. But Pauline would have none of it. Twenty minutes later, with whatever clothes we could grab, and our white Labrador at our feet, we drove away. Black smoke blurred our vision, and giant flames leapt beside us as we made our escape.

The house and outbuildings literally burned to the ground. A fireman told us later: "Eleven minutes and it was gone!" Our antique French furniture, all the mementos, paintings, photos and films, collected in our 30 years together, just vanished in flames.

We were totally devastated, and I think that, without many friends offering us a roof over our heads and clothing, etcetera, we might for a while have given up, but as my old star Dorothy McGuire stressed on us, life was not over — we were still alive and had our family.

Within ten days, we had rented a home just above Sunset Boulevard, and I returned to the cutting rooms and *Genghis Khan*. To my chagrin, I discovered through our most junior assistant, that Mr. Rispoli was secretly arranging to have my six-hour Director's Cut shipped back to Italy. It became clear he was abandoning our cutting rooms, leaving big debts throughout Hollywood, and was clearly planning to throw myself and the editor overboard.

With legal help from the group who had put up loan-finance for Charlton Heston and Pat Morita, we managed to spike this scheme and keep the film in LA. Unfortunately Rispoli still held the negative in Rome, so both sides were spiked, and a few weeks later we heard that Rispoli's company had gone into bankruptcy! BUT THIS IS ANOTHER EPIC STORY STILL TO BE TOLD! *Genghis Khan* has not been finished – YET!!

As for the Annakin Family, malevolent Fate had not finished with us! We received a call from our granddaughter Alice in London, saying that Jane was in the hospital with cancer. We dropped everything, and for the next two months were beside her bed some part of every day.

Suddenly she had what appeared to be a miraculous remission, and announced that she was going to live to see her daughter Alice through Cambridge and see her first grandchild born! Over the next four years, this is exactly what she did; and in her capacity as a top agent, kept twenty-odd writers and directors content and in work. During this time she helped negotiate a remarkable deal, which enabled John Madden to make *Shakespeare in Love*. John was so grateful that he insisted that Jane should be given a posthumous dedication at the end of this Oscar-winning movie!

Unfortunately the cancer returned with a vengeance, and she passed away in the Royal Marsden Hospital, aged fifty- three, taking with her the love and respect of a host of Brits involved in theatre and cinema.

Back in America, Pauline and I hugged each other, and decided we must, once again, put down roots and buy a home because each and every day was to be lived. We would never get over our terrible loss, but for Jane's sake, we must be there for Alice and her new family and, of course, for Debbie who was now working for Disney. We bought a house in Beverly Hills and I, after making a number of fruitless efforts to revive and re-finance *Genghis Khan*, was given another break by my good-luck Angel.

Because of my connection with old airplanes, I was brought together with a group of air-buffs who call themselves Amelia Exploration. They and the author of a book called 'Amelia Earhart Lives' have poured upon me so many generally unknown sensational facts to prove what really happened to Amelia Earhart, that I sat down and wrote probably my best-ever screenplay!

The world has been led to believe that Amelia just vanished into the Pacific Ocean while on the last leg of her 1937 world flight. That is definitely not so! Amelia Earhart was shot down over the island of Truk while her navigator, Fred Noonan, was taking spy pictures of secret Japanese fortifications. The Japanese pilot who shot her down is still alive in Tokyo. For reasons we will reveal in the film, Emperor Hirohito would not allow the truth to be told.

Amelia survived the war and was found in a Japanese internment camp for priests and nuns in North China. We have the cooperation of the American officer who was sent to get her out, as well as the brother of the man she later married under a covert identity. Amelia and her husband lived quietly for over 20 years on the east coast of America. This is a powerful human drama based on newly discovered facts. Amelia Earhart was a pioneer aviator who proved over and over that there is no job in the air that a woman cannot tackle as well as a man.

The signs for making this film look good. A lot of people with money see the project's commercial potential. Although I am regarded as a veteran-veteran in Hollywood, perhaps even at 86 I will direct my 50th movie! It will be called *Redwing*.

And so, the lad born in the small English market town of Beverley, East Yorkshire, is now living in Beverly (without the "e") Hills, California. Not in my wildest dreams did I ever think this was possible.

I have travelled the globe and had fabulous adventures. With the help of wonderful colleagues, I have created quite a few movies I can be proud of. With TV, Cable, Videos and DVD, I hope they will give pleasure to audiences for years to come.

Pauline and I are still together and lovingly happy after forty-one years, and Debbie now has a small son, Matthew, whom at this moment is more difficult to teach English words to, than Ando was, years ago! And I am still in the movie business!

If you 'wanna be a director', no matter how far away from that goal you may seem to be at the moment, I say, STRIKE OUT, and believe in yourself. TAKE RISKS, but cover yourself by learning every angle and new technique of your job. Keep batting away through thick and thin, and YOU CAN SUCCEED in this tough but most gratifying of professions.

KEN ANNAKIN FILMOGRAPHY

DOCUMENTARIES
THE SIXTEEN TASKS OF MAINTAINING MOTORISED VEHICLES (1941)
GB b/w
Ministry of Information/Verity Films
Prd: Max Munden Ph: Reg Wyer, Camera Assistant: Ken Annakin

(NO TITLE: FILM ABOUT LAND WORKERS) (1941)
GB b/w
Ministry of Information/Verity Films
Prd: Max Munden Dir: Ralph Keene Ph: Ken Annakin

BREAST FEEDING (1941)
GB b/w
Ministry of Information/Verity Films
Prd: Max Munden Dir: Ken Annakin Ph: Peter Hennessy

A RIDE WITH UNCLE JOE (1941)
GB b/w
Ministry of Information/Verity Films
Prd: Max Munden   Dir: Ken Annakin   Ph: Ray Elton

WE SERVE (1941)
GB b/w
Ministry of Information
Dir: Carol Reed Ph: Ken Annakin

THE NEW CROP (1941)
GB b/w
British Council/Green Park Productions
Prd: Ralph Keene Dir: Ken Annakin Ph: Reg Wyer

CROP ROTATION (1942)
GB Technicolor
British Council/Green Park Productions
Prd: Ralph Keene Dir: Ken Annakin Ph: Jack Cardiff, Geoff Unsworth, Cyril Knowles

THREE CADETS (1942)
GB b/w
Ministry of Information/Verity Films
Prd: Max Munden Dir: Ken Annakin Ph: Peter Hennessy

LONDON 1942 (1942)
GB 31 mins b/w
Ministry of Information/Verity Films
Prd: Sydney Box Sc/Dir: Ken Annakin Ph: Reg Wyer, Ray Elton, Peter Hennessy,
Ken Annakin

IT BEGAN ON THE CLYDE (1943)
GB b/w
Ministry of Information/Verity Films
Prd: Ronny Riley Dir: Ken Annakin Ph: Reg Wyer

MAKE FRUITFUL THE LAND (1943)
GB b/w
British Council/Greenpark Productions
Prd: Ralph Keene Dir: Ken Annakin Ph: Peter Hennessy

A FARM IN THE FENS (1944)
GB b/w
British Council/Greenpark Productions
Prd: Ralph Keene Dir: Ken Annakin Ph: Peter Hennessy

WE OF THE WEST RIDING (1944)
GB b/w
British Council/Greenpark Productions
Prd: Ralph Keene Dir: Ken Annakin Ph: Peter Hennessy

PACIFIC THRUST (1945)
GB b/w
Ministry of Information/Verity Films
Prd: Sydney Box Sc/Dir: Ken Annakin Ph: compiled from stock materials from
Service Cameramen from all over the world, plus animation by Jim Larkin.

**KNOW YOUR ENEMY: THE JAPANESE ARMY AND HOW IT BECAME WHAT IT IS
TODAY (1945)**
GB b/w
Ministry of Information/Verity Films
Prd: Ronny Riley Dir: Ken Annakin Ph: compiled from stock materials from Service
Cameramen from all over the world, plus animation by Jim Larkin.

CAMERA COVERAGE OF THE WAR IN EUROPE (1945)
GB b/w
Ministry of Information/War Office Archives, etc.
Prd: Paul Rotha Dir: Ken Annakin Ph: Ken Annakin (with Eymo Camera)

BRITISH CRIMINAL JUSTICE (1946)
GB b/w
British Council/Greenpark Productions
Prd: Ralph Keene Dir: Ken Annakin Ph: Ray Elton

FEATURE FILMS
HOLIDAY CAMP (1946)
GB 97mins b/w
GDF/Gainsborough/J Arthur Rank Films
Cast: Jack Warner, Kathleen Harrison, Flora Robson, Dennis Price, Hazel Court, Jimmy Hanley, Diana Dors (uncredited).
Prd: Sydney Box Dir: Ken Annakin Sc: Muriel and Sydney Box, Ted Willis, Peter Rogers, Mabel and Denis Constanduros. Story: Godfrey Winn Ph: Jack E. Cox

BROKEN JOURNEY (1947)
GB 89mins b/w
Gainsborough/Sydney Box Productions
Cast: Phyllis Calvert, James Donald, Margot Grahame, Francis L Sullivan, Raymond Huntley, David Tomlinson.
Prd: SydneyBox Dir: Ken Annakin Sc: Robert Westerby Ph: Jack E. Cox

MIRANDA (1948)
GB 80mins b/w
GDF/Gainsborough/Sydney Box Productions
Cast: Glynis Johns, Griffith Jones, Googie Withers, Margaret Rutherford, David Tomlinson.
Prd: Betty Box Dir: Ken Annakin Sc: Peter Blackmore Ph: Ray Elton

HERE COME THE HUGGETTS (1948)
GB 93mins b/w
Gainsborough/J Arthur Rank Films
Cast: Jack Warner, Kathleen Harrison, Petula Clark, Jimmy Hanley, Diana Dors
Prd: Betty Box Dir: Ken Annakin Sc: Muriel and Sydney Box, Peter Rogers, Mabel and Denis Constanduros. Ph: Reg Wyler

QUARTET (1948)
GB 120mins b/w
Gainsborough/J Arthur Rank Films
(Ken Annakin directed segment: "The Colonel's Lady")
(Arthur Crabtree directed segment: "The Kite")
(Harold French directed segment: "The Alien Corn")
(Ralph Smart directed segment: "The Facts of Life")
Cast: Cecil Parker, Ernest Thesiger, Wilfred Hyde White, Linden Travers, Mai Zetterling, Nora Swinburne, Felix Aylmer, Henry Edwards.
Prd: SydneyBox Anthony Darnborough Sc: W. Somerset Maugham, R. C. Sherriff stories by W. Somerset Maugham Ph: Ray Elton Reginald H. Wyer (segment: "The Colonel's Lady")

FILMOGRAPHY

VOTE FOR HUGGETT (1949)
GB 93mins b/w
Gainsborough/J Arthur Rank Films
Cast: Jack Warner, Kathleen Harrison, Petula Clark, Jimmy Hanley, Diana Dors
Prd: Betty Box Dir: Ken Annakin Sc: Muriel and Sydney Box, Peter Rogers, Mabel and Denis Constanduros. Ph: Reginald H. Wyer

LANDFALL (1949)
GB 88mins b/w
Associated British Productions
Cast: Michael Denison, Patricia Plunkett, Edith Sharpe, Margaret Barton, Charles Victor, Kathleen Harrison, Denis O'Dea, Margaretta Scott, Sebastian Shaw, Maurice Denham, David Tomlinson, Nora Swinburne.
Prd: Victor Skuzetzky Dir: Ken Annakin Sc: Gilbert Gunn, Talbot Jennings, Anne Burnaby, novel by Neville Shute Ph: Wilkie Cooper

THE HUGGETTS ABROAD (1949)
GB 89mins b/w
Gainsborough/J Arthur Rank Films
Cast: Jack Warner, Kathleen Harrison, Petula Clark, Jimmy Hanley, Diana Dors
Prd: Betty Box Dir: Ken Annakin Sc: Gerard Bryant, Mabel and Denis Constanduros.
Ph: Reginald H. Wyer

TRIO (1950)
GB 91mins b/w
Gainsborough/J Arthur Rank Films
(Ken Annakin directed segment: "The Verger")
(Ken Annakin directed segment: "Mr Know-All")
(Harold French directed segment: "Sanatorium")
Cast: James Hayter, Kathleen Harrison, Michael Hordern, Felix Aylmer, Nigel Patrick, Michael Rennie, Raymond Huntley, Andre Morell, Wilfid Hyde White, Michael Medwin, Bill Travers
Prd: Sydney Box Anthony Darnborough Sc: W. Somerset Maugham, R. C. Sherriff, Noel Langley from short stories by W. Somerset Maugham. Ph: Geoffrey Unsworth, Reginald H. Wyer

DOUBLE CONFESSION (1950)
GB 85mins b/w
Associated British Productions
Cast: Peter Lorre, Esme Cannon, Leslie Dwyer, Derek Farr, Kathleen Harrison, William Hartnell, Vida Hope, Joan Hopkins, Ronald Howard, Edward Rigby, Mona Washbourne, Naughton Wayne, George Woodbridge
Prd: Harry Reynolds Dir: Ken Annakin Sc: William Templeton, novel by John Garden. Ph: Geoffrey Unsworth

HOTEL SAHARA (1951)
GB 96mins b/w
GFD/ Tower
Cast: Peter Ustinov, Yvonne de Carlo, David Tomlinson, Roland Culver, Albert
Lieven, Bill Owen, Sidney Tafler, Ferdy Mayne
Prd: George H. Brown Dir: Ken Annakin Sc: George H. Brown, Patricia Kirwan
Ph: Geoffrey Unsworth

THE PLANTER'S WIFE (1952)
aka Outpost In Malaya; aka White Blood (USA)
GB 91mins b/w
J Arthur Rank Films/ Pinacle
Cast: Claudette Colbert, Jack Hawkins, Anthony Steel, Ram Gopal, Jeremy Spenser,
Tom Macauley, Helen Goss, Alfie Bass
Prd: John Stafford Dir: Ken Annakin Sc: Peter Proud, Guy Elmes Ph: Geoffrey
Unsworth and Peter Henessy

THE STORY OF ROBIN HOOD AND HIS MERRIE MEN (1952)
aka The Story Of Robin Hood (USA)
USA 84mins colour
Walt Disney Productions
Cast: Richard Todd, Peter Finch, Michael Hordern, Bill Owen, Bill Travers, James
Robertson Justice, James Hayter, Martita Hunt, Joan Rice
Prd: Pearce Pierce Dir: Ken Annakin Sc: Lawrence Edward Watkin, Ph: Guy Greene

THE SWORD AND THE ROSE (1952)
aka When Knighthood Was In Flower (USA) TV Title
USA 92mins colour
Walt Disney Productions
Cast: Richard Todd, Glynis Johns, James Robertson Justice, Michael Gough, Peter
Copley, Jane Barrett
Prd: Pearce Pierce Dir: Ken Annakin Sc: Lawrence Edward Watkin, novel by Charles
Major Ph:Geoffrey Unsworth

THE SEEKERS (1954)
aka Land Of Fury (USA)
GB 90mins colour
GDF/ Fanfare
Cast: Jack Hawkins, Glynis Johns, Inia Te Wiata, Kenneth Williams, James Copeland,
Francis De Wolff, Noel Purcell, Laya Raki
Prd: George H. Brown Dir: Ken Annakin Sc: William Fairchild Ph: Geoffrey
Unsworth

FILMOGRAPHY

YOU KNOW WHAT SAILORS ARE (1954)
GB 91mins colour
J Arthur Rank Films
Cast: Akim Tamiroff, Donald Sinden, Sarah Lawson, Naughton Wayne, Bill Kerr, Dora Bryan, Michael Hordern, Leslie Phillips
Prd: Peter Rogers Dir: Ken Annakin Sc: Peter Rogers, novel by Roger Hyams Ph: Reg Wyer

VALUE FOR MONEY (1955)
GB 93mins colour
J Arthur Rank Films/ Group Films
Cast: John Gregson, Diana Dors, Susan Stephen, Derek Farr, Ernest Thesiger, Joan Hickson, James Gregson, Donald Pleasence, Leslie Phillips
Prd: Sydney Box, Sergei Nolbandov Dir: Ken Annakin Sc: R.F. Delderfield,William Fairchild, novel by Derick Boothroyd, Ph: Geoffrey Unsworth

LOSER TAKES ALL (1956)
GB 88mins colour
British Lion Productions
Cast: Glynis Johns, Rossano Brazzi, Robert Morley, Tony Britton, Felix Aylmer, A.E. Mathews
Prd: John Stafford Dir: Ken Annakin Sc: Graham Greene novel by Graham Greene ,
Ph: Georges Perinal

THREE MEN IN A BOAT (1956)
GB 84mins colour
Romulus
Cast: Jimmy Edwards, David Tomlinson, Laurence Harvey, Adrienne Corri, Ernest Thesiger, Shirley Eaton, Martita Hunt, Jill Ireland, Robertson Hare, Miles Malleson
Prd: James Woolf Dir: Ken Annakin Sc: Hubert Greg, Vernon Harris novel by Jerome K. Jerome, Ph: Eric Cross

ACROSS THE BRIDGE (1957)
GB 103mins b/w
J Arthur Rank Films/ Pinacle
Cast: Rod Steiger, David Knight, Marla Landi, Noel Willman, Bernard Lee
Prd: John Stafford Dir: Ken Annakin Sc: Guy Elmes, Denis Freeman, story by Graham Greene Ph: Reg Wyer

NOR THE MOON BY NIGHT (1958)
aka Elephant Gun (USA)
GB 92mins colour
J Arthur Rank Films
Cast: Belinda Lee, Michael Craig, Patrick McGoohan, Anna Gaylor, Eric Pohlmann
Prd: John Stafford Dir: Ken Annakin Sc: Guy Elmes, novel by Joy Packer Ph: Harry Waxman

THIRD MAN ON THE MOUNTAIN (1959)
aka Banner In The Sky (USA) TV Title
USA 105mins colour
Walt Disney Productions
Cast: Michael Rennie, James MacArthur, Janet Munro, James Donald, Herbert Lom,
Laurence Naismith, Lee Patterson, Walter Fitzgerald, Nora Swinburne, Ferdy Mayne
Prd: William Anderson Dir: Ken Annakin Sc: Eleanore Griffin, novel by James
Ramsey Ullman Ph: Harry Waxman

SWISS FAMILY ROBINSON (1960)
USA 126mins colour
Walt Disney Productions
Cast: John Mills, Dorothy McGuire, James MacArthur, Janet Munro, Sessue
Hayakawa, Tommy Kirk, Kevin Corcoran, Cecil Parker, Andy Ho, Milton Reid, Larry
Taylor
Prd: Bill Anderson, Basil Keys Dir: Ken Annakin Sc: Lowell S. Hawley, novel by
Johann David Wyss Ph: Harry Waxman Storyboard Sketches: John Jensen

THE HELLIONS (1961)
GB 80mins colour
Columbia/ Irving Allen Productions/ Jamie Uys
Cast: Richard Todd, Lionel Jefferies, James Booth, Jamie Uys, Ronald Fraser, Anne
Aubrey, Zena Walker, Marty Wilde, Colin Blakely
Prd: Harold Huth Dir: Ken Annakin Sc: Harold Swanton, Patrick Kirwan, Harold
Huth Ph: Ted Moore

VERY IMPORTANT PERSON (1961)
aka A Coming Out Party (USA)
GB 98mins b/w
J Arthur Rank Films/ Independant Artists
Cast: James Robertson Justice, Stanley Baxter, Leslie Phillips, Eric Sykes, Richard
Wattis, Colin Gordon
Prd: Julian Wintle, Leslie Parkyn Dir: Ken Annakin Sc: Jack Davies, Henry Blyth,
Ph: Harry Waxman

FILMOGRAPHY

THE LONGEST DAY (1962)
USA 169mins b/w

TCF

(Ken Annakin directed: "British Sequence", "French Resistance", "Free French Attack on Casino" and "All Amercian Studio Exteriors")

(Andrew Marton directed: "American Exteriors")

(Gerd Oswald directed: "Parachute Drop Scene")

(Bernhard Wicki directed: "German Scenes")

Cast: John Wayne, Robert Mitchum, Henry Fonda, Robert Ryan, Rod Steiger, Robert Wagner, Paul Anka, Fabian, Tommy Sands, Richard Beymer, Mel Ferrar, Jeffrey Hunter, Sal Mineo, Roddy McDowell, Stuart Whitman, Steve Forrest, Eddie Albert, Edmond O'Brien, Red Buttons, Richard Burton, Donald Huston, Kenneth More, Peter Lawford, Richard Todd, Leo Genn, John Gregson, Sean Connery, Michael Medwin, Leslie Phillips, Irina Demich, Curt Jurgens, Gert Frobe, Christopher Lee, Richard Wattis

Prd: Darryl F. Zanuck, Elmo Williams, Sc: Cornelius Ryan, Romain Gary, James Jones, David Pursall, Jack Seddon, novel by Cornelius Ryan Ph: Henri Persin, Walter Wottitz, Pierre Levent, Jean Bourgoin

CROOKS ANONYMOUS (1962)
GB 87mins b/w

Anglo Amalgamated

Cast: James Robertson Justice, Stanley Baxter, Leslie Phillips, Julie Christie, Wilfred Hyde White, Robertson Hare, Charles Lloyd Pack

Prd: Nat Cohen Dir: Ken Annakin Sc: Jack Davies, Henry Blyth, Ph: Ernest Steward

THE FAST LADY (1962)
GB 95mins colour

J Arthur Rank Films/ Group Films

Cast: James Robertson Justice, Stanley Baxter, Leslie Phillips, Julie Christie, Dick Emery

Prd: Teddy Baird Dir: Ken Annakin Sc: Jack Davies, Henry Blyth, Ph: Reg Wyer

THE INFORMERS (1965)
aka Underworld Informers (USA)

GB 104mins b/w

J Arthur Rank Films

Cast: Nigel Patrick, Colin Blakely, Derren Nesbitt, Margaret Whiting, Catherine Woolville

Prd: William MacQuitty Dir: Ken Annakin Sc: Alun Falconer, novel by Douglas Warner Ph: Reg Wyer

THOSE MAGNIFICENT MEN IN THEIR FLYING MACHINES, OR HOW I FLEW FROM LONDON TO PARIS IN 25 HOURS 11 MINUTES (1964)
GB 133mins colour
TCF
Cast: Sarah Miles, Stuart Whitman, Robert Morley, Eric Sykes, Terry-Thomas, James Fox, Alberto Sordi, Gert Frobe, Jean-Paul Cassel, Karl Michael Vogler, Irina Demick, Benny Hill, Flora Robson, Sam Wannamaker, Red Skelton, Fred Emney, Cicely Cortneidge, Gordon Jackson, John Le Mesurier, Tony Hancock, William Rushton
Prd: Stan Margulies Dir: Ken Annakin Sc: Jack Davies, Ken Annakin, Ph: Christopher Challis

BATTLE OF THE BULGE (1965)
USA 167mins colour
Warner/ United States Pictures
Cast: Henry Fonda, Robert Shaw, Robert Ryan, Telly Savalas, Dana Andrews, George Montgomery, Ty Hardin, Pier Angeli, Barbara Werle, Charles Bronson, James MacArthur, Werner Peters
Prd: Sidney Harmon, Milton Sperling, Philip Yordan Dir: Ken Annakin Sc: Milton Sperling, Philip Yordan John Melson , Ph: Jack Hildyard and John Cabrera

THE LONG DUEL (1966)
GB 115mins colour
J Arthur Rank Films
Cast: Trevor Howard, Yul Brynner, Harry Andrews, Charlotte Rampling, Virginia North, Andrew Keir, Lawrence Naismith, Maurice Denham
Prd: Ken Annakin Dir: Ken Annakin Sc: Peter Yeldham, Ph: Jack Hildyard

THE BIGGEST BUNDLE OF THEM ALL (1967)
USA 110mins colour
MGM/ Shaftel-Stewart
Cast: Edward G. Robinson, Raquel Welch, Robert Wagner, Vittorio de Sica, Godfrey Cambridge, Davy Kaye
Prd: Joe Shaftel Dir: Ken Annakin Sc: Josef Shaftel, Sy Salkowitz, Rod Amateau
Ph: Pierro Portalupi

MONTE CARLO OR BUST (1969)
aka Those Daring Young Men in Their Jaunty Jalopies (USA)
USA/ Italy/ France 125mins colour
Paramount/ Dino de Laurentiis/ Miarianne
Cast: Peter Cook, Dudley Moore, Terry-Thomas, Bourvil, Walter Chiari, Susan Hampshire, Jack Hawkins, Gert Frobe, Eric Sykes, Tony Curtis
Prd: Ken Annakin, Basil Keys Dir: Ken Annakin Sc: Jack Davies, Ken Annakin, Ph: Gabor Pogany

CALL OF THE WILD (1972)
GB/ Norway/ Spain/ Italy/ France 105mins colour
Towers Films/ Massfilms/ CCC/ Izaro/ Oceania/UPF
Cast: Charlton Heston, Michele Mercier, Raimund Harmstorf, George Eastman
Prd: Harry Alan Towers Dir: Ken Annakin Sc: Harry Alan Towers, Wyn Wells, Peter
Yeldhan, novel by Jack London Ph: John Cabrera, Dudley Lovell

PAPER TIGER (1974)
GB 99mins colour
Maclean & Co
Cast: David Niven, Toshiro Mifune, Hardy Kruger, Ando, Ivan Desny, Irene Tsu,
Miko Taka, Ronald Fraser, Jeff Corey
Prd: Euan Lloyd Dir: Ken Annakin Sc: Jack Davies Ph: John Cabrera

THE FIFTH MUSKETEER (1977)
aka Behind The Iron Mask (USA)
Austria /106mins colour
Sascha Wien Film/ Ted Richmond
Cast: Beau Bridges, Sylvia Kristel, Ursula Andress, Cornel Wilde, Lloyd Bridges, Alan
Hale Jnr., Jose Ferrer, Rex Harrison, Olivia De Havilland, Ian McShane, Helmut
Dantine
Prd: Hal Richmond Dir: Ken Annakin Sc: David Ambrose, Ph: Jack Cardiff

CHEAPER TO KEEP HER (1980)
USA/ colour
Regal/Media Home Ent./Heron Comm.
Cast: Mac Davis, Tovah Feldshuh, Bruce Flanders, Steven M. Gagnon, Jack Gilford,
Patrick Gorman, Chuck Hicks, Gwen Humble, Priscilla Lopez, Rose Marie, Rod
McCary, Ian McShane, Art Metrano, Pat O,Malley
Prd: Lenny Isenberg Dir: Ken Annakin Sc: Timothy Harris, Herschel Weingrod, Ph:
Ossie Smith

THE PIRATE MOVIE (1982)
Australia 105mins colour
20th Century Fox/ Hamilton International Pictures
Cast: Kristy McNichol, Christopher Atkins, Ted Hamilton, Bill Kerr, Maggie
Kirkpatrick, Garry McDonald
Prd: David Joseph Dir: Ken Annakin Sc: Trevor Farrant based on the operetta The
Pirates of Penzance by William S. Gilbert, Ph: Robin Copping

THE NEW ADVENTURES OF PIPPI LONGSTOCKING (1986)
Sweden/USA 100mins colour
Columbia Pictures/ Svensk Filmindustri
Cast: Tami Erin, David seaman Jnr., Cory Crow, Eileen Brennan, Dennis Dugan, Dianne Hull, George DiCenzo, J.D. Dickenson, Chub Bailly, Dick Van Patten, John Schuck, Branscombe Richmond, Evan Adams, Fay Masterson
Prd: Gary Mehlman, Walter Moshay Dir: Ken Annakin Sc: Ken Annakin based on the book by Astrid Lindgren, Ph: Roland 'Ozzie' Smith

JOSEPH AND EMMA (1992-1994)
PROJECTS ABANDONED DUE TO LACK OF FINANCE
Jande Productions
Prd: John Harmer, Ph: Ossie Smith

GENGHIS KHAN (1994-96)
Kirgistan, Kazkhstan and China
ICC (Italy)
Cast: Richard Tyson, Charlton Heston, Julia Nickson-Soul, Pat Morita, Jas. Mitchum, Scott Hoxby, Tricia O'Neil, Rodney Grant, John Saxton, Daniel Greene plus 60 Russina and Mongolian Actors and 15 Chinese Actors.
Principal photography completed but due to Italian bankruptcy not yet shown.
Prd: Enzo Rispoli Dir: Ken Annakin Ph: John Cabrera

REDWING (1997-2000)
USA colour
Script completed – now casting and negotiating distribution.
Prd: Ken Annakin Sc/Dir: Ken Annakin Ph: John Cabrera

MOVIES MADE FOR TELEVISION
MURDER AT THE MARDI GRAS (1977) TVM
USA 90mins colour
Paramount Television
Cast: David Wayne, Harry Morgan, Wolfman Jack, Ron Silver, Barbi Benton
Dir: Ken Annakin Sc: Stanley Ralph Ross

HAROLD ROBBINS' THE PIRATE (1978) TVM
USA /colour
Warner Brothers Television
Cast: James Franciscus, Christopher Lee, Olivia Hussey, Ian McShane, Armand Assante, Eli Wallach, Jeff Corey, Franco Nero
Dir: Ken Annakin Sc: Julius J. Epstein, from novel by Harold Robbins

FILMOGRAPHY

INSTITUTE FOR REVENGE (1979) TVM
USA colour
Paramount/ Dino de Laurentiis/ Miarianne
Cast: Anne Bellamy, Lane Brinkley, Patience Cleveland, Robert Coote, Natalie Core, John Davey, Robert Emhardt, Ernie Fuentes, Sam Groom, George Hamilton. Jim Hess, Rawn Hutchinson, Lauren Hutton, James Karen, Paul Lawrence, Leslie Neilson, Ray Walston
Dir: Ken Annakin Sc: Bill Driskill,

INGRID (1985) TVM
USA colour
Wombat Productions
Cast: Jose Ferrer, John Guilgud, Liv Ullmann
Dir: Ken Annakin

INDEX

INDEX